Poverty Dynamics

Interdisciplinary Perspectives

Edited by
Tony Addison, David Hulme, and Ravi Kanbur

OXFORD
UNIVERSITY PRESS

OXFORD

UNIVERSITY PRESS

Great Clarendon Street, Oxford ox2 6DP

Oxford University Press is a department of the University of Oxford.
It furthers the University's objective of excellence in research, scholarship,
and education by publishing worldwide in

Oxford New York

Auckland Cape Town Dar es Salaam Hong Kong Karachi
Kuala Lumpur Madrid Melbourne Mexico City Nairobi
New Delhi Shanghai Taipei Toronto

With offices in

Argentina Austria Brazil Chile Czech Republic France Greece
Guatemala Hungary Italy Japan Poland Portugal Singapore
South Korea Switzerland Thailand Turkey Ukraine Vietnam

Oxford is a registered trade mark of Oxford University Press
in the UK and in certain other countries

Published in the United States
by Oxford University Press Inc., New York

© Oxford University Press 2009

The moral rights of the author have been asserted
Database right Oxford University Press (maker)

First published 2009

British Library Cataloguing in Publication Data

Data available

Library of Congress Cataloging in Publication Data

Poverty dynamics : interdisciplinary perspectives / edited by
  Tony Addition, David Hulme, and Ravi Kanbur.
    p. cm.
  ISBN 978–0–19–955754–7
1. Poverty–Measurement. 2. Social isolation. 3. Social structure.
4. Social mobility. 5. Economic policy. I. Addison, Tony.
II. Hulme, David. III. Kanbur, S. M. Ravi.
HC79.P6P6835 2008
339.4'6–dc22   2008035834

Typeset by SPI Publisher Services, Pondicherry, India
Printed in Great Britain
on acid-free paper by
CPI Antony Rowe, Chippenham, Wiltshire

ISBN 978–0–19–955754–7 (Hbk.)
ISBN 978–0–19–955755–4 (Pbk.)

1 3 5 7 9 10 8 6 4 2

David Hulme dedicates this book to his parents
Walter and Jessie Hulme,
for all their loving care and support over the decades

Preface

Research on poverty has never been as vigorous as it is now. The very notion of poverty—how we conceptualize what it means to be poor—and how we measure it is generating a rich debate involving anthropologists, economists, human geographers, political scientists, sociologists, and other social scientists. And whereas previously the subject tended to be split between those who pursued primarily quantitative approaches to poverty measurement (from the economics and social statistics traditions) and those pursuing qualitative approaches (from the other social sciences) there is now much greater interaction and discussion between researchers from different disciplinary backgrounds.

This book reflects our belief that there are three main fronts on which progress must be made if we are to dramatically deepen the understanding of why poverty occurs, and significantly improve the effectiveness of poverty reduction policies.

First, poverty research needs to focus on *poverty dynamics*—over the life course, across generations, and between different social groups. There is now a wide acceptance that static analyses have limited explanatory power and may conceal the processes that are central to the persistence of poverty and/or its elimination.

Second, there is a need to move efforts to measure poverty dynamics beyond mere income and consumption to more *multidimensional concepts and measures* of poverty. This is increasingly common in static analyses but is rare in work on poverty dynamics. This might involve economic assets or, more ambitiously, using the concepts of human development or well-being.

Third, there is a growing consensus that a thorough understanding of poverty and poverty reduction requires *cross-disciplinary* research and the development of 'Q-squared methodologies' (*quantitative and qualitative*). Quantitative studies may be representative but by concentrating on what is readily measurable they risk missing out on crucial variables and find it hard to go beyond identifying correlates. Qualitative studies can capture the complexity of poverty dynamics and the processes that underpin poverty but they can be dismissed for not being able to explain how their findings relate to wider populations. Cross-disciplinary and Q-squared approaches offer the possibility of combining the strengths of different disciplines and methods to produce deeper understandings.

In this volume we examine the opportunity for the evolution of innovative, cross-disciplinary analyses to poverty dynamics by presenting the reader with the latest thinking from a group of eminent researchers. The book is divided into three parts.

1. *Introduction*: this provides an overview and argues that the present conversation about poverty dynamics reveals a divide, between economists and other social scientists, about the concepts and methods that will push forward the frontier of poverty analysis. However, it also reveals that there is a strong desire, and increasingly frequent attempts, to bridge this divide.

2. *Poverty Dynamics: Poverty Measurement and Assessment*: this focuses on cutting-edge approaches to analysing poverty dynamics. It covers non-income poverty measures, assessments of the likelihood of future poverty, the incorporation of time duration into the FGT poverty measures, asset-based approaches, and analyses based on life histories and participatory methods.

3. *Explanatory Frameworks for Understanding Poverty Dynamics*: this section focuses upon differing explanatory frameworks. These include political economy, social ordering, contemporary social theory, capabilities approaches, and the intergenerational transmission of poverty.

The overarching aim of the book is to push forward the conceptualization of poverty dynamics and generate knowledge that will ultimately advance the goal of poverty reduction.

This book arises from the ongoing research of the Chronic Poverty Research Centre (CPRC). It derives from a workshop of leading scholars on 'Concepts and Associated Methods for Analysing Poverty Dynamics' held at the University of Manchester, 23–4 October 2006. The workshop was convened by the CPRC at the University's Institute for Development Policy and Management (IDPM) and Brooks World Poverty Institute (BWPI). More than twenty papers were presented and discussed at the workshop (see <www.chronicpoverty.org> for the original papers and full details). Fourteen of these papers have been revised for this volume.

Mounting such a workshop and producing a book have involved the efforts of many organizations and people. Our thanks to CPRC for financing and organizing the workshop, and to the UK's Department for International Development (DFID) for its financial support to CPRC. The workshop and this volume would not have been possible without the efforts and energy of many people. Our especial thanks to: Denise Redston, the workshop organizer (who has also coordinated the preparation of this book); Karen Moore at CPRC for helping to develop the original idea, structure the workshop, and for reviewing many of the papers; David Clark for advice and support; CPRC's theme coordinators (Armando Barrientos, Bob Baulch, Kate Bird, Sam Hickey, and Andy McKay) for advice and reviewing papers; the participants at the workshop who provided detailed criticism and encouragement that has greatly strengthened the collection; and to the many others who reviewed papers and/or provided practical support.

Finally a word of thanks to the many poor people around the world who have patiently answered the questions of enumerators and interviewers and participated in the participatory exercises that have provided the ideas and data for much of the work in this volume. Their unremitting efforts to improve their own and their children's lives serve as an inspiration to those of us fortunate to be privileged with the task of trying to deepen the understanding of poverty and poverty reduction. All royalties from this book are donated to BRAC in Bangladesh to support its programmes which help some of the world's poorest people to improve their lives.

Tony Addison, Manchester
David Hulme, Manchester
Ravi Kanbur, Ithaca

Contents

Contents

List of Figures

List of Tables

List of Contributors

Tony Addison is Professor of Development Studies and Executive Director of the Brooks World Poverty Institute at the University of Manchester, and Associate Director of the DFID-funded Chronic Poverty Research Centre. His research focuses on poverty and development, in particular policies towards chronic poverty reduction in Asia and Africa.

Jo Boyden is a social anthropologist with the Department of International Development at the University of Oxford. Since 2005 she has been the director of the Young Lives Project, a longitudinal study of child poverty in Ethiopia, India, Peru, and Vietnam. Her research has focused on child poverty with reference to armed conflict, forced migration, and coping and resilience.

César Calvo is a Departmental Teaching Associate at Oxford University. He also holds a post at the Universidad de Piura in Peru. His research focuses on the analysis and measurement of poverty and vulnerability.

Michael R. Carter is Professor of Agricultural and Applied Economics at the University of Wisconsin-Madison, and directs the BASIS Research Program on Poverty, Inequality, and Development.

Elizabeth Cooper is a doctoral student in social anthropology at the University of Oxford. Her doctoral research is concerned with children's, families', and institutions' responses to orphaning in western Kenya. Elizabeth's previous research has focused on the situations of children and youth in refugee camps in Kenya and Uganda.

Peter Davis is Lecturer in International Development at the University of Bath. His research has focused on poverty dynamics, livelihoods, and welfare regimes with special reference to Bangladesh.

Stefan Dercon is Professor of Development Economics at the University of Oxford. His work focuses on applied theory and empirical research on problems of development. Recent research focuses on themes of poverty, risk, migration, and institutions, with empirical work focusing on longitudinal data from Ethiopia, Tanzania, and India.

Andrew Felton is a Ph.D. student in the Public Policy department of the University of Maryland and a financial economist at the Federal Deposit

Insurance Corporation. Previously, he worked as a Senior Research Analyst at the Brookings Institution.

James E. Foster is Professor of Economics at Vanderbilt University. He has worked extensively on the measurement of poverty and inequality as well as literacy, health, education, and human development more generally. He is currently working on external capabilities and the distribution of well-being in Mexico.

Maia Green is Professor of Social Anthropology at the University of Manchester and was formerly Deputy Director of the Global Poverty Research Group at the Universities of Manchester and Oxford. Her research has focused on poverty, development, and social institutions in East Africa and witchcraft in Tanzania.

Isabel Günther finished her Ph.D. in 2007 at the Department of Economics at the University of Göttingen. Since then she has been a postdoctoral fellow at Harvard University. Her main research interests are poverty and inequality analysis as well as applied health and population economics with a regional focus on sub-Saharan Africa.

John Harriss is Professor of International Studies at Simon Fraser University in Canada. He has long-standing research interests in the political economy of development, and in politics and society in South Asia. His early work focused on the peasant economy and agrarian change, environmental change, labour markets, and the informal sector. More recently he has engaged in debates on the concept of social capital and about civil society and politics, and popular representation, especially with regard to India.

David Hulme is Professor of Development Studies at the University of Manchester, Associate Director of the Chronic Poverty Research Centre, and Associate Director of the Brooks World Poverty Institute. He currently holds a Leverhulme Senior Research Fellowship. His current research interests focus on integrating time into poverty analysis, the concept and practice of global poverty reduction, combining quantitative and qualitative research approaches, understanding poverty dynamics (Bangladesh), the role of social protection in poverty reduction strategies (global), natural resource management and livelihoods (Africa), and microfinance.

Munenobu Ikegami is a Ph.D. student at the University of Wisconsin-Madison. He will join International Livestock Research Institute as a post-doctoral scientist in summer 2008. He is working on dynamic models of asset accumulation and their implications for the design and implementation of social policies.

Ravi Kanbur is T. H. Lee Professor of World Affairs, International Professor of Applied Economics and Management, and Professor of Economics at Cornell University. He previously held a number of posts at the World Bank including principal adviser to the chief economist. His main areas of research are public economics and development economics. He is particularly interested in bridging the worlds of rigorous analysis and practical policy making. He has published extensively in leading journals and directed the *World Development Report 2000/01: Attacking Poverty.*

Stephan Klasen is a Professor of Development Economics at the University of Göttingen, Germany. He holds a Ph.D. in economics from Harvard University and has held positions at the World Bank, King's College, Cambridge, and the University of Munich. His research is focused on the measurement and analysis of poverty and inequality in developing countries.

Anirudh Krishna (Ph.D. in Government, Cornell, 2000; Masters in Economics, Delhi, 1980) is Associate Professor of Public Policy and Political Science at Duke University. His research investigates how poor communities and individuals in developing countries cope with the structural and personal constraints that result in poverty and powerlessness.

Caroline Moser is Professor of Urban Development and Director of the Global Urban Research Centre, School of Environment and Development, University of Manchester. She is also an External Senior Fellow at Brookings Institution. Previously she was Lead Specialist Social Development, Latin America and the Caribbean Region, in the World Bank and prior to that a lecturer at the London School of Economics. She has published widely on asset accumulation and urban poverty reduction, violence and insecurity, household vulnerability under structural adjustment, the informal sector, and gender and development.

S. R. Osmani is Professor of Development Economics at the University of Ulster. He has published widely on issues related to poverty, employment, inequality, hunger, famine, nutrition, rights-based approach to development, and development problems in general, and his publications include *Economic Inequality and Group Welfare, Nutrition and Poverty, Macroeconomics of Poverty Reduction: The Case Study of Bangladesh, Macroeconomics of Poverty Reduction: The Case Study of Bhutan,* and *The Employment Nexus between Growth and Poverty: An Asian Perspective.*

Agnes R. Quisumbing, an economist, is a senior research fellow at the International Food Policy Research Institute, where she conducts research on gender, poverty, and economic mobility.

Andries du Toit is Deputy Director of the Programme for Land and Agrarian Studies at the University of the Western Cape in South Africa. He has worked on chronic poverty, the sociology of labour relations, and agro-food restructuring in South Africa.

Michael Woolcock is Professor of Social Science and Development Policy, and Research Director of the Brooks World Poverty Institute, at the University of Manchester. His research draws on a range of disciplinary theories and methods to explore the social dimensions of economic development, in particular the role that social networks play in the survival and mobility strategies of the poor, in managing local conflict, and in shaping the efficacy of legal and political institutions. He has an MA and Ph.D. in sociology from Brown University.

Part I

Introduction

1

Poverty Dynamics

*Measurement and Understanding from an
Interdisciplinary Perspective*

Tony Addison, David Hulme, and Ravi Kanbur

1.1. Introduction

There are three main fronts on which progress must be made if we are to
deepen our understanding of why poverty occurs, and significantly improve
the effectiveness of poverty reduction policies. First, poverty research needs
to focus on *poverty dynamics*—over the life course and across generations.
There is now a wide acceptance that static analyses have limited explanatory
power and may conceal the processes that are central to the persistence of
poverty and/or its elimination. Second, there is a need to move efforts to
measure poverty dynamics beyond mere income and consumption to more
multidimensional concepts and measures of poverty. This is increasingly common in static analyses but is rare in work on poverty dynamics. This might
involve assets or, more ambitiously, using concepts of human development
or well-being. Third, at the same time there is a growing consensus that
a thorough understanding of poverty and poverty reduction requires *cross-
disciplinary research*, using the strengths of different disciplines and methods,
and of quantitative and qualitative approaches to poverty analysis.

Thus, we believe that the next frontier in poverty research is at the intersec-
tion of dynamics and cross-disciplinarity. This chapter introduces a significant
new multidisciplinary collection of studies of poverty dynamics, presenting
the reader with the latest thinking by a group of researchers who are leaders
in their respective disciplines.[1] In this Introduction we set the papers in

---

[1] The papers in this volume, together with others, were presented at the CPRC Workshop
on 'Concepts and Methods for Analysing Poverty Dynamics and Chronic Poverty', held at
the University of Manchester, 23–5 October 2006 (<www.chronicpoverty.org>).

context, beginning in section 1.2 with the issue of how to bring time into the measurement of poverty and into the analysis of trajectories in and out of poverty. We then compare qualitative and quantitative approaches and address the issue of cross-disciplinarity in section 1.3. Section 1.4 presents an overview of the chapters in the volume. Section 1.5 concludes by highlighting areas where we believe future research on poverty dynamics should focus.

1.2. Time and Poverty[2]

Time is a troubling and ambiguous concept in philosophy and in social analysis. The complexities are apparent in Adam's (2004) characterization: 'Time is lived, experienced, known, theorized, created, regulated, sold and controlled. It is contextual and historical, embodied and objectified, abstracted and constructed, represented and commodified' (Adam, 2004, p. 1).

Set against the notion of time as an abstract relation between the past, present, and the future, in the tradition of St Augustine and Kierkegaard, is what Adam (2004, p. 49) calls the 'clock-time perspective' of Aristotle, Newton, Marx, Weber, and Durkheim. This is the dominant conceptualization in the social sciences, and one that underpins the chapters in this volume.[3]

Even within the 'clock-time' frame, it is possible to introduce time into the conceptualization of poverty in one of two ways. The first of these involves treating time as an ordinary dimension of well-being and poverty, as in the World Bank's *Voices of the Poor* (see Narayan et al., 2000, esp. pp. 21, 34, 92–3). In this approach time, or lack of it, is merely another dimension of poverty. A person is defined as time poor if he or she lacks the necessary time to achieve things of value, such as adequate sleep and rest, being with family and friends, or income (see Clark, 2002, ch. 4). In effect, time is viewed as one, of many, scarce resources (Becker, 1965). This approach fits well into approaches that emphasize the multidimensionality of well-being and poverty.

The second approach may be identified with the 'poverty and well-being dynamics' perspective, with a focus on how well-being evolves over time, what determines this evolution, and how different patterns of evolution are to be evaluated for policy. This is the approach that characterizes the chapters in this volume. They provide detailed examples of the ways in which information about poverty dynamics can be acquired.

- *Panel data methods*—this method is considered the most reliable by virtually all quantitative researchers and by many qualitative researchers. It involves conducting questionnaire surveys or semi-structured interviews with the same individual or household at different points in time. This

---

[2] Parts of this section derive from Clark and Hulme (2005).
[3] Bevan (2004) distinguishes three approaches: clocks and calendars, rhythms, and histories, and considers ways of incorporating rhythms and histories into poverty analysis.

permits objective data to be collected for key measures and the collection of information about the ways in which the individual/household explain the changes that are occurring in their lives. Moser and Felton (this volume) illustrate this method for both quantitative and qualitative data. The strengths of this method are its rigour and the comparability of the data it collects at different points in time. Its disadvantages are its costs and the significant delay in analysis that it entails. Additional problems include interviewee fatigue, matching households in large datasets, and systematic sample attrition (see earlier).

- *One-off indicators*—given the difficulties of collecting panel data it is logical to seek to identify 'one-off' indicators (i.e. measures collected at a single point in time) that provide information about poverty duration. The most obvious type of indicator for this purpose is 'nutrition' oriented—on the grounds that certain nutritional measures reveal what has been happening to an individual over an extended period of time. Researchers who have adopted this approach have favoured child stunting as a measure indicating that a child has been undernourished for an extensive period of time and, by implication, that her or his household has been poor for an extended period of time as it has been unable to provide an adequate diet. Radhakrishna et al. (2006) have used this method to measure and analyse chronic poverty in India. The great advantage of this method is that it permits partial analyses of poverty dynamics for any population for which an anthropometric survey is available: so, it can be low cost and rapid. There are, however, severe challenges. These include questions about the accuracy of data on height and age; the assumption that stunting is caused by undernourishment, rather than by health problems, cultural practices, and/or genetic factors; and the difficulty of moving beyond simply identifying factors that correlate with stunting.

- *Retrospective data*: another means of avoiding the costs and delays of collecting panel data is to ask interviewees to provide data about their past circumstances at the same time as they are providing data about their present condition. Many researchers are highly suspicious of this method, however, because of the well-known problems of recall. These include the difficulty of identifying the exact time that is to be recalled and of remembering what conditions were like at that time. For some indicators— attending school, formal employment status—data may be reasonably accurate. But for others—income, consumption, food availability— quantitative data is unlikely to be reliable. In addition, over time people tend to develop selective memories and may be perceived as 'rewriting' parts of their lives.[4] As a result, many researchers do not regard this as a

---

[4] This is not a conscious attempt to lie, but a part of extremely complex psychological and cognitive processes that are common, but highly varied, across humanity.

credible method for collecting quantitative, cardinal data. It is used extensively to collect qualitative data, often to triangulate other data, and/or to understand the ways in which people subjectively interpret change over time. In recent years this method has become popular as a component of participatory poverty assessments (PPAs). Arguably, the group-based methods used in PPAs make data more reliable as interviewees debate each other's recall and researchers can triangulate data between groups.

Until the late 1980s the main ways in which time featured in poverty analysis was in terms of poverty trends, seasonality, the timing of experiences, and historical accounts of poverty. Poverty trends commonly contrasted headcounts of poverty across a population at two (or more) different times. However, comparing poverty trends in this sense does not tell us whether individuals or households are persistently poor or if they typically move into and/or out of poverty over time (see Hulme and Shepherd, 2003; Carter and Barrett, 2006; Hulme, 2006). For example, Lawson, McKay, and Okidi (2003) record that between 1992 and 1999 consumption poverty in Uganda fell by about 20 per cent as the headcount rate fell from 55.7 per cent to 35.2 per cent. However, moving beyond conventional static poverty analysis by looking at the dynamics of poverty (i.e. what actually happened to individual households over time) provides a richer picture. Almost 30 per cent of poor households in 1992 managed to move out of poverty by 1999, but around 10 per cent of non-poor households fell into poverty. About 19 per cent of households that were poor in 1992 remained poor in 1999 (ibid. 7 and table 1). Rather than getting the false impression that life has improved for everyone we gain a nuanced understanding of the ups and downs of welfare status.

The seasonality (or timing) of income, consumption, and access to food has been another focus with particular interest in the annual cycles of relative plenty and food shortage/hunger that occur in many rural areas (Chambers, Longhurst, and Pacey, 1981; Chambers, 1983). The significance of specific poverty experiences at certain times in the life course has also been highlighted with a particular focus on lack of access to food/nutrition for pregnant women and education for children. A lack of access to nutrition, basic health services, or education in early life (foetal and infant) can have irreversible effects on the physical stature and cognitive ability of people (Loury, 1981; Strauss and Thomas, 1998). Historical accounts of poverty—seeking to lay out and interpret the main experiences and events in a chronological order—also continued (Hufton, 1974; Haswell, 1975; Geremek, 1994), although Iliffe's (1987) work moved things forward through its contrast of structural and conjunctural poverty in Africa which went beyond the static poverty analyses typical of his era.

Since the late 1980s there has been growing interest in examining the duration of poverty. Economists initially led the way through studies of transitory and chronic poverty, poverty dynamics, and patterns of poverty spells (Bane and Ellwood, 1986; Gaiha, 1988). While these studies have helped to put duration on the research agenda, their narrow focus on income or consumption poverty means that they have, at best, only tangentially linked up with the conceptual advances promoted by Amartya Sen and others (e.g. Sen, 1985, 1999).[5] This pattern has continued and Hulme and McKay (2008) report that out of the 28 panel datasets available on developing countries, 26 assess the standard of living in terms of income or consumption and for 23 of these datasets they are the only poverty measures available. Baulch and Masset (2003) have produced one of the few studies that broaden panel dataset analysis to human development measures.

We believe that the duration aspect of time merits particular attention for four main reasons. First, there is a simple logic that says if x has experienced the same forms and depths of poverty as y, but for a much longer period, then a moral concern with helping the more disadvantaged requires that x be prioritized and supported as she or he has experienced more deprivation than y.[6] Second, a failure to analyse the distribution of spells in poverty in a population is likely to lead to weak analyses of 'why' people are poor and, potentially, to weak policies. For example, hypothetically two different countries might have the same scores for the headcount, depth, and severity of poverty. Apparently, poverty in both of these countries is similar. However, in the first country poverty is largely transitory and is a phenomenon that many of its population experience but only for short durations. In the other, most of the population are non-poor but a minority are trapped in poverty for most or all of their lives. In the former country policies need to help those experiencing short spells of poverty—unemployment insurance and benefits, reskilling, microcredit, temporary social safety nets, health services. In the latter, deeper structural problems must be addressed—inclusion of the poor in access to health and education services, asset redistribution, tackling social exclusion, and regional infrastructural development.

Third, recent important work (Barrett, 2005; Carter and Barrett, 2006) has revealed the linkages between the depth of poverty, in terms of material and social assets, and duration with a focus on household-level poverty traps. The assumption behind this work is that low levels of assets lead to persistent poverty (at least in the absence of financial markets and safety nets), but a conceptualization is needed that will also permit an analysis of the ways in which the duration of poverty leads to depleted asset levels. Finally, the

[5] Alkire (2002) and Clark (2002, 2006a) discuss much of the relevant literature.

[6] In effect this is arguing that the breadths, depths, and durations of the deprivations x and y experience should be multiplied and thus x will score a higher level of deprivation than y. If this computation were pursued it would be necessary to decide whether duration was computed as absolute time or relative time, i.e. the proportion of x and y's lives spent in poverty.

duration of time spent in poverty has important implications for individual or household future strategies. This is in terms of physical and cognitive capabilities and the ways in which past experience shapes the agency (motivation, preferences, and understandings) of people.

1.3. Methods and Disciplines

Over the past decade, there has been growing interaction between two strands of, or two approaches to, poverty analysis in developing countries—the qualitative and the quantitative. Interaction between these two approaches has been forced to some extent by the strengthening (in some cases mandated) requirement by development agencies to expand the traditional quantitative base of their poverty assessments with a qualitative component. The best-known cases of this trend are the World Bank's Poverty Assessments. But other agencies such as the United Kingdom Department for International Development have also encouraged and often insisted on the incorporation of qualitative methods in poverty analysis and development analysis more generally. While 'mixed methods' frameworks have of course been present in the literature outside of development, and in the academic literature more generally, it is undoubtedly true that the degree of interest in such methods for poverty analysis in developing countries has heightened considerably in the last ten years. There is now a website dedicated to such analysis and a series of conferences attest to the growing body of work in this area.[7]

What exactly is meant by a 'quantitative' versus a 'qualitative' approach in the context of poverty analysis? From the discussions reported in Kanbur (2003), the following are among the key elements characterizing analyses that the literature recognizes as falling into the 'quantitative' category:

- The information base comes from statistically representative income/expenditure type household surveys (which may also have a wide range of modules covering other aspects of well-being and activity).

- The questionnaire in these surveys is of a 'fixed response' type, with little scope for unstructured discussion on the issues.

- Statistical/econometric analysis is carried out to investigate and test causality.

- 'Neoclassical homo-economicus' theorizing underlies the development of hypotheses, interpretation of results, and understanding of causality.

---

[7] For example, conferences at Cornell in 2001 and at Toronto in 2004, which led to the publications Kanbur (2003) and Kanbur and Shaffer (2007a), and the conference in Hanoi, 2007. Details are available at <www.q-squared.ca>.

Similarly, the following seem to be some of the key characteristics of analyses that fall into the 'qualitative' category:

- Unstructured interviews, the outcomes from which are then analysed with textual analysis methods.
- Related to the above, use of interviews to develop 'life histories' of individuals.
- Participatory Poverty Analysis, where a community as a whole is helped to discuss, to define, and to identify poverty.
- Ethnography, involving immersion of the analyst into the community in question over a significant length of time to get a deeper understanding of the context.
- Related to all of the above, anthropological and sociological theorizing to understand results and discuss causality.

Three further points can be made on the above characterization. First, notice that while the quantitative category is relatively uniform, the qualitative category is relatively diverse. The unifying (homogenizing) force of the economic method is felt in the former, while the latter is a battleground across disciplines and indeed within disciplines such as anthropology.[8] Second, some analyses do combine elements of both, and are on a continuum between the qualitative and the quantitative, rather than being strictly one or the other. Thus the qualitative–quantitative distinction might best be viewed as a tendency rather than as a discrete divide. Third, the qualitative–quantitative divide to some extent aligns with, and to some extent cuts across, disciplinary divides in poverty analysis, especially as between economics and the other social sciences.

The advantages and disadvantages of the two types of approaches are becoming better understood and are well illustrated by Adato's (2007) mixed-methods study on assessing conditional cash transfers. The quantitative part of the appraisal was statistically representative, and addressed econometrically the difficulties in attributing causality to the programme from 'before and after' or 'with and without' comparisons. Moreover, it does appear that, at least to some extent, policy makers tend to put greater weight on statistically representative 'large sample' assessments than on a small number of case studies. It is now generally accepted that the quantitative assessments of Mexico's conditional cash transfer programme played a key role in convincing a new administration to continue a programme started by the previous administration.

---

[8] The case for cross-disciplinary research on poverty in the social sciences is discussed at length elsewhere (Hulme and Toye, 2006). See also Harris (2002), Kanbur (2002), and Clark (2006b).

However, Adato's (2007) assessments from the qualitative approach throw up key issues which policy makers and analysts ignore at their peril. For example, while the quantitative assessments have generally praised these programmes for being well targeted to beneficiary groups (low 'leakage'), and indeed have recommended the tightening up of monitoring to reduce what leakage there is, the qualitative assessments reveal a great deal of incomprehension and resentment on the ground by those who are left out of the beneficiary group, when they see their near neighbours being included. Thus, whatever the 'objective' criteria laid out at the centre and developed through quantitative surveys and analysis, what is important is the meaning ascribed to those criteria on the ground. The tensions caused by such factors, identified as being serious in the qualitative assessment, could undermine support for the programme.

This suggests that qualitative approaches are better suited to emphasizing deeper processes, and the context generating the outcomes revealed by the study. This is clearly relevant for understanding, and also for the local-level implementation of policy. That quantitative studies do not (or cannot) do this is in part the burden of the critique advanced by Harris (this volume) and du Toit (this volume), who criticize not only quantitative approaches but also the related economic approaches to measurement and understanding. On the other hand, whether a phenomenon is widespread, or perhaps only locally relevant, is better addressed by studies in the quantitative tradition. Statistical analysis on representative samples is also better suited, for example, to going beyond 'before and after' or 'with and without' comparisons of policy or other events, as revealed by interviews with individuals, no matter how context relevant.

The benefits of combining quantitative and qualitative approaches are thus not to be doubted, and are revealed in a large number of recent studies.[9] Further, as Harriss (2002, p. 494) says, 'disciplines need to be saved from themselves'. Effective cross-disciplinarity seeks to capture the 'productive' aspects of disciplinarity which 'produces the conditions for the accumulation of knowledge and deepening of understanding' while avoiding the 'constraining' effects of disciplinarity which can lead 'to the point where it limits thought...and even [becomes] repressive' (Harriss, 2002, pp. 487–8).

However, this is not to say that there are no problems. While conducting studies side by side, or making quantitative studies a little more qualitative (for example, by conducting a participatory appraisal prior to designing the survey questionnaire, or by adding an unstructured portion at the end of a questionnaire), or by making the qualitative studies a little more qualitative (for example, by choosing the sites for the qualitative assessment on the basis of a national sampling frame, or by generating numerical values from coding

---

[9] See Kanbur and Shaffer (2007a) and <www.q-squared.ca>.

of the unstructured interviews), there remain fundamental issues of discipline and epistemology that will not simply go away. Kanbur and Shaffer (2007b) identify some deep philosophical issues about different conceptions of the nature of knowledge in different disciplinary traditions that are bound to bedevil 'deep integration' of the different approaches. For example, it is not entirely clear that national-level policy making is well served by community-level measures of poverty which are based on community perceptions of what it means to be poor. These practical issues also have their roots in whether poverty can and should be identified 'objectively' by 'brute data', or whether it is inherently to do with intersubjective meanings. Kanbur and Shaffer (2007b) come out strongly in favour of mixed methods, but caution that there are pitfalls that we should be aware of.

The above discussion applies to poverty analysis in general. Consider now an application of the above discussion to poverty dynamics in particular, and especially to the chapters in this volume. As discussed in the previous section, time adds novel and irreducible dimensions to the conceptualization, measurement, and understanding of poverty. For example, the economic theory of poverty measurement is very well developed for the static case. Going back at least as far as Sen's (1976) classic exposition, axioms have been proposed to capture basic intuitions on what constitutes 'poverty' and 'higher poverty', and poverty measures that satisfy these axioms have been described which are now the workhorse of empirical poverty analysis in the quantitative tradition (for example, the famous FGT measure, Foster, Greer, and Thorbecke, 1984). But all this is for the static case. The introduction of time into the economic theory of poverty measurement is relatively recent, and the chapters by Foster (this volume) and Calvo and Dercon (this volume) represent the state of the art. The issues that arise hinge on how to aggregate individual poverty experiences over time, in conjunction with aggregation across individuals into a poverty measure for the society as a whole. Defining and separating out risk, vulnerability, transient poverty, and chronic poverty are the concerns of the current economic literature on poverty measurement (for example the chapters mentioned above and also Günther and Klasen (this volume) and Carter and Ikegami (this volume).

However, there are significant conceptual, methodological, and empirical questions that face the standard economic approach. Empirically, to implement any of these measures we need surveys of panels of individuals or households who are followed over time. If the object is to take a medium-term perspective on time, and especially if we wish to take a longer, inter-generational or dynastic, perspective, then panels of twenty years or more are needed by definition. There has been a recent flowering of panel dataset collection in a few developing countries. Effective use of this information for analysis to poverty and well-being dynamics is well illustrated by the review in Quisumbing (this volume). However, a majority of developing countries do not have panel data at all, certainly not of the national representative variety. And no countries have comparable panels over twenty years or more. Quantitative panel-based analysis on poverty dynamics, therefore, is largely an analysis of fairly short-run fluctuations in well-being and poverty, for the small number of countries that have them.

One way to obtain information about the past when we do not have actual intertemporal panels is to ask people about their past and record and utilize this information. This is often done in quantitative analysis (see papers referred to in Quisumbing, this volume). The method, of probing people about their past, is related to the life history method in qualitative poverty analysis, as exemplified by Davis (this volume). Each individual is engaged in a semi-structured discussion about their life course. The objective is not only to find out about the trajectory of well-being, but also the causes underlying it—as seen by the individual. Some quantitative information can be collected, on incomes, purchase of assets, value of dowry, etc. But the main focus is on the narrative and interpretation of the narrative. The 'stages of progress' approach of Krishna (this volume) is also a backward-looking self-assessment, but this operates at the community level, and there is a stronger push towards present-ing at least some numerical indicators of changes over time. While there is an interesting discussion to be had on the relative strengths of individual-focused versus community-based histories, it is clear that both share the feature of semi-structured interviews of the qualitative approach, as distinct from the (largely) fixed-response questionnaire method of the quantitative approach. The contextual detail emerging from the narratives is not something that is intended to be replicated in standard panel survey instruments. Moreover, especially if the panel-based survey is, say, every few years (which is the case for most panels in developing countries), then (apart from the 'attrition bias' from people leaving the sample, which quantitative analysts are well aware of) major twists and turns in the life course will be missed in the panel (except to the extent that they are reflected in the next snapshot of the household or the individual several years later). However, such events can be picked up in a life history discourse, and put to good analytical use, as is shown in Davis (this volume).

The chapter by Moser and Felton (this volume) is an interesting amalgam of the qualitative and quantitative approaches. It combines relatively standard quantitative information (sufficient to allow econometric regressions to be run) with ethnographic detail and long-term engagement with the communities studied—over twenty years, in fact. There are of course many anthropologists who have had similar long-term engagement with small numbers of communities (sometimes only one). But it is unlikely that information they have collected can be fed directly into quantitative type analysis—nor would they wish it to be. However, one possibility is to do for analysis of poverty dynamics what Ostrom (1990) and her colleagues did for analysis of the commons, namely build a bridge between qualitative and quantitative analysis by conducting a textual analysis of the reports and using coding to generate quantitative measures for further analysis from different perspectives. We leave this as a suggestion and an open question.

Finally, it should be recognized that, unlike in the static case, the combination of qualitative and quantitative approaches, and indeed cross-disciplinarity, in a single study, or in studying the same specific problem, is relatively rare. The papers in Kanbur and Shaffer (2007a) bear ample testimony to how far things have come in the static case. The chapters in this volume, however, show how far we have to go in poverty dynamics in advancing mixed-methods approaches. As a collectivity the chapters do highlight the benefits from combining quantitative and qualitative approaches, as discussed above. However, except for Moser and Felton, Boyden and Cooper, and Woolcock, the chapters are largely in one tradition or the other. It is to be hoped that the lead given by these chapters, and by recent papers such as Baulch and Davis (2007) and Lawson (2007), and the benefits of combination shown by bringing the two traditions together in this volume, will continue in poverty dynamics the trend that is already well under way in the static analysis of poverty.

1.4. Poverty Dynamics: Measurement and Understanding

This volume is divided into three parts. After Part I, which consists of this introduction and overview, Part II explores poverty measurement and assessment, with a focus on cutting-edge approaches to incorporating poverty dynamics, using both quantitative and qualitative methods. Part III focuses upon differing explanatory frameworks for understanding poverty dynamics.

Introducing time into poverty measurement and analysis is a major challenge, which researchers in developing countries have only begun to really address over the last decade. Dividing the past into discrete time periods ('spells') for the purpose of measuring living standards is a well-established practice, often accompanied by analysis of poverty mobility using tools such as 'poverty transition matrices' applied to individuals or groups (Baulch and Hoddinott, 2000). More ambitious are efforts to develop a single intertemporal measure of poverty to summarize different poverty paths; the best known is Ravallion's chronic poverty measure which uses the average poverty level (using the FGT poverty measures over the entire period for which (consumption) data is available). However, to derive satisfactory intertemporal measures we must be very clear about what underlying assumptions are being made. In particular, should we treat all spells of poverty equally and if not then how should they be weighted? How do we incorporate risk into the measure (a big concern of the poor, constantly voiced in surveys), especially when we are concerned to project poverty forward and individuals cannot be assumed to have perfect foresight? Much effort has gone into incorporating vulnerability—the unpredictability and riskiness found in the lives of the poor—into static poverty measures, but the effort is only just beginning with dynamic measures (Elbers and Gunning, 2006). Finally, different individuals and groups will experience different patterns of spells of poverty and non-poverty; how is this information to be combined?

In Chapter 2 César Calvo and Stefan Dercon argue that existing approaches have not been explicit enough about their underlying assumptions, and they set themselves the task of deriving a number of axioms which satisfactory measures should possess. The axiomatic approach is valuable because it forces us to be explicit about our values. Thus, do different time periods carry equal weight? To what extent can a period in poverty be compensated by future higher income (a key question for assessing the poverty impact of policy reforms that often generate short-term adjustment costs with the promise of long-term gains)? And to what extent are you the same person across time (a question raised by the philosophy of identity)? Calvo and Dercon illustrate their discussion with a panel of Ethiopian household data, finding substantial differences between static and intertemporal poverty measures.

One of Calvo and Dercon's theoretical propositions is likely to be controversial: they reject the notion of *time discounting* which prevails in other areas of economics when intertemporal welfare effects are being compared (in the cost–benefit analysis of environmental impacts, for example). Instead, they appeal to the principle of 'universalism' which argues strongly for valuing distress equally whatever the time period in which it has occurred—a principle that is used by Anand and Hanson (1997) to reject the use of time discounting in deriving intertemporal measures of health status. Some may feel that this goes too far; there is by no means unanimity among health economists as regards the use of time discounting and there are strong proponents for it (see Smith and Gravelle, 2000). But those who favour discounting poverty (as with health) must consider a major difficulty: what is to be the rate of discount? And if it varies across countries (because of differences in rates of time preference, in their turn influenced by cross-country variation in life expectancies) does this undermine the comparison of intertemporal poverty across countries? In summary, in seeking to clarify the theoretical basis of intertemporal poverty measures, Calvo and Dercon open a Pandora's box of important issues for future theoretical and empirical research.

The FGT measure (Foster, Greer, and Thorbecke, 1984) has been the most widely used poverty measure of the last two decades but it takes no account of duration. Since the length of time in poverty negatively affects outcomes, especially for children (see Chapter 13 by Boyden and Cooper) this is clearly a very important missing dimension of poverty measurement. Yet filling this gap raises major conceptual issues. In Chapter 3 James Foster takes up the challenge of introducing time into the measurement of chronic poverty, specifically by incorporating the duration of time spent in poverty into the FGT poverty measures. He creates a measure which obeys a number of crucial axioms and conditions (such as the need for the measure to be subgroup decomposable) with two cut-off points defining the chronically poor: a standard (absolute) poverty line and a duration line. As with Calvo and Dercon, an earlier period in poverty is given the same weight as a later period (i.e. no time discounting is used). Foster reports on an application of this new poverty measure to a panel for Argentina, with the duration-adjusted FGT measure yielding a significantly different estimate of poverty (with a large variation in spatial chronic poverty). Foster notes one criticism of this new measure: it is confined to income. The next step is to create multidimensional, duration-adjusted measures of chronic poverty, but this is an exceptionally demanding task (not least in making commensurate the different dimensions of well-being to construct a single measure). Notwithstanding this remaining challenge, Foster's duration-adjusted FGT measure is work that promises to revolutionize the measurement of poverty dynamics in the way that the original FGT measures revolutionized static poverty measurement.

Part II offers a spectrum of different dimensions of well-being and poverty. Chapter 4 analyses the dynamics of non-income poverty measures which are as important as those of income and consumption measures of changes in poverty status. Working within a capabilities framework, Isabel Günther and Stephan Klasen analyse nutrition, health, and education poverty indicators for Vietnamese panel data, selecting households with at least two generations present. They argue that non-income indicators can be as good (and sometimes better) as income at capturing intergenerational poverty transmission: income tells only part of the story. Vietnam is especially relevant since the economy is experiencing fast growth and structural change. There has been a sharp decline in income poverty, but nutrition and health indicators show fewer households escaping from poverty (overall there is a lower correlation between non-income and income measures than one would expect). Günther and Klasen find intergenerational education poverty remains particularly strong: many households with low education among the older generation also have low education among the young.

In Chapter 5 Caroline Moser and Andrew Felton apply a principal components analysis to panel data from urban Ecuador (collected over 1978–2004) and construct an asset index to measure asset accumulation. They inductively construct the index on the basis of longitudinal anthropological research (rather than building an index and then applying it to the data), a methodology they term 'narrative econometrics'. Moser and Felton argue that it is imperative to understand the social context of assets and how they vary in their importance; simply plugging assets into an index is highly unsatisfactory. Their chosen assets are: physical capital (including housing); financial/productive capital; human capital and social capital (natural capital is not included as this is an urban study). Different asset indices deploy different weighting methodologies and the three most common are: weighting by asset prices (but these are difficult to obtain and it is hard to impute a price for non-marketed assets); equal weights (which has obvious problems since it assumes all assets have equal value (a computer and a horse for example); and principal components analysis (using correlations to estimate the underlying unobservable variable, following Filmer and Pritchett, 2001). Moser and Felton adopt the latter. The distribution of each type of capital is then calculated over different points in time to highlight asset shifts.

Crucially the importance of assets can vary over time due to structural changes in the economy as well as economic policy which affect the returns to specific assets (asset indices can be used to identify the effect of macro-economic shocks). Thus Guayaquil has seen large changes in labour demand due to globalization; imports of cheap Chinese-made goods have reduced the demand for artisanal male skills which provided a reasonable income in the 1970s. And the shift from community-based services to market-provided services (the result of privatization) is showing up in changes in social capital at the community level.

Assets are a long-running theme in the poverty debate from the 1970s paradigm of 'redistribution of growth' (Chenery et al., 1974) through to the WDR-2000 and WDR-2005 policy discussions, and in livelihood approaches to poverty analysis (Scoones, 1998; Ellis, 2000). Assets (*stocks*) generate income and consumption *flows* (and stocks may be more easily measured than flows); they enable households to withstand shocks (within limits); the level and composition of assets determines whether a household is in a poverty trap (and its chances of escape); and helping the poor to build assets (including human capital) has policy traction—although there is much debate about which assets are the most important in the many livelihood contexts that the poor face (Hulme, Moore, and Shepherd, 2001). Fundamentally, assets bring the *production* dimension into poverty measurement, adding to the income, consumption, and human development dimensions (and telling us more about how levels of these latter three dimensions arise in households).

The methodology of assets-based approaches has become increasingly sophisticated (and is (panel) data intensive), particularly in incorporating time into the formal models to address a key question: who among the currently poor are likely to be poor in the future? Dynamics are therefore centre stage in this approach, with a theory of poverty traps underlying empirical applications (Buera, 2005; Carter and Barrett, 2006). Drawing upon this recent literature, and in a model applied to data from KwaZulu-Natal, Michael Carter and Munenobu Ikegami (Chapter 6) introduce new theory-based measures of chronic poverty and vulnerability and illustrate their feasibility using South

African data. They identify three types of poor people each with different future prospects: (i) the low-skilled with few livelihood possibilities who are in a low-level equilibrium trap (the *Economically Disabled*); (ii) a middle-ability group that will move either up or down the income scale depending upon their initial asset level (the *Multiple Equilibrium Poor*); and (iii) a high-ability group who can move out of poverty given enough time (the *Upwardly Mobile*).

Forward-looking measures of poverty are then derived. In the FGT measure poverty is measured using an income gap, but it is possible to see poverty as an asset gap as well, and this is what Carter and Ikegami do, to calculate the percentage of people who will stay poor under different assumptions of asset dynamics. Asset shocks are then simulated in this model, with individuals reacting to the risk of shocks by, for example, being unwilling to forgo present consumption in order to accumulate assets that they may well lose. Different policy recommendations are developed for each group. The economically disabled are candidates for social protection while the middle-ability group need protection to reduce their risk and asset transfers to put them over the asset threshold and to give them a fighting chance of exiting poverty.

The final two chapters in Part II focus on the measurement and assessment of poverty through subjective approaches. Peter Davis's chapter examines the role of individual/household life history methods in assessing poverty dynamics, while Anirudh Krishna uses participatory methods to assess changes in poverty and well-being at the community level.

By providing contextual and historical detail, life histories constitute a valuable complement to quantitative approaches. Peter Davis (Chapter 7) demonstrates their ability to reveal phenomena concealed by other methods, including: events with multiple causation; 'last-straw' threshold effects (the culmination of a series of adverse trends); outcomes based on the ordering of a sequence of events; and events associated with household breakdown which tend to be masked in household survey approaches. For rural Bangladesh, Davis constructs household resource profiles before conducting the life history interviews and seeks out a high level of historical and contextual detail (both Davis and Krishna use 'referencing'—mapping events and changes at the household level to a template of easily recalled national events). Davis finds that most improvements tend to only happen gradually, whereas declines are often more sudden (in this Davis's work links to that of Paul Farmer, 2005, on the structural violence that poor people face) and he develops trajectory patterns: saw-tooth patterns in trajectories are more common among the poor than smooth paths. Davis also deploys the methodology of 'fuzzy sets' in identifying chronic poverty. However, the very richness of life histories means that the number of cases studied is generally small, limiting generalization across larger populations.

Whereas Peter Davis focuses on one country (Bangladesh), Anirudh Krishna (Chapter 8) tracks households in five countries: four developing countries and the United States. He aims to capture poverty dynamics through a 'stages of progress' methodology. This has seven steps: (i) get together representative community group; (ii) discuss the objectives of the exercise; (iii) define poverty collectively in terms of stages of progress, then ask the question: if a poor household gets a bit more money what do they do with it? (typically they specify food for the family as their first priority); (iv) define 'x years ago' in terms of a well-known signifying event; (v) list all village households, and then ask about each household's stage at the present time and x years ago; (vi) categorize all present-day households into chronically poor or not; and then (vii) take a random sample within each category to ascertain reasons for change or stability. To cross-check the reliability of the method the researchers share the results with key informants, before leaving the community, to see whether they agree with the findings.

Krishna finds that health and healthcare expenses were a primary event in the descent into poverty (41 per cent of cases in North Carolina and 88 per cent in Gujarat, India). Other reasons were more context specific: funerals and marriage (important in four countries), debt (important in India), drought, and loss of land (Uganda and Peru). Among the reasons for successful escape from poverty, interviewees cited a supplemental income source (mainly city-based informal sector) as the most important.

As will have become clear, many of the chapters in Part II, although primarily about measurement, also address the understanding of poverty dynamics. Indeed, in some of the chapters measurement is a route into understanding, so a simple division between the two is not possible. Similarly, the chapters in Part III, although primarily about understanding, also broach questions of measurement.

Part III begins with two chapters that offer a critique of measurement. In Chapter 9 Harriss argues that most poverty research is working with a model of knowledge from the natural sciences: that is to say, there are objective facts to be discovered; methods for uncovering these facts improve over time as better techniques are discovered and employed; and, predictive theories that can be universally applied across all societies will eventually emerge. But this approach is doomed to disappointment, argues Harriss, for the focus is on measurement and on the characteristics of individuals and households with very little attention to the structural processes that move people in and out of poverty. Numerous studies identify the same set of factors (assets, household characteristics, demographics) as being associated with poverty dynamics, yet these are proximate factors only. This supposedly 'value-neutral' approach depoliticizes poverty. Harriss highlights similarities between the new asset-based approaches and research during the 1970s on agrarian differentiation and class formation—although the social context is much less explicit in the former (a consequence of the household being the primary unit of analysis). Thus a key but outstanding question is why the poor come to have so few assets and the role of wealthy elites in blocking their asset-accumulation strategies (including historical and contemporary expropriation). Clearly, there is considerable scope for qualitative research to inform quantitative data collection in this area.

In Chapter 10 Andries du Toit emphasizes the need to engage with the structural dimensions of persistent poverty and therefore with social relations, agency, culture, and subjectivity. He illustrates his argument with examples from South Africa. While welcoming the recent dialogue between quantitative and qualitative research, he emphasizes the need to go beyond the positivist assumptions underlying econometric approaches which at their worst constitute a 'mystifying narrative' of what poverty means and how we come to understand it. Drawing on the work of James Scott (1998) and others, du Toit argues that the process of abstraction in poverty measurement results in a decontextualization of poverty; certain information (that which can be standardized and quantified) is given preference in building a narrative of the poor and the processes that result in impoverishment. In South Africa, government officials have become fixated on finding unambiguous and quantifiable systems of indicators of structural vulnerability, to the detriment of really understanding the role of national and local history and power relations. By focusing on what is readily measurable at the individual and household level, measurement approaches neglect culture, identity, agency, and social structure that are central to creating wealth and poverty (see Chambers, 1983; Bevan, 2004) and the policy conclusions do not connect to the realities of poor societies.

The next two chapters offer attempts at understanding poverty dynamics within a recognizably economics/quantitative framework. In Chapter 11 Siddiqur Osmani develops a dynamic approach to capabilities; people may develop or lose specific capabilities over time, and their opportunities are often changing as economic change favours some skills, and downgrades others. Poverty traps for both households and individuals then result from a mismatch between the structure of endowments and the structure of opportunities. Osmani contrasts the roles of level and structure of assets/endowments in explaining chronic poverty. Chronic poverty has an inherent time dimension, but the analysis to date is insufficiently explicit—for example how long do people have to be poor to be categorized as chronically poor? Most discussion adopts a backward-looking approach, whereas in Osmani's view we need to be more forward looking—someone is in a poverty trap indefinitely unless something changes for the better. Since even a chronically poor person can move above the poverty line, the key point is that for most of the time a chronically poor person is below the poverty line—unable to accumulate to get out during their working lifetime. He develops a definition of chronic poverty with *expected* income as its core, with expected income in turn conditional on the expected accumulation of assets over time as well as initial exogenous circumstances. If that conditional expected income lies below the poverty line then that person is chronically poor. With limited endowments a person can be chronically poor without being caught in a poverty trap (for the fortunate their income may be on a time path to move them out of poverty even if they are chronically poor at present). For policy it is then essential to look at the *pattern* of growth and not just its rate, for the former restructures the pattern of opportunities, devaluing some initial asset investments while raising the returns on others (as will economic policy change, for example market liberalization). Targeted interventions to improving endowments and putting people on upward accumulation paths out of chronic poverty must take account of the changing pattern of growth. Assets are also socially constructed (a theme echoed by Maia Green) and a mismatch between endowments and opportunities can arise when social relations, not just the economy, change.

A key assumption in existing models is that individuals cannot borrow against their future earnings to build present assets (which in turn yield higher (future) income flows) and must save instead. A threshold of initial assets exists below which accumulation through saving is not a viable strategy for moving out of poverty and, with a binding credit constraint, the household cannot become a successful entrepreneur—even if it has the skills and knowledge to do so.[10]

Conceptually, many different types of asset have been identified: natural capital, physical capital, human capital, social capital, and financial capital, with further refinements within each (for example Hulme, Moore, and Shepherd (2001) divide social capital into socio-cultural and socio-political assets). But data on human capital and physical capital are the most readily available, and in Chapter 12 Agnes Quisumbing focuses on these in an analytical survey of how intergenerational asset transfers can create (or block off) escape routes from poverty. The poor are typically constrained in their ability to trade off present for future consumption (exacerbated by credit constraints) and an inability to invest in human capital persists across generations (there is plenty of evidence from the Philippines that the children of parents with little schooling and/or assets have lower school participation, and the children of credit-constrained households are shorter than those of unconstrained households).

Quisumbing argues that context matters greatly in determining which assets work best for poverty reduction. Thus in Ghana more land is better for increasing women's income than more education given the low returns to

[10] There is a growing literature on modelling credit constraints; using United States data, Buera (2006) finds that the welfare cost of such constraints is significant (about 6% of the household's lifetime consumption), and there is clearly much scope for applying these tools to simulate the impact of microfinance on future poverty trajectories.

female schooling in rural labour markets. If asset accumulation takes time and is difficult for the poor, then assets at marriage largely determine lifetime prosperity. The marriage market therefore plays a central role, and evidence from Ethiopia shows that assortative mating increases inequality and reduces social mobility (due to intergenerational transfers at marriage)—thereby continuing social stratification from one generation to the next. For the poor to transfer assets across generations they must first accumulate them; hence the need to strengthen property rights, reduce the initial costs of acquiring capital, and provide savings instruments (and provide mechanisms to maintain the poor people's asset base in the face of shocks). More mechanisms for human capital investment by the credit constrained are essential (Mexico's PROGRESA is a model).

An alternative disciplinary approach is presented by Jo Boyden and Elizabeth Cooper (Chapter 13) to address the concept of 'resilience' in research and practice concerning children's poverty and the life course and intergenerational transmission of poverty. 'Resilience' means the strategies that people use to cope with adversities, such as income poverty or violent conflict. For children much attention has been paid to the issue of whether they can in some way overcome initial disadvantages. Unfortunately children are more susceptible to the effects of poverty than adults, particularly to the effect of under-nutrition. Boyden and Cooper argue that while superficially attractive the resilience concept has not yet proved to be a useful tool for poverty research. Resilience lacks a satisfactory definition, it is impossible to observe directly, and indeed the concept disguises multivariate phenomena. Thus the correlation between inputs (mother's education, for example) and outputs (child health, for example) are derived from the analysis of datasets that cover many different parental and community characteristics. In short, research in this area has been highly mechanistic (prematurely identifying direct cause and effect), thereby failing to take account of moderating forces. Moreover, what is often taken for granted in the policy debate is not borne out by recent research; for example, current research challenges assumptions about the foundational role of the family in child development. Static models of human development often underpin the conventional wisdom on the effects of deprivation in early childhood, whereas more dynamic approaches are called for in which child-development trajectories are constantly modified (implying that it is better to speak in terms of probabilities). Boyden and Cooper argue that much more attention must be given to the interaction of genetic and environmental impacts on poverty, as well as the structural influences.

In much of the analysis of assets there have been attempts to understand the social context that gives assets their value, a point emphasized by Moser and Felton (this volume) and further developed in Chapter 14 by Maia

Green who argues that the 'mystery of capital' lies in social relationships; hence entitlements do not exist in the abstract but within networks of moral relationships. The latter determine what different categories of people can expect. Most importantly, these categories can shift radically. Building on Barbara Harris-White's (2005) work on social exclusion, Green argues that social ordering sanctions harm to some, but not to others, illustrating this point with an examination of witchcraft in contemporary Africa which is used to change relationships within and between families (including control over assets and the value attached to them). In Green's view the concept of chronic poverty usefully highlights a situation but does not really explain it, tending to yield frameworks that are far from local conceptions of poverty, and local concerns. To get deeper insights we need to develop the idea of *durable* poverty (based on deprivation) rather than chronic poverty, for the former concept is better able to handle the institutional factors that keep people poor.

The idea of the multidimensionality of poverty is now firmly embedded in the policy discourse, and we have already discussed non-income poverty dynamics in the contribution by Günther and Klasen to this volume. Yet there is still much to do. In Chapter 15, Michael Woolcock highlights how the need for a broader social theory of chronic poverty must look to systems of social relations, rules, and meaning. Thus understanding how groups are defined is key to a better understanding of the social relations that underlie chronic poverty (a point also made by Maia Green). Rules systems, which constitute everything from constitutions and contracts to languages and social norms, can lie at the heart of 'legal inequality traps' that condemn people to chronic poverty. A better understanding of meaning systems (how people make sense of what happens in the world and to them) is essential to deepen our knowledge of chronic poverty since groups can sometimes subvert practices that are 'clearly' in their best interests. A clear model of human behaviour is needed (one that goes beyond microeconomics); better explanations of why poverty persists as part of broader processes of economic and social change; more insight into how power is created, maintained, and challenged; and more attention to how we can best learn from the new generation of poverty reduction policies and practices. Woolcock illustrates his argument with cases from Australia, Cameroon, and China. Each of these cases shows how social relations are central to understanding responses to economic and social change.

Fundamentally, Woolcock argues for a shift away within social theory from what he terms 'endless critiques' and yet more 'conceptual frameworks' and a more constructive engagement with the most pressing and vexing concerns around chronic poverty. Much of development can be said to be about facilitating 'good struggles' in areas where there is no technical solution, but rather progress is crafted by dialogue and negotiation.

1.5. Conclusion

In this volume the reader will encounter a rich menu of perspectives and methodologies in some of the latest research on poverty. Our introduction has provided the first course. Conceptually and methodologically poverty dynamics are challenging but a number of clear conclusions emerge.

The first of these is about the duration of poverty. It is imperative to bring time into analytical frameworks for measuring and understanding poverty. There are many ways forward, including panel datasets (of which we need many more, since they are still confined to a small subset of countries) and life history methods. Major conceptual problems do however remain. These include the degree to which we do or do not place equal value on different spells in poverty (time discounting).

Second, multidimensionality is essential. It is time to get out of the rut of income/consumption measures. Poverty dynamics can look very different when non-income measures are used, and these are critical as both a cross-check on trends in income measures, as well as giving us a broader picture of how well-being in all its dimensions is moving over time (essential if we are to track the poverty impact of growth). Multidimensional, duration-adjusted measures of poverty remain the next big challenge in measurement.

Third, interdisciplinary work is possible and desirable, despite the difficulties discussed in this chapter. In other words, the boundaries of our interdisciplinary conversation are becoming clearer, and the points of commonality and difference are now more sharply in focus. We need to encourage further the trend towards combining qualitative and quantitative approaches in the analysis of poverty dynamics. The present conversation about poverty dynamics reveals a divide, between economists and other social scientists (sociology, anthropology, politics, and geography). However, it also reveals that there is a strong desire, and increasingly frequent attempts, to bridge this divide. We hope that this volume will support that process, encouraging others to join in the debate, and to tackle the conceptual and methodological hurdles that still lie ahead.

References

Adam, B. (2004), *Time*, Cambridge: Polity Press.

Adato, M. (2007), 'Combining Survey and Ethnographic Methods to Evaluate Conditional Cash Transfer Programs', paper presented at the conference on Q-Squared in Policy, Hanoi, 7–8 July.

Alkire, S. (2002), *Valuing Freedoms: Sen's Capability Approach and Poverty Reduction*, Oxford: Oxford University Press.

Anand, S., and Hanson, K. (1997), 'Disability-Adjusted Life Years: A Critical Review', *Journal of Health Economics*, 16: 685–702.

Bane, M., and Ellwood, D. (1986), 'Slipping into and out of Poverty: The Dynamics of Spells', *Journal of Human Resources*, 21(1): 1–23.

Barrett, C. B. (2005), 'Rural Poverty Dynamics: Development Policy Implications', in D. Colman and N. Vink (eds.), *Reshaping Agriculture's Contributions to Society*, Oxford: Blackwell.

Baulch, B., and Davis, P. (2007), 'Poverty Dynamics and Life Trajectories in Rural Bangladesh', paper presented at the conference on Q-Squared in Policy. Hanoi, 7–8 July.

—— and Hoddinott, J. (2000), 'Economic Mobility and Poverty Dynamics in Developing Countries: Introduction to a Special Issue', *Journal of Development Studies*, 36(1): 1–24.

—— and Masset, E. (2003), 'Do Monetary and Non-Monetary Indicators Tell the Same Story about Chronic Poverty? A Study of Vietnam in the 1990s', *World Development*, 31(3): 441–53.

Becker, G. S. (1965), 'A Theory of the Allocation of Time', *Economic Journal*, 299: 495–517.

Bevan, P. (2004), 'Exploring the Structured Dynamics of Chronic Poverty', WeD Working Paper No. 6, University of Bath.

Buera, F. (2005), 'A Dynamic Model of Entrepreneurship with Borrowing Constraints', processed paper, Northwestern University.

—— (2006), 'Persistency of Poverty, Financial Frictions and Entrepreneurship', processed paper, Northwestern University (March).

Carter, M. R., and Barrett, C. B. (2006), 'The Economics of Poverty Traps and Persistent Poverty: An Asset-Based Approach', *Journal of Development Studies*, 42(2): 178–99.

Chambers, R. (1983), *Rural Development: Putting the Last First*, London: Heinemann.

—— Longhurst, R., and Pacey, A. (eds.) (1981), *Seasonal Dimensions to Poverty*, London: Frances Pinter.

Chenery, H., Ahluwalia, M. S., Bell, C. L. G., Duloy, J. H., and Jolly, R. (1974), *Redistribution with Growth*, Oxford: Oxford University Press.

Clark, D. A. (2002), *Visions of Development: A Study of Human Values*, Cheltenham: Edward Elgar.

—— (2006a), 'Capability Approach', in D. A. Clark (ed.), *The Elgar Companion to Development Studies*, Cheltenham: Edward Elgar, 32–45.

—— (2006b), 'Development Studies in the Twenty First Century', in D. A. Clark (ed.), *The Elgar Companion to Development Studies*, Cheltenham: Edward Elgar, pp. xxvi–xli.

—— and Hulme, D. (2005), 'Towards a Unified Framework for Understanding the Depth, Breadth and Duration of Poverty', GPRG Working Paper 20, Universities of Manchester and Oxford.

Elbers, C., and Gunning, J. W. (2006), 'Poverty, Risk, and Accumulation: Pro-Poor Policies when Dynamics Matter', paper presented at the CSAE 2006 Conference.

Ellis, F. (2000), *Rural Livelihoods and Diversity in Developing Countries*, Oxford: Oxford University Press.

Farmer, P. (2005), *Pathologies of Power*, Berkeley and Los Angeles: University of California Press.

Filmer, D. and Pritchett, L. (2001) 'Estimating Wealth Effects without Expenditure Data—Or Tears: An Application to Educational Enrollments in States of India', *Demography*, 38(1): 115–32.

Foster, J., Greer, J., and Thorbecke, E. (1984), 'A Class of Decomposable Poverty Measures', *Econometrica*, 52(3): 761–6.

Gaiha, R. (1988), 'Income Mobility in Rural India', *Economic Development and Cultural Change*, 36(2): 279–302.

Geremek, B. (1994), *Poverty: A History*, Oxford: Blackwell (original Italian edition pub. 1986).

Harriss, J. (2002), 'The Case for Cross-disciplinary Approaches in International Development', *World Development*, 30(3): 487–96.

Harriss-White, B. (2005), 'Destitution and the Problem of its Politics: With Special Reference to South Asia', *World Development*, 33(6): 881–92.

Haswell, M. (1975), *The Nature of Poverty: A Case History of the First Quarter-Century after World War II*, London: Macmillan.

Hufton, O. (1974), *The Poor of Eighteenth Century France*, Oxford: Clarendon Press.

Hulme, D. (2006), 'Chronic Poverty', in D. A. Clark (ed.), *The Elgar Companion to Development Studies*, Cheltenham: Edward Elgar, 61–7.

——and McKay, A. (2008), 'Identifying and Measuring Chronic Poverty: Beyond Monetary Measures', in N. Kakwani and J. Silber (eds.), *The Many Dimensions of Poverty*, London: Palgrave Macmillan.

——Moore, K., and Shepherd, A. (2001), 'Chronic Poverty: Meanings and Analytic Frameworks', Chronic Poverty Research Centre Working Paper 2, CPRC, University of Manchester.

——and Shepherd, A. (2003), 'Conceptualizing Chronic Poverty', *World Development*, 31(3): 403–24.

——and Toye, J. (2006), 'The Case for Cross-disciplinary Social Science Research on Poverty, Inequality and Well-Being', *Journal of Development Studies*, 42(7): 1085–107.

Iliffe, John (1987), *The African Poor: A History*, Cambridge: Cambridge University Press.

Kanbur, R. (2002), 'Economics, Social Science and Development', *World Development*, 30(3): 477–86.

——(ed.) (2003), *Q-Squared: Combining Qualitative and Quantitative Methods in Poverty Appraisal*, Delhi: Permanent Black.

——and Shaffer, P. (eds.) (2007a), *Experiences of Combining Qualitative and Quantitative Approaches in Poverty Analysis*, special issue of *World Development*, 35(2), February.

————(2007b), 'Epistemology, Normative Theory and Poverty Analysis: Implications for Q-Squared in Practice', *World Development*, 35(2): 183–96.

Lawson, D. (2007), 'Methodological Issues Associated with Combining Quantitative and Qualitative Approaches in Understanding Poverty Dynamics: Evidence from Uganda', paper presented at the conference on Q-Squared in Policy, Hanoi, 7–8 July.

——McKay, A., and Okidi, J. (2003), 'Poverty Persistence and Transitions in Uganda: A Combined Qualitative and Quantitative Analysis', CPRC Working Paper 38, Institute for Development Policy and Management, University of Manchester.

Loury, G. (1981), 'Intergenerational Transfers and the Distribution of Earnings', *Econometrica*, 49(4): 843–67.

Narayan, D., Chambers, R., Shah, M. K., and Petesch, P. (2000), *Voices of the Poor: Crying out for Change*, New York: Oxford University Press for the World Bank.

Ostrom, E. (1990), *Governing the Commons: The Evolution of Institutions for Collective Action*, New York: Cambridge University Press.

25

Radhakrishna, R., Rao, K. Hanumantha, Ravi, C., and Reddy, B. Sambi (2006), 'Estimation and Determination of Chronic Poverty in India: An Alternative Approach', paper presented at the CPRC Workshop on 'Concepts and Methods for Analysing Poverty Dynamics and Chronic Poverty', Chancellors Conference Centre, University of Manchester, 23–5 October.

Scoones, I. (1998), 'Sustainable Rural Livelihoods: A Framework for Analysis', IDS Working Paper 72, Brighton: Institute for Development Studies.

Scott, J. (1998), *Seeing Like a State: How Certain Schemes to Improve the Human Condition Have Failed*, New Haven: Yale University Press.

Sen, A. K. (1976), 'Poverty: An Ordinal Approach to Measurement', *Econometrica*, 44: 219–31.

——(1985), *Commodities and Capabilities*, Oxford: Elsevier Science Publishers.

——(1999), *Development as Freedom*, Oxford: Oxford University Press.

Smith, D. H., and Gravelle, H. (2000), *The Practice of Discounting in the Economic Evaluation of Health Care Interventions*, York: Centre for Health Economics, University of York.

Strauss, J., and Thomas, D. (1998), 'Health, Nutrition and Economic Development', *Journal of Economic Literature*, 36(2): 766–817.

Part II

Poverty Dynamics

Poverty Measurement and Assessment

2

Chronic Poverty and All That

The Measurement of Poverty over Time

César Calvo and Stefan Dercon

2.1. Introduction

A vast literature has developed on the measurement of poverty. Poverty is considered a state of deprivation, with a living standard below some minimal level. Much debate has focused on ways to approach the underlying standard of living. For example, in recent years much attention has been given to finding appropriate ways to address the multidimensionality in assessing living standards and poverty (Tsui, 2002; Bourguignon and Chakravarty, 2003). In this chapter we focus on another issue often ignored in the standard poverty literature: that the standard of living is not a static, timeless state, but a state that evolves over time. The standard of living follows a trajectory, a path with a history and a future. As a consequence, to assess poverty over time for a particular individual or society, we could explore how we should assess different trajectories of the standard of living, rather than just focusing on the standard of living and poverty in each period, as if neither past nor future poverty experiences had any bearing on the meaning of present hardship. In this chapter, we provide some tentative steps to address this issue.

Both theory and empirical evidence provide reasons why careful attention to time paths may be important. If we are interested in well-being over a long time span, information about present outcomes can only be sufficient in a very stable world, where individuals need not exert any effort to ensure that their outcomes remain invariant. It is hard to think of such a scenario. In practice, first, a myriad of reasons for fluctuations exist, and smoothing efforts are often impossible, e.g. in the case of health, which cannot be transferred from the present to the future, nor vice versa. While some storing technology may be available for other well-being dimensions, the individual may still find it hard to fully smooth away all variations, since such technology will rarely be perfect. For instance, in the case of consumption, credit market failures disallow some people to resort to high future consumption flows in the face of current hardship. Secondly, in a world with uncertainty, random shocks may push outcomes above or below the expected time-invariant target. If insurance mechanisms are imperfect, then the individual will be exposed to the consequences of shocks she failed to foresee.

In this chapter, fluctuations are interesting in their own right. However, this does not mean that their long-term effects on living conditions are overlooked. Surely enough, fluctuations may turn into serious persistence: a temporary shortfall may translate into a long period of low well-being, with slow and uneven recovery, if at all. Also, in their quest for stability, households may react to the threat of fluctuations by resorting to smoothing efforts with some cost in terms of long-run growth. For instance, a street vendor may prefer not to commit to items exhibiting great seasonality, even if they are very profitable.

The issues arising as soon as we pay attention to time trajectories are thus manifold. Policy implications also promptly crop up. For instance, this concern can be directly linked to policy discussion related to concepts of 'chronic' poverty: we should be concerned with poverty that does not easily resolve itself, that has a persistence attached to it. Obviously, this is a statement about a future state, yet not just about one future period, but related to a permanent escape or the lack of escape from poverty, persisting in different periods. In order to assess different paths over time, means of ordering and/or valuing these trajectories are required.

This chapter therefore explores issues related to the assessment of poverty over a lengthy *period* of time for an individual. By 'lengthy' we mean that this period can be decomposed into *spells*. In each spell, we observe the level of the standard of living, which for simplicity we will call consumption. Each spell is long enough for consumption flows to be observed and measured. For instance, we may think of a five-year *period*, with consumption data for each single year. Let us use 'spell' to refer to the time units (indexed by t) where consumption flows c_t are measured (in the example, one year), and 'period' to refer to that 'lengthy' stretch which we are interested in (i.e. all five years together).

While, for the sake of concreteness, in this note we prefer to speak of consumption, the discussion equally applies to any other dimension of well-being, such as nutritional status. Define poverty in a T-spell period as

$$P_T(y_1, y_2, \ldots, y_T),$$

where y_t stands for consumption at spell t. Let z be the poverty line. We assume this line to be time invariant for simplicity. Alternatively, if poverty lines did vary over time, our analysis would still hold only if outcomes in every spell were to be normalized with respect to their spell-specific poverty lines.

Put differently, in our setting, consumption changes over time must reflect variations in the ability of the individual to reach decent living standards, above the minimum acceptable norm.

It would be wrong to suggest that the concerns addressed have no precedents. A vast empirical literature has developed that assesses the 'dynamics' of poverty, by following the poverty status over time of particular individuals or groups. For example, Baulch and Hoddinott (2000) summarize a number of studies, using panel data, by counting 'poverty spells', whereby they mean how often people are observed to be poor in a particular period, and also using simple concepts of poverty mobility, based on poverty transition matrices, identifying who moved in and out of poverty, and who stayed poor. The best-known summarizing measure of poverty assessed over time is Ravallion's 'chronic poverty' measure. This measure assesses chronic poverty as the level of poverty obtained based on a Foster–Greer–Thorbecke measure, using the average level of consumption over the entire period as the underlying standard of living measure (Jalan and Ravallion, 2000).

In this chapter, we will argue that these approaches are particular, certainly suggestive, but still arbitrary choices among many different others that could be made to make sense of poverty over a particular period.[1] We will present a number of measures and document some of the specific underlying normative choices based on specific alternative axioms. Our approach may be best motivated by considering a few imaginary scenarios. First, let Figure 2.1a act as a benchmark description of consumption flows of a given individual. There, each poverty-free spell is succeeded by hardship, which in turn lasts for only one spell and is followed by a fresh episode of sufficient consumption. How should this scenario compare to those in the other three charts? In Figure 2.1b, the same pattern exists, except consumption is higher in non-poor spells, whereas poor episodes remain just as bad. Should we say that period-long poverty has lessened? This raises the issue of *compensation* of poverty spells by non-poverty spells, and the first issue tackled below. As we will show, different plausible measures of poverty of time take a different stance on this issue. In static poverty measurement, across individuals, the issue barely arises by using the focus axiom: the non-poor's outcomes are considered as if they just have reached the poverty line. When considering the poverty over time of a specific individual, this is not self-evidently resolved, as some may argue that hardship at some point in life may be acceptable if it is followed by much better outcomes in other periods. In our measures, we will show that how such judgements can be incorporated.

---

[1] Some of the concerns explicitly considered in this chapter related to compensation over time and discounting are also discussed in a very different context, related to adjusting poverty measures to handle differential mortality across a population, in Kanbur and Mukherjee (2006).

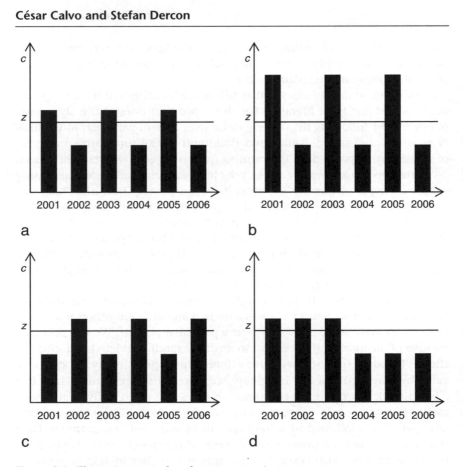

Figure 2.1. Illustrative examples of poverty experiences

Next, compare 2.1a with 2.1c. As seen from 2006, the salient difference lies now in the fact that poverty episodes were suffered further back in the past. The alternation pattern is otherwise still in place. The question is then whether the assessment of period-long poverty must pay the same attention and attach the same weight to all isolated poverty spells, regardless of how far in the past each occurred. This may be the case if the affliction of human deprivation is seen as an irremediable loss, but on the other hand, its burden can also be imagined to die out as time passes. This is a second issue explicitly discussed: is there any case for using 'discount rates', judgements on the relative importance of the present relative to the future or past?

The same question arises as we lastly take Figure 2.1d. Keeping Figure 2.1a as the benchmark, 2002 and 2005 seem to swap consumption levels. However, a new issue comes forth, since poverty spells are now contiguous, and the individual faces a prolonged episode of poverty (2004–2006). Should the

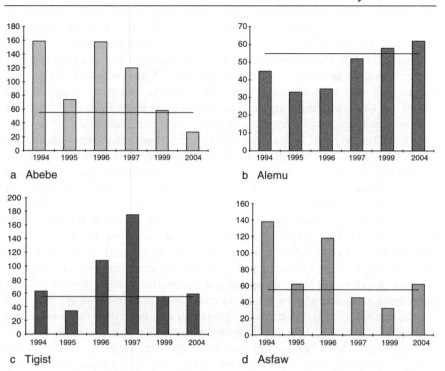

Figure 2.2. Examples of poverty experiences from the Ethiopian panel data survey

distress of hardship compound over time, such that a three-spell episode of poverty should cause greater harm than three isolated poverty spells? This is the third question to tackle as we turn to our intent to propose poverty measures over a lengthy period.

While these stylized examples show some of the choices involved, trajectories observed in actual data look messier. For example, take four trajectories found in the Ethiopian rural household panel data survey, with six observations in the period 1994 to 2004. While these consumption levels may well be measured with error, the patterns are not simple, and general judgements about how to order these in terms of poverty over time are not self-evident. For example, the household of Abebe (Figure 2.2a) appears to have been going downhill in the last four years of the data, but has only one spell in poverty, while Alemu (Figure 2.2b) has four poverty spells, but by the end of the period has two years above the poverty line. Tigist and Asfaw's families (Figures 2.2c and 2.2d) both have spells below the poverty line, but at different times in the sequence.

It is clear that many judgements will be required to summarize such trajectories of the standard of living in one single index of intertemporal poverty.

This chapter aims to present a number of possible indices, even though its main aim is to make some of these normative judgements explicit.

Foster (2007) in this collection has a related objective, but aims to explicitly construct a class of measures of 'chronic poverty'. Below we will highlight the similarities with at least one of our own measures, but there is one crucial difference worth commenting on now. His measure starts from the identification within the data of who is chronically poor, and then proceeds in ways not dissimilar to ours. In his paper, a 'chronic' poor person is someone who experiences at least a specific percentage of poverty over time. His measure of chronic poverty then values the depth and severity of poverty for such persons, excluding the non-chronically poor. While internally fully consistent and sensible, and a chronic poverty equivalent of the Foster–Greer–Thorbecke measure, one key requirement is a judgement of a cut-off for classifying someone as 'chronic' poor, irrespective of how far below the poverty line this person is. By introducing a further threshold beyond the poverty line, the result is that people with just over the required number of spells for chronic poverty, but with all spells just below the poverty line, would be considered chronically poor, while someone with marginally fewer but more serious spells is counted as transitory poor. Our approach does not resolve this issue at all—it just ducks it—by considering measures of 'a poor life', or more precisely the extent, depth, and severity of 'poverty over a period of time', using a means of weighing all poverty spells in one aggregate across time, irrespective of the frequency of spells.

In the next section, we offer the basic set-up, discussing the key decision needed regarding applying a focus on poverty, transformation of outcomes and aggregation over time. In section 2.3, we present a number of core axioms that may guide these choices, and the resulting choice of measures. In section 2.4, a set of measures are presented, ordered by the particular sequence in terms of applying focus, transformation, and aggregation. They can be shown to satisfy (or not) some of the suggested axioms for intertemporal poverty assessment. The rest of the chapter will offer extensions. In section 2.5, a discussion is introduced on the role of time preference, while in section 2.6, the idea of sensitivity to prolonged poverty is introduced. In section 2.7, we reintroduce risk and derive a forward-looking measure of the threat of long-term poverty, building on our previous work on vulnerability. Finally, in section 2.8, we offer some examples of how some of the measures may be applied using data from Ethiopia.

2.2. Basic Set-up

Unless otherwise stated, and for most of the chapter, we will imagine the world to be uncertainty free. All consumption levels are perfectly known, regardless of the point we take in time. For instance, as seen from the final spell, a backward-looking assessment of poverty throughout the period has the benefit of hindsight, and no uncertainty clouds the view of past consumption levels. Our assumption intends to put forward-looking assessments on a similar standing, by granting the individual the gift of perfect foresight. To see what this implies, imagine periods are seen (ex post) from their final spells and ranked according to some intertemporal poverty measure, and also that some ranking reshuffling occurs if the standing point is brought forward (ex ante) to their first spells. In our world, uncertainty cannot act as an explanation for such reshuffling, at least for now. In the final section of the chapter, we will suggest an extension in which this perfect foresight is dropped and uncertainty is reintroduced.

By assuming away uncertainty, we can focus both ex post and ex ante analyses on our central question, which is to identify a metric for *how much suffering or deprivation was or will be endured over a particular period*. This concern must be distinguished from the *current experience* of suffering which may be caused by a grim *future* (a sense of hardship to come), or by unhappy memories of *past* deprivation. For instance, if we speak about poverty between 2007 and 2015, we will enquire how much poverty will be 'accumulated' by the end of 2015 (and not how much future hardship impinges ex ante on well-being in 2007). In this note, we think of period poverty as the cumulative result of spell-specific poverty episodes.

In the vein of the distinction between 'identification' and 'aggregation' in the measurement of aggregate poverty (as in Sen), let us propose the following three stages for our analysis:

- *Focus.* It is well known that all measures of aggregate poverty (e.g. Foster, Greer, and Thorbecke, 1984) build on some form of focus axiom, whereby outcomes above z are censored down to the poverty line itself, since the poverty of the poor is not meant to be alleviated by the richness of others. For instance, a society will not be said to be less poor simply because the rich become richer, with no change in consumption levels among the poor. Thus, it is this focus condition that 'identifies' the relevant outcomes. Let this stage be related to a function $f(u)$, such that $f(u) \equiv \text{Min}[u, z_u]$, where z_u is the relevant poverty threshold, e.g. $z_u = z$ if $y = u$.

- *Transformation.* To motivate this stage, recall the well-known Pigou–Dalton condition, whereby aggregate poverty rises if consumption is transferred from the very poor to the not-so-poor. In our case, we may require period poverty P_T to rise as a consequence of a transfer from a poor spell to a not-so-poor spell, in the presumption that the drop in the former will outweigh the gain in the latter. This however is a presumption that cannot be taken for granted in our case, since the locations in time of these two spells may matter and have not been determined yet. For instance, the poorer spell may have occurred such a long time ago that its loss in consumption may be meaningless. The 'aggregation' step turns to such issues shortly.

Nonetheless, we can still say that *for equally valued spells* (in the way that all individuals are equally valued by the Pigou–Dalton condition), a transfer for the benefit of a not-poor spell should result in greater intertemporal poverty P_T. In practical terms, this implies that outcomes y_t must at some point be transformed by a suitable strictly convex function, *either before or after some correction for the value of their time location has been made*.

Let function $g(u)$, with $g'(u) < 0$ and $g''(u) > 0$ account for the possibility of this strictly convex transformation.

- *Aggregation*. Thirdly, spell-specific inputs must combine into one single measure of total, period-long poverty P_T. To be clear, we deal here with an aggregation over time spells, and not over individuals (as in the usual poverty measures). Hence, aggregation methods may well differ from the standard procedure. For instance, they will need to account for weight differences across time spells, e.g. if we were to decide that spells further back in the past should be paid less attention than more recent ones.

  Let function $A_T(u_1, u_2, \ldots, u_T)$ perform this aggregation. To keep the convex, Pigou–Dalton-like transformation as a separate issue, let A_T be *linear in each of its arguments*. This restriction has no major drawback—except for the transfer argument described above, there is no obvious reason why changes in any spell should be allowed to have any bearing on the effect on P_T of further changes in that same spell.

How these three stages come together is a question with no unique answer. Will we first apply focus, then transform and then aggregate over the entire period, or will we change the order of these actions? As will be shown below, this sequence matters. But which order we choose will depend on our view on the set of desirable properties of a period-long poverty measure. To develop this further, we will in section 2.4 give examples of the possible permutations related to focus, transformation, and aggregation. In the next section, we will first discuss some possible desiderata.

2.3. Formalizing the Axioms

In this section, we offer a few possible axioms that can guide us in choosing particular measures of individual, period-long poverty. The set of these axioms is not exhaustive, in the sense that no combination of them determines uniquely a particular family of measures. These desiderata will nevertheless offer routes to decide among different permutations of focus, transformation, and aggregation.

The first two axioms are quite general and hardly debatable.

Monotonicity in outcomes. Since consumption rises can under no circumstances cause a rise in poverty, we impose

$$\text{For } d > 0, P_T(y_1, y_2, \ldots, y_t + d, \ldots, y_T) \leq P_T(y_1, y_2, \ldots, y_t, \ldots, y_T) \quad (2.1)$$

A narrower definition specification is only possible if we decide when the focus stage will enter. For instance, if the focus function f is allowed to come first, then we could go further and require

$$\text{For } d > 0 \text{ and } y_t < z, P_T(y_1, y_2, \ldots, y_t + d, \ldots, y_T) < P_T(y_1, y_2, \ldots, y_t, \ldots, y_T)$$
$$(2.1')$$

In words, this alternative version imposes that a consumption rise during a poverty spell will reduce overall poverty. In (2.1), since focus has not yet been enforced, $y_t < z$ is not enough to take for certain that the reduction in P_T will occur, and we can only rule out a rise in poverty.

Increasing cost of hardship. This axiom echoes the Pigou–Dalton condition, whose exact translation to our setting would impose that a consumption transfer from a very-poor spell to a not-so-poor spell should raise overall poverty. However, we cannot readily resort to this formulation here, since the time location of these spells must also be specified, unless we assume that regardless of these locations, all spells are equally valued. While the Pigou–Dalton assumption that all individuals (with equal consumption) receive equal attention faces no major objection, here we must allow for the case where some time spells receive greater weight than others.

An alternative formulation can build on the effect of consumption changes at *one single spell*, and thus steer clear of the risk of committing to valuations of changes in two different spells. The spirit of this condition remains unchanged—*consumption losses hit harder if consumption is already low to begin with*. We may phrase it as the increasing cost of hardship. Formally,

$$\text{For } d > 0 \text{ and } y_K < z, P_T(y_1, \ldots, y_K, \ldots, y_T) - P_T(y_1, \ldots, y_K + d, \ldots, y_T)$$
$$> P_T(y_1, \ldots, y_K + d, \ldots, y_T) - P_T(y_1, \ldots, y_K + 2d, \ldots, y_T) \quad (2.2)$$

Next, one may invoke an axiom providing the basis for comparison across periods of different lengths. While 'total' poverty over a given T-span is necessarily dependent on its length T, one may wish to speak of poverty at an 'average' spell, i.e. the spell-specific poverty level which, if repeated in every single spell of the period, would lead to the observed period-long poverty level. To formalize this, let $P_T(y_1, y_2, \ldots, y_T)$ increase proportionally to a k-fold repetition of the period at hand, which we may write as

Full-period repetitions.

$$P_{kT}(y_1', y_2', \ldots, y_{kT}') = kP_T(y_1, y_2, \ldots, y_T), \tag{2.3}$$

where $y_{i+k(t-1)}' = y_t$ for $t = 1, 2, \ldots, T$ and $i = 1, 2, \ldots, k$.

In (2.3), we imagine that the complete period is lengthened by allowing the first spell to repeat k times before the outcome of the (initially) second spell obtains, which then repeats k times before the third outcome occurs, and so forth. Consider the following alternative formulation (2.3′), where the whole period unfolds and is then followed by an identical sequence of T spells, and then by another, and so forth until it is repeated k times:

$$P_{kT}(y_1', y_2', \ldots, y_{kT}') = kP_T(y_1, y_2, \ldots, y_T), \tag{2.3′}$$

where $y_{t+k(i-1)}' = y_t$ for $t = 1, 2, \ldots, T$ and $i = 1, 2, \ldots, k$

The difference between (2.3) and (2.3′) is trivial only if we impose two assumptions which we shall discuss further on, namely that all outcomes are equally valued, regardless of the time when they occur, and also that hardship is assessed in each spell separately, e.g. with no chance for the immediately preceding outcomes to matter. Otherwise, if either of these assumptions fails, then a choice between (2.3) and (2.3′) is required. Both assumptions are also underlying the two remaining axioms of this section.

Note that this axiom is clearly akin to the population invariance axiom of aggregate poverty measurement. It also plays a similar role here in contributing to a linear specification of the aggregation function A_T. In the spirit of Foster and Shorrocks (1991), we will approach linearity by imposing this full-period repetitions axiom and also a 'sub-period consistency' axiom. The latter is meant to impose Gorman separability and hence needs $P_T(y_1, y_2, \ldots, y_T)$ to be a transform of a linear combination of $y_1, y_2, \ldots, y_T$ as long as $T \geq 3$. The axiom on full-period repetitions then generalizes this result to $T \geq 1$.

To formalize, and further mirroring the aggregate poverty literature, allow the period to be decomposed into (any) two sub-periods and focus on the reaction of period-long poverty to changes in these sub-periods.

Sub-period consistency.

$$P_T(y_1', y_2', \ldots, y_K', y_{K+1}, \ldots, y_T) > P_T(y_1, y_2, \ldots, y_K, y_{K+1}, \ldots, y_T) \tag{2.4}$$

if $P_K(y_1', y_2', \ldots, y_K') > P_K(y_1, y_2, \ldots, y_K)$ and $P_{T-K}(y_{K+1}', y_{K+2}', \ldots, y_T') = P_{T-K}(y_{K+1}, y_{K+2}, \ldots, y_T)$.

If some sub-period exhibits a rise in poverty (while poverty remains unaltered in all other sub-periods), then P_T must also rise for the entire period. This sensitivity is what we mean by 'consistency'. Its interpretation may gain from noting that it restricts the ability of some spells (those from $K+1$ to T) to impinge on the effect of other spells (from 1 to K) on P_T. We may see the seed of a linear specification here, which however needs a stronger axiom to be fully imposed. Such axiom can be phrased as 'sub-period decomposability', whereby total period-poverty is a weighted sum of both sub-period poverty indices.

Sub-period decomposability.

$$P_T(y_1, y_2, \ldots, y_K, y_{K+1}, \ldots, y_T) = \frac{K}{T} P_K(y_1, y_2, \ldots, y_K)$$

$$+ \frac{(T-K)}{T} P_{T-K}(y_{K+1}, y_{K+2}, \ldots, y_T) \quad (2.5)$$

Needless to say, this axiom is reminiscent of subgroup decomposability in the aggregate poverty literature. Again, note both that timing is assumed to have no bearing on the valuations of a given spell, and any information in the *sequence* of poverty spells can be ignored: the valuation of a poverty spell is unrelated to its history, such as whether the person was poor before or not—sequences are quite freely broken into sub-pieces.

Even though this set of axioms is relatively limited, they are enough for a clarifying discussion on some possible measures, linked to particular permutations of the choices related to focus, transformation, and aggregation.

2.4. Choices as a Matter of Sequencing

We said that alternative P_T specifications follow from alternative sequencing choices for three crucial stages (Focus, Transformation, and Aggregation). Even though six orderings thereof are possible (FTA, TFA, FAT, TAF, AFT, and ATF), in this section we only consider four of them, prior to giving the general specification of the corresponding period-long poverty measures, as well as a number of specific examples. Four orderings are enough to characterize the existing alternatives, since it can be easily shown that focus and transformation can swap positions with no practical consequence, provided aggregation is not inserted between them. Thus, FTA exhausts all the insights in TFA, and likewise AFT can stand for ATF.

Case 1: Focus–Transformation–Aggregation (FTA).

$$P_T(y_1, y_2, \ldots, y_T) \equiv A_T(g(f(y_1), f(y_2), \ldots, f(y_T))) \quad (2.6)$$

In this case, imposing first focus implies that consumption levels are immediately censored. Hence, this specification rules out compensations *across time spells*, in the same spirit of the focus axiom in aggregate poverty measures, which discards compensations across individuals. In our case, the intuition could be phrased as follows: 'poverty episodes cause shock and distress to such an extent that they leave an *indelible mark*—no future or past richness episode can make up for them.'

Under FTA, convexity is imposed next, before aggregation. Unsurprisingly, the resulting families of measures are reminiscent of the well-known Chakravarty (1983) and Foster, Greer, and Thorbecke (1984) measures of aggregate poverty. To see this, consider in particular the first two of the examples below, where $\tilde{y}_t \equiv \text{Min}[z, y_t]$ and aggregation allows for some time adjustment, as by β^t. For now, and for the rest of this section, we may take this factor as given, until we turn to discuss it in section 2.4.

$$P_T(y_1, y_2, \ldots, y_T) = \sum_{t=1}^{T} \beta^{T-t} \left(1 - \frac{\tilde{y}_t}{z}\right)^{\alpha}, \text{ with } 1 < \alpha \text{ and } \beta > 0. \quad (2.7)$$

$$P_T(y_1, y_2, \ldots, y_T) = \sum_{t=1}^{T} \beta^{T-t} \left[1 - \left(\frac{\tilde{y}_t}{z}\right)^{\alpha}\right], \text{ with } 0 < \alpha < 1 \text{ and } \beta > 0. \quad (2.8)$$

Measure (2.7) is a simple multi-period version of the FGT measure, where aggregation has acted upon time spells, rather than individuals. Formula (2.8) offers a similar idea for the Chakravarty measure. In terms of formal desiderata, FTA does rather well in capturing at least some of the basic desiderata. *Both Monotonicity and Increasing cost of hardship apply.* Transformation ensures the latter because it applies before aggregation, i.e. before all spell-specific outcomes merge into some form of total consumption, where no distinction between poor and not-so-poor spells would be possible. Likewise, *Sub-period decomposability* is also possible due to the fact that aggregation comes last, so that the linearity of the final specification is not endangered—thus, total-period poverty can be written as a weighted average of sub-period poverties. This equally allows *Full-period repetitions*.

A limiting case of (2.7) is familiar, imposing $\beta = 1$ and $\alpha = 0$. It would result in a period-long poverty measure that simply counts the number of spells below the poverty line. But unlike (2.7), by imposing $\alpha = 0$, it would fail both the *Monotonicity* and the *Increasing cost of hardship* axioms. Nonetheless, the simplicity of this specification makes it a useful starting point for summarizing total-period poverty. It has been used among others by Baulch and Hoddinott (2000), when counting poverty spells and its distribution across a population.

Measure (2.7) is probably the most straightforward and relevant for empirical analysis. It aggregates individual period-by-period poverty spells into one aggregate measure of poverty over a period of time consisting of T spells. It is also close to the ideas behind Foster (2007) in this collection, with one crucial difference: we do not restrict this measure to be zero for those who experience a frequency of spells below the 'chronic poverty' threshold.

Case 2: Focus–Aggregation–Transformation (FAT).

$$P_T(y_1, y_2, \ldots, y_T) \equiv g\left(A_T\left(f(y_1), f(y_2), \ldots, f(y_T)\right)\right) \quad (2.9)$$

A different set of families obtains if aggregation occurs before a convex transformation is enforced. Since focus retains the first move, it is still true that poverty episodes remain the crucial concern. We do not take into account any outcomes above the poverty line: there is no weight attached to being better off in good years. For example, Figures 2.1a and 2.1b will still be equally valued and period-long poverty will still be the same for both cases. However, in (2.9), the severity of poverty is paid attention to not in every single spell, but only after all spell-specific outcomes are summarized into one single value. *It is overall severity that matters.*

Take the following few examples, which can read as a transformation of some form of 'present value of censored consumption':

$$P_T(y_1, y_2, \dots, y_T) = \left(\sum_{t=1}^{T} \beta^{T-t} \left[1 - \frac{\tilde{y}_t}{z} \right] \right)^{\alpha}, \text{ with } 1 < \alpha \text{ and } 0 < \beta. \qquad (2.10)$$

Given the sequencing of the three stages, it is clear that *Monotonicity* still holds, unlike *Sub-period decomposability* and *Full-period* repetitions, which must be weakened down to *Sub-period consistency*. Finally, *Increasing cost of hardship* also fails to hold, which may be undesirable on a number of accounts—very bad poverty spells are brushed aside as long as, on average, poverty spells are not too severe. This result, which clearly follows from the location of transformation at the final position of the sequence, may explain why no instances of this specification can be found in the literature. Nonetheless, other cases where transformation also comes last do exist in the literature, as we see next.

Case 3: Aggregation–Focus–Transformation (AFT).

$$P_T(y_1, y_2, \dots, y_T) \equiv g(f(A_T(y_1, y_2, \dots, y_T))) \qquad (2.11)$$

Here, transformation remains last, and even more importantly, focus is removed from the first position. Note that this second choice implies that some degree of *compensation does occur across spells*. As opposed to the view underlying FTA and FAT, what matters here is not so much whether the individual faced severe hardship at any particular point in time (regardless of how she performs at other points). The main concern is rather that outcomes realized in the rest of the period may not be high enough to compensate for observed hardship episodes. In other words, *poverty does not imply an irremediable loss*, since the case is also possible, where hardship does occur, but high consumption in other spells does 'save' the period. Looking back at our illustrative examples, Figure 2.1a has more poverty than Figure 2.1b.

Put it differently, (2.11) would be consistent with poverty assessed in relation to some form of intertemporal utility-based measure of poverty, whereby, given instantaneous or direct utility in a particular spell, the present value of these utilities is calculated as the sum of discounted direct utility, to which then some benchmark norm is applied. While this is open to argument, it does make somewhat unsatisfactory reading since period-long poverty can be reduced by focusing on spells of already high consumption well above the poverty line, say in the form of temporary opulence and feasts. Nevertheless, some intuitive examples can be shown of measures in this case:

$$P_T(y_1, y_2, \ldots, y_T) = \left\{ 1 - \text{Min}\left[1, \frac{\sum_{t=1}^{T} \beta^{T-t} y_t}{\sum_{t=1}^{T} \beta^{T-t} z} \right] \right\}^{\alpha}, \text{ with } 1 < \alpha \text{ and } 0 < \beta. \quad (2.12)$$

$$P_T(y_1, y_2, \ldots, y_T) = 1 - \left\{ \text{Min}\left[1, \frac{\sum_{t=1}^{T} \beta^{T-t} y_t}{\sum_{t=1}^{T} \beta^{T-t} z} \right] \right\}^{\alpha}, \text{ with } 0 < \alpha < 1 \text{ and } 0 < \beta. \quad (2.13)$$

Since transformation comes last, *Increasing cost of hardship* fails to hold. More strikingly, *Sub-period consistency* also does (which of course rules out *Sub-period decomposability* as well). To see why, take the following example. Imagine outcomes in a four-spell period changes from (8,8,8,40) to (4,4,8,40), with $z = 10$. Poverty has risen in the sub-period comprising the first two spells (while the rest of the period is unaltered), and yet poverty for the entire period remains at zero. Again, the reason must be found in the fact that compensations across spells are possible.

This may therefore seem an unappealing measure. However, one of the most commonly used 'measures of chronic poverty', based on Jalan and Ravallion (2000), is directly nested in this case, for $\beta = 1$. The measure reduces then to $P_T(y_1, y_2, \ldots, y_T) = \{1 - \text{Min}[1, \sum_{t=1}^{T} y_t / Tz\}^{\alpha}$, which is an FGT measure of poverty applied to *mean* consumption in the period. It rests strongly on the case for compensations across periods.

Case 4: Transformation–Aggregation–Focus (TAF).

$$P_T(y_1, y_2, \ldots, y_T) \equiv f(A_T(g(y_1), g(y_2), \ldots, g(y_T))) \quad (2.14)$$

Again, removing focus from the first position does matter, since compensations are allowed. For instance in the following examples, the main comparison takes place between the norm and some aggregation of the stream of consumption flows (say, its present value):

$$P_T(y_1, y_2, \ldots, y_T) = \text{Max}\left[0, \sum_{t=1}^{T} \beta^{T-t} \left(1 - \frac{y_t}{z} \right)^{\alpha} \right], \text{ with } 1 < \alpha \text{ and } 0 < \beta. \quad (2.15)$$

$$P_T(y_1, y_2, \ldots, y_T) = \text{Max}\left[0, \sum_{t=1}^{T} \beta^{T-t} \left[1 - \left(\frac{y_t}{z} \right)^{\alpha} \right] \right], \text{ with } 0 < \alpha < 1 \text{ and } 0 < \beta \quad (2.16)$$

Note that, in fact, these specifications may allow $P_T = 0$ even if $y_t < z$ for some t—this may well be the case if y_t is sufficiently above z in some other spells.

In terms of our desiderata, *Increasing cost of hardship* applies (since transformation is enforced before aggregation), but again, *Sub-period consistency* is dropped, along with *Sub-period decomposability*. In addition, *Monotonicity* is risked, since cases where $y_t > z$ will display the troublesome feature of greater *positive* gaps between y_t and z raising both spell-specific and period-long poverty. Unsurprisingly, no instance of this specification exists in the literature.

The result of this discussion is that a number of choices can be made in terms of the sequence of aggregation, transformation, and the application of a focus criterion, but only a relatively limited set is consistent with some desiderata. For example, (2.7) and (2.8) or (2.12) and (2.13), building on the Foster–Greer–Thorbecke and Chakravarty families of measure, have been taken as acceptable candidates. A key issue is the extent of compensation between spells that is allowed—a normative choice we can only point to. However, the discussion opens avenues for applications and extensions. In the next few sections, we will address three further issues: first, whether there is any primacy of particular spells in our assessment of period-long poverty. For example, should the last state be given any special weight, as the end-point of our assessment? The second issue is whether there are any normative issues related to the particular sequencing of spells—in particular, should any additional attention be paid to repeated spells and therefore prolonged periods of poverty? Finally, what would happen if we move to forward-looking measures, which take into account that the world is uncertain?

2.5. Equally Valued Spells

In all the examples thus far we have not been explicit about the choice of the parameter β beyond requiring that it is positive. The coefficient β determines the rate of time discounting: the weight we attach to consumption and poverty spells in different periods. Standard economic analysis assesses the value of some future flow of a variable of interest (such as income or consumption) by assuming the rate of time discounting to give nearby flows a higher weight. For instance, in (2.7), where $P_T(y_1, y_2, \ldots, y_T) = \sum_{t=1}^{T} \beta^{T-t}(1 - \frac{y_t}{z})^\alpha$, as seen from the outset at $t = 1$, we would require $\beta > 1$, so that outcomes in the distant future receive less attention. However, in our assessment of poverty spells, we argue that in fact, the choice is not as self-evident. For example taking $\beta = 1$, meaning not to exert any discount, or even $\beta < 1$, may be a sensible decision, given our purposes.

While time discounting is made undisputed use of in most intertemporal economic problems, it is not self-evident that it should apply when assessing hardship spells. Severe hardship must cause some irremediable impact on human life, or at least this seems to be the spirit underlying the whole of the literature on poverty. Poverty episodes are spells of misfortune which cannot be compensated for (in the spirit of FTA). Note how close this argument comes to the rationale behind the cases above, where focus is given the first priority, as opposed to those where the focus applies after some aggregation has been performed and outcomes are allowed to compensate for one another across spells, such as in the case of AFT. Even if some compensation were allowed for, it would seem reasonable to require that compensation comes at least at some serious cost. In any case, allowing some compensation is not an argument to dismiss poverty spells, simply because they occur far away in the future. In other words, discounting spells would sit uncomfortably with a concept of period-long poverty.

There is a corollary in the literature on health measures. In the context of the measurement of health, Anand and Hanson (1997) refuse to accept time discounts in the calculation of DALYs:

We can see no justification for an estimation of the time lost to illness or death which depends on when the illness or the calculation occurs. Suppose a person experiences an illness today and another person, identical in all respects, experiences an illness of exactly the same description next year. Discounting amounts to concluding that the quantity of the (same) illness is lower in the latter case. This does not accord with intuition or even with common use of language.

We are inclined to agree with this view. 'A principle of universalism would argue strongly for a common intrinsic valuation of human life, regardless of the age at (or the time period in) which it is lived.'

An axiomatic formulation for this stance ($\beta = 1$) allows reshuffles across time positions to occur with no bearing on total, period-long poverty. Timing does not matter. Thus, we could impose

Symmetry over time positions.

$$P_T(y_1, y_2, \ldots, y_T) = P_T(y_{\sigma(1)}, y_{\sigma(2)}, \ldots, y_{\sigma(T)}), \tag{2.17}$$

where $\sigma(u)$ is a one-to-one function whose co-domain is identical to its domain $(1,2,\ldots,T)$.

All the measures described before could be trivially adjusted to allow for (2.17) by setting $\beta = 1$.

But other arguments could be made. In evaluating trajectories, one may well be tempted to value more the spells at the end of period rather those at the beginning. Gradually drifting into poverty is then viewed as worse than evolving from spells in poverty out of poverty, even if the number and extent of spells in poverty may be equal in both cases. 'All is well that ends well' may be a sentiment that could be reflected in our value judgements. An example could be Figure 2.1d, compared to the reverse of this graph whereby the three 'non-poor' spells come at the end: the latter would then be considered better. One way of introducing this in our evaluation of trajectories would be to consider $\beta < 1$: spells later on are given a higher weight. Other choices are also possible: β could become period dependent and particular periods in the future could be given a much higher weight.[2]

2.6. Axioms of a Sequence-Sensitive Specification

An arguably strong assumption is that some form of linearity is always present in our measures of period-long poverty. To be more precise, note that our aggregation fuction A_T rules out any cross-effect across spells, i.e. $\frac{\partial^2 A_T}{\partial y_s \partial y_t} = 0$. This linearity is at the basis of the fact that the valuation of a poverty spell is unrelated to its history, such as whether the person was poor before or not. This is ensured by the linearity-related axioms above, but it can also be summarized by an underlying axiom ensuring

Independence of other time spells.

$$P_T(y_1, \ldots y_{K-1}, y_K', y_{K+1}, \ldots, y_T) - P_T(y_1, \ldots y_{K-1}, y_K, y_{K+1}, \ldots, y_T)$$
$$= P_T(y_1', \ldots y_{K-1}', y_K', y_{K+1}, \ldots, y_T') - P_T(y_1', \ldots y_{K-1}', y_K, y_{K+1}, \ldots, y_T') \quad (2.18)$$

However, the case against such independence exists. Indeed, one may prefer to imagine that prolonged, uninterrupted poverty is less acceptable than a situation of equally frequent, but intermittent poverty episodes. For instance, within a $T = 3$ period, two poverty episodes in a row may be harder to bear than the same two poverty episodes with a recovery spell in between.

Of course, this is a normative issue. It may also be phrased on the grounds of *technology-related mechanisms*, which we may even provide with the support of some empirical evidence—e.g. body strength is progressively undermined by continuous hardship and makes further poverty harder to bear, or more plainly, low consumption comes hand in hand with asset depletion. However, we prefer to say that prolonged poverty can be particularly bad *per se*.[3] The quality of a human life may be eroded more harshly if poverty is sustained for a lengthy string of spells.

In this case, we may define

Prolonged poverty.

$$P_T(y_1, y_2, \ldots, y_{K-1}, y_K + d, \ldots, y_T) - P_T(y_1, y_2, \ldots, y_{K-1}, y_K, \ldots, y_T)$$
$$\leq P_T(y_1, y_2, \ldots, y_{K-1} + e, y_K + d, \ldots, y_T)$$
$$- P_T(y_1, y_2, \ldots, y_{K-1} + e, y_K, \ldots, y_T), \quad \text{for} \quad d, e \geq 0. \quad (2.19)$$

[2] This sentiment is not unknown in the policy discourse, where targets are set: the Millennium Development Goals have a well-defined deadline—2015—and this deadline is seemingly far more important than, say, outcomes in the preceding years.

[3] Another way of putting this is that we assume here that our underlying standard of living indicator comprehensively incorporates these concerns, so that there is no more information on the spell-specific standard of living required, for example on one's asset position, once the standard of living is known. Our concern with the sequence of poverty spells relates to assessing the sequence of spell-specific standard of living outcomes: repeated spells have an additional welfare cost and there is information in the sequencing of spells.

César Calvo and Stefan Dercon

This axiom implies that some form of path dependence exists. A change in any given spell can only be assessed with knowledge of outcomes in previous spells. In particular, greater poverty in a spell implies that a drop in consumption in the following spell will hit harder. Our specification in (2.19), however, can only be taken as a starting point, since it narrows the concept of prolonged poverty down to a dependence only on the immediately pre-ceding spell, whereas one may just as well allow spells further back to matter likewise.

Note that this concern with prolonged poverty is not just one more form of smoothing behaviour. In fact, it may actually run against such behaviour. For instance, in the face of three consecutive spells where the consumption level remains invariant and below the poverty line, $P_T(y_1, y_2, \ldots, y_T)$ may drop if the neat, smooth sequence is broken by raising the middle consumption level above the poverty line, at the expense of a decrease in the other two spells. In other words, individual preferences may or may not favour smoothing efforts, and yet sensitivity of $P_T(y_1, y_2, \ldots, y_T)$ to prolonged poverty persists all the same. Our measure has a normative role, consisting in no more than reporting the extent of poverty-related suffering over a stretch of time, quite regardless of the features of the objective function of the individual.

For instance, take the following specification:

$$P_T (y_1, y_2, \ldots, y_T) = \sum_{t=1}^{T} \beta^{T-t} h (\tilde{y}_t, \tilde{y}_{t-1}), \text{ with } 0 < \beta \qquad (2.20)$$

and where some standard value for $\tilde{y}_0$ could be added as a convention to prevent $h(\tilde{y}_t, \tilde{y}_{t-1})$ from being undefined for $t = 1$. One particular specification for this sequence-sensitive measure could be

$$P_T (y_1, y_2, \ldots, y_T) = \sum_{t=1}^{T} \beta^{T-t} \left(\left(1 - \frac{\tilde{y}_t}{z}\right) \left(1 - \frac{\tilde{y}_{t-1}}{z}\right)^{\rho} \right)^{\alpha}, \qquad (2.21)$$

with $1 < \alpha, 0 < \beta$ and $0 < \rho < 1$

The measure in (2.21) can be seen as one example of a FTA measure: first focus is applied, and then a transformation takes place, and finally, aggrega-tion over spells. This last stage includes however a new element, as it allows the preceding spell to act as a weight. In particular, note that quite naturally a poverty-free spell ($\tilde{y}_t = z$) does not add to period-long poverty, either in the same spell or in the following one. However, if poverty does hit the individual, then the resulting burden increases in the severity of hardship in the recent past (since $\rho > 0$). And likewise, this new poverty episode impinges on the weight of future deprivation. The restriction $\rho < 1$ simply aims to rule out the case where in the assessment of hardship at time t, the poverty gap at $t - 1$ receives more attention than the actual gap at t.

Note that this specification imposes that $\tilde{y}_t$ and $\tilde{y}_{t-1}$ must be seen as com-plements as we assess the contribution of poor consumption in spell t to total, period-long poverty P_T. In other words, whenever we assess the extent of consumption shortfall in a particular spell, our valuation includes the memory of the shortfall if any in the last period. There is a close similarity to the literature on multidimensional poverty, where different attributes are assessed in relation to each other. Just as in multidimensional assessment, the fact that consumption (shortfalls) in any two spells must be combined into one composite leaves the gate open to questions on whether they complement (or substitute for) each other. In our case, complementarity is the only intuitive answer, since it is the fear that poor previous consumption may compound current hardship that motivates the *Prolonged poverty* axiom. The measure in (2.21)—one of many possibilities—allows for this complementarity, ensuring that poverty spells are valued higher in overall period poverty if they follow after another poverty spell.

2.7. Vulnerability in a Dynamic World

The entire discussion thus far has considered poverty in a world with time, but with no risk. When constructing a measure of poverty over time ex post, building on past observed outcomes in the standard of living, then this may be acceptable. Such a measure values actual realizations of a trajectory of the standard of living. However, using the earlier analysis when looking forward into the future to assess different paths of the standard of living, we implicitly assume perfect foresight: we know the realization of the standard of living without any uncertainty. In themselves, such exercises are useful: for example, to compare trajectories under different policies or interventions. But one striking feature of such assessment is that it is unlikely to be done in a world of certainty, and risk should feature.

In Calvo and Dercon (2006), a measure of vulnerability as the 'threat of poverty' has been derived. In particular, a set of desiderata has been proposed, borrowing from the standard poverty literature, and incorporating axioms that capture desirable properties stemming from the need to aggregate over states of the world. In the annexe, an extract of this paper is given. The intuition is to provide an aggregate over some transformation of outcomes in all states of the world, whereby outcomes in each state are assessed relative to the poverty line. This gives a metric of the threat of poverty, before uncertainty has been resolved, and not of poverty itself. As Appendix 2.1 shows, the desiderata include a focus axiom, symmetry over states, continuity and differentiability, scale invariance, normalization, probability-dependent effect of outcomes, a probability-transfer axiom between states, and risk sensitivity (so increased risk raises vulnerability). If we impose an assumption of constant relative risk sensitivity, then it is shown that the preferred vulnerability measure will be the expected value of the Chakravarty measure of poverty:

$$V_{(a)} = 1 - E \left(\frac{\tilde{y}_t}{z} \right)^{\alpha}, \quad \text{with} \quad 0 < \alpha < 1. \tag{2.22}$$

E is the expected value operator, and α regulates the strength of risk sensitivity—as α rises to 1, we approach risk neutrality. It is crucial to note that, as defined by (2.22), vulnerability becomes greater whenever uncertainty rises, even if all in all expected outcomes remain unaltered. Thus, a normative choice is made to ensure that risk *per se* is bad and compounds expected hardship.

Note also that $\tilde{y}_t$ is a vector consisting of $\tilde{y}_{it}$, censored outcomes for each state of the world i at time t. Although forward looking, this measure is still essentially timeless: possible outcomes in timeless states are considered before the veil of uncertainty is lifted and before a particular state has been realized. Nevertheless, its desirable properties when constructing a measure of the threat of poverty mean that it could be used as a candidate for period-by-period outcomes before aggregation in an intertemporal measure of poverty. In particular, consider a amended version of (2.8), which in itself was based on the Chakravarty measure of poverty:

$$V_T(y_1, y_2, \ldots, y_T) = \sum_{t=1}^{T} \beta^{T-t} \left[1 - E \left(\frac{\tilde{y}_t}{z} \right)^{\alpha} \right], \quad \text{with} \quad 1 < \alpha \text{ and } 0 < \beta \tag{2.23}$$

This can be considered a forward-looking and dynamic measure of vulnerability, consistent with a form of 'FTAA'-case, where allowing for uncertainty requires that the final stage (after focus in each state and transformation) is extended to a double exercise: aggregation first takes place over all states of the world in each t, and then it operates over all periods of time. In each period, it satisfies set desiderata that appear reasonable when assessing poverty ex ante in a risky world, as a metric of the threat of poverty. Even if the presence of risk will affect the exact formulation of the intertemporal desiderata, it appears clear that versions of the intertemporal axioms related to *Monotonicity*, *Increasing cost of transfers*, and *Sub-period decomposability* apply as well.

In other words, we have a measure of forward-looking intertemporal poverty, as a measure of the extent of the threat of poverty in the future, providing a clear ordering of different possible trajectories for individuals. It comes closer than any of its predecessors to providing a direct measure of 'chronic' poverty, in that it does not just assess poverty in one period, nor assess poverty in a risk-free world. It offers an exact way of ordering very different and complex trajectories, including the threat of poverty and deprivation implied ex ante for those whose trajectory in expectation contains serious spells of severe deprivation, even if ex post they do not always become realized.

2.8. An Example from Ethiopia

To illustrate the insights that can be gained from a variety of measures of intertemporal poverty, we use data from rural Ethiopia. The Ethiopian Rural Household Survey has collected data on about 1,450 households over the course of ten years, in the form of six unequally spaced rounds. Here we drop round 2, which was collected in the second half of 2004, as it was collected in a distinctly different season and only about six months after the first round of 2004. The result is data from 1994, 1995, 1997, 1999, and 2004. We use data on consumption per capita, deflated to be expressed in 1994 prices. The consumption aggregate is based on careful recording of consumption from own production, purchased items, and gifts, and is predominantly food, at about 75 per cent reflecting the relative poverty of households in rural Ethiopia. The data is relatively highly clustered, from only fifteen communities, but reasonably well spread across the country. Round-by-round attrition was low, although we focus in the rest of the analysis on 1,187 observations with complete information in all rounds. More details can be found in Dercon and Krishnan (2000). Using a poverty line not dissimilar to the national poverty line, at about US$8.50 per capita per month, we find that the headcount of poverty declined in this period, from 48 per cent in 1994 and even 55 per cent in 1995, to 33 per cent by 1997 (an exceptionally good harvest year) and 36 and 35 per cent in respectively 1999 and 2004. Still, there is considerable churning, and combined with the gradual decreasing poverty levels and possibly some problems of measurement error, we find that only 18 per cent of the households were never poor and 7 per cent were poor in all rounds (Table 2.1).

Using these data, we calculated a number of different poverty measures summarizing these poverty experiences, using 1,187 observations. First, and for comparison, we calculated the squared poverty gap (the Foster–Greer–Thorbecke measure with $\alpha = 2$) in the base year, 1994, and the final year, 2004. We find that it almost halved from 0.120 to about 0.065. In terms

Table 2.1. Poverty episodes 1994 to 2004 (based on five rounds)

	Percentage of households (1)
Never poor	18
Poor once	22
Poor in 2 out of 5 rounds	23
Poor in 3 out of 5 rounds	16
Poor in 4 out of 5 rounds	14
Poor in all rounds	7

Source: Ethiopia Rural Household Survey (based on 1,187 observations with data in all 5 rounds).

Table 2.2. Spearman rank correlation between different poverty measures

	Sq Pov Gap 1994	Sq Pov gap 2004	FTA (7)	AFT (12)	Seq FTA (22)	FTA (7), ($\beta = 0.85$)	FTA (7), ($\beta = 1.15$)
Sq Pov Gap 1994 ($\alpha = 2$)	1						
Sq Pov gap 2004 ($\alpha = 2$)	0.166	1					
FTA (7), ($\beta = 1, \alpha = 2$)	0.690	0.462	1				
AFT (12) ($\beta = 1, \alpha = 2$)	0.553	0.468	0.689	1			
Seq FTA (22) ($\beta = 1, \alpha = 2, \rho = 0.90$)	0.662	0.371	0.824	0.715	1		
FTA (7), ($\beta = 0.85, \alpha = 2$)	0.751	0.404	0.993	0.678	0.821	1	
FTA (7), ($\beta = 1.15, \alpha = 2$)	0.633	0.516	0.994	0.690	0.813	0.974	1

Source: Calculated from the Ethiopian Rural Household Survey by authors.

of intertemporal measures, we calculated measure (2.7) with $\alpha = 2$, an FGT-style measure in which the focus axiom is applied before transformation and aggregation, so that no compensation is allowed between periods. We also use the assumption of equal-valued spells, i.e. $\beta = 1$. Although measure (2.7) is not scaled by the number of periods, dividing it by 5 gives a direct way to compare it with the period-by-period squared poverty gaps. Its scaled mean value of 0.089 is consistent with the nature of the decline in poverty in this period. Next, we calculated measure (2.12), effectively the Jalan and Ravallion (2000) measure, a squared poverty gap measure based on mean consumption in this period, allowing for compensation and equal-valued spells (with $\alpha = 2$ and $\beta = 1$). Its mean value of 0.025 suggests how strong the impact is of allowing for compensation, i.e. for aggregation before the focus axiom is applied. Further, we calculated two indices of poverty, based on (2.7) but relaxing the assumption of equal-valued spells, by focusing on an index that values more recent years less than the past ($\beta = 0.85$) and an index that values the present more than the past ($\beta = 1.15$). Finally, we introduced sequence sensitivity, using measure (2.22), which values poverty gaps only to the extent that one was poor in the previous year, using $\rho = 0.90$, nesting it with the other cases by choosing $\alpha = 2$ and $\beta = 1$. The actual values of these last three indexes cannot quite be compared with the other indices shown.

For empirical relevance, we need to ask whether these different measures of poverty give us any different messages about poverty. As these measures are different non-linear transformations of underlying consumption measures, a first appropriate way to compare these measures would be to look at rank correlations: do they order people differently? Table 2.2 gives Spearman correlation coefficients for all these measures.

As could be expected, all measures are positively (significantly) correlated, but some interesting differences emerge. Poverty in 1994 and in 2004 is relatively weakly correlated, partly reflecting the overall decline. Among the intertemporal measures, using the FTA (2.7) measure with different discount rates does not appear to matter much for the ranking of households, with high correlations with each other. Choices on the sequence of focus, transformation, and aggregation appears to matter most, with a correlation of about 0.69 between the AFT (2.12) and the FTA (2.7) measures with otherwise equal values for α and β. Adjusting for the sequence of poverty outcomes matters, but the correlation remains high with the other AFT measures. At least in these data, choices on allowing for compensation appear to be most important, while cross-section poverty estimates for a population may give the wrong impression on intertemporal poverty outcomes and rankings.

Of course, much of this difference may be due to a different treatment of measurement error in welfare outcomes, entailed by each of these intertemporal poverty measures. More in general, the differences in poverty may be due to individual specific attributes hardly observable to a researcher. One way of assessing whether our interpretation on the nature of poverty is different across measures is by constructing a 'poverty profile', a multivariate description of the correlates of poverty in these data, effectively whether we identify different types of households to be poor using these different measures. This is definitely not an exploration of a causal relationship between any of the factors identified and poverty—more careful analysis would be required— but it can give some sense of whether different concepts of intertemporal poverty result in different implications; for example, when trying to target poor population on the basis of generic characteristics. Table 2.3 gives the correlates of some of the different poverty measures used in Table 2.2: the poverty gap in 1994, the FTA (2.7), the AFT (2.12), and the sequential FTA. The last two FTA measures, with different discount rate, were not used as they are very highly correlated with the FTA (2.7). As the poverty measures used are all censored, we use a Tobit model with censoring at zero. Table 2.3 reports the coefficients.

The correlates used include educational characteristics of the head (whether completed primary education or more, and whether some primary education, with the base group no education), land holding in hectares and per capita, the sex of the head, demographic composition of the household (number of male and female adults, children, and elderly), and a number of village characteristics: the distance to the nearest town in kilometres, whether there is a road passing the village that is accessible to trucks, buses, and cars, and the coefficient of variation of rainfall in the village; and finally, a few mean village characteristics, such as the mean land holding per capita, and the mean number of female and male adults per household (as there are substantial differences in land holdings and in demographic composition across villages).

Table 2.3. Correlates of poverty measures (Tobit model)

	Poverty gap 1994	AFT (7)	FTA (12)	Seq AFT (7)
Head at least primary ed.	-0.094 [2.35]**	-0.054 [4.66]***	-0.088 [3.36]***	-0.025 [3.56]***
Head some primary	-0.075 [2.68]***	-0.02 [2.39]**	-0.013 [0.77]	-0.006 [1.29]
ln land per capita (ha)	-0.046 [3.48]***	-0.019 [4.89]***	-0.03 [3.64]***	-0.008 [3.42]***
Sex of the head is male	-0.068 [2.49]**	-0.007 [0.83]	0.001 [0.04]	-0.005 [0.97]
No. of female adults	0.029 [3.13]***	0.01 [3.32]***	0.013 [2.24]**	0.006 [3.95]***
No. of girls 5-15	0.026 [2.69]***	0.005 [1.84]*	0.008 [1.37]	0.004 [2.61]***
No. of girls 0-5	0.031 [2.18]**	0.021 [4.83]***	0.041 [4.74]***	0.011 [4.42]***
No. of females 65+	0.037 [1.17]	0.004 [0.46]	-0.011 [0.50]	0.009 [1.59]
No. of male adults	0.015 [1.61]	0 [0.12]	-0.007 [1.11]	0.001 [0.63]
No. of boys 5-15	0.039 [4.14]***	0.014 [4.85]***	0.02 [3.40]***	0.006 [3.67]***
No. of boys 0-5	0.056 [3.80]***	0.022 [4.88]***	0.038 [4.26]***	0.011 [4.45]***
No. of males 65+	-0.047 [0.96]	-0.006 [0.43]	-0.024 [0.76]	-0.008 [0.93]
Distance to town (km)	0.021 [10.60]***	0.006 [10.43]***	0.013 [9.04]***	0.004 [10.84]***
Coeff. variation rainfall	0.006 [5.69]***	0.002 [4.82]***	0.003 [3.86]***	0.001 [3.45]***
Is road accessible trucks	-0.22 [7.56]***	-0.072 [8.66]***	-0.164 [7.42]***	-0.04 [7.75]***
Village mean land p.c.	0.228 [7.48]***	0.051 [5.64]***	0.066 [3.55]***	0.026 [5.03]***
Village mean male adults	-0.049 [0.71]	-0.039 [1.87]*	0.052 [1.17]	-0.024 [1.98]**
Village mean fem adults	0.397 [6.29]***	0.188 [9.93]***	0.178 [4.58]***	0.095 [8.79]***
Constant	-0.619 [7.90]***	-0.212 [9.14]***	-0.597 [10.33]***	-0.152 [10.99]***
Observations	1125	1125	1125	1125

Absolute value of t statistics in brackets. * significant at 10%; ** significant at 5%; *** significant at 1%.

Table 2.4. Percentage change in poverty index from marginal change in characteristics

	AFT (7)	FTA (12)	Seq AFT (7)
From no education to primary completed	−0.43	−0.39	−0.48
Doubling land per capita	−0.17	−0.19	−0.18
Reducing distance to town by one kilometre	−0.05	−0.08	−0.09
From bad or no road to road accessible for trucks/bus	−0.63	−1.01	−0.91

Source: Calculated from results in Table 2.3.

The most striking insight from the table is that the differences between the different intertemporal measures of poverty appear relatively small: in any case, in terms of significance, the same variables appear to stand out, with the expected signs: education, land, distance to towns, road access, and weather variability. Demographic characteristics also matter but not the sex of the head. Strikingly, even the profile based on the 1994 squared poverty gap offers broadly a similar set of correlates. Obviously, this does not mean that the same people are being predicted as being poor across equations.

It is difficult to interpret the differences in the size of the coefficients across equations, as the left-hand side variables are rather different and most are not directly comparable. To highlight better the different interpretations across the regressions, we can compare the marginal effects *relative* to the mean of each left-hand size variable. In other words, we can establish the percentage change on each poverty measure from a change in one of the explanatory variables. The relevant marginal effects are not the coefficients given in Table 2.3 as the zeros in the data can be given direct meaning (a zero squared poverty gap is a zero squared poverty gap, and not some unobserved negative poverty). The coefficients in Table 2.3 give the marginal effects relative to the underlying latent variable of the statistical model which is assumed to take on negative values. Instead, we use marginal effects based on the unconditional expected value, evaluated at the mean of all explanatory variables. Expressing these as a percentage of the mean dependent variable for each poverty measure, we obtain Table 2.4.

These results are suggestive, as there are some interesting differences in the order of magnitudes of the relative marginal effects. The most striking differences relate to the infrastructure variables: using the FTA (2.12) measure (i.e. allowing for compensation over time) suggests that living nearer to towns or with better roads is associated with considerably lower poverty than implied by the AFT (2.7). Education improvements are more strongly related to the AFT measures, especially the measure that effectively only counts repeated poverty episodes. In short, when using poverty measures over time, the way aggregation over time is done will affect the characteristics that will be especially highlighted in poverty profiles as correlated with lower poverty.[4]

2.9. Conclusions

This chapter has offered a discussion of a number of issues related to measuring poverty over time. It has highlighted some of the key normative decisions that have to be taken. In particular, we have highlighted the role of compensation over time (whether poverty spells can be compensated for by non-poverty spells); the issue of the discount rate (whether each spell should be given an equal weight); and the issue of the role of persistence (whether repeated spells should be given a higher weight). We have offered a number of plausible poverty measures, each with different assumptions regarding these key issues. We have also shown how these insights can be used to construct a forward-looking measure of vulnerability. Applying a number of these measures to data from rural Ethiopia, it is shown that while correlations are high, there would still be considerable differences in ranking households by poverty according to different measures, especially those that have different views on the role of compensation. Turning to a multivariate poverty profile, it was shown that while similar factors are significant, their relative importance in identifying intertemporal poverty is different according to the measure used to summarize poverty.

Appendix 2.1

A Family of Individual Vulnerability Measures (Based on Calvo and Dercon, 2006)

Let individual vulnerability (V) be measured by $V = v(z,\mathbf{p},\mathbf{y})$, where z is the poverty line, and $\mathbf{p}$ and $\mathbf{y}$ are k-dimensional vectors, containing state-of-the-world probabilities and outcomes, respectively—i.e. p_i is the probability of the i-th state occurring, with outcome y_i. We impose $y_i \geq 0$. It may be easiest to think of these outcomes as consumption levels in each possible state of the world, especially if poverty is defined as usual as a shortfall in consumption. We remark that we mean outcomes *after all consumption-smoothing efforts have been deployed*. In other words, their variability across states is taken as a final word, with no scope for reducing it further, e.g. by formal insurance, risk sharing, or precautionary savings.

---

[4] As is well known with poverty profiles, these results have only limited policy implications, as these correlates are not shown to be causal factors, and even if they were, the relative cost of intervening in terms of infrastructure, land, or education would have to be taken into account.

For each state, define 'censored outcome' $\tilde{y}_i$ by $\tilde{y}_i \equiv \mathrm{Min}(y_i,z)$, and the 'rate of coverage of basic needs' x_i by $x_i \equiv \tilde{y}_i/z$, so that $0 \le x_i \le 1$. Vectors $\tilde{\mathbf{y}}$ and $\mathbf{x}$ are defined correspondingly. $\mathbf{e}_i$ stands for a k-dimensional vector whose elements are 0, except for the i-th one, which equals 1. We close our notation with vectors $\mathbf{y}$ and $\tilde{\mathbf{y}}^c$. Their elements are all equal to y and $\tilde{y}^c$, respectively, which in turn are defined by $\hat{y} = \sum_{i=1}^{k} p_i \tilde{y}_i$ and $v(z,\mathbf{p},\tilde{\mathbf{y}}) = v(z,\mathbf{p},\tilde{\mathbf{y}}^c)$. Note that $\tilde{y}^c$ can be written as a function $\tilde{y}^c(z,\mathbf{p},\tilde{\mathbf{y}})$ and will shortly be called the risk-free equivalent to the set of prospects described by $(z,\mathbf{p},\mathbf{y})$, in the sense that it yields the same degree of vulnerability; $\hat{y}$ is the expected value of $\tilde{y}_i$.

We propose eight desiderata. The first is the Focus Axiom, which imposes $v(z,\mathbf{p},\mathbf{y}) = v(z,\mathbf{p},\tilde{\mathbf{y}})$. Our measure will thus disregard outcome changes above the poverty line. If vulnerability is understood as a burden caused by the threat of future poverty, it should not be compensated by simultaneous (ex ante) possibilities of being well off. In consequence, high vulnerability is not necessarily tantamount to grim overall expected well-being (as arguably in Ligon and Schechter, 2003), since the 'promise' of richness in some states can raise welfare expectations, with no bearing on vulnerability.

Imagine that a farmer faces two scenarios: rain (no poverty) or drought (poverty). Does she become less vulnerable if the harvest in the rainy scenario improves? Our answer is 'no'. *Poverty is as bad a threat as before.* It is as likely as before, and it is potentially as severe as before.

According to this axiom, 'excess' outcomes $y_i - z > 0$ are 'wasteful' and can be ignored, as far as vulnerability is concerned. Taking this for granted, the remaining axioms can be presented as follows:

Symmetry over States: $v(z,\mathbf{p},\tilde{\mathbf{y}}) = v(z,\mathbf{Bp},\mathbf{B}\tilde{\mathbf{y}})$, where $\mathbf{B}$ is any $k \times k$ permutation matrix. All states receive the same treatment, and the only relevant difference between two states of the world i and j is the difference in their outcomes (y_i, y_j) and probabilities (p_i, p_j).

Continuity and Differentiability. Function $v(z,\mathbf{p},\tilde{\mathbf{y}})$ is continuous and twice-differentiable in $\mathbf{y}$, for tractability and to preclude abrupt reactions to small changes in outcomes.

Scale Invariance. $v(z,\mathbf{p},\tilde{\mathbf{y}}) = v(\lambda z,\mathbf{p},\lambda\tilde{\mathbf{y}})$ for any $\lambda > 0$. Our measure will not depend on the unit of measure of outcomes.

Normalization. $\mathrm{Min}_{\tilde{y}}[v(z,\mathbf{p},\tilde{\mathbf{y}})] = 0$ and $\mathrm{Max}_{\tilde{y}}[v(z,\mathbf{p},\tilde{\mathbf{y}})] = 1$. We impose closed boundaries to facilitate interpretation and comparability.

Probability-Dependent Effect of Outcomes. For $-c < \tilde{y}_i < z$ and $p_i p_i' \neq 0$, $v(z,\mathbf{p},\tilde{\mathbf{y}}) - v(z,\mathbf{p},\tilde{\mathbf{y}}+c\mathbf{e}_i) = v(z,\mathbf{p}',\tilde{\mathbf{y}}') - v(z,\mathbf{p}',\tilde{\mathbf{y}}'+c\mathbf{e}_i)$ if and only if $p_i = p_i'$ and $\tilde{y}_i = \tilde{y}_i'$. Should $\tilde{y}_i$ change, the consequent effect on vulnerability is not allowed to depend on the outcomes or probabilities of other states of the world—for a given p_i, the change in vulnerability depends only on $\tilde{y}_i$.[5] In the opposite direction, the effect must be

---

[5] A possible counterargument could run: 'in fact, there could be some relief in considering that one could have done much better had the odds been more fortunate' (or to the contrary, 'one may rue having missed a better possible outcome, through no fault on one's own part, and thus one's misery will be greater'). We ignore such counterarguments for the sake of tractability. In doing so, we simply adhere to the common concept of poverty as mere failure to reach a poverty line, with no regard for 'subjective' subtleties.

sensitive to the likelihood of that particular state of the world. Note that $p_i p_i' \neq 0$ discards 'impossible' states ($p_i = p_i' = 0$).

PROBABILITY TRANSFER. For every $p_j \geq d > 0$, $v(z,\mathbf{p}+d(\mathbf{e}_i-\mathbf{e}_j),\bar{\mathbf{y}})\left\{{\leq\atop\geq}\right\}v(z,\mathbf{p},\bar{\mathbf{y}})$ if $\bar{y}_i\left\{{\geq\atop\leq}\right\}\bar{y}_j$.

If $\bar{y}_i$ is greater than or at least equal to $\bar{y}_j$, then vulnerability cannot increase as a result of a probability transfer from state j to state i. Likewise, if $\bar{y}_i$ is lower than or at most equal to $\bar{y}_j$, then vulnerability cannot decrease. Going back to the example of the farmer facing rain and drought, we say that she becomes more vulnerable if a drought becomes more likely, at the expense of the rainy scenario (or at least, her vulnerability does not lessen as a result).

RISK SENSITIVITY. $v(z,\mathbf{p},\bar{\mathbf{y}}) > v(z,\mathbf{p},\mathbf{y})$. Vulnerability would be lower if the expected (censored) outcome $\hat{y}$ were attained in all states of the world and uncertainty were thus removed. In other words, greater risk raises vulnerability.[6] Thus we link up with our first intuition about vulnerability, as a concept aiming to capture the burden of insecurity, the fact that hardship is also related to fear of future threats.

Alternatively, resorting to the risk-free equivalent $\bar{y}^c$, the same axiom could be expressed as $\bar{y}^c/\hat{y} < 1$. Expected outcome is unevenly and 'inefficiently' spread across states of the world, in the sense that a similarly low degree of vulnerability would result from $\bar{y}^c < \hat{y}$ being secured in every state. $\bar{y}^c/\hat{y}$ reflects this 'efficiency loss'.

CONSTANT RELATIVE RISK SENSITIVITY. For $\kappa > 0$, $\kappa\bar{y}^c(z,\mathbf{p},\bar{\mathbf{y}}) = \bar{y}^c(z,\mathbf{p},\kappa\bar{\mathbf{y}})$. A proportional increase by κ in the outcomes of all possible states of the world leads to a similar proportional increase in the risk-free equivalent $\bar{y}^c$. While risk sensitivity ensures $\bar{y}^c/\hat{y} < 1$, we now require this ratio (or 'efficiency loss') to remain constant if all state-specific outcomes increase proportionally.

As compared to the previous axioms, this final property seems less compelling. Still, we find it attractive for its contribution both to narrowing down the families of acceptable measures to only one, and to securing that risk sensitivities receive an appropriate treatment. As for this second point, Ligon and Schechter (2003) were the first to point out that some existing vulnerability measures hid some awkward assumptions, e.g. risk sensitivity increasing in initial income, at odds with most empirical findings on risk attitudes (e.g. Binswanger 1981).

Needless to say, we are avoiding here terms such as 'risk aversion' or 'utility'. We intend our choice of language to convey our view of vulnerability as distinct from expected utility, if only to stress our departure from proposals where vulnerability boils down to some form of bad 'overall' expectations (e.g. Ligon and Schechter, 2003). On the other hand, parallels should be obvious. In fact, the proof of the following theorem heavily draws on results from expected utility theory (mainly Pratt, 1964), necessarily with some departures due to the specific traits of our vulnerability concept. For this reason and for brevity, it is not provided, but it is available on request.

THEOREM 1—If all the axioms above are satisfied, then

$$V_{(a)} = 1 - E[x^a], \text{ with } 0 < a < 1. \tag{.24}$$

---

[6] We implicitly define the increase in risk as a probability transfer 'from the middle to the tails', in keeping with one of the Rothschild–Stiglitz senses of risk.

E is the expected value operator, and we recall $x_i \equiv \bar{y}_i/z$ is the rate of coverage of basic needs, and $0 \le x_i \le 1$. We highlight the simplicity of this single-parameter family of measures $V_{(\alpha)}$.[7] Of course, α regulates the strength of risk sensitivity—as α rises to 1, we approach risk neutrality.

A few remarks are in place. First, for those facing no uncertainty and with known $x_i = x^* < 1$ for all i, $V_{(\alpha)} > 0$. If vulnerability is about the threat of poverty, certainty of being poor is but a dominant, irresistible threat. The concept is not confined to those whom the winds might blow into poverty or out from it. Vulnerability is about risk, but not only about it.

Second, it is easy to prove that $V_{(\alpha)}$ is equal to the probability of being poor only if outcomes are expected to be zero in every state of the world where the individual is poor. If vulnerability were measured as expected FGT_0 (as in Chaudhuri and Jalan, 2002), then vulnerability would be overestimated. Ligon and Schechter (2003) have pointed out the shortcomings of other FGT choices.[8]

Finally, $V_{(\alpha)}$ can still be assimilated into the expected-poverty approach to vulnerability, provided poverty is measured as in Chakravarty (1983). In some sense, one of the contributions of this chapter is to identify the Chakravarty poverty index as the best choice if the poverty analysis moves from static poverty on to vulnerability.

References

Anand, S., and Hanson, K. (1997), 'Disability-Adjusted Life Years: A Critical Review', *Journal of Health Economics*, 16: 685–702.

Baulch. B., and Hoddinott, J. (2000), 'Economic Mobility and Poverty Dynamics in Developing Countries', introduction to special issue, *Journal of Development Studies*.

Binswanger, H. P. (1981), 'Attitudes toward Risk: Theoretical Implications of an Experiment in Rural India', *Economic Journal*, 91(364): 867–90.

Bourguignon, F., and Chakravarty, S. R. (2003), 'The Measurement of Multidimensional Poverty', *Journal of Economic Inequality*, 1(2): 1569–721.

Calvo, C., and Dercon, S. (2006), 'Vulnerability to Poverty', mimeo, Oxford University.

Chakravarty, S. R. (1983), 'A New Index of Poverty', *Mathematical Social Sciences*, 6: 307–13.

Chaudhuri, S., and Jalan, J. (2002), 'Assessing Household Vulnerability to Poverty from Cross-sectional Data: A Methodology and Estimates from Indonesia', Columbia University Discussion Paper 0102-52.

Dercon, S., and Krishnan, P. (2000), 'Vulnerability, Poverty and Seasonality in Ethiopia', *Journal of Development Studies*, 36(6): 25–53.

Foster, J. (2007), 'A Class of Chronic Poverty Measures', mimeo.

——Greer, J., and Thorbecke, E. (1984), 'A Class of Decomposable Poverty Measures', *Econometrica*, 52(3): 761–6.

——and Shorrocks, T. (1991), 'Subgroup Consistent Poverty Indices', *Econometrica*, 59(3): 689–709.

---

[7] For instance, if our last axiom (constant relative risk sensitivity) were replaced by constant absolute risk sensitivity $[\kappa + \bar{y}^c(z,\mathbf{p},\bar{\mathbf{y}}) = \bar{y}^c(z,\mathbf{p},\bar{\mathbf{y}} + \kappa)$, for $\kappa > 0]$, the less attractive measure $V_{(\beta)} = 1 - E[\{e^{\beta(1-x)} - 1\}/\{e^\beta - 1\}]$, with $\beta > 0$, would result.

[8] More precisely, we should speak about expected individual poverty, as measured by the function implicit in the corresponding aggregate FGT index, as in Foster, Greer, and Thorbecke (1984).

Jalan, J., and Ravallion, M. (2000), 'Is Transient Poverty Different? Evidence from Rural China', *Journal of Development Studies*, 36(6): 82–99.

Kanbur, R., and Mukherjee, D. (2006), 'Premature Mortality and Poverty Measurement', mimeo, Cornell University.

Ligon, E., and Schechter, L. (2003), 'Measuring Vulnerability', *Economic Journal*, 113(486): C95–C102.

Pratt, J. W. (1964), 'Risk Aversion in the Small and in the Large', *Econometrica*, 32(1/2): 122–36.

Tsui, K. (2002), 'Multidimensional Poverty Indices', *Social Choice and Welfare*, 19(1): 69–93.

3

A Class of Chronic Poverty Measures

James E. Foster

3.1. Introduction

Traditional measures of poverty based on cross-sections of income (or consumption) data provide important information on the incidence of material poverty, its depth and distribution across the poor. However, they have little to say about another important dimension of poverty: its duration. Empirical evidence suggests that increased time in poverty is associated with a wide range of detrimental outcomes, especially for children.[1] If so, then this would provide a strong rationale for using a methodology for evaluating chronic poverty that explicitly incorporates 'time in poverty'. This chapter presents a new class of chronic poverty measures that can account for duration in poverty as well as the traditional dimensions of incidence, depth, and severity.

There are several methodologies available for measuring chronic poverty using panel data. Two broad categories may be discerned, each with its own distinctive strategy for identifying the chronically poor.[2] The *components* approach, exemplified by Jalan and Ravallion (1998), constructs an average or permanent component of income and identifies a chronically poor person as one for whom this component lies below an appropriate poverty line.[3] Variations in incomes across periods are ignored by this identification process and by the subsequent aggregation step when the data are brought together into an overall measure. The components approach to chronic

---

[1] For example, longer exposure to poverty is associated with: increased stunting, diminished cognitive abilities, and increased behavioural problems for children (Brooks-Gunn and Duncan, 1997); worse health status for adults (McDonough and Berglund, 2003); lower levels of volunteerism when poor children become adults (Lichter, Shanahan, and Gardner, 1999); and an increased probability of staying poor (Bane and Ellwood, 1986; Stevens, 1994). See also the conceptual discussions of Yaqub (2003) and Clark and Hulme (2005).

[2] This division is due to Yaqub (2000); see also McKay and Lawson (2002).

[3] Examples of the components approach can be found in Duncan and Rodgers (1991), Rodgers and Rodgers (1993), Jalan and Ravallion (1998), and Dercon and Calvo (2006), among others.

poverty measurement is not especially sensitive to the time a family spends in poverty and, hence, may not be the best framework for incorporating duration into poverty measurement.

A second approach to evaluating chronic poverty—called the *spells* approach—focuses directly on the period-by-period experiences of poor families, and especially on the time spent in poverty. The identification of the chronically poor typically relies on a duration cut-off as well as a poverty line: Gaiha and Deolalikar (1993), for example, take the set of chronically poor to be all families that have incomes below the poverty line in at least five of the nine years of observations, hence have a duration cut-off of 5/9. As for the aggregation step, most proponents of the spells approach use a very simple index of chronic poverty based on the number of chronically poor.[4] While the number (or percentage) of chronically poor may be an important statistic to keep in mind, it is a rather crude indicator of overall chronic poverty. In particular, it ignores the time a chronically poor family spends in poverty and hence violates a 'time monotonicity' property that is especially relevant in the present context. In addition, other key dimensions of poverty, namely its depth and distribution, are utterly ignored by the index.

The present chapter adopts the general methodology of the spells approach. Two distinct cut-offs are used for identifying the chronically poor—one in income space (the usual poverty line $z > 0$) and another governing the percentage of time in poverty (the duration line $0 < \tau \leq 1$). In other words, a family is considered to be chronically poor if the percentage of time it spends below the poverty line z is at least the duration cut-off τ. For the aggregation step, this chapter presents a new class of chronic poverty measures based on the P_α family proposed by Foster, Greer, and Thorbecke (1984), appropriately adjusted to account for the duration of poverty. All of the measures satisfy time monotonicity and an array of basic axioms, while certain subfamilies satisfy the multiperiod analogues of (income) monotonicity and the transfer principle. Associated measures of *transient* poverty are defined to account for poverty that is shorter in duration. Each chronic poverty measure (and its transient dual) satisfies decomposability, thus allowing the consistent analysis of chronic poverty by population subgroup. In particular, profiles of chronic poverty can be constructed to understand the incidence, depth, and severity of poverty in a way analogous to the standard static case.

The chapter proceeds as follows. Section 3.2 provides a brief overview of poverty measurement in a static environment to help ground the discussion of chronic poverty measurement. Section 3.3 introduces time into the analysis. The identification and aggregation steps are specified and the new family

---

[4] See for example *The Chronic Poverty Report 2004–05*, p. 9, which uses a simple headcount. Duncan, Coe, and Hill (1984) and Gaiha and Deolalikar (1993) use the headcount ratio, or the percentage of the population that is chronically poor.

of chronic poverty measures is defined. Section 3.4 provides a brief application of the technology to data from Argentina, while Section 3.5 concludes.

3.2. Traditional Poverty Measurement

Following Sen (1976), poverty measurement can be broken down into two conceptually distinct steps: first, the identification step, which defines the criteria for determining who is poor and who is not; and, second, the aggregation step, by which the data on the poor are brought together into an overall indicator of poverty. The identification step is typically accomplished by setting a cut-off in income space called the *poverty line* and evaluating whether a person's resources are sufficient to achieve this level. There are several varieties of poverty lines, each with its own information basis and method for updating over time. *Subjective* poverty lines consider information from surveys that ask participants how much it takes to get along. *Relative* poverty lines depend on the current income standard in a given society: a common example sets the poverty line at 50 per cent of the median income. *Absolute* poverty lines may be purely arbitrary (such as the US$1 or US$2 per day lines used in World Bank illustrations) or may be initially derived from consumption studies. Note that in principle each type of line can be located at the low end or the high end of conceivable cut-offs (e.g. a relative line at 1 per cent of the median and an absolute line at US$15 per day); consequently, the use of an absolute line does not identify a person as being 'absolutely impoverished'. Instead, the term 'absolute' typically refers to the fact that the poverty line is to remain fixed during the time frame under consideration. In contrast, a thoroughgoing relative (or subjective) approach will have a different poverty line at each point in time as the income standards (or norms) change.[5] This chapter assumes that an absolute poverty line has been selected and that it is applicable at all time periods under consideration.

The aggregation step is typically accomplished by selecting a *poverty index* (or *measure*). Each index is a method of combining the income data and the poverty line into an overall indicator of poverty. Formally, it is a function associating with each income distribution and poverty line a real number, namely, the measured level of poverty. The simplest and most widely used measure is the *headcount ratio*, which is the percentage of a given population that is poor. It is sometimes helpful to view the headcount ratio as a specific population average; indeed, if every person identified as being poor is assigned a value of '1' while every person outside the set of the poor is assigned a value of '0', then the headcount ratio is simply the mean of the resulting '0–1' vector.

[5] One could also imagine alternative types of hybrid approaches to setting poverty lines across space and time. See Foster and Székely (2006).

A second method of aggregation is given by the *(per capita) poverty gap*, which is the aggregate amount by which poor incomes fall short of the poverty line, measured in poverty line units, and averaged across the entire population. It too can be seen as a population average, with those outside the set of the poor being assigned a value of '0', as before, and those inside being represented by their *normalized shortfall*, or the difference between their income and the poverty line, divided by the poverty line itself. In contrast to the 'all or nothing' approach of the headcount ratio, the poverty gap uses the normalized shortfall as a continuous measure of individual poverty and views overall poverty as its average value across society. Consequently, it satisfies a standard *monotonicity axiom* for poverty measures, which requires poverty to rise when the income of a poor person falls (ceteris paribus). The headcount ratio does not.

A general method of aggregation suggested by Foster, Greer, and Thorbecke (1984) proceeds as above, but first *transforms* the normalized shortfalls of the poor by raising them to a non-negative power a to obtain the associated P_a measure. This approach actually includes both of the foregoing measures: P_0 is the headcount ratio and P_1 is the poverty gap measure. The *squared gap* measure P_2 from this family takes the square of each normalized shortfall, which has the effect of diminishing the relative importance of very small shortfalls and augmenting the effect of larger shortfalls—and hence emphasizing the conditions of the poorest poor in society. As a simple average of the squared normalized shortfalls across the population, P_2 satisfies the *transfer* axiom, which requires poverty to rise whenever a poor person transfers income to a richer poor person. All the P_a measures satisfy a range of basic axioms as well as a property linking subgroup and overall poverty levels that has been used extensively in the empirical literature: *Decomposability* requires overall poverty to be the weighted average of subgroup poverty levels, where the weights are the population shares of the respective subgroups. While there are several other poverty measures in common use, this chapter will focus on the P_a class in general and the three measures P_0, P_1, and P_2, in particular, in developing a new class of chronic poverty measures.[6]

3.3. The Measurement of Chronic Poverty

A main premise of chronic poverty evaluation is that poverty repeated over time has a greater impact than poverty that does not recur. This section discusses how poverty measurement can be altered to take into account the

[6] Other measures can be found in Sen (1976), Clark, Hemming, and Ulph (1981), Chakravarty (1983), for example; see also Foster and Sen (1997), Zheng (1997), and Foster (2006).

additional dimension of time in poverty. The first part begins with some important definitions and notation.

3.3.1. Notation

The basic data are observations of an income (or consumption) variable for a set $\{1, \ldots, N\}$ of individuals at several points in time.[7] Let $y = (y_i^t)$ denote the matrix of (non-negative) income observations over time, where the typical entry y_i^t is the income of individual $i = 1, 2, \ldots, N$ in period $t = 1, 2, \ldots, T$. We adopt the convention that y is a $T \times N$ matrix (having height T and length N), so that each column vector y_i lists individual i's incomes over time, while each row vector y^t gives the distribution of income in period t. It will prove helpful to use the notation $|y| = \Sigma_i \Sigma_t y_i^t$ to denote the sum of all the entries in a given matrix, and to define an analogous notation for vectors (hence $|y_i| = \Sigma_t y_i^t$ is the sum of i's incomes across all periods while $|y^t| = \Sigma_i y_i^t$ is the total income in period t). It is assumed that incomes have been appropriately transformed to account for variations across time and household configurations so that a common poverty line z can be used to establish who is poor in each period.

It is sometimes useful to express the data in terms of (normalized) shortfalls rather than incomes. Let g be the associated matrix of normalized gaps, where the typical element g_i^t is zero when the income of person i in period t is z or higher, while $g_i^t = (z - y_i^t)/z$ otherwise. Clearly, g is a $T \times N$ matrix whose entries are non-negative numbers less than or equal to one. When an entry g_i^t is equal to zero, this indicates that the person's income is at least as large as the poverty line and hence is not in poverty; when an entry is positive, this indicates that the person's income falls below the line, with g_i^t being a measure of the extent to which that person is poor.[8] We can similarly define the matrix s of squared normalized shortfalls by squaring each entry of g; i.e. the typical entry of s is $s_i^t = (g_i^t)^2$.

Counting-based approaches to evaluating poverty ignore the extent of the income gap and instead only take into account whether the gap is positive or zero. It is therefore helpful to create another matrix h by replacing all positive entries in g with the number '1'. Thus the typical entry h_i^t of h is '0' when the income of person i in period t is *not* below z, and '1' when y_i^t is below z. One statistic of interest in the present context is the *duration* of person i's poverty, or the fraction of time the person is observed to have an income below z. Denote this by d_i and note that it can be obtained by summing the entries in

---

[7] The income variable can be any single-dimensional, cardinally meaningful indicator of well-being. In the present case, where per-period values are *not* transferable across time, this may be more consistent with consumption than with income, per se.

[8] In this chapter a person with an income of z is not poor; the alternative assumption (that z itself is a poor income level) could be adopted with a slight change in notation.

h_i (the i-th column of h) and dividing by the number of periods; i.e. $d_i = |h_i|/T$. In essence the duration is analogous to a headcount ratio, but defined for a *given* person over time, not across *different* people within the same period of time.

This chapter's approach to chronic poverty will be based on the percentage of time a person spends in poverty. Toward this end, it will be useful to derive matrices from g (and also from s and h) that ignore persons whose duration in poverty falls short of a given cut-off $\tau \geq 0$. Let $g(\tau)$ (and $s(\tau)$ and $h(\tau)$) be the matrix obtained from g (respectively s and h) by replacing the i-th column with a vector of zeros when $d_i < \tau$. In other words, the typical entry of $g(\tau)$, namely $g_i^t(\tau)$, is defined by $g_i^t(\tau) = g_i^t$ for all i satisfying $d_i \geq \tau$ while $g_i^t(\tau) = 0$ for all i having $d_i < \tau$ (with the analogous definition holding for s and h).

As the duration cut-off τ rises from 0 to 1 the number of non-zero entries in the associated matrix falls, reflecting the progressive censoring of data from persons who are not meeting the poverty duration requirement. The specification $\tau = 0$ would not alter the original matrices at all, so that $g(0) = g$, $s(0) = s$, and $h(0) = h$. Every poverty observation would be included, regardless of a person's duration in poverty. At the other extreme, the cut-off $\tau = 1$ ensures that any person who was out of poverty for even a single observation would have a column of zeros; in other words, $g(1)$, $s(1)$, and $h(1)$ consider a person who fell out of poverty for *one period* indistinguishable from a person who was *always* out of poverty.

As in the static case, the measurement of chronic poverty can be divided into an identification step and an aggregation step. There are many potential strategies for identifying the chronically poor, but all have the effect of selecting a set Z of chronically poor persons from $\{1, \ldots, N\}$. The aggregation step takes the set Z as given and associates with the income matrix y an overall level $K(y; Z)$ of chronic poverty. The resulting functional relationship K is called an *index*, or *measure*, of chronic poverty.

3.3.2. Identifying the chronically poor

What can panel data reveal that cross-sectional observations cannot? By following the same persons over several periods, they can help discern whether the poverty experienced by a person in a given period is an exceptional circumstance or the usual state of affairs.

With panel data, there are several income observations linked to each individual, and this in turn leads to a wide array of potential methods for deciding when a person is chronically poor. One approach employed by Jalan and Ravallion (1998) bases membership in Z on a single comparison between the poverty line z and a composite indicator of the resources an individual has available through time. The specific income standard employed by Jalan and Ravallion is $\mu(y_i) = |y_i|/T$, the average or mean income over time; hence their method identifies as chronically poor any person whose mean income is below the poverty line. As noted above, this approach is not particularly sensitive to the duration of poverty. Nonetheless, it may make good sense when incomes are perfectly transferable across time and, accordingly, consumption can be completely smoothed. Anyone with an average income below z would in the best case be poor for every period; while a person with a mean of z or above could be out of poverty in every period. However, the assumption of perfect transferability may be difficult to sustain, particularly for poorer individuals; and if per-period incomes are even slightly less than perfectly substitutable, this procedure could easily misidentify persons.[9]

At the other extreme is the 'spells' approach to identifying the chronically poor, which bases membership in Z upon the frequency with which one's income falls below the poverty line. So, for instance, one might require a person to be poor 50 per cent of the time or more, before identifying the person as chronically poor. A higher cut-off (say 70 per cent of the time or more) would probably lead to a smaller set of persons being identified as chronically poor, while a lower cut-off (such as 30 per cent) would probably expand the set. Note, though, that this approach also contains within it an implicit assumption—that there is *no* possibility of transferring income across periods. Indeed, it is not entirely clear why a person with a tremendous amount of income (or expenditure) in period one, who is just barely below the poverty line in the remaining periods, would be considered chronically poor, as may be required under this approach. Nonetheless, if (1) the poverty line is considered to be a meaningful dividing line between poor and non-poor and (2) the observed data on income (or consumption) in each period faithfully reflects the constraint facing the person in the given period, then identifying chronic poverty with sufficient time in poverty makes intuitive sense.

This chapter uses a dual cut-off 'spells' approach to identifying the chronically poor: The first cut-off is the *poverty* line $z > 0$ used in determining whether a person is poor in a given period; the second is the *duration* line τ (with $0 < \tau \geq 1$) that specifies the minimum fraction of time that must be spent in poverty in order for a person to be chronically poor. Given the income matrix y and the poverty line z, the matrix h depicts the poverty spells for each person, and this in turn yields d_i, the fraction of time that person i is observed to have an income below z. Then, given τ, the set of chronically poor persons is defined to be $Z = \{i : d_i \geq \tau\}$, or the set of all persons in poverty at least τ share of the time. Since Z depends on z and τ, the poverty index can be written as a function $K(y; z, \tau)$ of the income matrix and the pair of parametric cut-offs. The next section constructs several useful functional forms for $K(y; z, \tau)$.

---

[9] The case of imperfect substitutability is considered by Foster and Santos (2006).

3.3.3. *Chronic poverty and aggregation*

The first question that is likely to arise in discussions of chronic poverty is: How many people in a given population are chronically poor? The answer comes in the form of the *headcount* $Q(y; z, \tau)$ defined as the number of persons in Z. This statistic is often highlighted in order to convey meaningful information about the magnitude of the problem; however, when making comparisons, especially across regions having different population sizes, the *headcount ratio* $H(y; z, \tau) = Q(y; z, \tau)/N$ is commonly used, where N is the population size of y. The measure H focuses only on the frequency of chronic poverty in the population and ignores all other aspects of the problem, such as the average time the chronically poor are in poverty, or the average size of their normalized shortfalls.

An example will help illustrate these concepts. Consider the income matrix

$$y = \begin{bmatrix} 3 & 9 & 7 & 10 \\ 7 & 3 & 4 & 8 \\ 9 & 4 & 2 & 12 \\ 8 & 3 & 2 & 9 \end{bmatrix}$$

where the poverty line is $z = 5$ and the duration line is $\tau = 0.70$. The associated matrices of normalized poverty gaps, g, and of poverty spells, h, are given by

$$g = \begin{bmatrix} 0.4 & 0 & 0 & 0 \\ 0 & 0.4 & 0.2 & 0 \\ 0 & 0.2 & 0.6 & 0 \\ 0 & 0.4 & 0.6 & 0 \end{bmatrix} \qquad h = \begin{bmatrix} 1 & 0 & 0 & 0 \\ 0 & 1 & 1 & 0 \\ 0 & 1 & 1 & 0 \\ 0 & 1 & 1 & 0 \end{bmatrix}$$

Summing the entries of h vertically and dividing by $T = 4$ yields the duration vector $d = (d_1, d_2, d_3, d_4) = (0.25, 0.75, 0.75, 0)$ and hence we see that $Q(y; z, \tau) = 2$ and so $H(y; z, \tau) = 0.5$; in this population, half of the persons (namely numbers 2 and 3) are chronically poor.

Now consider a thought experiment in which person 3 in the above example receives an income of 3 rather than 7 in period 1, and hence the normalized gap in that period becomes 0.40 and the entry in h becomes one. Then person 3 would still be chronically poor, but would have a poverty duration of $d_3 = 1.0$ rather than 0.75. What would happen to H? Clearly, it would be *unchanged* even though a chronically poor person has experienced an increment in the time spent in poverty. In other words, H violates an intuitive *time monotonicity* axiom: if the income in a given period falls for a chronically poor person in such a way that the duration in poverty rises, then the level of chronic poverty should increase.[10] It can be argued that, while H conveys meaningful information about one aspect of chronic poverty, and

---

[10] See Foster (2007) for a precise statement of this axiom.

hence is a useful 'partial index', it is a bit too crude to be used as an overall measure.[11]

There is a very direct way of transforming H into an index that is sensitive to changes in the duration of poverty. Consider the matrix $h(\tau)$ defined above, which leaves a column unchanged if the person is chronically poor, and otherwise replaces the column with zeros. Let $d_i(\tau) = |h_i(\tau)|/T$ denote the associated duration level of person i, so that $d_i(\tau) = d_i$ for each chronically poor person and $d_i(\tau) = 0$ otherwise. Then the *average duration* among the chronically poor is given by $D(\tau) = (d_1(\tau) + \cdots + d_N(\tau))/Q$. This is a second partial index that conveys relevant information about chronic poverty, namely, the fraction of time the average chronically poor person spends in poverty. Combining the two partial measures yields an overall index that is sensitive to increments in the time a chronically poor person spends in poverty as well as to increases in the prevalence of chronic poverty in the population. Define the *duration-adjusted headcount ratio* $K_0 = HD$ to be the product of the original headcount ratio H and the average duration D or, equivalently, $K_0 = (d_1(\tau) + \cdots + d_N(\tau))/N$.

K_0 offers a different interpretation of our thought experiment from the one provided by H. Return to the original situation in which person 3 is not poor in period 1. For $\tau = 0.70$, the relevant $h(\tau)$ matrix is given by

$$h(\tau) = \begin{bmatrix} 0 & 0 & 0 & 0 \\ 0 & 1 & 1 & 0 \\ 0 & 1 & 1 & 0 \\ 0 & 1 & 1 & 0 \end{bmatrix}$$

and the respective column averages are given by $d_1(\tau) = d_4(\tau) = 0$ and $d_2(\tau) = d_3(\tau) = 0.75$. The headcount ratio is $H = 0.50$ while the mean duration is $D = 0.75$ so that the duration-adjusted headcount ratio K_0 is initially 0.375. Now when person 3's income in period 1 becomes 3 rather than 7, the fraction of time spent in poverty rises to 1 for that person, while the mean duration among all chronically poor rises to 0.875. Consequently, even though H is unchanged, K_0 rises to about 0.438, with this higher overall level of chronic poverty being due to person 3's increased time in poverty.

The above example also shows that $K_0 = \mu(h(\tau)) = |h(\tau)|/(TN)$; in words, K_0 is the mean of the entries in matrix $h(\tau)$ or, equivalently, the total number of periods in poverty experienced by the chronically poor, as given by $|h(\tau)|$, divided by the total number of possible periods across all people, or TN. In the above example, it is easy to see that the mean of the sixteen entries in $h(\tau)$ is $6/16 = 0.375$, and hence this is the duration-adjusted headcount index K_0. Notice that if a chronically poor person were to have an additional period in poverty, this would raise an entry in the matrix $h(\tau)$ from zero to one,

---

[11] See the discussion of partial indices in Foster and Sen (1997).

thereby causing the average value K_0 to rise, as noted above. In other words, K_0 satisfies the time monotonicity axiom.

There is no doubt that K_0 is less crude than H as an overall measure of chronic poverty. However, it too may not fully reflect the actual conditions of the chronically poor. The matrix $h(\tau)$, upon which K_0 is based, is unaffected by changes in incomes (or normalized gaps) that preserve the signs of the entries of $g(\tau)$, even if the magnitudes of the entries in $g(\tau)$ change dramatically. For example, if the income of person 3 in period 2 were decreased from 4 to 2, so that the normalized gap g_3^2 rose from 0.2 to 0.6, the corresponding entry in h would obviously be unchanged (namely, $h_3^2 = 1$), and hence K_0 would remain the same. So a chronically poor person is now much poorer in period 2, and yet this fact goes unnoticed by the duration-adjusted headcount measure. This is a violation of the (income) *monotonicity* axiom, which states that if a chronically poor person's income is below the poverty line in a given period, lowering that income further should increase the measured level of chronic poverty.[12]

What is missing from this measure of chronic poverty is information on the *magnitudes* of the normalized gaps. Consider the matrix $g(\tau)$ defined above whose non-zero entries are the normalized gaps of the chronically poor. The number of non-zero entries in $g(\tau)$—and hence $h(\tau)$—is $|h(\tau)|$, while the sum of the non-zero entries in $g(\tau)$ is $|g(\tau)|$. The ratio $|g(\tau)|/|h(\tau)|$ indicates the average size of the normalized gaps across all periods in which the chronically poor are in poverty. The resulting *average gap* $G(\tau) = |g(\tau)|/|h(\tau)|$ provides exactly the type of information that would usefully supplement the adjusted headcount ratio. Define the *duration-adjusted poverty gap index* $K_1 = K_0 G$ to be the product of the duration-adjusted headcount ratio K_0 and the average gap G or, equivalently, $K_1 = HDG$, the product of the three partial indices that respectively measure the prevalence, duration, and depth of chronic poverty.

This chronic poverty index provides a third perspective from which to view our numerical example. Given the duration cut-off $\tau = 0.70$, the matrix $g(\tau)$ associated with the original situation in which person 3 has an income of 4 in period 2 is given by

$$g(\tau) = \begin{bmatrix} 0 & 0 & 0 & 0 \\ 0 & 0.4 & 0.2 & 0 \\ 0 & 0.2 & 0.6 & 0 \\ 0 & 0.4 & 0.6 & 0 \end{bmatrix}$$

The respective sum of entries is $|g(\tau)| = 2.4$ while the number of periods in poverty is $|h(\tau)| = 6$, and hence the average gap is $G = 0.40$. Given $H = 0.50$ and $D = 0.75$ from before, the resulting level of the duration-adjusted poverty gap measure is $K_1 = 0.15$. Now suppose that the period 2 income of person

---

[12] See Foster (2007) for a rigorous statement of this axiom.

3 falls from 4 to 2. Clearly H and D are unaffected by this change, and so K_0 would likewise be unchanged. However, the average gap G would rise to about 0.47, and hence the duration-adjusted gap would now be $K_1 = 0.175$, reflecting the worsened circumstances for person 3. K_1 rises as a result of the income decrement since it satisfies the monotonicity axiom.

The duration-adjusted gap measure has a simple expression as the mean of the entries of the matrix $g(\tau)$, so that $K_1 = \mu(g(\tau)) = |g(\tau)|/(TN)$. In words, K_1 is the sum of the normalized shortfalls experienced by the chronically poor, or $|g(\tau)|$, divided by TN, which is the maximum value this sum can take.[13]

While K_1 is sensitive to magnitude of the income shortfalls of the chronically poor, the specific way the gaps are combined ensures that a given sized income decrement has the same effect on overall poverty whether the gap is large or small. One could argue that a loss in income would have a greater effect the larger the gap, in which case the *square* of the normalized gaps, rather than the gaps themselves, could be used. For example, suppose that the initial level of income is 4 and the poverty line is 5, so that the normalized gap is 0.20 and the squared (normalized) gap is 0.04. Decreasing the income by one unit will increase the squared gap to 0.16, an increase of 0.12. Now suppose that the initial level of income is 2, so that the normalized gap is 0.60 and the squared gap is 0.36. The unit decrement would raise the squared gap to 0.64, which represents a much larger increase of 0.28. Using squared gaps, rather than the gaps themselves, places greater weight on larger shortfalls.

Consider the matrix $s(\tau)$ whose non-zero entries are the squared normalized gaps of the chronically poor. The number of non-zero entries is $|h(\tau)|$ so that the *average squared gap* over these periods of poverty is given by $S(\tau) = |s(\tau)|/|h(\tau)|$. If this partial index is used instead of $G(\tau)$ to supplement the duration-adjusted headcount ratio, the resulting chronic poverty index would place greater weight on larger shortfalls. The resulting *duration-adjusted FGT measure* $K_2 = K_0 S$ is a chronic poverty analogue of the usual FGT index P_2 (just as K_0 and K_1 respectively correspond to P_0 and P_1 of the same class). K_2 has a straightforward expression as the product of partial indices $K_2 = HDS$ and as the mean of the entries of the matrix $s(\tau)$ of squared gaps $K_2 = \mu(s(\tau)) = |s(\tau)|/(TN)$. It is the sum of the squared (normalized) gaps of the chronically poor, divided by the maximum value this sum can take.

Referring once again to the numerical example, the matrix of squared gaps is given by

$$s(\tau) = \begin{bmatrix} 0 & 0 & 0 & 0 \\ 0 & 0.16 & 0.04 & 0 \\ 0 & 0.04 & 0.36 & 0 \\ 0 & 0.16 & 0.36 & 0 \end{bmatrix}$$

[13] TN is the value of $|g(\tau)|$ that would arise in the extreme case where all incomes were 0.

James E. Foster

and hence $K_2 = \mu(s(\tau)) = (1.12)/16 = 0.07$. Now recall that the income of person 2 in period 3 is $y_2^3 = 4$, so that a unit decrement in income causes the squared normalized gap to rise from 0.04 to 0.16, and raising K_2 by about 0.008. In contrast, a unit decrement from $y_3^3 = 3$ raises the squared normalized gap from 0.16 to 0.36, and lifting K_2 by about 0.013. With K_2, the impact of a unit decrement is larger for lower incomes than for higher incomes.

Analogous reasoning demonstrates that K_2 is sensitive to the distribution of income among the poor. Let i and j be two chronically poor persons with income vectors y_i and y_j. Suppose that their income vectors are replaced with $y_i' = \lambda y_i + (1 - \lambda)y_j$ and $y_j' = (1 - \lambda)y_i + \lambda y_j$, respectively, for some $\lambda \varepsilon (0,1/2]$. This represents a uniform 'smoothing' of the incomes of persons i and j, with the value $\lambda = 1/2$ yielding the limiting case where $y_i' = y_j' = (y_i + y_j)/2$ is a simple average of the two vectors. A transformation of this type is a multidimensional analogue of a progressive transfer (among the poor) and it is easy to show that K_2 will not rise; indeed, if their associate normalized gap distributions g_i and g_j were not initially identical, K_2 would fall as result of the progressive transfer.[14] In the numerical example, if the income vectors of persons 2 and 3 are replaced by the average vector (with $\lambda = 1/2$), then K_2 falls from 0.07 to about 0.54. In contrast, this smoothing of incomes affects neither the average duration of poverty, nor the average shortfall among the chronically poor, and hence K_0 and K_1 are entirely unaffected. The property requiring such a transformation to lower chronic poverty is called the *transfer* axiom.[15] The measure K_2 satisfies this axiom while K_0 and K_1 both violate it.

The general approach to constructing chronic poverty measures can be applied to obtain analogues of all of the indices in the FGT class. For any $a \geq 0$ let $g^a(\tau)$ be the matrix whose entries are the a powers of normalized gaps for the chronically poor (and zeros for those who are not chronically poor).[16] The *duration-adjusted P_a measures* are the general class of chronic poverty measures defined by $K_a(y; z, \tau) = \mu(g^a(\tau)) = |g^a(\tau)|/(TN)$; in other words, K_a is the sum of the a power of the (normalized) gaps of the chronically poor, divided by the maximum value that this sum could take. It can be shown that time monotonicity is satisfied by all K_a; monotonicity is satisfied by K_a for $a > 0$; and the transfer axiom is satisfied by K_a for $a > 1$.

The K_a measures satisfy a wide range of general properties for chronic poverty measures, some of which are direct analogues of the static poverty

[14] See Kolm (1977) and Tsui (2002). The condition g_i and g_j rules out the case mentioned by Tsui (2002) where the two chronically poor persons are poor in the same periods and have the same incomes below the poverty line.

[15] See Foster (2007) for a rigorous definition of this axiom.

[16] For $a = 0$, the entries of the matrix are more precisely defined as the limit of the entries of $g^a(\tau)$ as a tends to 0.

axioms and others more explicitly account for the time element in chronic poverty.[17] One axiom that deserves special mention due to its importance in empirical work is the following:

Decomposability. For any distributions x and y we have

$$K(x, y; z, \tau) = \frac{N(x)}{N(x, y)} K(x; z, \tau) + \frac{N(y)}{N(x, y)} K(y; z, \tau).$$

According to this property, when a distribution is broken down into two subpopulations, the overall chronic poverty level can be expressed as a weighted average of subgroup chronic poverty levels, with the weights being the respective subgroup population shares.[18] All the measures in the K_a class satisfy decomposability and hence are well suited for the analysis of chronic poverty by population subgroup.

For each measure of chronic poverty K_a, a corresponding measure of *transient* poverty can be defined to account for spells of poverty among those who are not chronically poor. Applying K_a to a cut-off of $\tau = 0$ removes all the restrictions concerning the duration of poverty. The resulting quantity $K_a(y; z, 0) = \mu(g^c)$ takes into account *every* spell of poverty for *all* persons, including those who are not chronically poor, and, in fact, is the overall (or average) level of measured poverty (using P_a) across the T periods. In contrast, $K_a(y; z, \tau)$ limits consideration to the shortfalls of the chronically poor, and hence the difference $R_a(y; z, \tau) = K_a(y; z, 0) - K_a(y; z, \tau)$ is an intuitive measure of transient poverty. The shares of overall poverty that are chronic $K_a(y; z, \tau)/K_a(y; z, 0)$ and transient $R_a(y; z, \tau)/K_a(y; z, 0)$ are helpful tools for understanding the nature of poverty over time, and are used in the empirical application below.

3.4. An Empirical Illustration

In this section, the new chronic poverty measures are applied to panel data from Argentina's Encuesta Permanente de Hogares carried out by Instituto Nacional de Estadísticas y Censos (INDEC), covering 2,409 households during the four waves of October 2001, May 2002, October 2002, and May 2003. The income variable used is equivalent household income, calculated by dividing total household income in each period by the number of equivalent adults (using the equivalent adult scale provided by INDEC).[19] The Instituto also provides a separate poverty line for each region and each period in order to

[17] The first group of axioms includes *anonymity, replication invariance, focus, and subgroup consistency*; the second includes *time anonymity* and *time focus*. See Foster (2007).

[18] This expression can be generalized to any number of subgroups by repeated application of the two-subgroup formula.

[19] In periods where an income is missing or zero for a given household, the methodology of Little and Su (1989) is followed, which calculates an imputed income using the household's incomes at other dates and other household incomes at the same date. In the few cases where

Table 3.1. Chronic poverty in Argentina: estimated levels for various measures and durations

	Measure			
	H	K_0	K_1	K_2
$\tau = 0.25$	0.61	0.44	0.21	0.124
$\tau = 0.50$	0.50	0.42	0.20	0.122
$\tau = 0.75$	0.40	0.37	0.19	0.116
$\tau = 1.00$	0.27	0.27	0.15	0.096
% Chronic[a]	66.3	83.1	90.7	93.5
% Transient	33.7	16.9	9.3	6.5

[a] The duration cut-off is $\tau = 0.75$. Since there are four periods, $\tau = 0.25$ yields the same values as overall poverty, and Percentage Chronic can found by dividing the third row by the first row. Percentage Transient is 100 minus Percentage Chronic.

capture spatial variations in the cost of living as well as inflation over time. Normalized gaps for a household are found by subtracting the equivalent income from the appropriate poverty line and dividing this difference by the same line. Since there are $T = 4$ periods, there are four relevant duration cut-offs τ, namely, 0.25, 0.50, 0.75, 1.00. Table 3.1 provides the resulting levels of chronic poverty for each of the measures H, K_0, K_1, and K_2, at each of the four duration cut-offs.

Notice that for each index, the measured level of chronic poverty rises as the duration requirement τ falls. For $\tau = 1$, the headcount and duration-adjusted headcount have the same value since the average duration in this special case is precisely 1. In general, for fixed τ the value of H is higher than that of K_0, which in turn is higher than K_1, and so forth, reflecting the mathematical properties of the measures. However, it is important to remember that actual poverty comparisons should only be made using the same poverty measure and with the same duration cut-off.

The first row provides the chronic poverty level when the duration in poverty is at least 0.25, and for K_a this is clearly the same as the level when the minimum duration is 0. This latter level $K_a(y; z, 0)$ is precisely the static poverty level that would arise if the data from all periods were merged into a single distribution and evaluated by P_a, or equivalently, $\Sigma_t P_a(y^t; z)/T$, the average static poverty level across all periods. Now given a minimum duration of $\tau = 0.75$, the difference between this overall poverty level $K_a(y; z, 0)$ and the chronic poverty level $K_a(y; z, \tau)$ is the level of transient poverty, $R_a(y; z, \tau)$ as defined above.[20] The final two rows provide the percentage of overall poverty due to chronic poverty and transient poverty respectively for $\tau = 0.75$ given

the household reports zero income in all four periods, an income equal to the lowest social welfare transfer was assumed.

[20] For H, overall poverty is the limit of $H(y; z, \tau)$ as τ tends to zero; this also equals the value at $\tau = 0.25$.

Table 3.2. Chronic poverty profile for Argentina

	Pop. share (%)	K_0	% contrib.	K_1	% contrib.	K_2	% contrib.
				Measure[a]			
GBA	12	0.18	8.3	0.10	8.0	0.065	8.1
NE	15	0.44	25.2	0.26	26.3	0.174	27.1
NW	22	0.34	28.4	0.19	28.1	0.120	27.4
C	28	0.22	23.5	0.13	24.1	0.085	24.6
MW	11	0.24	10.0	0.13	9.6	0.080	9.1
S	12	0.10	4.6	0.05	4.0	0.029	3.6
Total	100	0.27	100.0	0.15	100.0	0.096	100.0

[a] Duration cut-off is $\tau = 1.00$. Percentages may not sum to 100% due to rounding errors.

each measure. It is interesting to note that as the poverty measure changes from H to K_0 to K_1 to K_2, the share of chronic poverty becomes larger while the share of transient poverty falls. For K_2 the chronic poverty share is 93.5 per cent, suggesting that the transient poverty spells generally do not involve large shortfalls.

Table 3.2 provides a profile of chronic poverty in each of the six regions of Argentina, namely, Greater Buenos Aires (GBA), the North-East (NE), the North-West (NW), the Center of the country (C), the Midwest (MW), and the South (S). In this example, chronically poor means poor in all four periods; hence the duration cut-off is $\tau = 1$. The first column in the table gives the population shares of the six regions. The second, fourth, and sixth columns provide the regional chronic poverty levels for K_0, K_1, and K_2, respectively; while the third, fifth, and seventh columns give the percentage contribution of each region to total poverty (or the population share times the regional poverty level over the total poverty). Notice that the North-East has only 15 per cent of the population, yet accounts for at least 25.2 per cent of the chronic poverty in Argentina; in contrast, the South has 12 per cent of the total population, but only contributes 4.6 per cent or less to total chronic poverty.

3.5. Conclusions

This chapter has presented a new family K_a of chronic poverty measures based on the P_a measures of Foster, Greer, and Thorbecke (1984). Each measure has an intuitive interpretation as a 'duration-adjusted P_a measure' and can be readily calculated as the mean of a particular matrix. All the measures satisfy a series of general axioms for chronic poverty measures, and an additional set of axioms that are applicable to measures based on a spells approach to chronic poverty. Within the class, there is a range of measures satisfying a monotonicity axiom, and a smaller subset satisfying a transfer axiom.

In particular, K_2, the duration-adjusted analogue of the usual P_2 measure, satisfies all of the properties discussed in this chapter. The usefulness of the class of chronic poverty measures has been illustrated using panel data from Argentina.

One powerful criticism of the general framework for evaluation used here is that, being limited to a single income variable, it cannot utilize data on other dimensions of relevance to poverty and well-being. The approach is indeed restrictive, and when panel data containing information on other capabilities become more widely available, multidimensional measures of chronic poverty will need to be developed. Of course, there remain serious difficulties in formulating effective multidimensional poverty measures, even in the static context. The identification step for multidimensional poverty depends crucially on assumptions about substitutability across different dimensions; and the aggregation step has seemingly endless possibilities for bringing the various dimensions of deprivation into a single coherent index. The problem of measuring multidimensional chronic poverty is not likely to be solved anytime soon.

The measurement approach presented in this chapter is based on a very simple treatment of time in poverty: an earlier period in poverty is given the same weight as a later period in poverty. Indeed, such a position could be justified using the traditional 'no discounting' argument of Ramsey (1928). However, other plausible alternatives exist. For example, one might argue that greater weight should be placed on income received in *earlier* periods, as is typically done by discounting (see Rodgers and Rodgers, 1993, or Dercon and Calvo, 2006). This could be justified ex ante where there may be greater perceived or actual value from receiving income earlier. However, when viewed from an ex post perspective, there may also be good reason to view earlier incomes as having less weight (see, for example, the discussion in Ray and Wang, 2001). An additional problem with discounting (one way or the other) is deciding *what* to discount: the income received by the chronically poor person, the utility level, or some function of the gap. And if the discounting procedure delivers a different ordering depending on the base period for evaluation, this could certainly make the procedure less attractive.

There are other aspects of the above approach that might be altered. Some have argued that continuous spells of poverty should have larger weight in the evaluation of chronic poverty. As noted by Mckay and Lawson (2002), there are significant data problems from trying to implement this using panel data. Another perspective might consider placing greater weight on observations from a chronically poor person who is in poverty longer. This could indeed be done either via a new functional form or through dominance orderings over time, but this will have to await future work.

References

Atkinson, A. B. (1987), 'On the Measurement of Poverty', *Econometrica*, 55: 749–64.

Bane, M., and Ellwood, D. (1986), 'Slipping into and out of Poverty: The Dynamics of Spells', *Journal of Human Resources*, 21: 1–23.

Brooks-Gunn, J., and Duncan, G. J. (1997), 'The Effects of Poverty on Children', *Children and Poverty*, 7: 55–70.

Chakravarty, S. (1983), 'A New Index of Poverty', *Mathematical Social Sciences*, 6: 307–13.

Chronic Poverty Research Centre (2005), *The Chronic Poverty Report 2004–05*, Manchester: University of Manchester.

Clark, C. R., Hemming, R., and Ulph, D. (1981), 'On Indices for the Measurement of Poverty', *Economic Journal*, 91: 515–26.

Clark, D., and Hulme, D. (2005), 'Towards a Unified Framework for Understanding the Depth Breadth and Duration of Poverty', mimeo, Manchester.

Dercon, S., and Calvo, S. (2006), 'Chronic Poverty and All That: The Measurement of Poverty Over Time', mimeo, University of Oxford.

Duncan, G. D. J., Coe, R. and Hill, M.S. (1984), 'The Dynamics of Poverty' in G.J. Duncan (ed.) *Years of Poverty, Years of Plenty*, Ann Arbor: Institute of Social Research, pp. 33–70.

Foster, J. E. (2006), 'Poverty Indices', in Alain de Janvry and Ravi Kanbur (eds.), *Poverty, Inequality and Development: Essays in Honor of Erik Thorbecke*, Berlin: Springer Verlag.

—— (2007), 'A Class of Chronic Poverty Measures', working paper, Department of Economics, Vanderbilt University.

—— Greer, J., and Thorbecke, E. (1984), 'A Class of Decomposable Poverty Indices', *Econometrica*, 52: 761–6.

—— and Santos, M. E. (2006), 'Measuring Chronic Poverty', mimeo, Vanderbilt University.

—— and Sen, A. (1997), 'On Economic Inequality: After a Quarter Century', annexe to the enlarged edition of Amartya Sen, *On Economic Inequality*, Oxford: Clarendon Press.

—— and Shorrocks, A. F. (1988), 'Poverty Orderings and Welfare Dominance', *Social Choice and Welfare*, 5: 179–98.

—— (1991), 'Subgroup Consistent Poverty Indices', *Econometrica*, 59: 687–710.

—— and Székely, M. (2006), 'Poverty Lines over Space and Time', mimeo, Vanderbilt University.

Gaiha, R., and Deolalikar, A. B. (1993), 'Persistent, Expected and Innate Poverty: Estimates for Semi Arid Rural South India', *Cambridge Journal of Economics*, 17: 409–21.

Hulme, D., Moore, K., and Shepherd, A. (2001), 'Chronic Poverty: Meanings and Analytical Frameworks', CPRC Working Paper 2, Manchester: IDPM, University of Manchester.

—— and Shepherd, A. (2003), 'Conceptualising Chronic Poverty', *World Development*, 1(3): 403–25.

Jalan, J., and Ravallion, M. (1998), 'Determinants of Transient and Chronic Poverty: Evidence from Rural China', Policy Research Working Paper 1936, World Bank.

Kanbur, R., and Mukherjee, D. (2006), 'Premature Mortality and Poverty Measurement', mimeo, Cornell University.

Kolm, S.-C. (1977), 'Multidimensional Egalitarianisms', *Quarterly Journal of Economics*, 91: 1–13.

Lichter, D. T., Shanahan, M. J., and Gardner, E. L. (1999), 'Becoming a Good Citizen? The Long-Term Consequences of Poverty and Family Instability during Childhood', mimeo, Russell Sage.

Little, R. J. A., and Su, H.-L. (1989), 'Item Non-Response in Panel Surveys', in D. Kasprzyk, G. Duncan, and M. P. Singh (eds.), *Panel Surveys*, New York: John Wiley.

McDonough, P., and Berglund, P. (2003), 'Histories of Poverty and Self-Rated Health Trajectories', *Journal of Health and Social Behavior*, 44: 198–214.

McKay, A., and Lawson, D. (2002), 'Chronic Poverty: A Review of Current Quantitative Evidence', CPRC Working Paper No. 15, Manchester: University of Manchester.

——— (2003), 'Assessing the Extent and Nature of Chronic Poverty in Low Income Countries: Issues and Evidence', *World Development*, 31: 425–39.

Ramsey, F. (1928), 'A Mathematical Theory of Savings', *Economic Journal*, 38: 543–59.

Ravallion, M. (1994), *Poverty Comparisons*, Chur: Harwood.

Ray, D., and Wang, R. (2001), 'On Some Implications of Backward Discounting', mimeo, New York University.

Rodgers, J. R., and Rodgers, J. L. (1993), 'Chronic Poverty in the United States', *Journal of Human Resources*, 18: 25–54.

Sen, A. (1976), 'Poverty: An Ordinal Approach to Measurement', *Econometrica*, 44: 219–31.

Shorrocks, A. F. (1992), 'Spell Incidence, Spell Duration and the Measurement of Unemployment', Working Papers of the ESRC Research Centre on Micro-social Change, No. 12, University of Essex.

Stevens, A. H. (1994), 'The Dynamics of Poverty Spells: Updating Bane & Ellwood', *American Economic Review: Papers and Proceedings*, 84: 34–7.

Tsui, K.-Y. (2002), 'Multidimensional Poverty Indices', *Social Choice and Welfare*, 19: 69–93.

Yaqub, Shafin (2000), 'Poverty Dynamics in Developing Countries', IDS Development Bibliography, University of Sussex, April.

——— (2001), 'At What Age Does Poverty Damage Most?', mimeo, University of Sussex.

——— (2003), 'Chronic Poverty: Scrutinizing Estimates, Patterns, Correlates and Explanations', CPRC Working Paper 21, University of Manchester.

Zheng, B. (1997), 'Aggregate Poverty Measures', *Journal of Economic Surveys*, 11(2): 123–62.

4

Measuring Chronic Non-Income Poverty*

Isabel Günther and Stephan Klasen

4.1. Introduction

In recent years, the research agenda on poverty in developing countries has moved beyond static assessments of poverty levels to consider dynamic trajectories of well-being over time. The main reason for this shift in emphasis was the recognition that there is considerable mobility of well-being over time and that only a share of the poor are affected by persistent (or chronic) poverty, while a much larger share of the total population experiences transient poverty, or vulnerability to poverty.

Since the two groups were found to be quite different in terms of their characteristics and in terms of their needs regarding policy interventions, the research community has developed two largely distinct research agendas, one focusing on chronic poverty, the other focusing on vulnerability to poverty. The research agendas complement one another, with chronic poverty focusing on poverty traps and poverty persistence and vulnerability focusing on risks and shocks and poverty dynamics.

The distinction between chronic and transient poverty is usually closely linked to conceptualizing poverty in the monetary dimension. This is largely related to the fact that the stochastic nature of the income-generating process is well recognized in economics for decades, going back to Friedman's Permanent Income Hypothesis, which already made a distinction between permanent and transitory incomes (Friedman, 1957). In line with that hypothesis, consumption is used as the preferred welfare indicator in many applications in developing countries as it is believed to be a better reflection of long-term

*We would like to thank Bob Baulch, Stephan Dercon, Michael Grimm, David Hulme, Stephen Jenkins, John Mickleright, an anonymous referee, and participants at a workshop in Manchester for very useful comments on a first draft of this chapter.

or permanent incomes.[1] In this sense, low consumption (i.e. consumption below a poverty line) is seen as a reflection of a chronic inability to generate sufficient incomes to leave poverty, even though households might temporarily escape income poverty.

But empirically it has been shown that in developing countries also households' consumption fluctuates greatly, in fact often not much less than income. This could be for three reasons. First, households, particularly poor households, are not able to smooth their consumption due to a lack of assets and access to credit and/or insurance markets (e.g. Townsend, 1995; Deaton, 1997). Second, 'permanent' incomes of households change as a result of permanent shocks affecting the lifetime earning paths of individuals, thus forcing households to re-optimize their consumption decisions. Last, consumption (and/or incomes) is measured with error and thus much of the fluctuation is spurious and related to these errors.[2]

To figure out which households are facing permanently low consumption, i.e. are chronically poor, and which households are 'only' transitory poor and which households (currently non-poor) are facing a high risk of becoming poor is thus a very important and at the same time quite difficult task and it is not surprising that a large literature has dedicated itself to this subject. And with the help of an increasing number of panel data in developing countries, dynamic assessments of consumption, i.e. an analysis of chronic poverty as well as vulnerability to poverty, have indeed become more feasible in an increasing number of countries, thus underpinning the analysis of poverty dynamics.

At the same time, this exclusive emphasis on incomes in the assessment of chronic poverty and vulnerability has clear limitations and shortcomings (see also Hulme and McKay, 2005), as it is well recognized that income (or consumption) is an inadequate indicator of well-being. If we conceptualize well-being from a capability perspective, income is but one (and for some capabilities a rather poor) means to generate capabilities such as the ability to be healthy, well educated, integrated, clothed, housed, and the like (see Sen, 1995, 1999; Klasen, 2000); nor do equal incomes translate into equal capabilities for different individuals, due to the heterogeneity of people in translating incomes into well-being. It is therefore preferable to study well-being *outcomes* directly (e.g. capabilities or functionings; see Klasen, 2000[3])

---

[1] There are other reasons to prefer consumption to incomes as a welfare measure in developing countries. See Deaton (1997) and Deaton and Zaidi (2002).

[2] This is a difficult issue to sort out with the type of panel data available for developing countries which typically have only two or three waves and thus do not allow the application of common methods to control for measurement error (such as instrumental variable techniques).

[3] In principle, it is preferable to study capabilities to understand the choices people have at their disposal. In practice, we usually can only observe functionings and thus most studies are analysing functionings instead of capabilities (e.g. Klasen, 2000).

rather than study a specific well-being *input*. However, there have been few attempts to integrate the insights from the static analysis of non-income dimensions of well-being into a dynamic setting and thus investigate chronic poverty and vulnerability from a non-income perspective. In addition, apart from the conceptual advantage of studying chronic poverty from a non-income perspective, there are several advantages (but also limitations) from a measurement perspective to studying non-income chronic poverty, which we discuss in more detail below.

The purpose of this chapter is to try to conceptualize chronic poverty and hence also poverty dynamics from a non-income perspective and then illustrate ways to explore this topic empirically. Section 4.2 discusses the potentials as well as limitations of conceptualizing chronic poverty in a non-income perspective. Section 4.3 presents a first approach to empirically measure chronic non-income poverty, focusing on critical functionings related to health and education, using a panel survey of Vietnam from 1992/3 and 1997/8. Section 4.4 shows the results of this application. Section 4.5 concludes with highlighting open issues and suggestions for further research.

4.2. Conceptualizing Chronic Non-Income Poverty

It is clear that in principle it should be useful to study chronic poverty in non-income dimensions (using for example applications of Sen's capability approach) as it would allow us to track well-being *outcomes* rather than simply track an important well-being *input* (income) over time. Thus it would allow us to measure well-being itself rather than only a proxy of it. The same theoretical reasoning to prefer non-income to income indicators to measure well-being as in a static framework certainly applies in a dynamic well-being framework (see e.g. Sen, 1985). In addition, there are some specific advantages (and limitations) of studying poverty using non-income indicators that emerge particularly in a *dynamic* poverty framework.

4.2.1. Potentials

Analysing non-income poverty dynamics would first of all allow an assessment of the relationship between income and non-income chronic and transitory poverty. Identifying those households where the two approaches converge would identify those households who are chronically poor from a multidimensional perspective and thus possibly most deprived and arguably most deserving of support. This would enrich our assessment of dynamic well-being. Conversely, where the two approaches fail to converge in identifying the chronic poor, we would learn more about the dynamic relationship between income and non-income poverty. This is directly interesting for policy purposes as policy makers are interested in reducing income and non-income poverty and thus knowing the temporal relationship between the two, e.g. whether improvements in income will eventually improve health outcomes (but only with a lag), or vice versa, is critical.

The measurement of non-income poverty dynamics might also shed some new light on the causes of the less than perfect correlation between income and non-income dimensions of poverty in a static framework (see e.g. Klasen, 2000). In particular, the lack of correlation at one point in time might be related more to different dynamics of the two well-being approaches, rather than the lack of a contemporaneous causal relation between the two. More precisely, for example in a two-wave panel, static assessments of poverty in both periods could yield the same result regardless of whether income and non-income dimensions are used. However, the two (income and non-income) approaches could also agree in the static assessment of poverty in the first period, but differ in the dynamics between the first and second periods, suggesting that different drivers affect these dynamics. Similarly, the two approaches could agree in the static assessment of poverty in the second period, but differ in the dynamics, and thus would not agree in the static assessment of poverty in the first period. Last, the two approaches might also disagree on classifying households in both periods but agree on the dynamics over time. Thus analysing income and non-income poverty dynamics simultaneously we are able to separate static and dynamic disagreements in identifying the poor.[4] If we only examined the two periods separately, we would either find a lack of overlap in the first period or a lack of overlap in the second period. But we would not be able to tell whether this is due to different dynamics between two periods or whether there is a permanent disagreement between the two approaches to identifying the poor.

However, even if it turned out that chronic income and non-income poverty dynamics are highly correlated, there could still be practical advantages focusing on the measurement of non-income poverty, as many indicators of non-income deprivation (e.g. education or housing) are easier to measure and less prone to measurement error than income (or consumption) measures.[5] In fact, at times it may be useful to use non-income measures of well-being as instruments to correct poorly measured incomes (and or consumption).

A second measurement advantage is that information on past dynamics of non-income well-being are often easier to get and more reliable than information on past income series—even when using cross-sectional surveys. For example, it is easier to get reliable information about the educational

---

[4] If we had more waves, we could also say more about the temporal relationship between the two variables by explicitly examining leads and lags.

[5] See, for example, Zeller et al. (2006) for an example of a short-cut approach to poverty measurement using non-income indicators.

history of a person than that person's income history. Moreover, some current non-income indicators can already provide some information about historical trends in access to critical functionings. For example, the height of an adult reflects past nutritional status and the current grade enrolled for a child at a certain age reveals important aspects of that child's past educational history.

In addition, many capabilities/functionings (e.g. education and health) can be measured at the individual level while income/consumption poverty can only be assessed at the household level, due to the presence of household-specific public goods which are impossible to attribute to individual members (see Klasen, 2000, 2007a, for a discussion). This therefore allows an assessment of intra-household poverty dynamics which is impossible using income data but might be quite important for studying intra-household inequalities (see also Haddad and Kanbur, 1990). This advantage, which is already present in a static assessment of poverty using a capability/functioning framework, might be easily extended within a dynamic framework, as we illustrate below.

4.2.2. Limitations

Apart from stating some advantages of an extension of chronic poverty to non-income dimensions, it is also important to name some problems. Probably the most important objection to such an extension is that it would not yield very useful new information as many non-income dimensions of well-being do not change much over time. Moreover, change in some non-income measures usually means improvements, at least in the way it is measured. The most extreme example of this would be to use years of schooling to track education poverty of individual adults. This indicator is likely to stay the same for the vast majority of adults once they have left the educational system and if it changes, it will only go up, but never down (as surveys usually only keep track of improvements in education, but not of loss of knowledge/skills over time).

Thus many non-income measures of well-being seem to exhibit a great deal of inertia and most non-income poor would be *chronically* non-income poor and there would be no point in distinguishing between them and the small number of transitory non-income poor (see McKay and Lawson, 2003). In contrast, the evidence on income poverty is that there is a great deal of churning, and in many countries most of the poor at any point in time are transitory poor while a smaller share of households are chronically poor (see Baulch and Hoddinott, 2000).

There are several possible replies to this objection. First, to the extent that these non-income measures adequately reflect the functioning shortfall in question, the inertia in these measures correctly suggests that in many developing countries many people are chronically deprived of critical functionings. For example, those adults (of whom many are female) in developing countries

81

that never had the chance to be schooled will be chronically educationally poor. Stating this might be obvious but from a well-being perspective we need to occasionally remind ourselves that all attempts to achieve universal enrolments for children will do nothing to combat education poverty among adults. In these cases it is particularly interesting to see whether these chronically non-income poor are also chronically income poor and how the two measures are related in a static and dynamic context.

Second, some indicators of measuring non-income well-being achievements are not adequately reflecting the functioning in question. For example, adult height only reflects the nutritional status during the phase of growing up, but not the current one. Also, years of schooling say nothing about the level of functional education a person has at a point in time. To track this we would need different measures such as test scores and functional literacy and numeracy surveys which only exist in some countries (e.g. OECD, 2000). These scores are likely to move more over time and can go up or down for adults.

Third, despite the fact that a well-being indicator for an *individual* is not changing over time, it may sometimes be useful to consider a *household* perspective. For example, while being educated oneself is clearly valuable in and of itself, sometimes there are also individual benefits of education of other household members. To the extent this is the case, it might be useful to consider the average education of household members or possibly even the highest education level existing in the household (see Basu and Forster, 1998). These indicators will clearly move more over time than individuals' educational level.

Fourth, for some indicators there is considerable movement for children, but little (or no) movement among adults (e.g. years of schooling). Thus it might be useful to separately track changes in non-income poverty of children and adults which will generate different insights. Lastly, we show in section 4.4 that there are a range of indicators where there is quite a lot of dynamics over time so that there indeed is an empirical justification to examine chronic (and transitory) poverty in a non-income perspective.

A second objection is that current survey instruments lack the tools to systematically track poverty in the non-income dimension. There is clearly a valid point as many surveys do not systematically track, for example, the health or nutrition status of all individuals across time using comparable measures. In the survey that we use, there are also shortcomings in this respect. However, this objection can only lead to efforts to improve survey design rather than abandon this interesting approach.

A third objection is that it is difficult to interpret the linkages between income and non-income poverty dynamics for two reasons. One is the differing magnitude of measurement error in income and non-income dimensions of poverty which might make it difficult to interpret differences in chronic income vs. non-income poverty. While this is an important issue which we also discuss below, it focuses attention on the role of measurement error in the assessment of chronic poverty and a comparison between chronic income and non-income poverty might actually help shed light on this important issue.[6] The second problem of interpretation deals with the fact that the income indicator will always refer to households, whose size and composition might have changed over time, thereby affecting the poverty status of that household. In contrast, the non-income assessment of poverty will usually focus on individuals that are present in both periods. While one indeed has to bear in mind this difference when household chronic poverty is compared with individual non-income chronic poverty, one can just as easily use the existing household boundaries to calculate non-income household poverty (as we do below).

A last objection is that when measuring non-income poverty dynamics several new conceptual questions arise. For example, what is education and health poverty among children? How can one define such poverty to be chronic or persistent? Am I education poor only if I am out of school? Or also if I am falling behind in progressing through school? Or if I also have a worsening performance? When do I become chronically education poor? Similarly, is stunting already an indicator of chronic poverty since it is related to persistent lower than required energy intake (UNICEF, 1998) or is only persistent stunting an issue? Clearly these are serious questions and below we explore the empirical impact of some choices of answers relating to these difficult questions. But also here, the call is for more work extending the concept of chronic poverty to these cases rather than to abandon the enterprise.

Thus we believe that it is well worth studying chronic non-income poverty and the approach we take here in this chapter is to simply explore whether, given data and measurement constraints, reasonable ways to conceptualize and measure non-income poverty can be extended across time and whether they will generate useful additional information about static and dynamic aspects of well-being.

4.3. Methodology

4.3.1. *Measurement of chronic poverty*

To measure chronic poverty two methods have been proposed: the 'spells' (McKay and Lawson, 2003) and 'component' (Jalan and Ravallion, 1996) approach. The 'spells' approach defines households as chronically poor who

---

[6] Also, in longer panels, it would be possible to control for this problem through appropriate econometric techniques.

have always been poor, i.e. whose per capita household consumption has been below the poverty line in all observed points in time. The transient poor are those who have only temporarily been poor. In contrast, the 'component' approach distinguishes permanent (average) consumption of a household from temporary variations in household consumption. Hence, whereas the 'spells' approach classifies households as either chronic poor or transient poor the 'component' approach calculates the 'chronic' and 'transient' component of households' poverty and a classification of households into chronic and transient poor households is not possible.

In this study we opt for the 'spells' approach as we only have a two-wave panel at hand. We define individuals to be chronically poor in the non-income dimension if they are poor in both periods considered. Those who are poor in either period but not chronically poor are thus the transitory poor and those being poor in neither period are defined as the non-poor. In a two-wave panel it is difficult to assess whether observed transient poverty is caused by fluctuating welfare indicators or whether transient poverty is caused by individuals falling into poverty or escaping from poverty, i.e. we cannot say whether we observe stochastic or structural changes in the well-being of individuals.

Similar to the income dimension, we will define 'poverty lines' for the non-income dimensions based on reasonable (but essentially arbitrary) notions of who should be considered as poor in the relevant dimension (see below for details). Also, we will, in line with the literature on chronic income poverty, treat poverty in the income and non-income dimensions as a dichotomous yes/no question and thus will not consider depth or severity of poverty.[7] In addition, as both from a theoretical perspective as well as from a measurement perspective non-income poverty for adults and children is often defined and measured differently and thus should show different dynamics, we further-more analyse poverty dynamics for these two subgroups of the population separately.

4.3.2. *Indicators of non-income poverty*

The question arises which non-income indicators should be analysed. Whereas for a theoretical discussion of temporary and long-term well-being an analysis of a very broad range of functionings might be appropriate, when undertaking empirical studies it should be more useful to focus on a smaller subset of basic functionings. We therefore focus on education and

---

[7] Clearly, considering depth and severity of income and non-income poverty and considering the correlations between income and non-income dimensions in them would yield additional useful information and should be taken into account in further work.

health (approximated with the nutritional status of individuals[8]), since these are probably some of the most critical and commonly agreed capabilities (Hulme and McKay, 2005). These non-income indicators have the additional advantage that they are measured at the individual level in contrast to e.g. housing or service access which can (as income) only assess chronic poverty of households.

For children who are below the age of 18 years we use stunting as an indicator of health or nutritional deprivation, whereas for adults of 18 years and older we use the body mass index (BMI). Moderate (severe) under-nutrition (or nutrition poverty) is defined as being below a z-score of -2 for children or being below a BMI of 18.5 for adults.

The z-score is calculated as the height for a child minus the median height of a reference standard (of children of the same age), divided by the standard deviation of that reference standard. The reference standard used is the commonly used US-based reference standard recommended for use by the World Health Organization (WHO) for monitoring under-nutrition everywhere since 1987 (see Klasen, 2007b, for further details).

While most analysts agree that the z-score is particularly accurate in measuring nutrition problems of children below the age of 6, there are questions with regard to its applicability to populations outside the USA for children older than the age of 6, as growth after 6 seems to differ even in well-nourished populations across the world (see WHO, 1995, for a discussion). Thus one should view the application of this indicator until the age of 18 with some caution.

One should also note that this measure of anthropometric shortfall essentially makes a probabilistic assessment of the likelihood that a child is undernourished. As a result, some well-nourished children might be wrongly classified as under-nourished because they have genetically short parents while other children might wrongly be classified as well nourished even though they are under-nourished but this does not show up in their height due to their genetically tall parents. Thus we expect some noise in these anthropometric data. However, while this noise will affect static assessments of undernutrition, it should not seriously affect the dynamics of under-nutrition.

For adults, height is not an indicator of current nutritional status, and the BMI as a measurement for under-nutrition is thus chosen instead. The BMI is defined as the weight in kilograms divided by the height squared in metres of individuals. While a low BMI is surely an indicator of severe nutritional problems, the precise cut-off is controversial. Also, due to secular changes in

---

[8] In an earlier version, we also considered a morbidity indicator, but this measure only captured very recent illnesses and not a more general health status and is therefore not very suited for an analysis of 'health' poverty. Clearly, this is an issue that could be solved by including more detailed health questions in household surveys. See Schultz (2002, 2003) for a discussion of particularly useful health indicators.

dietary patterns and exercise in developing countries, malnourished people might have an adequate BMI or even show up as overweight, but still lack important nutrients and access to healthy foods. Thus some 'health' poor might not be captured using this indicator.[9]

Moderate (severe) education poverty for adults of 16+ years of age is defined as having less than nine (four) years of education. Moderate education poverty for children of 6–15 years of age is defined as being out of school within the first nine (four) years of education. Four years of education refer to completed primary school. Nine years of education refer to completed lower secondary school. In addition, we do not only consider children who have been in school in one observation period but not in school in the other observation period as transient poor, but also those children who were in school in both observation years n and $n + t$, but did not complete t years of schooling during the observation period, are considered as transient poor.

Clearly, while the choice of the schooling variable seems defensible for adults, the choice is somewhat arbitrary for children. One could equally well consider only those children who are out of school in the two observation periods as poor as well as consider all children who are behind in their educational programme, taking account of their age (in either years), as educational poor. This would include children who are behind in their education programme already in the first observation period as well as children who fall behind during the observation period, i.e. children who progress less than the number of years between the two waves of the panel. All of these problems could be circumvented by the use of educational test scores, but hardly any household surveys, let alone panel surveys, collect such data on a regular basis.

Examining several non-income indicators, which is inevitable when studying well-being from a functioning/capability perspective, the question of an appropriate aggregation and weighting arises if one wants to generate summary measures of well-being (e.g. Atkinson and Bourguignon, 2000; Ramos and Silber, 2005). Alternatively, one can simply report the individual functionings/capabilities without weighting and aggregating them, thus generating partial orderings of well-being outcomes.

In this study, we opt for the latter approach and did not calculate a composite indicator but examine chronic and transitory deprivation in these indicators separately. In addition to the usual problems that emerge when aggregating and weighting different non-income indicators, it is particularly difficult to interpret such a composite measure in a dynamic perspective, as different non-income indicators show quite different dynamics. For example, education poverty using our indicators is largely irreversible as people have reached adulthood, while nutrition poverty can be reversed as general conditions improve. Moreover, when analysing multidimensional poverty in

---

[9] See, for example, Henderson (2005) for a discussion.

a dynamic perspective not only the aggregation and weighting of different non-income indicators becomes an issue but also how to do this over time.[10]

4.3.3. Research questions

Applying the described non-income indicators to the study of chronic under-development, we first analyse if and to what extent income and non-income indicators show the same poverty dynamics. We study both the level of chronic (and transient) non-income and income poverty as well as the cor-relation of income and non-income poverty dynamics. The first analysis assesses from a macro-perspective whether the same share of individuals suffer from chronic income and non-income poverty whereas the latter approach analyses from a micro-perspective if the same individuals would be identified as chronically poor whether income or non-income indicators are used.

In a second step we study individual poverty dynamics within households, which includes an analysis of the differences between individual and house-hold poverty dynamics, as well as intergenerational poverty dynamics, which analyses the persistence of poverty of different generations living in the same household. Such an analysis of individual chronic poverty is usually not possible with income indicators.

Last, we might also define chronic poverty as multidimensional poverty, i.e. examine the number of dimensions of deprivation (including income and non-income dimensions) at a point in time and over time.

4.4. Data

The data we use are the Vietnam Living Standard Survey (VLSS), which is a two-wave panel conducted in 1992/3 and 1997/8. The first round comprises a sample of 4,799 (23,838) and the second round a sample of 5,999 (28,509) households (individuals). Four thousand three hundred and five of these households were interviewed in both years, which allows to track 17,829 indi-viduals over a five-year time period. As we limited our analysis to households and individuals that were present in both years, there might be a problem of attrition bias in the sense that the households and individuals studied do not fully represent the population. However, simple probits indicate that the attrition bias in the VLSS is quite low, i.e. basically random (Baulch and Masset, 2003).

[10] For example, should an individual who is poor in one dimension in the first period but not so in the latter, but who is *not* poor in a second dimension in the first period, but poor in the second period, be considered as chronic poor (deprived of one non-income dimension in either period) or as transient poor (altering deprivation)?

Also children below the age of 5 years in 1997 are excluded from the sample as they were not yet born in 1992. For comparison with non-income poverty dynamics we also calculate income poverty dynamics. We define moderate poverty as per capita household consumption below the official poverty line and severe poverty as per capita household consumption below the official food poverty line. The official (food) poverty line, which is provided by the General Statistical Office in Vietnam, is 1.160.000 (750.000) Vietnamese Dong for 1992 and 1.790.000 (1.287.000) Vietnamese Dong for 1997, respectively. Note that in this study we use per capita household consumption.[11]

4.5. Empirical Results

4.5.1. *Level of chronic poverty*

Table 4.1 shows the extent of chronic and transient poverty measured with income and non-income indicators. Depending on the measures we use (and whether we observe adults or children) we come to quite different conclusions about poverty dynamics and the level of chronic poverty in Vietnam.

In general one can however state that nutritional and particularly educational well-being, with a transient poverty component of 25.8 per cent and 15.0 per cent respectively, fluctuate less than income poverty, with a transient poverty component of 33.0 per cent. Also, the well-being of adults seems to be much more stable than the well-being of children. Whether stable well-being is positive or negative from a normative perspectives depends on whether an individual is poor or non-poor in a certain well-being dimension. For the poor, steady indicators mean poverty traps; for the non-poor steady indicators mean higher permanent well-being. But for all human development indicators (except education for adults) there is a significant transient component, i.e. it is well worth studying the dynamics of non-income dimensions of well-being.

Some important cautionary remarks have to be made concerning the interpretation of poverty dynamics across different well-being dimensions. The first issue relates to the fact that we often only have a two-wave panel at hand, where high-income transient poverty might largely be caused by general economic development. In our case, Vietnam experienced significant economic growth which led to a massive decrease in income poverty there between 1992/3 and 1997/8 (see also Bonschab and Klump, 2007), with the headcount poverty rate falling from about 61 per cent to 34 per cent. All measures of non-income poverty show much smaller improvements.

[11] We thus do not apply equivalence scales. White and Masset (2003) have recently shown the 'bias' induced by ignoring household size and composition on poverty profiles for Vietnam in a static context. In a further study it might hence be interesting to analyse the impact of equivalence scales (and hence also household dynamics) on measured income (or consumption) poverty dynamics; see also the discussion on household size below.

Table 4.1. Poverty rates and dynamics

	Income			Nutrition			Education		
	Total	Adult	Child	Total	Adult	Child	Total	Adult	Child
Poverty 1992	61.5	56.6	69.7	43.2	33.6	54.9	58.1	64.1	29.4
Poverty 1997	34.2	31.2	40.3	34.5	30.9	41.5	49.7	57.9	17.7
Chronic	31.4	27.8	38.2	26.0	23.0	32.6	43.7	57.9	14.6
Transient	33.0	32.2	33.6	25.8	18.6	29.7	15.0	6.2	32.9
Non-poor	35.6	40.0	28.2	48.2	58.4	37.7	31.3	35.9	52.5

With a two-wave panel in this economic boom environment, it is therefore difficult to distinguish whether high-income poverty dynamics are caused by income fluctuations or by a move out of structural poverty of a large part of the population. Likewise, we do not know whether we observe higher chronic non-income poverty because human development indicators are more stable (i.e. are less volatile) or because they adjust more slowly (i.e. with some delay) than income indicators to economic development. The interesting question here then is whether dynamics of non-income indicators rather reflect past, whereas income poverty dynamics reflect current, poverty dynamics.

In addition, differences between income and non-income poverty dynamics might also be explained by the somewhat 'arbitrarily set' level, i.e. poverty line, in different poverty dimensions. In other words, chronic poverty rates are certainly positively correlated with the extent of total poverty and negatively related to poverty reduction (or increases) over time: i.e. the higher the static poverty rate the higher chronic poverty, and the higher poverty reduction (or increase) the higher transient poverty. Hence, differences in the extent of chronic poverty using income and non-income indicators might just stem from the fact that the extent of total (static) poverty rates is different.

We deal with this potential measurement problem by equalizing poverty rates across the different indicators. For example, Table 4.2 shows 'fitted' income poverty rates for the case of nutritional and income poverty, where we first align income poverty rates to the level of nutrition poverty in 1992, i.e. the consumption poverty line is endogenously set so that total static income poverty rate is equal to the level of static nutrition poverty in the first year. If we do this, the share of transitory income poverty remains about the same and much higher than the share of transitory nutrition poverty, while the share of chronically poor falls as expected. Thus the higher transitory component is not related to the initial setting of the poverty line. If, however, we equalize income total (static) poverty rates to nutritional (static) poverty rates in both years 1992 and 1997, the differences between income and non-income chronic and transitory poor largely disappears; thus much of the transitory component of income poverty is indeed related to a quicker escape from income than non-income poverty in Vietnam during that era. However,

Table 4.2. Poverty dynamics using *fitted* income poverty rates

	Income	Nutrition	Education	Income adj. to Nutrition		Income adj. to Education	
Poor 1992	61.5	43.2	58.1	43.2	43.2	58.1	58.1
Poor 1997	34.2	34.5	49.7	34.5	17.0	30.8	49.7
Chronic poor	31.4	26.0	43.7	26.4	14.6	27.7	41.5
Transient poor	33.0	25.8	15.0	25.1	31.2	33.6	24.9
Non-poor	35.6	48.2	31.3	48.5	54.2	38.7	33.6

Note: In the first set of adjusted poverty rates we adjust the income poverty rate to the nutritional (educational) poverty rate in the first year and then inflate it with the inflation rate implied by the official poverty line inflation between 1992 and 1997, while in the second adjustment we adjust income poverty rates in both years to nutritional (educational) poverty.

if we adjust income poverty rates to education poverty rates in both years, still the transient component of income poverty is much higher than the transient component of educational poverty, indicating that educational well-being is indeed much more stable over time than income poverty (and nutritional poverty).

Two further measurement issues that might explain the higher transient component in income poverty dynamics are household dynamics and measurement error. As stated above, we consider the total household for a calculation of per capita incomes and thus income poverty, while we only consider individuals present in both surveys for our non-income analysis. Household dynamics, i.e. increasing or decreasing household size, will have a significant influence on per capita income and thus affect poverty dynamics (by affecting the denominator by which existing household income is divided or by additionally affecting the numerator if the additional person is contributing incomes), while they do not directly affect the non-income well-being of individuals tracked (see discussion in section 4.3). With regard to measurement error, income (or consumption) is likely to be measured with higher measurement error than non-income indicators; thus a considerable part of transient income poverty might indeed be caused by measurement error. And with only a two-wave panel at hand there is little scope for appropriate instruments to control for measurement error (see Woolard and Klasen, 2005, for a discussion). Bhatta and Sharma (2006) have nevertheless lately applied the proposed method of Luttmer (2002), of error-adjusted consumption measures, to a two-wave panel in Nepal, which might deserve further consideration, although some rather stringent assumptions have to be made.

4.5.2. *Correlation of poverty dynamics*

Even if national levels of income and non-income poverty were the same at a point in time or across time, it could still be the case that the income chronic

Table 4.3. Correlation of income and non-income dynamics

Income	Nutrition			Education		
	Chronic	Transient	Non-poor	Chronic	Transient	Non-poor
Chronic	33.5	27.5	39.0	49.8	18.7	31.6
Transient	26.9	27.5	45.6	43.4	15.8	40.9
Non-poor	18.5	22.6	58.9	39.3	11.3	49.3

(transient) poor are different from the non-income chronic (transient) poor, i.e. depending on the measures used we might identify different households (individuals) as chronically poor. This is most important from a policy perspective as it would affect the targeting of anti-poverty policies.[12]

Table 4.3 illustrates the correlation between income and the diverse non-income poverty dynamics. The numbers show row percentages: that is, they show the percentage of the income chronic (transient, non-) poor that are also non-income chronic (transient, non-) poor, i.e. each row sums to 100 per cent.[13]

Although there is a positive correlation between income and non-income poverty dynamics the correlation is quite low. In fact, it is astounding how many chronic income poor are never poor in a nutrition and education perspective and vice versa.[14] For example, 39.0 per cent of the chronic income poor are never nutritionally poor. The correlation is even lower for transient poverty. For example, the likelihood to be nutritionally transient poor does not (or not much) increase if the individual is income transient poor: 27.5 per cent of the chronic income poor as well as only 27.5 per cent of the transient income poor are also nutritionally transient poor.

One could again argue that part of the low correlation between income and non-income indicators is a consequence of general differences in poverty levels (see previous section). However, if we use fitted income poverty dynamics, i.e. we set income poverty rates in 1992 and 1997 equal to nutritional and educational poverty, the correlation between income and non-income poverty dynamics does not improve significantly. This low correlation between the income and non-income poverty dynamics even if we use fitted income poverty rates could then be explained by two other major factors which we explore in turn: either there is already a low correlation between different dimensions of static poverty (see Table 4.4) or different dimensions of well-being show very different dynamics (see Table 4.5).

---

[12] See Klasen (2000) for a discussion in a static context.

[13] Alternatively, one could have calculated the percentage of the non-income chronic (transient, non-) poor which are also income chronic (transient, non-) poor. As we came to the same conclusions applying this latter approach, we only report the former.

[14] See Baulch and Masset (2003) for a similar finding.

Table 4.4. Correlation of static income and non-income poverty

	Nutrition 1992		Education 1992	
	Poor	Non-poor	Poor	Non-poor
Income 1992				
Poor	29.9	31.6	31.3	27.9
Non-poor	13.3	25.3	18.7	22.1
Income 1997				
Poor	14.5	19.9	17.0	16.8
Non-poor	20.1	45.7	26.7	39.5

Table 4.4 shows the static correlation between income and non-income poverty in 1992 and 1997. Each year and each human development dimension sums to 100 per cent. It can be observed that the income poor are not necessarily the non-income poor. For example, in 1992 29.9 per cent of the population is both income and nutrition poor whereas 25.3 per cent of the population is neither income nor nutrition poor. However, 44.9 per cent of the population is either income poor and not nutrition poor or nutrition poor but not income poor. In 1997, due to significant economic development in Vietnam in the 1990s, the share of the poor in both dimensions has decreased whereas the share of the non-poor in both dimensions has significantly increased, but still 40.0 per cent of the population is only poor in one dimension but not poor in the other. The same trends can be observed if we analyse educational poverty instead. Thus the extent of differences in static poverty is very large, in fact larger than in some other studies where income poverty was compared with composite non-income measures of well-being (e.g. Klasen, 2000).[15]

To separate differences in static poverty from differences in dynamics across the various well-being dimensions, in Table 4.5 we analyse the correlation of different poverty dynamics of only those individuals who show the same static well-being in 1992. More precisely, we only analyse those individuals who were either both income and non-income poor or *neither* income nor non-income poor in 1992. Hence we exclude those individuals who were poor in one but not in the other well-being dimension. The figures show row percentages, i.e. show the percentage of income chronic (transient, non-) poor that are non-income chronic (transient, non-) poor. It should be clear that if we exclude individuals who were initially income poor but not non-income

---

[15] Part of this difference is, as discussed above, surely related to the 'noise' in the anthropometric indicator which only gives a probabilistic assessment of a true nutritional deficit of an individual.

Table 4.5. Correlation of income and non-income dynamics

Income	Nutrition			Education		
	Chronic	Transient	Non-poor	Chronic	Transient	Non-poor
Chronic poor	65.3	34.7	0.0	87.9	12.1	0.0
Transient	52.9	38.2	8.9	80.9	15.0	4.1
Non-poor	0.0	11.4	88.6	0.0	12.1	87.9

Note: Only initial poor/non-poor in both income and non-income dimension are considered.

poor (and vice versa), there can be no individuals who are chronically poor in one dimension but non-poor in another dimension.

If we analyse differences in pure poverty dynamics, i.e. poverty dynamics controlled for differences in static poverty, the correlation between poverty dynamics of income and non-income indicators increases significantly. Especially the income non-poor also seem to stay non-income non-poor: approximately 80 per cent of the income non-poor also stay non-poor in other dimensions of well-being. To a large extent also the chronic income poor remain (chronically) poor in non-income dimensions. In contrast the transient income poor, i.e. mostly those individuals who move out of poverty, often stay chronically poor in other dimensions, which could be caused by delayed dynamics, where non-income indicators change *after* income well-being has changed (i.e. transient non-income poverty reflects past poverty dynamics whereas transient income poverty reflects current poverty dynamics).

In general, though, the dynamics of income and non-income poverty are more similar than their static correlation, which is an interesting and important finding. It suggests that the (unmeasured) characteristics that affect this lack of static correlation between income and non-income poverty do not change much over time as the dynamic correlation for those who were identified as poor/non-poor in both dimensions is quite similar.

4.6. Intra-Household Poverty Dynamics

As discussed above, a particular advantage of examining non-income dimensions of well-being is the ability to study intra-household differences in well-being levels and trends. In this section we explore household non-income poverty dynamics, i.e. analyse the difference between (aggregate) household and individual non-income poverty dynamics, which cannot be captured by income or consumption measures of poverty dynamics which always assume that either everyone or no one in the household is income poor. Differences in household and individual poverty dynamics might, as already discussed above, also be partly responsible for the very low correlation between income

Table 4.6. Household non-income poverty dynamics

	Nutrition			Education		
	Total	Adult	Child	Total	Adult	Child
Homogeneous non-income dynamics						
Chronic poor	2.5	7.1	13.7	9.1	37.7	2.2
Transient poor	1.4	4.5	9.5	0.1	1.1	10.3
Non-poor	11.7	34.5	20.7	14.8	18.0	53.1
	15.6	46.1	43.9	24.0	56.8	65.6
Heterogeneous non-income dynamics						
Transient and chronic poor	6.8	6.9	18.8	10.9	5.8	2.7
Transient and non-poor	22.4	18.9	16.2	8.2	3.4	28.1
Chronic and non-poor	55.3	28.1	21.1	56.8	34.0	3.7
	84.5	53.9	56.1	76.0	43.2	34.4

and non-income poverty dynamics, with the former measuring household and the latter measuring individual poverty dynamics.

Table 4.6 shows intra-household poverty dynamics of the various non-income indicators. The indicated percentages refer to individuals (or adults and children) who live in households where all members are chronically, transient, or non-poor (homogeneous poverty dynamics) or where some are transient while others are chronically poor or non-poor, or where some household members are chronically poor whereas others are non-poor (heterogeneous poverty dynamics). One should be very cautious looking at the total population and should rather analyse adults and children separately, as a lot of differences in poverty dynamics between adults and children are caused by differences in measurement (e.g. the nutritional status of adults is measured weight over height, whereas the nutritional status of children is measured height over age).

Whether we look at nutrition or education, the percentage of individuals who live in households where all adult or child members show the same poverty dynamics is only around 40–60 per cent. What is most surprising is that up to one-third of individuals even live in households where some household members are never poor in a particular non-income dimension while others are always poor in that same dimension.

This high heterogeneity of individual poverty dynamics within households can also explain part of the low correlation of income and non-income poverty dynamics at the micro-level (section 4.4.2) as well as on the aggregate macro-level (section 4.4.1). In contrast to non-income indicators, income indicators ignore differences in poverty dynamics within households. We illustrate this in Table 4.7, where we compare *individual* nutritional (and educational) poverty rates with per capita *household* average nutritional (and educational) poverty rates. If we use the household average instead

Table 4.7. Average household poverty dynamics

	Nutrition		Education	
	Individual[a]	Household[b]	Individual[a]	Household[b]
Poverty 1992	33.6	25.7	64.1	77.6
Poverty 1997	30.9	21.6	57.9	72.6
Chronic	23.0	14.5	57.9	70.4
Transient	18.6	18.9	6.2	9.2
Non-poor	58.4	66.6	35.9	20.4

[a] Poverty rates refer to the individual BMI and years of schooling for adults 18+.

[b] Poverty rates refer to per capita average household BMI and schooling. Rates only for adults of age 18+.

of individual rates the transient poverty rate (relative to the chronic part) becomes significantly larger. So part of the lower transient non-income poverty rate—in comparison to income poverty—stems from the fact that we use individual instead of average household (scaled up to household members) well-being indicators. If one individual improves his or her welfare all other household members become better/worse off as well, so we artificially increase transient poverty if we work with household means. Also absolute chronic poverty rates change significantly if we work with household averages instead of individual poverty rates. But whereas for the nutritional poverty rate the chronic component decreases—in comparison to individual rates— for the educational poverty rate chronic poverty would significantly increase if we worked with household poverty rates.

Lastly, non-income well-being indicators, or intra-household poverty dynamics, can also be used to analyse long-term (intergenerational) poverty dynamics, which is usually not possible with income indicators. Intergenerational chronic poverty, which refers to poverty that is passed from one generation to the next, i.e. the most severe form of chronic poverty, can be assessed by comparing the well-being of two generations within the same households. Table 4.8 shows nutritional and educational poverty for all households, where at least two generations were present in the household.[16] *Poor elderly* indicates the poverty rate of individuals of the older generation within a household, whereas *Poor young* refers to the poverty rate of individuals belonging to the younger generation within a household. *Poor* refers to individuals that are living in households where both the older and younger generations are poor, i.e. where intergenerational chronic poverty persists. By definition, all generations within the same household are either income poor or not. However, there is quite a significant share of individuals who live in households where one generation is non-income poor whereas the other generation is

[16] Poverty rates were calculated based on the average consumption, BMI, and educational level of adults older than 18 years belonging to one of the two generations within households.

95

Isabel Günther and Stephan Klasen

Table 4.8. Intergenerational chronic poverty (1997)

	Income	Nutrition	Education
Poor elderly	31.1	24.4	67.6
Poor young	31.1	22.6	55.5
Poor	31.1	8.9	50.7
Poor/non-poor	0.0	34.8	31.9
Non-poor	69.9	56.4	17.4

Note: Rates are shown for the cross-section data of 1997. However, we obtain the same trends if we use the data from 1992 instead.

not non-income poor. But a large part of individuals live in households where particularly educational poverty is passed from one generation to the next, and we should very much be concerned about these households where poverty persists over very long time horizons.

4.7. Multidimensional Poverty as Chronic Poverty

Several authors have argued that chronic poverty might also be characterized by multidimensional poverty (see e.g. Hulme, Moore, and Shepherd, 2001), i.e. individuals who are poor in several dimensions are more likely to stay chronically poor. We test this hypothesis by analysing the correlation of the number of dimensions an individual is deprived of in 1992 and 1997 in Table 4.9. For example 7.3 per cent of the total population have been poor in one well-being dimension in 1992 and in one well-being dimension in 1997, whereas 4.1 per cent of the population have been poor in all three dimensions (income, nutrition, and education) in 1992 and 1997.

What is striking is that although the correlation of poverty dynamics of different well-being indicators seems to be rather low, i.e. moving out of income poverty does not mean moving out of non-income poverty (and vice versa), the number of well-being dimensions an individual is deprived of seems to be quite stable over time. Fifty per cent of individuals have not changed the number of dimensions in which they are poor (the sum of the diagonal shares)

Table 4.9. Chronic poverty as multidimensional poverty

1992	1997			
	Non-dimensional	One dimensional	Two dimensional	Three dimensional
Non-dimensional	11.6	2.6	0.4	0.0
One dimensional	10.5	19.4	4.0	0.5
Two dimensional	3.9	14.7	15.8	3.5
Three dimensional	0.4	2.9	6.2	4.1

and very few (8.2 per cent) have changed by more than one dimension. This finding could to some extent even explain the low correlation of income and non-income poverty dynamics, if we assume that poor individuals alternate between, for example, low educational or low health functionings or between income and non-income poverty. So here the extent of poverty would be defined as the number of well-being dimensions a person is deprived of. If she is poor in one dimension in one year it is very likely that she is also poor in one dimension in the following years, but the dimension can change. One intriguing interpretation would be that individuals are forced to choose between different forms of deprivation and make different choices over time. This issue certainly deserves closer attention in future research.

4.8. Conclusion and Further Research

The main findings from this exploratory analysis to study chronic poverty and/or poverty dynamics from a non-income perspective are, first, that there are sound theoretical as well as practical empirical arguments for moving in such a direction. It generates important new insights about the dynamics of well-being outcomes over time, their relationship to incomes, and intra-household and intergenerational dynamics. In particular, in our empirical assessment there is more dynamics in non-income dimensions of poverty than commonly presumed, although non-income poverty is certainly more stable over time than income poverty. Moreover, the correlation between chronic poverty in the income and non-income dimensions is very low. This seems to be mostly caused by the low static correlation between the two rather than by different dynamics over the observed period. Fourth, we observed a rather high heterogeneity in intra-household non-income poverty dynamics, which would not be captured by income poverty measures. Last, the number of well-being dimensions individuals are deprived of is surprisingly stable over time. Given the limitations of the data we had at our disposal, these are interesting findings worth exploring more.

But clearly one implication of our research is that more effort must be directed into generated comparable panel datasets that fully capture important non-income well-being outcomes in a comparable fashion. Among the most important improvements to tackle are better measures of health status (see Schultz, 2002, 2003, for possible suggestions) and the inclusion of educational test scores for all in the household.

In addition, this largely descriptive analysis leaves a number of questions unanswered which should be the topic for further research. Most important is a formal regression-based analysis of the determinants of income and non-income poverty dynamics to further understand the surprisingly low correlation between the two as well as the high heterogeneity of poverty dynamics within households. To date, most related regressions have only examined the determinants of chronic and transient income poverty where some non-income dimensions of well-being (particularly human assets such as health and education) are seen as important determinants (e.g. Woolard and Klasen, 2005). Such regression approaches could be extended to also explain dynamics of non-income poverty. Controlling for measurement error and endogeneity will clearly be an issue here, which can be more easily achieved if one can use lagged values as instruments in panels that have more than two waves. Such analyses should usefully consider the actual levels of income and non-income deprivation rather than be based on dichotomous poverty definitions as used here in our exploratory analysis.

Moreover, one can more systematically examine whether some households are chronically worse at turning incomes into non-income achievements. This can be done by examining the persistence of positive and negative residuals of non-income regressions among households across time or applying quantile regressions. This would uncover and define households that are chronically underperforming in turning incomes into functionings as chronically poor.

Secondly, the question of household structure dynamics and equivalence scales deserves closer examination. As shown for example by Woolard and Klasen (2005), changes in household size and structure are an important determinant of income mobility over time and we also know that static poverty assessments are sensitive to equivalence scale assumptions. Both of these issues were raised here but deserve further analysis, particularly when comparing income to non-income poverty dynamics.

Thirdly, one can examine the whole *distribution* of income and non-income well-being dynamics, i.e. using continuous measures rather than dichotomous indicators to study chronic poverty in a non-income dimension. Here the research of Grosse, Harttgen, and Klasen (e.g. Grosse, Harttgen, and Klasen, 2005; Klasen, 2005) in combination with the work of Grimm (2006) could be extended to study non-income poverty dynamics across the entire well-being distribution of households.

A last interesting extension of our work would be to derive multidimensional measures of non-income poverty dynamics, which go beyond a partial ordering of well-being outcomes. The challenging question here is not only how to weight and aggregate different well-being dimensions but in addition how to weight and aggregate different time dimensions. Such work could build on studies by Bossert and D'Ambrosio (2006) and Chakravarty and D'Ambrosio (2006) who axiomatically derive relative and absolute measures of social exclusion, i.e. chronic capability failure. For them, social exclusion is the (weighted) sum of individual functionings from which an individual is excluded over time. The chapter is much concerned with the aggregation to a social exclusion score for the society and with comparisons with other societies using dominance relations, which could be a helpful start for such work. In this context, it might also be fruitful to combine the study of Duclos, Sahn, and Younger (2006) with the one of Gräb and Grimm (2006), with the former concentrating on robust multidimensional and the latter focusing on robust multi-period poverty comparisons in non-income dimensions.

References

Atkinson, A. B., and Bourguignon, F. (2000), *Handbook of Income Distribution*, Amsterdam: North Holland.

Basu, K., and Foster, J. (1998), 'On Measuring Literacy', *Economic Journal*, 108: 1733–49.

Baulch, B., and Hoddinott, J. (2000), 'Economic Mobility and Poverty Dynamics in Developing Countries', *Journal of Development Studies*, 36(6): 1–24.

——and Masset, E. (2003), 'Do Income and Non-Income Indicators Tell the Same Story about Chronic Poverty? A Study of Vietnam in the 1990s', *World Development*, 31(3): 441–53.

Bhatta, S. D., and Sharma, S. K. (2006), 'The Determinants and Consequences of Chronic and Transient Poverty in Nepal', CPRC Working Paper 66, Manchester: Chronic Poverty Research Center.

Bonschab, T., and Klump, R. (2007), 'Pro-Poor Growth in Vietnam: Explaining the Spatial Differences', in M. Grimm, A. McKay, and S. Klasen (eds.), *Determinants of Pro-Poor Growth: Determinants of Pro-Poor Growth: Analytical Issues and Findings from Country Cases*, London: Palgrave Macmillan.

Bossert, W., and D'Ambrosio, C. (2006), 'Deprivation and Social Exclusion', *Economica*, forthcoming.

Chakravarty, S., and D'Ambrosio, C. (2006), 'The Measurement of Social Exclusion', *Review of Income and Wealth*, 52(3): 377–98.

Clark, D., and Hulme, D. (2005), 'Towards a Unified Framework for Understanding the Depth, Breadth and Duration of Poverty', Global Poverty Research Group Working Paper 20, Manchester: Chronic Poverty Research Center.

Deaton, A. (1997), *The Analysis of Household Surveys*, Baltimore: Johns Hopkins University Press.

——and Zaidi, S. (2002), 'Guidelines for Contructing Consumption Aggregates for Welfare Analysis', LSMS Working Paper No. 135, Washington: World Bank.

Duclos, J. Y., Sahn, D., and Younger, S. D. (2006), 'Robust Multidimensional Spatial Poverty Comparisons in Ghana, Madagascar, and Uganda', *World Bank Economic Review*, 20(1): 91–113.

Friedman, M. (1957), *A Theory of the Consumption Function*, Princeton: Princeton University Press.

Gibson, J. (2001), 'Measuring Chronic Poverty without a Panel', *Journal of Development Economics*, 65: 244–63.

Gräb, J., and Grimm, M. (2006), 'Robust Multiperiod Poverty Comparisons', paper prepared for the Chronic Poverty Research Center.

Grimm, M. (2007), 'Removing the Anonymity Axiom in Assessing Pro-Poor Growth', *Journal of Economic Inequality*, 5(2): 179–97.

Grosse, M., Harttgen, K., and Klasen, S. (2005), 'Measuring Pro-Poor Growth Using Non-Income Indicators', Ibero-America Institute Working Paper 132, Göttingen: University of Göttingen.

———— (2008), 'Measuring Pro-Poor Growth in Non-Income Dimensions', *World Development*, 36(6): 1021–47.

Haddad, L., and Kanbur, R. (1990), 'How Serious is the Neglect of Intra-Household Inequality?', *Economic Journal*, 100: 866–81.

Henderson, R. M. (2005), 'The Bigger the Healthier: Are the Limits to BMI Risk Changing over Time?, *Economics and Human Biology*, 3: 339–66.

Hulme, D. (2003), 'Chronic Poverty and Development Policy: An Introduction', *World Development*, 31(3): 399–402.

—— and McKay, A. (2005), 'Identifying and Understanding Chronic Poverty: Beyond Income Measures', Manchester: Chronic Poverty Research Center.

—— Moore, K., and Shepherd, A. (2001), 'Chronic Poverty: Meanings and Analytical Frameworks', CPRC Working Paper 2, Manchester: Institute of Development Policy and Management.

—— and Shepherd, A. (2003), 'Conceptualizing Chronic Poverty', *World Development*, 31(3): 403–23.

Jalan, J., and Ravallion, M. (1996), 'Transient Poverty in Rural China', Policy Research Working Paper 1616, Washington: World Bank.

Jensen, R. (2000), 'Agricultural Volatility and Investments in Children', *American Economic Review*, 90(2): 399–404.

Klasen, S. (2000), 'Measuring Poverty and Deprivation in South Africa', *Review of Income and Wealth*, 46: 33–58.

—— (2005), 'Economic Growth and Poverty Reduction: Measurement and Policy Issues', OECD Development Centre Working Paper 246, Paris: OECD.

—— (2007a), 'Gender-Related Indicators of Well-Being', in M. McGillivray (ed.), *Human Well-Being: Concept and Measurement*, London: Palgrave, 167–92.

—— (2007b), 'Poverty, Undernutrition, and Child Mortality: Some Inter-regional Puzzles and their Implications for Research and Policy', *Journal of Economic Inequality*, forthcoming.

—— (2008a), 'Economic Growth and Poverty Reduction: Measurement Issues using Income and Non-Income Indicators,' *World Development*, 36(3): 420–45.

—— (2008b), 'Poverty, Undernutrition and Child Mortality: Some Inter-regional Puzzles and their Implications for Research and Policy'. *Journal of Economic Inequality*, 6(1): 89–115.

Luttmer, E. F. P. (2002), 'Measuring Poverty Dynamics and Inequality in Transition Economies: Disentangling Real Events from Noisy Data', NBER Working Paper.

McKay, A., and Lawson, D. (2003), 'Assessing the Extent and Nature of Chronic Poverty in Low Income Countries: Issues and Evidence', *World Development*, 31(3): 425–39.

Moradi, A. (2006), 'Nutritional Status and Economic Development in Sub-Saharan Africa, 1950–1980', working paper, Oxford: University of Oxford.

OECD (2000), *Literacy in the Information Age*, Paris: OECD.

Ramos, X., and Silber, J. (2005), 'On the Application of Efficiency Analysis to the Study of the Dimensions of Human Development', *Review of Income and Wealth*, 51: 285–310.

Schultz, T. P. (2002), 'Health and Labor Force Participation of the Elderly in Taiwan', Yale University Economic Growth Center Discussion Paper No. 846.

—— (2003), 'Human Capital, Schooling, and Health', *Economics and Human Biology*, 1: 207–22.

Sen, A. (1985), *The Standard of Living*, Cambridge: Cambridge University Press.

—— (1999), *Development as Freedom*, Oxford: Oxford University Press.

Townsend, R. (1995), 'Consumption Insurance: An Evaluation of Risk-Bearing in Low-Income Economies', *Journal of Economic Perspectives*, 9(3): 83–102.

UNICEF (1998), *The State of World's Children: Focus on Nutrition*, New York: UNICEF.

White, H., and Masset, E. (2003), 'Constructing the Poverty Profile: An Illustration of the Importance of Allowing for Household Size and Composition in the Case of Vietnam', *Development and Change*, 34(1): 105–26.

WHO (1995), *Physical Status: The Use and Interpretation of Anthropometry*, WHO Technical Report Series No. 854, Geneva: WHO.

Woolard, I., and Klasen, S. (2005), 'Income Mobility and Household Poverty Dynamics in South Africa', *Journal of Development Studies*, 41: 865–97.

Yaqub, S. (2003), 'Chronic Poverty: Scrutinizing Patterns, Correlates and Explorations', CPRC Working Paper 21, Manchester: University of Manchester.

Zeller, M., Sharma, M., Henry, C., and Lapenu, C. (2006), 'An Operational Method for Assessing the Poverty Outreach Performance of Development Policies and Projects', *World Development*, 34: 446–64.

5

The Construction of an Asset Index

Measuring Asset Accumulation in Ecuador

Caroline Moser and Andrew Felton

5.1. Introduction

In the past decade development economists have increasingly advocated the use of assets to complement income and consumption-based measures of welfare and wealth in developing countries (Carter and May, 2001; Filmer and Pritchett, 2001). Income has long been the favoured unit of welfare analysis, because it is a cardinal variable that is directly comparable among observations, making it straightforward to interpret and use in quantitative analysis. However, by the 1990s this was often superseded by consumption-based measures (Ravallion, 1992). The analysis of assets and their accumulation is intended to complement such measures, by extending our understanding of the multidimensional character of poverty and the complexity of the processes underlying poverty reduction (Adato, Carter, and May, 2006).

Closely linked to the asset-based approach is recent methodological work on the measurement of assets with a range of new techniques developed to capture aggregate ownership of different assets into a single variable. The objective of this 'technical' chapter is to contribute to the debate about the measurement of assets. It describes the particular methodology developed to construct an asset index based on a longitudinal panel dataset from

The authors gratefully acknowledge Michael Carter, who as adviser to the Guayaquil project has provided invaluable guidance and positive feedback as we have grappled with creating the asset index. Thanks also to James Pickett, John Hoddinott, Jesko Hentschel, Michael Woolcock, and Peter Sollis for advice. The latest stage of the Guayaquil project has been supported by the Ford Foundation, New York. Particular thanks to vice president Pablo Farias for his commitment to this work.

Guayaquil, Ecuador. It then outlines its application in terms of the different components of the asset index, before concluding by identifying several continuing methodological problems.

5.2. Contextual Background

5.2.1. *The research methodology*

The construction of an asset index is grounded in a research project on 'Intergenerational asset accumulation and poverty reduction in Guayaquil, Ecuador between 1978 and 2004'. A community study such as this, which combines a range of qualitative, participatory, and quantitative methodological approaches used over a twenty-six-year research period, poses challenges relating to its statistical robustness, or representativeness. This was also the case in an earlier research phase when the data were included in a World Bank study on the 'social impact' of structural adjustment reforms in four poor urban communities in different regions of the world that included not only Guayaquil, Ecuador, but also Lusaka, Zambia, Budapest, Hungary, and Metro Manila, the Philippines (Moser, 1996, 1998). At the time the results were dismissed by World Bank economists as not representative at the national level, nor robust in terms of cross-country comparisons; at best they provided interesting case study 'anecdotal information' on community and household coping strategies in 'crisis situations' (Moser, 2002).

To address this challenge the research methodology for this final study builds on earlier cross-disciplinary combined methodologies including the pioneering work of Ravi Kanbur to address the 'qual–quant' divide (Kanbur, 2002) but pushes the envelope further by including the econometric measurement of the quantitative data on capital assets. The methodology, which we have called 'narrative econometrics', combines the econometric measurements of change with in-depth anthropological narratives that identify the social relations within households, communities, and broader institutional structures that influence well-being and assist in identifying the associated causality underpinning economic mobility. In so doing we also seek to develop methodological tools that can bridge the divide in current debates about the limitations of measurement-based poverty analysis that disregards context and therefore 'cannot address the dynamic, structural and relational factors that give rise to poverty' (Harriss, 2007; see also Green and Hulme, 2005; Green, 2006). This chapter, however, is limited to the elaboration of the index methodology and therefore complements further analysis that seeks to bring together the 'econometric' and the 'narrative' (see for instance Moser and Felton, 2007).

5.2.2. *Assets and income*

While economists often use income to measure wealth, welfare, and other indicators of well-being, income data has limitations in both accuracy and measurement, particularly in the context of developing countries. For instance, for people living in informal labour markets incomes are often highly variable. Income can be seasonal, such as when earned from farming or the tourist market, or just variable and lumpy for small-business owners. Taking a snapshot of income at one point in time may therefore produce a less reliable picture of these types of workers than those who receive regular pay cheques. Furthermore, they may be engaged in barter and other non-monetary forms of trade. In all of these cases there is a high potential for error in data based on the recollection and value of all sources of income. This means that income itself does not necessarily provide a reliable measure of well-being.

Expenditures and consumption are also commonly used to measure well-being (Chen and Ravallion, 2000; Ellis, 2000). Expenditures solve some of the problems of income, such as seasonality. Households can save their income from flush times as a buffer against bad times. This 'consumption smoothing' is both theoretically appealing and has empirical regularity. Households also tend to be more forthcoming about expenditures, which lack the sensitivity that some have towards divulging income data. However, a number of the same difficulties of income also apply to expenditure, such as measuring the value of bartered goods. Work done for oneself, such as house improvement, also tends to be missing from expenditures. In addition, although economists have shown that consumption data provide more robust information on well-being than income data (particularly in rural areas), income data are still used in a number of research studies such as in the Guayaquil study.[1]

When asking people what they own from a list of assets, there is often less likelihood of recall or measurement problems. Furthermore, assets may provide a better picture of long-term living standards than an income snapshot because they have been accumulated over time and last longer. However, a list of assets lacks money's advantages of cardinality and fungibility. The following section explores the theoretical difficulties of creating a set of 'asset' variables.

---

[1] Longitudinal anthropological research in this urban context revealed that even people's short-term recall of consumption expenditures was often inaccurate or underestimated. People buying many of their basic consumption items on a daily basis simply did not remember what they spent. Data from expenditure diaries, for instance, proved to be widely inconsistent with expenditure data from anthropological participant observation. In contrast, working in a community where trust had been established, there was a high level of compatibility across the 51 households in the panel data in terms of income relating to both formal and informal sector earnings. For this reason the study used income measures.

Suppose that a household's capital portfolio can be measured in terms of a number I of types of capital, C^i, where $i \in [1, 2, \ldots I]$. Each type of capital C^i is composed of J types of assets $a^{i,1} \ldots a^{i,J}$. Each of these a's may be measured using a binary, ordinal, or cardinal variable. We want to assign a weight w to each item and then sum up the weighted variables to arrive at our estimate of C^i, as in equation 5.1.

$$C^i_{n,t} = \sum_{j=1}^{J} w^{i,j}_t a^{i,j}_{n,t}$$ (5.1)

where
  n = Household number
  i = Type of capital
  j = Type of asset
  t = Time period

The rest of this section describes different ways to measure the w's.

Method 1: Prices. One intuitive way to weight the assets is to use monetary values, so that $w^{i,j}_t = p^{i,j}_t$ where $p^{i,j}_t$ is the price (or some other monetary measure of value) of asset (i,j) at time t. The sum $\sum_{j=1}^{J} w^{i,j}_t a^{i,j}_{n,t}$ would then be the total monetary value of the household's asset wealth. However, this approach is problematic for some of the same reasons that income data are. Price data can be difficult to obtain in some contexts, especially in economies that have high levels of barter. Even more fundamental is the problem that it is difficult or impossible to assign prices to intangible assets, such as human or social capital. Of course, assigning any numbering to those types of capital is tenuous, but the ordinal scale that we develop in this chapter seeks to overcome the implied fungibility of prices.

Method 2: Unit values. Another method is to simply sum up the number of assets owned, which is equivalent to setting $w = 1$ for each w. This method has the virtue of simplicity, but also has the limitation of assigning equal weight to ownership of each asset. For example, this method would assign equivalent worth to owning a radio and a computer, although in reality their contributions to the capital variable are surely different.

Method 3: Principle components analysis. Recently, development economists have followed the recommendation made by Filmer and Pritchett (2001) to use principle components analysis (PCA) to aggregate several binary asset ownership variables into a single dimension. PCA is relatively easy to compute and understand, and provides more accurate weights than simple summation.

The intuition underlying this method is that there is a latent (unobservable) variable $\tilde{C}^i$ for each type of capital C^i that manifests itself through ownership of the different assets $a^{i,1} \ldots a^{i,J}$. For example, suppose household n owns asset $a^{i,1}$ if $\tilde{C}^i > w^{i,1}$. It turns out that the maximum likelihood estimators

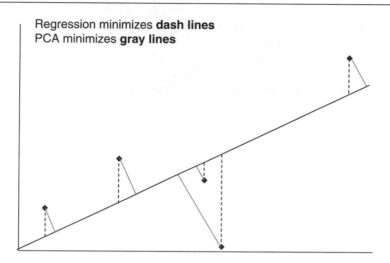

Figure 5.1. Difference between regression and PCA

of the w's are the eigenvectors of the covariance matrix, also known as the *principle components* of the dataset.[2] Usually only the eigenvector with the highest eigenvalue is used, because it is the vector that provides the most 'information' about the variables.[3] The first eigenvector is the vector that minimizes the squared distances from the observations to a line going through the various dimensions.

This is an appealing method for combining variables for two reasons. First, it is technically equivalent to a rotation of the dimensional axes, such that the variance from the observations is minimized. This is equivalent to calculating the line from which the orthogonal residuals are minimized. This is similar to a regression in terms of minimizing residuals, but in this case the residuals are measured against all of the variables, not just one 'dependent' variable. Figure 5.1 demonstrates how regression minimizes the squared residuals from a dependent variable to a line, while PCA minimizes the distances from points in multidimensional space to a line.

The second reason that PCA is a valuable approach is that the coefficients have a fairly intuitive interpretation. The coefficient on any one variable is related to how much information it provides about the other

---

[2] In fact a correlation matrix is usually used to equally scale the variables and avoid problems stemming from what measurement units are used.

[3] It is also possible to use the sum of a number of eigenvectors, based on some criteria. Using the sum of all the eigenvectors is equivalent to using unit coefficients for each variable. Some statisticians recommend using all eigenvectors with eigenvalues greater than one; others suggest the 'scree test'. However, these are more complicated to interpret than using just the first eigenvector (Jolliffe, 2002).

variables.[4] If ownership of one type of asset is highly indicative of ownership of other assets, then it receives a positive coefficient. If ownership of an asset contains almost no information about what other assets the household owns (its correlation coefficient is near zero), then it receives a coefficient near zero. And if ownership of an asset indicates that a household is likely to own few other assets, then it receives a negative coefficient. Higher and lower coefficients mean that ownership of that asset conveys more or less information about the other assets.

This makes PCA excellent for modelling a presumed underlying continuous variable, such as wealth. If ownership of a certain asset is highly correlated with owning the other assets that were asked about in the survey, then it is probably correlated with owning other types of assets that were not in the survey as well. To return to the earlier example, wealthy households are more likely to own a computer than poor ones, but radio ownership is spread evenly across the spectrum. Therefore, knowing that one household owns a computer provides us with more information about that household's wealth than a radio does, and it receives a higher weighting.

Filmer and Pritchett (2001) fail to adequately address the important methodological issue that the variables must positively correlate with the latent variable, and with each other. If all the variables are positively correlated, then the estimates will all be greater than or equal to 0 and bounded at the top by the value of the first eigenvalue (which is itself less than or equal to the number of variables in the matrix). If they are not, then the first eigenvector may have negative values, which means that the estimated latent variable would be *reduced* from ownership of an asset. This is only remedied by interpreting ownership of those assets as a sign of lower wealth. If this is plausible, then even negative values of estimated wealth are acceptable because the estimated variable is ordinal and can either be used as is or rescaled so that they are all positive.

Filmer and Pritchett (2001) use twenty-one types of assets from the Demographic and Health Surveys, covering both consumer durables and housing stock, to create a single 'wealth' variable. They show that the resulting variable has empirically plausible consequences and predicts school enrolment better than expenditure. The robustness tests on asset indices conducted by Sahn and Stifel (2003) demonstrate that the asset index reliably predicts poverty and serves as a proxy for long-term wealth with less error than data on expenditures.

Other papers advocate a variety of techniques. Sahn and Stifel (2003) use factor analysis, which is designed more for data exploration than dimensional reduction. Booysen, van der Berg, Burger, von Maltitz, and du Rand (2005)

---

[4] This has a precise mathematical definition in terms of Kullback–Leibler (1951) information.

use multiple correspondence analysis (MCA), which they promote as better at dealing with categorical variables than PCA. Finally, Kolenikov and Angeles (2004) describe a new technique, polychoric principle components analysis, which improves on regular PCA and is designed specifically for categorical variables. Unlike MCA it can also be used for continuous variables and is especially appropriate for discrete data. It supposes that the discrete data are observed values of an underlying continuous variable. Similar in spirit to an ordered probit regression, polychoric PCA uses maximum likelihood to calculate how that continuous variable would have to be split up in order to produce the observed data.

Polychoric PCA has a number of advantages over regular PCA. For instance, its coefficients are more accurately estimated than with regular PCA.[5] The main advantage, however, comes from its use of ordinal data. Many assets can be described as ordinal. Researchers often ask about the quality of construction of a home, for example, which might be recorded on a 1–4 scale. While Filmer and Pritchett (2001) advocate splitting this into four binary variables, this introduces a large amount of distortion into the correlation matrix, as the variables are automatically perfectly negatively correlated with each other. Furthermore, the knowledge that the researcher brings—that some values are better than others—is lost, as the PCA treats every variable as the same. Polychoric PCA solves these problems by assigning each the value of a discrete variable and ensuring that the coefficients of an ordinal variable follow the order of its values.

Another advantage of polychoric PCA is that it allows us to compute coefficients of both owning and not owning an asset. This is desirable because sometimes not owning something conveys more information than owning it. If almost every household owns indoor plumbing except for the very poorest, then the coefficient on owning indoor plumbing will be around zero (since it does not help distinguish household wealth among those that own it). However, not owning indoor plumbing will be negatively correlated to ownership of other assets and the coefficient of not owning it will be highly negative. This further distinguishes among wealth levels.

5.3. Multivariate Analysis

Most research so far has only used PCA and its related techniques to model ownership of a single type of asset, usually a variant of 'wealth'. However, social scientists are often interested in examining portfolios that include different asset types in order to better understand the specific root causes

---

[5] Kolenikov and Angeles (2004) run a Monte Carlo exercise on simulated data and find that polychoric PCA predicts the 'true' coefficients more accurately than regular PCA.

of poverty. Hulme and McKay (2005) provide an overview of techniques used for multivariate asset analysis, briefly mentioning index construction methods like PCA before moving on to a variety of other methods used by economists, sociologists, and anthropologists. Most of the examples of multivariate asset analysis cited do not use PCA or other sophisticated techniques of aggregating assets. For example, Klasen (2000) identifies fourteen components of well-being and sums up the number that are unsatisfactory for a given households to arrive at a 'deprivation index'. However, as Hulme and McKay point out,

while giving all components the same weight might appear to be 'fair', there is a complex set of value judgments built into such an assumption. For example, can nutrition (child stunting that may reduce an individual's capabilities over her lifecourse) be weighted the same as transport/mobility (where a low score may be a temporary inconvenience)?

They identify similar issues with multidimensional frameworks by Clark and Qizilbash (2002, 2005) and Barrientos (2003).

Among the papers that use PCA or similar methods, Sahn and Stifel (2003) come closest to implementing a multidimensional approach. They categorize their index components into three types of capital (household durables, household characteristics, and human capital) but they then combine them all together into a single index. Asselin (2002) also groups his variables into categories (economy and infrastructure, education, health, and agriculture) but then combines them all before his analysis. To the best of our knowledge, no paper so far uses PCA on the components of each type of capital before undertaking its analysis.

5.4. The Empirical Application of Polychoric PCA: The Guayaquil Panel Dataset

Below we present an application of multivariate analysis on a panel dataset of fifty-one households in a neighbourhood of Guayaquil, Ecuador, between 1978 and 2004. The analysis is based on the research presented in detail in Moser and Felton (2007) on the measurement and analysis of four dimensions of the five-dimensional asset framework (see for instance Carney, 1998; Moser, 1998; World Bank, 2000) in order to implement a quantitatively rigorous, multidimensional approach to asset accumulation and poverty dynamics.

While the asset index is grounded in an extensive literature review on livelihoods and asset accumulation (Moser, 2008), the specific assets chosen were determined by the questions available in the dataset. Here it is necessary to recognize constraints relating to the fact that this was not originally defined as a study of asset accumulation when the first stage of field research was undertaken living in the community. (This applies particularly to the social capital variables and employment data.)

5.4.1. *Data and contextual background*

The data come from a research project that focused on household asset accumulation strategies using twenty-six years of anthropological and sociological research in a poor urban community, Indio Guayas, in Guayaquil, Ecuador. Named after its community committee, this is an eleven-block neighbourhood area within the barrio of Cisne Dos, which in 2004 had an estimated 75,364 inhabitants (World Bank, 2004). Cisne Dos itself is one of a number of working-class suburbs in the *parroquia* of Febres Cordero located on the south-west edge of the city. This area, about seven kilometres from the central business district, was originally a mangrove swamp.

In 1978, when the research began, recently arrived settlers were consolidating the 10 by 30 metre waterlogged plots (*solars*) they had purchased cheaply from professional invaders. Households lacked not only dry land, but also basic physical services such as electricity, running water, plumbing, as well as adequate social services like education and health facilities. At this time it was a young population, struggling to make their way in the city, many just starting families. By 2004, Indio Guayas was a stable urban settlement with physical and social infrastructure, and, due to the city's rapid expansion, a community no longer on the periphery. By this time, children of the original settlers had reached adulthood and started families of their own, either in the same community or elsewhere. The study is contextualized within the broader macroeconomic and political structural context during different phases of Ecuador and Guayaquil's history; in brief these can be summarized as the 1975–85 democratization process, the 1985–95 economic structural adjustment policies, and the 1995–2005 globalization and dollarization period.

Three quantitative household surveys were undertaken in 1978, 1992, and 2004 that comprise a panel dataset of the inhabitants of fifty-one family plots. In 1978, a universe survey of 244 households was undertaken over the eleven-block area; in 1992 a random sample survey of 263 households undertaken in exactly the same spatial area picked up 56 households that had also been in the 1978 universe survey. In 2004, these same 56 households were tracked and 51 were re-interviewed (indicating a 9 per cent attrition rate).

5.4.2. *Analysis*

The Indio Guayas household asset index is based on the following sources: those defined in the literature, research based on local anthropological knowledge of asset vulnerability in the community (Moser, 1996, 1997, 1998), and the empirical data available from the panel data. The variables were adapted from the questionnaire data from the 1978–2004 panel data. Two types of physical capital were identified: housing and consumer durables. Financial capital was extended to incorporate productive capital, while human capital was limited to education because of a lack of panel data on health. Finally, social capital was disaggregated in terms of household and community social capital.[6]

Table 5.1 outlines each type of asset analysed, the category of capital that it belongs to, and the specific components that make up its index. The following section describes in detail the construction of the index to measure each of these capital types and the associated challenges. Polychoric PCA was used for many but not all of the asset categories; as we elaborate in the subsequent sections, its advantages and limitations become clearer when moving from theory to practice. As with any statistical technique, the devil is in the details and we lay out below exactly how and why we chose specific variables out of this detailed dataset for use with different techniques.

(I) PHYSICAL CAPITAL

Physical capital is generally defined as comprising the stock of plant equipment, infrastructure, and other productive resources owned by individuals, businesses, and the public sector (see World Bank, 2000). In this study, however, physical capital is more limited in scope. It is subdivided into two and includes the range of consumer durables households acquire, as well as their housing (identified as the land, and the physical structure that stands on it).

Housing is the more important component of physical capital. In Indio Guayas households squatting in severe conditions on a mangrove swamp rapidly constructed wooden stilts and a platform, and then incrementally built very basic houses with bamboo walls, wood floor, and corrugated iron roofs. However, such houses were insecure—bamboo walls could easily be split by knives, and the materials quickly deteriorated. Consequently, as soon as resources were available, households upgraded their dwellings. This started with infill to provide land, followed by permanent housing materials such as cement blocks and floors. This very gradual incremental upgrading took place over a number of years.

This process is reflected in the econometric findings on housing based on the four indicators: type of toilet, light, floor, and walls. These are ordered in terms of increasing quality (for instance 'incomplete' walls are those in the process of being upgraded from bamboo to either wood or brick/concrete),

---

[6] A fifth type of capital, natural capital, is commonly used in the assets and livelihoods literature. Natural capital includes the stocks of environmentally provided assets such as soil, atmosphere, forests, water, and wetlands. This capital is more generally used in rural research. In urban areas where land is linked to housing this is more frequently classified as productive capital as is the case in this study. However, since all households lived on similar plots this was not tracked in the dataset.

Table 5.1. Types of capital, asset categories, and components

Capital type	Asset index categories	Index components
Physical capital	Housing	Roof material
		Walls material
		Floor material
		Lighting source
		Toilet type
	Consumer durables	Television (none, b/w, colour, or both)
		Radio
		Washing machine
		Bike
		Motorcycle
		VCR
		DVD player
		Record player
		Computer
Financial/productive capital	Labour security	Type of employment:
		State employee
		Private sector permanent worker
		Self-employed
		Contract/temporary worker
	Productive durables	Refrigerator
		Car
		Sewing machine
	Transfer/rental income	Remittances
		Rental income
Human capital	Education	Level of education:
		Illiterate
		Some primary school
		Completed primary school
		Secondary school or technical degree
		Some tertiary education
Social capital	Household	Jointly headed household
		Other households on solar
		'Hidden' female-headed households
	Community	Whether someone on the solar:
		attends church
		plays in sports groups
		participates in community groups

with the data showing a high degree of inter-household correlation. The ordinal nature and positive correlation of the variables make this part of the data highly suitable for analysis using the polychoric PCA technique (see Table 5.2).

The estimated coefficients rise with the increasing quality of each asset, and greater numbers (either positive or negative) mean that the variable provides more 'information' on the household's housing stock. For example, the greatest negative coefficient is on having no electric lights. This means that a household that lacks electric lighting is extremely likely to fall into the lowest categories of the other types of assets: toilet, floor, and walls. Similarly, a household with a flush toilet (the highest level within the toilet category) is

Table 5.2. Housing stock polychoric PCA coefficients

Asset	Coefficient
Toilet: hole	−0.5629
Toilet: latrine	−0.0735
Toilet: toilet	0.4541
Light: none	−0.8869
Light: illegally tapped electricity	−0.2605
Light: mains electricity	0.4063
Floor: earth/bamboo	−0.8672
Floor: wood	−0.3052
Floor: brick/concrete	0.3658
Walls: earth/bamboo	−0.5687
Walls: incomplete	−0.1847
Walls: wood	−0.1340
Walls: brick/concrete	0.3631

likely to have scored highly on the other items as well. This is because flush toilets were owned by the fewest people, and it was only in 2004 that almost all households acquired one. In contrast, many people had connected to the main electrical grid, and upgraded their floors and walls to brick/concrete, by 1992.

The consumer durables variable illustrates a new type of difficulty with PCA. Because the data cover multiple time periods, the 'values' of many of these assets have changed between observations. For example, a black-and-white television was relatively more valuable in 1978 than in 2004. In 1978, it was a sign of wealth to own a black-and-white television, but in 2004, a sign of poverty, as colour televisions had become available. By 2004, a number of electronic items that had become available were simply not on the market previously.

This issue can be addressed either by conducting a separate analysis for each year, or by aggregating the data across time. The first three columns of Table 5.3, which calculate values for each item in each year, illustrate the changing values of many of the variables. In 1978, a black-and-white television had a strongly positive coefficient, as it was a sign of wealth. Its coefficient decreased during each time period as it became less indicative of wealth. This demonstrates that in addition to its ability to create a single variable, asset index construction is useful for tracking the relative value of items.

Aggregating the time periods proved to be the most efficacious method of combining the variables, as it allows relative comparisons across, as well as within, time periods. Items that were once luxury items can receive a negative score in later time periods, which means they are on average indicative of poverty. However, because we estimate the value of not owning the asset as well as the value of owning it, a household with a black-and-white TV

Table 5.3. Consumer durables polychoric PCA coefficients

Asset	1978	1992	2004	All years combined
No TV	−0.5358	−0.4168	−0.4687	−0.4616
B/w TV	0.5797	−0.0317	−0.2939	−0.0564
Colour TV		0.2782	0.0194	0.3093
Both b/w and colour TV		0.5229	0.3778	0.7321
No radio	−0.8888	−0.6856	−0.2631	−0.1069
Radio	0.1761	0.1358	0.0943	0.0277
No washing machine		−0.0402	−0.0914	−0.0492
Washing machine		1.4188	0.7685	0.7507
No bike		−0.1190	−0.1802	−0.1428
Bike		0.3009	0.1665	0.3973
No motorcycle		−0.0949	−0.0240	−0.0253
Motorcycle		0.7978	0.2020	0.3464
No VCR			−0.0623	−0.0258
VCR			0.6574	0.8706
No DVD player			−0.1477	−0.0580
DVD player			0.6507	0.8844
No record player	−0.1738		−0.1236	−0.0639
Record player	0.4394		0.6239	0.3718
No computer			−0.1100	−0.0519
Computer			0.4843	0.7910

in 1978, although receiving a 'negative' score in aggregate, still ranks much higher in 1978 than a comparable household that does not own a TV at all. In fact, the average household in 1978 had a negative score for their consumer durables capital, but the ordinal rankings remain the same as the coefficients were calculated separately for each year. Therefore, the rankings make sense both within and across time periods.

This method produces a feasible and accessible continuous variable representing ownership of consumer durables. Figure 5.2 shows the kernel density distributions for the consumer durables variable in each round. In 1978 and 1992, the variable is roughly normally distributed (when the households are just beginning to diverge from their equal starting points), but by 2004 it resembles the lognormal distribution commonly found in studies of income distribution (which parallels the actual growth of income and asset inequality in Guayaquil).

(II) HUMAN CAPITAL

Human capital assets refer to individual investments in education, health, and nutrition, which affect people's ability to use their labour and change the nature of their returns from their labour. Education is the only component in this index and therefore provides only a partial picture of human capital.[7]

[7] The study contains detailed information on health status, particularly in terms of shocks relating to serious illnesses or accidents, as well as the use and cost of health services.

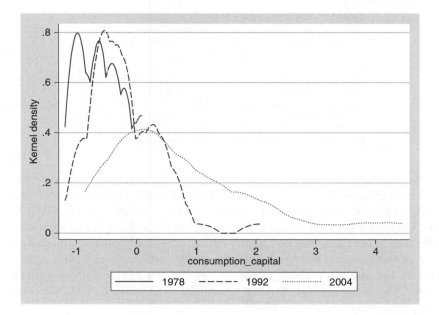

Figure 5.2. Consumer durables capital density estimates

Human capital presents a different challenge from previous categories because it is usually measured at the individual, not household level. If we want to measure human capital at the household level, we need to develop a method of aggregation. Furthermore, we have only one key measure of human capital at the individual level: years of education (or, alternatively, level of completed education). Since there is only one variable, we cannot use any of the varieties of PCA at the individual level because PCA measures the correlation between two or more variables. We could assign an equal weight to every year of education and add them up—but this brings us back to the earlier methods described above, with the same attendant problems. Instead, we make use of the fact that the survey contains the income earned by every individual, so are able to estimate the monetary return to education. The education variable was split into five levels: none, some primary, completed primary, completed secondary, and some tertiary (see Table 5.4).

Income earned from wages is regressed on the level of education, age and age squared to proxy for experience, and a gender dummy variable. The regression is estimated separately for each year because the value of each type of degree changes every year as the job market changes. Therefore, the value of the education capital of a household can change even though the actual level

However, the lack of an adequate methodology to translate these into a health asset index means that the information remains at the narrative level.

Table 5.4. Value of educational levels

Educational level	1978	1992	2004
Illiterate	3.52	2.15	3.18
Some primary	3.20	2.47	3.09
Completed primary	3.31	2.51	3.19
Completed high school or technical school	3.09	2.66	3.21
Tertiary education	3.98	3.12	3.37

Note: Coefficients for age, age squared, and gender not shown.

of education in the household did not. In 1978, there was very little difference in terms of wages in the value of being illiterate, having some primary education, or having completed primary school. These education levels accounted for almost 90 per cent of the young settlers of Indio Guayas's population at the time. Those few that had higher education earned considerably more in the labour market. Over time, however, being illiterate or without a primary degree became more disadvantageous because less-educated people earned lower wages. Meanwhile, the macroeconomic instability of 1992 decreased wages for every educational group.

Human capital is usually valued for its use in the labour market, so it is one type of capital that may be measured in monetary terms relatively easily using techniques similar to those described above. Years of education and salary are frequently available in surveys. On the other hand, endogeneity and other issues are problematic in this methodology. For example, many people with low education are not in the workforce—neither including them as zero income nor not including them is wholly satisfactory. If low-educated people are disproportionately absent from the formal economy, then the estimation of returns from low levels of education might be biased up, because only the most talented of the poorly educated have income. Table 5.4 shows that illiterate people often earn more than those with more education, suggesting that this problem may indeed exist in our data.

Furthermore, the use of other variables like age and gender, while important, also leads to complications. Younger generations on average had more educational opportunities, and the importance of education changes over the years as the economy develops. By using income as the dependent variable, we are measuring the market value of education, rather than some level of inherent human capital specific to the individual. Finally, we may disagree with the values the labour market places on human capital. For example, people with no education at all in 1978 earned more than any other group except those with college educations (only one person). However, we want to assign those people the lowest level of human capital. For these reasons, estimating the level of human capital using other variables may produce worse results than an arbitrary ranking.

Ideally, PCA or a similar technique can be used, given a variety of data on individuals assumed to be correlated with the unmeasurable 'human capital', such as test scores, grades, education, etc. In fact, the literature on measuring intelligence often uses PCA to collapse scores along a number of dimensions into one variable (Jensen, 2002). However, data of this nature are not usually available, especially in developing countries.

(III) FINANCIAL/PRODUCTIVE CAPITAL

Financial/productive capital comprises the monetary resources available to households. In developed countries, this usually translates into financial assets such as bank holdings, stock and bond investments, house equity, etc. that can be drawn on in case of need. However, few citizens of developing countries have any of these. In this case, a monetary measure is actually less useful than an asset index, because the assets are likely to be intangible and not easily quantified in monetary terms.

The financial/productive capital asset index comprises three components: labour security, which measures the extent to which an individual has security in the use of their labour potential as an asset; transfer/rental income which is non-earned monetary resources; and productive durables, which are durable goods with an income-generating capability. Table 5.5 shows the results of the polychoric analysis.

Labour security is undoubtedly the most challenging component in the index. However, it represents an effort to include labour as an asset?omitted so far in the work on asset indices—and to include employment vulnerability as linked to stability of job status. The composite component derives from combining two ILO work categories on employer type and work status, and is ranked in terms of vulnerability in the Guayaquil context through local anthropological knowledge: the most secure type of job is working for the state, the second is as a 'permanent worker' (with a formal, stable job)

Table 5.5. Financial/productive capital polychoric PCA coefficients

Asset	Coefficient (all years combined)
Sewing machine: no	−0.0158
Sewing machine: yes	0.0173
Refrigerator: no	−0.3344
Refrigerator: yes	0.3133
Car: no	−0.1351
Car: yes	0.8356
Home business income: no	−0.1036
Home business income: yes	0.4999
Rental income: no	−0.1152
Rental income: yes	0.9031
Remittances: no	−0.1326
Remittances: yes	0.4779

in the private sector, the third is self-employment, and the least secure is contract/temporary work. The ordering of the top two job types should be uncontroversial, but the latter two require some explanation. Entrepreneurs, even on a small scale, build up business knowledge, contacts, and habits that can help sustain them through a downturn. They can continue in their business even during times of reduced demand (Moser, 1981). Temporary workers, however, have less to fall back on when they are let go. Consequently we make the judgement that the self-employed have more job security than contract workers. Unfortunately, we must still arbitrarily assign weights to each type of job: we give temporary work a four on the vulnerability scale and move down to government work, which gets a weight of one. We then aggregate up to the household level by computing the average vulnerability of each household. Although this method retains some of the arbitrariness that we have been trying to avoid, we at least manage to turn labour security into an ordinal variable that can be used for polychoric PCA.

The main sources of unearned income are remittances, government transfers, and rent. The first two are transfers of income within society and the latter is a return on capital—similar to income from physical goods as analysed above. Non-wage income has increasingly played an important role in household income. Remittance income has risen most dramatically, linked to the explosion of Ecuadorian migrants in the late 1990s following dollarization and the banking crisis. The fact that this accounted for over 50 per cent of non-wage income in 2004 shows that having someone abroad is a real household asset. Remittance income comprised more than half total income for some households. Rental income is much smaller and more recent as households have specifically built on extra rooms to accommodate renters either at the back of their plots, or in additional floors to their house.

Finally, productive durable goods count as financial/productive capital because they represent a current or potential income stream. In the context of Guayaquil, sewing machines, refrigerators, and cars were popular examples of this type of goods, with each predominating during different time periods. Numerous families acquired sewing machines in the 1970s. Men primarily used them in their work as tailors, either as self-employed or as subcontracting outworkers. A lesser number of women had sewing machines for use both within the family but also to generate income through work as dressmakers (Moser, 1981). Refrigerators are generally used as the basis of a small enterprise selling ice, frozen lollies, and cold drinks such as Coca Cola. Car ownership is a more recent phenomenon and one that requires far more capital (usually based on credit loans). Almost all local men who own cars use them as taxis to generate an income. While in some cases these are full-time occupations, in other cases they supplement other jobs particularly when there is high demand—such as weekend nights.

Table 5.6. Community social capital polychoric PCA coefficients

Asset	Coefficient
Don't attend church	−0.7449
Attend church	0.2744
Don't participate in community activities	−0.3511
Participate in community activities	0.3650
Don't participate in sports league	−0.4358
Participate in sports league	0.6050

(IV) SOCIAL CAPITAL

Social capital, the most commonly cited intangible asset,[8] is generally defined as the rules, norms, obligations, reciprocity, and trust embedded in social relations, social structures, and societies' institutional arrangements that enable its members to achieve their individual and community objectives. Social capital is generated and provides benefits through membership in social networks or structures at different levels, ranging from the household to the marketplace and political system. The index differentiates between community-level social capital and household social capital. The latter is based on detailed panel data on changing intra-household structure and composition (see Moser, 1997, 1998). Social capital is usually considered extremely difficult for social scientists to measure because the assets are non-physical and difficult to translate into monetary terms. In the asset index framework, however, they are measured in terms of binary variables such as household participation in various different activities and groups.[9]

This dataset uses three variables to determine household social capital as identified in Table 5.1. The results are shown in Table 5.6. The index was constructed using polychoric PCA. The three variables are positively correlated with each other and participation in a sports league was the best indicator of social capital. Not attending church was the best indicator of a lack of social capital, garnering a large negative coefficient. Of the twelve observations in which a household had a member participating in a sports club, only one of those did not also have someone who either went to church or participated in community activities.

Household social capital as an asset is complex because it is both positive and negative in terms of accumulation strategies. On one hand, households act as important safety nets protecting members during times of vulnerability

---

[8] Social capital is the most contested type of capital (Bebbington, 1999). The development of the concept is based on the theoretical work of, for instance, Putnam (1993) and Portes (1998).

[9] Again it important to note that the original study in 1978 was not designed to 'measure' social capital; consequently the groups identified do not represent the universe but are those for which comparative data is available.

and can also create opportunities for greater income generation through effective balancing of daily reproductive and productive tasks (see Moser, 1993). On the other hand, the wealth of a household may actually be reduced by having to support less-productive members. Over time, households change in size and restructure their composition and headship in order to reduce vulnerabilities relating both to lifecycle and wider external factors.

Household social capital was defined as the sum of three indicator variables. The first component, jointly headed households, serves to indicate trust and cohesion within the family between partners, and is applied to both nuclear and couple-headed extended households. In 1978 when the community comprised young families nearly two-thirds were nuclear in structure.[10] By 1992 this had dropped to a third and in 2004 was only one in ten households. In contrast, the reverse was true for couple-headed extended households, growing from one-fifth in 1978 to two-fifths by 1992 and levelling off to slightly more by 2004. Within many extended households there are also 'hidden' female heads of household: unmarried female relatives raising their children within the household to share resources and responsibilities with others. This has grown from less than one in ten in 1978 to more than one in four in 2004. The third component is the presence of other family-related households living on the solar—usually the households of sons or daughters.

Unfortunately, none of the varieties of PCA could be used here because the variables are not all positively correlated, but we wanted to give them all a positive value. PCA or a similar technique would have given at least one of the coefficients a negative value. We therefore had to give them all equal weight (or some other arbitrary weight). This is an area where more research is needed.

5.4.3. *Preliminary analysis*

Longitudinal analysis of changing poverty levels based on income alone provides one measure of well-being, and shows movement between poverty levels. A more comprehensive understanding of household assets accumulation complements income data in helping to identify why some households are more mobile than others and how some households successfully pull themselves out of poverty while others fail.

Most assets increased fairly steadily between 1978 and 2004 (Figure 5.3). The greatest difference between households in the first and last periods was

[10] A nuclear household comprises a couple living with their children; an extended household comprises a single adult or couple living with their own children and other related adults or children; a female-headed household comprises a single-parent, nuclear, or extended household headed by a woman; if married she identifies herself as the head usually because her husband is not the main income earner; a woman is counted as a 'hidden' head of household if she: (1) lives on the family plot; (2) is unmarried; and (3) has at least one child.

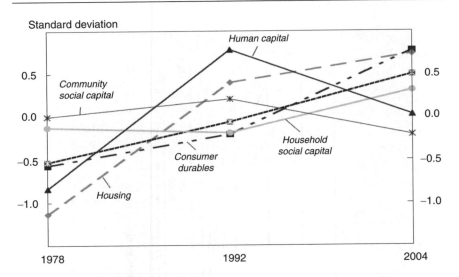

Figure 5.3. Household asset accumulation in Guayaquil, Ecuador, 1978–2004

in housing: the average household improved its housing stock by over two standard deviations. Community capital actually decreased from 1992 to 2004. These quantitative observations are supported by the anthropological research.

Asset analysis can be particularly useful when used in conjunction with income data. The following Figure 5.4 displays the level of housing and consumer durables owned by income group during each time period and demonstrate that households of all income levels have similar average levels of housing, but very different levels of consumer durables (especially in 2004). This implies that poor households place a much greater emphasis on accumulating housing than consumer durables.

These numbers are not adjusted for household size, although size is obviously significant. Poorer households tend to be larger households, with greater needs for housing space and physical infrastructure. Also, larger households, ceteris paribus, tend to have more people working and greater total income than smaller households, although large households tend to have lower per capita incomes than small households. This means that the larger household may have an advantage in accumulating assets and therefore look wealthier, but those assets have to be shared among a greater number of people. Some assets can be shared without diminishing their utility for any one person. A radio, for example, can be listened to by multiple people at once. Cars can be shared to some extent, but they cannot be driven by more than one person at the same time. Naturally, jobs and education are not shared. Finally, the index is not adjusted for household size because PCA techniques used to calculate

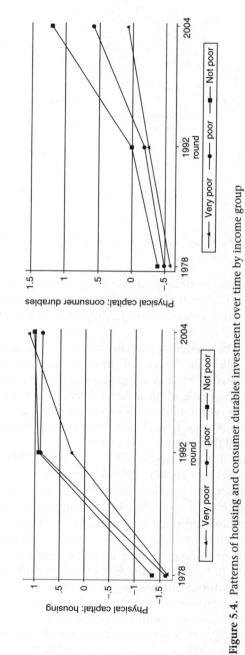

Figure 5.4. Patterns of housing and consumer durables investment over time by income group

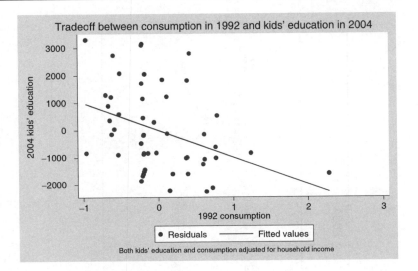

Figure 5.5. Trade-off between consumption and kids' education

the asset indices do not have units, and would therefore be unsuitable for interpreting variables on a per capita basis.

We can also use asset indices to examine how individual households make 'portfolio' choices between types and amounts of assets to accumulate. Figure 5.5 illustrates a trade-off between the level of consumer durables in a household in 1992 and the total amount of education that the household's children receive in 2004. By 1992 the original generation of settlers had reached middle age and most had school-age children. By 2004 many of the second-generation children had finished school and moved out on their own. The data in Figure 5.5 are adjusted for household income because wealthier households may be able to afford more consumer durables *and* educate their kids better. The kids' education is not per capita—it represents the total investment that households have put into their kids' human capital and is parallel to consumer durables ownership, which is also not per capita. The figure quantifies the stark choices that households—especially those with large numbers of children—make between acquiring two types of assets.

Figure 5.6 uses 'star graphs' to display the changing composition of household portfolios over time. Because this type of graph cannot display negative numbers, the estimated levels of assets were scaled so that the minimum score was 0 and average score was 1. The graphs display how the average portfolios increased in size and changed in shape. For example, there is a clear outward shift of financial capital and consumer durables by 2004, as well as a noticeable increase in variation.

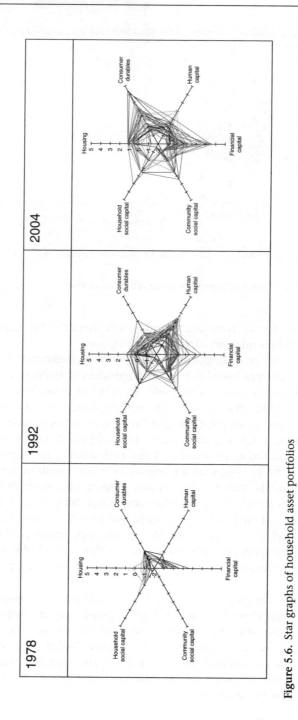

Figure 5.6. Star graphs of household asset portfolios

These simple diagrams suggest several directions in which the work could go. One would be the use of mathematical techniques to sort observations into groups based on a number of variables, such as cluster analysis and fuzzy set theory. By 2004, there is enough differentiation among the households that they may have sorted themselves into identifiable groups. One of the advantages of the asset-based analysis presented above is that it enables enough dimensional reduction to make other techniques more intuitive and easier to apply, because they can incorporate fewer key variables.

5.5. Conclusion

This study of assets provides an overview of recent research on the use of asset indices as well as illustrating a particular way of constructing an asset index. Much progress has been made over the last five years, but a number of issues remain. For example, principle components analysis, in all its variations, is still dependent on the observed variables being positively correlated. Another unresolved issue is how best to aggregate assets from the individual level to the household level without involving arbitrary methods like summation or averaging. Similarly, there is no clear way to adjust levels of assets for household size. Finally, this is obviously not a methodology that can be immediately applied to many datasets. It requires considerable knowledge of the different variables in order to select and transform them into appropriate subjects for polychoric PCA.

Nevertheless, existing techniques contribute to the accuracy and robustness of asset accumulation analysis. This chapter has demonstrated how grouping a large number of assets into a smaller number of dimensions facilitates an intermediate level of analysis. By examining how households allocate their resources using an asset index, the analysis of specific poverty mechanics is possible without examining an overwhelming quantity of individual variables. Asset indices are an important complement to pure income data because they paint a clearer picture of the strategies households in various income groups have employed to acquire different types of assets, and because they provide clues to poverty alleviation. The next step is to use these indices to understand poverty dynamics in greater detail.

References

Adato, M., Carter, M., and May, J. (2006), 'Exploring Poverty Traps and Social Exclusion in South Africa using Qualitative and Quantitative Data', *Journal of Development Studies*, 42(2): 226–47.

Asselin, L.-M. (2002), 'Composite Indicator of Multidimensional Poverty', unpublished paper, Institut de Mathématique Gauss.

Barrientos, A. (2003), 'Non-Contributory Pensions and Well-Being among Older People: Evidence on Multidimensional Deprivation from Brazil and South Africa', DEPP Working Paper, University of Manchester, IDPM.

Bebbington, A. (1999), 'Capitals and Capabilities: A Framework for Analysing Peasant Viability, Rural Livelihoods and Poverty', *World Development*, 27: 2021–44.

Booysen, F., et al. (2005), 'Using an Asset Index to Assess Trends in Poverty in Seven Sub-Saharan African Countries', paper presented at conference on Multidimensional Poverty hosted by the International Poverty Centre of the United Nations Development Programme (UNDP), 29–31 August, Brasilia.

Carney, D. (ed.) (1998), *Sustainable Rural Livelihoods: What Contribution Can We Make?*, London: Department for International Development (DFID).

Carter, M., and May, J. (2001), 'One Kind of Freedom: Poverty Dynamics in Post-Apartheid South Africa', *World Development*, 29(12): 1987–2006.

Chen, S., and Ravallion, M. (2000), 'How Did the World's Poorest Fare in the 1990s?', Policy Research Working Paper 2409, Washington: World Bank.

Clark, D. A., and Qizilbash, M. (2002), 'Core Poverty and Extreme Vulnerability in South Africa', Discussion Paper No. 2002–3, School of Economics, University of East Anglia.

—— —— (2005), 'Core Poverty, Basic Capabilities and Vagueness: An Application to the South African Context', GPRG Working Paper No. 26, Universities of Manchester and Oxford. Available online at <http://www.gprg.org/pubs/workingpapers/default.htm>.

Ellis, F. (2000), *Rural Livelihoods and Diversity in Developing Countries*, Oxford: Oxford University Press.

Filmer, D., and Pritchett, L. (2001), 'Estimating Wealth Effects without Expenditure Data—or Tears: An Application to Educational Enrollments in States of India', *Demography*, 38(1): 115–32.

Green, M. (2006), 'Representing Poverty and Attacking Representations: Perspectives on Poverty from Social Anthropology', *Journal of Development Studies*, 42(7): 1108–29.

—— and Hulme, D. (2005), 'From Correlates and Characteristics to Causes: Thinking about Poverty from a Chronic Poverty Perspective', *World Development*, 33(6): 867–89.

Harriss, J. (2006), 'Why Understanding Social Relations Matters More for Policy in Chronic Poverty than Measurement', paper presented at the Concepts and Methods Workshop, University of Manchester, October.

Hulme, D., and McKay, A. (2005), 'Identifying and Measuring Chronic Poverty: Beyond Monetary Measures', paper presented at conference on Multidimensional Poverty hosted by the International Poverty Centre of the United Nations Development Programme (UNDP), 29–31 August, Brasilia.

Jensen, A. (2002), 'Psychometric g: Definition and Substantiation', in R. Sternberg and E. Grigorenko (eds.), *The General Factor of Intelligence: How General Is It?*, Mahwah, NJ: LEA, Inc.

Jolliffe, I. T. (2002), *Principal Component Analysis*, New York: Springer-Verlag.

Kanbur, Ravi (ed.) (2002), *Qual–Quant: Qualitative and Quantitative Methods of Poverty Appraisal*, Delhi: Permanent Black.

Klasen, S. (2000), 'Measuring Poverty and Deprivation in South Africa', *Review of Income and Wealth*, 46: 33–58.

Kolenikov, S., and Angeles, G. (2004), 'The Use of Discrete Data in Principal Component Analysis: Theory, Simulations, and Applications to Socioeconomic Indices', Working Paper of MEASURE/Evaluation project, No. WP-04-85, Carolina Population Center, University of North Carolina.

Kullback, S., and Leibler, R. A. (1951), 'On Information and Sufficiency', *Annals of Mathematical Statistics*, 22(1): 79–86.

Moser, C. (1981), 'Surviving in the Surburbios', *Bulletin of the Institute of Development Studies*, 12(3): 19–25.

—— (1993), *Gender Planning and Development: Theory, Practice and Training*, New York: Routledge.

—— (1996), 'Confronting Crisis: A Comparative Study of Household Responses to Poverty and Vulnerability in Four Poor Urban Communities', Environmentally Sustainable Development Studies and Monograph Series No. 8, Washington: World Bank.

—— (1997), 'Household Responses to Poverty and Vulnerability, Volume 1: Confronting Crisis in Cisne Dos, Guayaquil, Ecuador', Urban Management Program Policy Paper No. 21, Washington: World Bank.

—— (1998), 'The Asset Vulnerability Framework: Reassessing Urban Poverty Reduction Strategies', *World Development*, 26(1): 1–19.

—— (2002), ' "Apt Illustration" or "Anecdotal Information": Can Qualitative Data Be Representative or Robust?', in R. Kanbur (ed.), *Qual–Quant: Qualitative and Quantitative Methods of Poverty Appraisal*, Delhi: Permanent Black, 79–89.

—— (2008), 'Assets and Livelihoods: A Framework for Asset-Based Social Policy', in C. Moser and A. Dani (eds.), *Assets, Livelihoods, and Social Policy*, Washington: World Bank.

—— and Felton, Andrew (2007), 'Intergenerational Asset Accumulation and Poverty Reduction in Guayaquil, Ecuador 1978–2004', in Caroline Moser (ed.), *Reducing Global Poverty: The Case for Asset Accumulation*, Washington: Brookings Institutional Press.

Portes, A. (1998), 'Social Capital: Its Origins and Applications in Modern Sociology', *Annual Review of Sociology*, 24: 1–24.

Putnam, R. (1993), *Making Democracy Work: Civic Traditions in Modern Italy*, Princeton: Princeton University Press.

Ravallion, M. (1992), 'Poverty Comparison: A Guide to Concepts and Methods', Living Standards Measurement Study Working Paper 88, Washington: World Bank.

Sahn, D., and Stifel, D. (2003), 'Exploring Alternative Measures of Welfare in the Absence of Expenditure Data', *Review of Income and Wealth*, 49(4): 463–89.

World Bank (2000), *World Development Report 2000/01: Attacking Poverty*, Washington: World Bank.

—— (2004), *Ecuador Poverty Assessment*, Washington: World Bank.

6

Looking Forward

Theory-Based Measures of Chronic Poverty and Vulnerability

Michael R. Carter and Munenobu Ikegami

6.1. From Backward-Looking to Forward-Looking Poverty Analysis

> [The historian] becomes a crab. The historian looks backward; eventually he also believes backward.
>
> (Friedrich Nietzsche, *Twilight of the Idols*)

Conventional quantitative poverty analysis invariably looks backwards to the most recent living standards survey to enumerate (the past) extent and nature of poverty. Living standards surveys, with their 7-day, 30-day, and 12-month recall periods, look yet further backward. While there is no reason to follow Nietzsche and assert that backward-looking poverty analysis 'believes backwards', there are clearly (forward-looking) questions that conventional poverty analysis is ill equipped to answer. Perhaps the most important of these questions concerns the future persistence of observed poverty status: Are the observed poor chronically poor, or are they in a transitory state?

Others have struggled with this question. One approach (used by the Chronic Poverty Research Centre, 2004) is empirical. With numerous repeated observations of the same households, the chronically poor can be identified as those who have been 'frequently' poor in the observed past. While this approach has much to recommend it, it is expensive and has an ad hoc element (how frequently must an individual be observed to be poor in order to be classified as chronically poor?). More importantly, it is also backward looking.

The approach put forward in this chapter is rather different. Using guidance from the microeconomic theory of poverty traps, this chapter uses the past to identify structural patterns of change—asset dynamics—rather than past levels of poverty. The statistical identification of these patterns then permits the creation of forward-looking poverty measures that tell us where we expect the poor to be in the future, not where they have been in the past.[1] While these new measures do not eliminate the need for other approaches (indeed, when combined with standard approaches they provide a more complete poverty dialogistic for a particular economy), they do offer a promising approach for the conceptualization and measurement of chronic poverty. They also carry important policy implications.

Building on the work of Buera (2005) and Barrett, Carter, and Ikegami (2007), section 6.2 of this chapter develops a theoretically grounded approach to chronic poverty that emphasizes the role of individual heterogeneity and clarifies the role that vulnerability to economic shocks plays in producing chronic poverty. The key theoretical construct that emerges from this analysis is the Micawber Frontier, defined as the level of assets below which an individual of a particular skill level is unable to successfully accumulate assets and move ahead economically over time.

Section 6.3 then shows how knowledge of the Micawber Frontier can be used to generate two classes of chronic poverty measures. The first class generalizes a suggestion put forward by Carter and Barrett (2006) and is based on the individual's distance from the Micawber Frontier. The second uses information on the Micawber Frontier to simulate future asset (and income) changes. When combined with the family of chronic poverty measures put forward by Calvo and Dercon (this volume), these asset dynamics open yet another window into chronic poverty that is forward looking and based on a theoretically well-specified model. Numerical simulation of a stylized 100-household economy is used to illustrate both sets of measures. In addition, both sets of chronic poverty measures can be used to derive well-structured measures of vulnerability, where vulnerability is understood as the fraction of all chronic poverty that would be eliminated in a world without economic shocks (or with perfectly well-positioned social safety nets).

Section 6.4 then takes some first steps toward implementing the ideas put forward in this chapter, using estimated asset dynamics in South Africa over the 1993 to 1998 period to calculate chronic poverty measures based on distance from the asset threshold. While based on somewhat stringent assumptions, these forward-looking estimated chronic poverty measures provide a more in-depth look at the nature of poverty than do standard

---

[1] This approach of course still relies on the past, but uses it to identify patterns of asset dynamics. If those past patterns of change are not stable, providing a poor guide to future patterns, then the approach put forward here also becomes backward looking.

FGT-based measures. At the same time, data from a later time period (2004) illustrate weaknesses of the estimated chronic poverty measures and point the way toward more reliable estimation needed to capture the full richness of a theory-based approach to chronic poverty. The chapter closes with some reflections on the implications of the analysis for the design of social protection policy which potentially will pay off with a double dividend of reduced chronic poverty.

6.2. A Theory-Based Approach to Chronic Poverty

This section summarizes recent theoretical work by Barrett, Carter, and Ikegami (2007) (hereafter cited as BCI) on the economics of poverty traps. Building on the dynamic model of Buera (2005) that explicitly incorporates the intrinsic capacity or ability differences of individuals, BCI show that there are two types of chronic poverty:

- *Intrinsic Chronic Poverty* suffered by those of relatively low skill and possibilities who are inevitably trapped in a poor, low-level equilibrium trap (given the structure of wages and opportunity in their economy); and

- *Multiple Equilibrium Chronic Poverty* suffered by a middle-ability group that has the potential to be non-poor in their extant economy, but whose histories have placed them below the minimum asset threshold needed to initiate and sustain the accumulation needed to escape poverty.

In addition to these two groups, the BCI model identifies a third, high-ability group that may be consumption poor for an extended period of time, but who are expected to surmount a poor standard of living given a sufficiently long period of time in which to accumulate assets. We refer to this third group as the *Intrinsically Upwardly Mobile*.

This section proceeds in two steps. First, it considers the implications of the BCI model in the absence of economic shocks. While unrealistic, this simplification underwrites basic insights into the economics of asset thresholds and chronic poverty. In addition, when paired with the analysis of shocks and risk pursued later in this section, the simplified model will suggest measures of vulnerability and its effect on chronic poverty.

6.2.1. Heterogeneous ability and poverty traps

Building on the model of Buera (2005), BCI assume that each individual is endowed with a level of innate ability (a) as well an initial level of capital (k_0). Every period t, the individual has the choice between two alternative

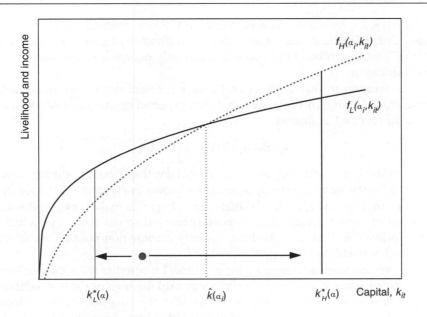

Figure 6.1. Assets and livelihood options

technologies for generating a livelihood, f:

$$f(a, k) = \begin{cases} f_L(a, k) = ak^{\gamma L} \text{ under the low technology} \\ f_H(a, k) = ak^{\gamma H} - E \text{ under the high technology} \end{cases},$$

Both technologies are skill sensitive (for any given technology, more able people can produce more than less able people). One technology (the 'high' technology) is subject to fixed costs, E, meaning that the technology is not worth using with low amounts of capital. Figure 6.1 illustrates these technologies for an individual with a given skill level a. As can be seen in the figure, the individual (interested in maximizing income or livelihood possibilities) will optimally shift to employing the high technology only after k reaches the critical level $\hat{k}(a) = \{k| f_L(a, k) = f_H(a, k)\}$.

Using this basic set-up, BCI analyse when it is possible and desirable for the individual to save and accumulate assets in order to surpass $\hat{k}(a)$, employ the high technology, and reach a higher standard of living. As summarized in Appendix 6.1, the BCI model assumes that individuals divide their total income (f) between consumption (c_t) and investment (i_t) in order to maximize their intertemporal stream of utility. Assets evolve according to the following rule

$$k_{t+1} = i_t + (1 - \delta)k_t. \tag{6.1}$$

where $i_t = f(a, k_t) - c_t$ is investment and δ is the rate at which capital depreci-
ates. Critically, the model assumes that the individual cannot borrow against
future earnings to build up capital and can only pursue autarchic accumulation strategies.

The solution to this intertemporal choice problem defines an investment
rule, $i^*(k_t|a)$. Using this rule, we can define expected capital stock of a house-
hold in year $t + 1$ as follows:

$$k_{t+1}^e(k_t|a) = i^*(k_t|a) + (1 - \delta)k_t$$

If individuals had access to only one technology, they would optimally accumulate capital up to the steady state values shown in Figure 6.1, $k_L^*(a)$ for the
low technology and $k_H^*(a)$ for the high technology.[2] To make it easy to discuss
the model, we will assume that the poverty line just equals $f(k_L^*(a))$ for a high-
skill individual. That is, individuals can only become non-poor if they adopt
the higher livelihood strategy.[3]

The key question addressed by the BCI model is whether individuals whose
initial capital stock is below $\hat{k}(a)$ gravitate toward the high or the low technology. Consider an individual who begins life with the asset position at the level
marked by the dot in Figure 6.1. Will this individual optimally move to the
right over time, accumulating assets and ending up at $k_H^*(a)$ and a non-poor
standard of living? Alternatively, will the individual de-accumulate, move to
the left, and settle into a poor standard of living with capital stock $k_L^*(a)$?[4]
More formally, is there an initial asset threshold, which we will denote $\bar{k}(a)$,
below which individuals stay at the low equilibrium (remaining chronically
poor), and above which they will move to the high equilibrium (eventually
becoming non-poor)?

As analysed by BCI, the answer to this question depends on the skill level
of the individual. In particular, there will be three classes of individuals
each exhibiting distinct dynamically optimal behaviour. Figure 6.2, which is
created through the numerical analysis of the BCI model, illustrates these
three classes (see Appendix 6.1 for the full specification of the dynamic
programming model). Along the horizontal axis are skill levels, ranging from
least to most able. The vertical axis measures the stock of productive assets.

---

[2] Note that these steady state values are increasing in the level of skill, a. The steady state
values are also influenced by the individual's discount rate, meaning his or her willingness to
sacrifice current consumption in order to save and gain higher future consumption.

[3] If this assumption is not true, individuals may get trapped at the low equilibrium, but
they would not necessarily be poor.

[4] Note that beyond the low-level equilibrium, $k_L^*(a)$, the immediate marginal returns to
additional capital are low and less than the value of the consumption that the individual
must sacrifice in order to accumulate additional capital. In the rationality of the model, an
individual will only make that sacrifice if future returns (when she finally accumulates at least
$\bar{k}(a)$ <sp>) are large enough close enough (and sufficiently certain, when there is uncertainty
in the model).

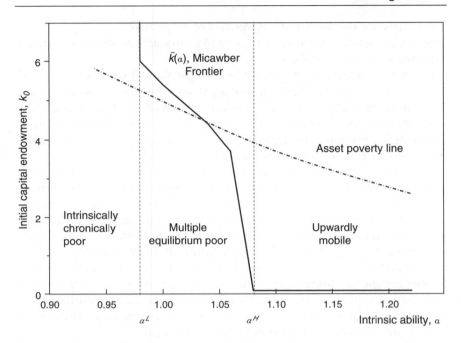

Figure 6.2. The Micawber Frontier (non-stochastic case)

The dashed curve is the asset poverty line, defined as the level of assets needed to generate an expected standard of living equal to the poverty line. The solid curve shows the asset level at which an individual is just indifferent between staying with the low technology versus building up stocks of assets such that a transition to the high technology eventually becomes feasible. Denote this frontier as $\bar{k}(a)$. An individual with ability level a will attempt to accumulate and move out of poverty if she enjoys a capital stock $k_0 > \bar{k}(a)$. Otherwise, she will only pursue the low technology, accumulating the modest levels of capital that it requires. Following Carter and Barrett (2006), we label $\bar{k}(a)$ as the Micawber Frontier as it divides those who have the wealth needed to accumulate from those who do not.[5]

As illustrated in Figure 6.2, the numerical analysis identifies three distinct regions in the space of ability and initial asset holdings. High-skill individuals are those with $a > a^H$ who will always move toward the high equilibrium even if they find themselves with a zero stock of assets (as $\bar{k}(a) = 0$ for these individuals). When they reach $\hat{k}(a)$ they will optimally switch to the higher technology. Irrespective of their starting position, these individuals steadily converge to the steady state asset value for the high technology. These

---

[5] As discussed by Carter and Barrett, the phrase Micawber Threshold was first used by Michael Lipton, and was then subsequently adopted by Zimmerman and Carter (2003), who give it a meaning similar to that used here.

individuals are the *intrinsically upwardly mobile*, perhaps consumption poor over some extended period as they save and accumulate assets, but eventually expected to become non-poor.

In contrast, those with an ability level below the critical level $a < a^L$ will never move toward the high technology if they find themselves with any finite stock of assets. These are *intrinsically chronically poor* individuals who lack the ability or circumstance to achieve a non-poor standard of living in their existing economic context (CPRC, 2004, gives examples of individuals who suffer such fundamental disabilities).[6]

Finally, and most interestingly, the intermediate skill group with $a^L < a < a^H$ have positive, but finite, values $\tilde{k}(a)$. If sufficiently well endowed with assets ($k_0 > \tilde{k}(a)$), these individuals—the *multiple equilibrium poor*—will accumulate additional assets over time, adopt the high technology, and eventually reach a non-poor standard of living. If they begin with assets below $\tilde{k}(a)$, these individuals will no longer find the high equilibrium attainable and will settle into a low standard of living. Like the intrinsically chronically poor, this subset of the multiple equilibrium poor will be chronically poor.[7] The total number of chronically poor in any society will thus depend on the distribution of households across the ability–wealth space shown in Figure 6.2. The chronic poverty measures developed below rely on this insight.

6.2.2. Shocks, risk, and poverty traps

While establishing the possibility of distinct types of poverty, the analysis in the prior section has ignored the reality of the economic shocks that threaten the well-being of less well-off people almost everywhere. In the presence of asset thresholds and poverty traps, economic shocks take on particular significance as Carter, Little, Mogues, and Negatu (2007) explore in an empirical analysis of Ethiopia and Honduras.

There are at least three types of shocks that could generate risks that might have a major impact on the accumulation decisions of poor people. The first type is income shocks where households receive more or less than the expected amount of income from their assets at any point in time. Second, the marginal utility of income is also subject to shocks. Households, for example, may suffer a severe illness, creating new needs for cash that effectively drive up the marginal utility of consumption. Third, assets themselves are subject to shocks. Livestock may die, businesses may burn down, or productive equipment may unexpectedly break or be stolen. All three types of shocks have the

---

[6] Addressing the poverty of such individuals will require transfers and perhaps efforts like the PROGRESA programme to assure that the next generation acquires adequate human capital.

[7] Unlike the disabled, this class can be helped to help themselves with safety nets and cargo nets.

capacity to derail households from the accumulation paths discussed in the prior section. We will here focus only on asset shocks.[8]

In the presence of asset shocks, next-period assets depend not only on prior stocks plus investments, but also on realized shocks. To represent this possibility, BCI rewrite the rule that determines the evolution of capital stock (6.1) as follows:

$$k_{t+1} = \theta_t[i_t + (1 - \delta)k_t], \tag{6.2}$$

where θ_t is a random variable realized every period t. Note that if $\theta = 1$, there is no shock, whereas $\theta < 1$ indicates a negative shock that destroys some fraction of assets. While in principle shocks could be positive ($\theta > 1$), such events seem unlikely and we will restrict the analysis here to the case where only negative shocks are possible.

As summarized in Appendix 6.1, the individual intertemporal choice problem can be modified with (6.2) and the assumption that the individual knows the distribution of θ and chooses consumption and investment every period in order to maximize the discounted stream of expected utility. Denote the investment rule in the presence of asset shocks as $i_s^*(k_t|\alpha, \Omega)$, where Ω represents the set of information on the probability distribution that generates random shocks.

The impact of shocks on investment and the long-term evolution of poverty can be broken down into two pieces, the ex post effect of realized shocks and the ex ante effect of risk. The ex post effect of shocks comes about simply because negative events may destroy assets, knocking people off their expected path of accumulation. For intrinsically upwardly mobile individuals, such shocks may delay their arrival at the upper-level equilibrium, or occasionally knock them down from it, necessitating a period of additional savings and asset reaccumulation.

For multiple equilibrium households, the ex post consequences of shocks can be rather more severe. Consider the case of a household that is initially only slightly above the Micawber Frontier. A shock that knocks it below that frontier will knock the household into the ranks of the chronically poor, as the household will (optimally) alter its strategy and give up trying to reach the high equilibrium. Figure 6.3 illustrates such a case derived from the numerical simulation of the BCI model. The horizontal axis shows time, and the vertical measures accumulated capital stock. The two illustrated time paths show two different histories for a household that begins with initial assets above the Micawber Frontier. Under the dashed line trajectory, the household avoids severe shocks (at least early on) and manages a long-term escape from

---

[8] The analysis of income and marginal utility shocks is more difficult, raising interesting issues of asset smoothing discussed theoretically by Zimmerman and Carter (2003) and analysed empirically by Hoddinott (2006).

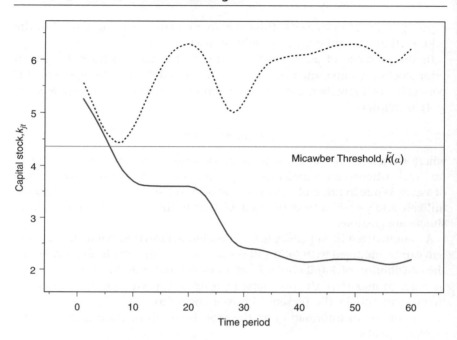

Figure 6.3. The irreversible consequences of shocks

poverty. The solid line trajectory shows that the household receives a more severe shock in year 5 and falls below the Micawber Threshold. From that point on, the household sinks into a long-term poverty trap. Under the more fortunate history, the household recovers and continues to move toward the high-equilibrium steady state.

While these ex post effects of shocks are important, the anticipation that they might take place would be expected to generate 'a sense of insecurity, of potential harm people must feel wary of—something bad can happen and "spell ruin"', as Calvo and Dercon (2005) put it. Analysis of the BCI model shows that this sense of impending ruin will indeed discourage forward-looking households from making the sacrifices necessary to reach the high equilibrium. Numerical analysis of the model shows that the Micawber Frontier shifts to the north-east once asset risk is introduced into the model. As shown in Figure 6.4, the solid line is the Micawber Frontier in the absence of risk (as in Figure 6.2 above), while the dashed curve is the Micawber Frontier in the face of risk. The boundaries marking the critical skill levels at which households move between the different accumulation regimes also shift right (to $a^{L'}$ and $a^{H'}$), meaning fewer intrinsically upwardly mobile households and more intrinsically chronically poor households.

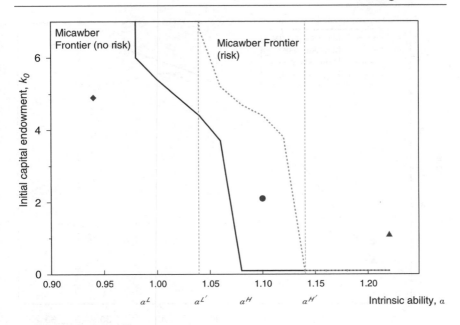

Figure 6.4. Vulnerability shifts out the Micawber Frontier

The most dramatic effects of risk are seen by considering a household whose skill and capital endowments place it between the two frontiers. Consider a household whose skill and initial asset endowments place it at the solid circle illustrated in Figure 6.4. Absent the risk of shocks, such a household would strive for the upper equilibrium and eventually escape poverty. In the presence of risk, such a household would abandon this accumulation strategy as futile and settle into a low-level, chronically poor standard of living. In the face of asset risk, the extraordinary sacrifice of consumption required to try to reach the high equilibrium is no longer worth doing, and the household will optimally pursue the low-level, poverty trap equilibrium. Again, shocks have their largest effects on mid-skill households.

Simulation of the BCI model provides additional insight into the impact of shocks and risk on dynamic behaviour and chronic poverty. Consider the following three simulations:

- *A Non-Stochastic Simulation* in which repeated application of the accumulation rule, $i^*(k_t|a)$, can be used to define the sequence of optimal capital stocks for any individual i with initial endowments k_{i0} and a_i. At each point in time, the implied income and consumption of the individual can also be calculated.

- *A Risk without Shocks Simulation* in which repeated application of the risk-adjusted optimal accumulation rule, $i_r^*(k_t|a, \Omega)$, is used to define a

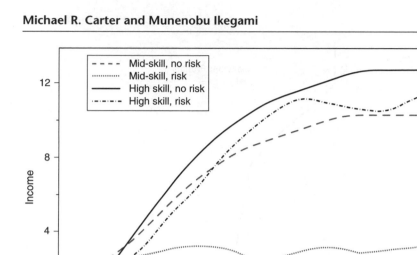

Figure 6.5. Vulnerability hurts 'average' individuals most

sequence of capital stocks. To isolate the pure ex ante effect of risk, no shocks are actually realized in this simulation (despite the fact that individuals fearfully behave as if shocks will occur).

- *A Full Stochastic Simulation*, in which the risk-adjusted optimal accumulation rule, $i_r^*(k_t|\alpha, \Omega)$, is applied, but after each application, the individual receives a random shock generated in accordance with the probability structure Ω. This simulation permits us to isolate the full effect of random events (both ex ante and ex post) on the time path of capital, income, and consumption for an individual.

Figure 6.5 illustrates the generated time paths when the Non-Stochastic and the Full Stochastic simulations are applied to the mid-skill and high-skill individuals whose initial endowment positions are shown in Figure 6.4 by the circle and triangle, respectively. The simulation was run for sixty time periods. As can be seen, in the non-stochastic simulation, both individuals move smoothly toward the high equilibrium.[9] Autarchic accumulation provides a pathway from poverty for both individuals. Both become non-poor around

---

[9] Note that the high-skill individual has a higher level of steady state capital stock because the marginal productivity of capital is boosted by her skill level.

Table 6.1. Simulations for archetypical individuals

	Non-stochastic	Risk without shocks	Full stochastic
Low skill ($a = 0.94$, $k_0 = 4.9$)			
Discounted stream of utility	2.7	2.7	1.2
Discounted stream of income	26	26	25
Dynamic asset gap $\bar{k}(c) - k_0$	∞	∞	∞
Calvo–Dercon $P^{fta}(0)$	60	60	60
Calvo–Dercon $P^{fta}(1)$	10.2	10.3	14.3
Middle skill ($a = 1.10$, $k_0 = 2.1$)			
Discounted stream of utility	4.0	3.8	3.3
Discounted stream of income	37	29	28
Dynamic asset gap $\bar{k}(c) - k_0$	0	2.3	2.3
Calvo–Dercon $P^{fta}(0)$	8	60	60
Calvo–Dercon $P^{fta}(1)$	0.6	2.8	3.9
High skill ($a = 1.22$, $k_0 = 1.1$)			
Discounted stream of utility	5.5	5.5	4.7
Discounted stream of income	44	43	40
Dynamic asset gap $\bar{k}(c) - k_0$	0	0	0
Calvo–Dercon $P^{fta}(0)$	4	5	6
Calvo–Dercon $P^{fta}(1)$	0.5	0.6	0.6

year 10 of the simulation as their achieved capital stocks exceed the asset poverty line.

In the stochastic simulation, the high-skill individual is occasionally buffeted about by shocks and must continually rebuild her assets in order to reattain the desired steady state capital stock.[10] In sharp contrast, the middle-skill agent undertakes a fundamental shift in strategy in the presence of risk. As seen in Figure 6.4, this individual has fallen below the Micawber Frontier once risk is taken into account. While this individual suffers fluctuations akin to those suffered by the high-skill individual, the more fundamental effect results from her retreat from trying to reach the high equilibrium (i.e. a pathway from poverty is no longer attainable or sustainable).

Table 6.1, which presents statistics related to all three simulations, further substantiates this latter point. The table includes results for the low-skill individual whose initial asset position is indicated by the triangle in Figure 6.4. For each of the three individuals, the table displays the discounted stream of utility which is obtained under each simulation. In addition, the discounted value of income produced by each individual over the simulation is also listed. In contrast to the mid-skill individual, the 'Risk without Shocks' simulation barely perturbs the time paths and outcomes of both the low-skill and high-skill agents as neither of these agents shifts strategy in the face

---

[10] Note that the desired steady state level of capital is reduced by the presence of risk.

of risk.[11] When shocks are actually realized (the Full Stochastic Simulation), then these agents suffer more substantial losses, especially in terms of utility.[12]

In contrast, for the mid-skill individual, the 'Risk without Shocks' simulations brings a major drop in production (from 37 to 29) and utility (from 4.0 to 3.8) compared to the Non-Stochastic simulation. While the Full Stochastic simulation brings some additional income losses for this individual, they are modest compared to the losses occasioned by the risk-induced strategy shift. Among other things, these simulations show that in the presence of critical asset thresholds, risk takes on particular importance for those individuals subject to multiple equilibria.

6.3. Forward-Looking Measures of Chronic Poverty and Vulnerability

The theoretical analysis in the prior section has used dynamic economic theory to elucidate the multiple dimensions of chronic and persistent poverty, and to demonstrate how vulnerability to economic shocks further increases chronic poverty. Building on those ideas and insights, this section puts forward two types of chronic poverty measures. The first generalizes a suggestion in Carter and Barrett (2006) and uses information on the Micawber Frontier to create a asset-based chronic poverty measure. The second uses the asset dynamics implied by the BCI model to create a forward-looking income stream that can then be used to calculate any of the income-based chronic poverty measures discussed by Calvo and Dercon (this volume). Both the asset and income-based measures can be utilized to create explicit chronic poverty vulnerability measures, where vulnerability is understood as the increase in the chronic poverty measure induced by risk and shocks.

The measures put forward in this section rely on structure of the standard, backward-looking Foster–Greer–Thorbecke (FGT) class of poverty measures defined as:

$$P(\gamma) = \frac{1}{M} \sum_{i=1}^{N} I_i \left(\frac{z - f_i}{z} \right)^{\gamma}$$

where M is the total population size (poor and non-poor), i indexes individual observations, c is the scalar-valued poverty line, c_i is the flow-based measure

---

[11] Their desired steady state values do diminish and hence production and consumption fall modestly, generating the changes shown in the table.

[12] Realized shocks affect utility more strongly than income. For example, for the low-skill agent, the discounted stream of the utility of consumption falls from 2.7 to 1.2, while the discounted stream of income only falls from 26 to 25. The proportionately larger drop in utility occurs because individuals will end up spending more of their income on reaccumulating assets destroyed by shocks.

of welfare (income or expenditures) as measured retrospectively at the time of the survey, I_i is an indicator variable taking value one if $f_i < z$ and zero otherwise, and γ is a parameter reflecting the weight placed on the severity of poverty. Setting $\gamma = 0$ yields the headcount poverty ratio $P(0)$ (the share of a population falling below the poverty line). The higher-order measures, $P(1)$ and $P(2)$, yield the poverty gap measure (the money-metric measure of the average financial transfer needed to bring all poor households up to the poverty line) and the squared poverty gap (an indicator of severity poverty that is sensitive to the distribution of well-being amongst the poor).

6.3.1. *Chronic poverty measures based on the Micawber Threshold*

As suggested by Carter and Barrett (2006), information on asset dynamics that permits identification of the Micawber Frontier opens the door to a forward-looking poverty measure. The standard, money-metric poverty line is frequently criticized as an arbitrary construct which has no behavioural foundation. In contrast, the Micawber Frontier is an empirical construct whose foundation is observed behaviour. Conceptually, the Micawber Frontier can separate households expected to be persistently poor from those for whom time is an ally that promises better standards of living in the future. Poverty measures based on the Micawber Frontier thus promise to help identify the long-run health of an economy as judged by its ability to facilitate growth in living standards amongst its least well-off members.

Generalizing the Carter and Barrett measure to allow for heterogeneous ability yields the following expression:

$$P_k(\gamma) = \frac{1}{M} \sum_{i=1}^{M} I_i^k \left(\frac{\bar{k}(a_i) - k_i}{\bar{k}(a_i)} \right)^{\gamma}, \qquad (6.3)$$

where k_i is asset stock of household i and the binary indicator variable $I_i^k = 1$ if $k_i < \bar{k}(a_i)$ and reflects whether the household i's asset stock is below the Micawber Frontier. When $\gamma = 1$, we can use the core part of this measure, $I_i^k(\bar{k}(a_i) - k)$, to define the 'dynamic asset poverty gap'. Table 6.1 reports this measure for three prototypical individuals whose initial asset positions are illustrated in Figure 6.4. The normalized asset poverty gap for the high-skill individual is always zero. For the mid-skill individual, the gap is zero in the absence of risk, but rises to 1.3 units of capital (or about 33 per cent of the Frontier value of 4) when the discouraging effect of risk shifts out the Micawber Frontier. For the low-skill person, the Micawber Frontier and the dynamic asset poverty gap are infinite as there is no level of capital stock from which this individual will find it desirable to sustain the high-level equilibrium.

The existence of the intrinsically chronically poor individuals (for whom the dynamic asset poverty gap is infinite) renders the poverty measure (6.3)

141

mathematically problematic as the portion of the expression in parentheses is undefined for these individuals. We thus modify the measure as follows:

$$\tilde{P}^k(\gamma) = \frac{1}{M} \sum_{i \varepsilon \tilde{M}} I_i^k \left(\frac{\bar{k}(a_i) - k_i}{\bar{k}(a_i)} \right)^\gamma ,$$

where $\tilde{M}$ is the subset of the total population for whom $\bar{k}(a_i)$ is finite. Setting $\gamma = 0$, this modified measure ($\tilde{P}^k(0)$) gives the headcount ratio of all non-intrinsically poor individuals who are below the Micawber Threshold and who would therefore be expected to be chronically poor in the sense of being trapped at the low-level equilibrium. Information on the fraction of the population that is intrinsically chronically poor ($\frac{M-\tilde{M}}{M}$) can be used to create a complete chronic poverty headcount measure, $CPHC = \tilde{P}^k(0) + (\frac{M-\tilde{M}}{M})$.

When $\gamma = 1$, $\tilde{P}^k(1)$ yields a normalized measure of the asset transfers that would be necessary to place multiple equilibrium chronically poor households in a position from which they can grow and sustain a non-poor standard living in the future. In the language of Carter and Barrett (2006), this $\tilde{P}^k(1)$ measure would indicate the resources needed for the cargo net transfers required to eliminate multiple equilibrium chronic poverty. Note that there are no asset transfers that will sustainably eliminate the chronic poverty of the intrinsically chronically poor.

To illustrate these ideas, we used the BCI model to conduct a sixty-year simulation of poverty and its evolution for an imaginary community of 100 households. We performed two sets of simulations using the procedures described in the prior section. First we performed the Non-Stochastic simulations (in which households follow the optimal accumulation rule defined by the non-stochastic version of the BCI model). Second we utilized the Full Stochastic in which each household follows the optimal accumulation rule defined by the stochastic version of the BCI model and each received their own random (idiosyncratic) shock in each time period.

For the simulation, it was assumed that 25 per cent of the households had sufficiently low skill endowments that they were in the intrinsically chronically poor category in the presence of risk (that is, $a_i < a^{L'}$). Another 50 per cent were in the mid-skill (multiple equilibrium) range, $a^{L'} < a_i < a^{H'}$, while the final 25 per cent were in the high-skill (intrinsically upwardly mobile) range ($a_i < a^{H'}$). While these assumptions are arbitrary, they do match the empirical findings of the Santos and Barrett (2006) study of East African pastoral households. Finally, initial asset endowment for each household was randomly distributed (using a uniform distribution) over the range of 0.1 to 10 units of capital.[13]

---

[13] In the real world, one would not expect to find 'initial' endowments uncorrelated with skill. However, for illustrative purposes, this egalitarian assumption permits us to more fully see the operation of the model.

Table 6.2. Simulated chronic poverty measures

	Non-stochastic simulation	Stochastic simulation	Vulnerability
'Backward-looking' measure			
FGT $P(0)$ at time $t = 1$	0.34 [0.07]	0.34 [0.07]	—
FGT $P(0)$ at time $t = 60$	0.21 [0.02]	0.55 [0.08]	—
Forward-looking chronic poverty measure			
Carter–Barrett threshold measures			
Intrinsic headcount, $\frac{M-\tilde{M}}{M}$	3%	24%	88%
$\tilde{P}^k(0)$ measure at time $t = 1$	18%	24%	25%
Complete headcount, $CPHC$	21%	48%	—
$\tilde{P}^k(1)$ measure at time $t = 1$	10%	15%	—
Calvo–Dercon income stream Measures			
$P_i^{fta}(0)$ (average)	13 [22%]	28.5 [48%]	54%
$P_i^{fta}(1)$ (average)	1.5	3.7	59%

Included in the table are the standard (backward-looking) Foster–Greer–Thorbecke (FGT) poverty measures for both the initial period ($t = 1$) and final period of the simulation ($t = 60$). Under the scenario that assumes away economic shocks, the standard poverty headcount drops over the period of the simulation from 34 per cent to 21 per cent of the population. This latter figure exactly equals the period 1 dynamic asset poverty threshold headcounts of the chronically poor (both the intrinsically and multiple equilibrium chronically poor). As this simple example shows, the forward-looking threshold-based measure captures the dynamics of the system and thus provides a more informative portrayal of the expected long-run evolution of poverty.[14] Combining the two pieces of information would permit us to say (in period 1) that 34 per cent of the population is currently poor and that we would expect (under existing dynamics) to see 13 per cent of the population escape poverty, and the other 21 per cent to remain chronically poor. The $\tilde{P}^k(1)$ measure of the size of the dynamic asset poverty gap shows that, on average, the chronically poor have assets that are 10 per cent below the Micawber Frontier.

When shocks (and risk) are brought into the model, the results change rather significantly as shown in the second column of Table 6.2. Over the sixty-year period of the simulation, the FGT headcount rises from 34 per cent to 55 per cent. In this case, the backward-looking FGT measure overstates the long-run health of the economy. In contrast, the year 1 Carter–Barrett asset-based CPHC indicates that 48 per cent of the population is chronically poor (with this fraction split evenly between the intrinsically chronically poor and the multiple equilibrium chronically poor). This 48 per cent figure is in fact an understatement of the functioning of the economy as it fails to account

---

[14] The BCI model assumes that the underlying structural dynamics of the economic do not change over the period of the simulation, a stricture unlikely to be met in the real world.

for multiple equilibrium households that are knocked below the Micawber Threshold over the time period of the simulation.[15] The $\tilde{P}^k(1)$ measure rises to 15 per cent, indicating that the depth of dynamic asset poverty rises for the multiple equilibrium poor. The cargo net transfers needed to lift these individuals over the Micawber Frontier have thus increased. As in the non-stochastic case, the combination of the FGT and the dynamic asset poverty measures provides a more comprehensive view of the nature of poverty and its likely future evolution.

6.3.2. Using asset dynamics to create forward-looking income-based chronic poverty measures

In addition to underwriting chronic poverty measures based on the Carter–Barrett dynamic asset poverty gap, information on asset dynamics can be used to project future asset and income levels. When combined with the income-based chronic poverty measures of Calvo and Dercon (this volume), these projections open up another class of forward-looking chronic poverty measures.

Calvo and Dercon suggest a number of ways of consistently analysing a sequence of income levels for a given household over T time periods. While they are primarily thinking of sequences of past incomes, they suggest that their methods can be applied to estimated future income streams. The analysis here follows this suggestion.

For purposes here, we will limit our attention to what Calvo–Dercon call the FTA (Focus–Transformation–Aggregation) chronic poverty measure. Letting z denote the standard income poverty line, and f_{it} denote the income of household i in period t, we can write the FTA measure (P^{fta}) as:

$$P_i^{fta}(\gamma) = \sum_{t=1}^{T} \beta^{T-t} I_{it}^{fta} \left(\frac{z - f_{it}}{z} \right)^{\gamma}, \tag{6.4}$$

where I_{it}^{fta} is an indicator variable that takes the value of one if $f_{it} < z$, and β is the discount factor. Note that measure (6.4) is specific to a particular individual and does not aggregate across individuals. For illustrative purposes here, we set $\beta = 1$, so that all poverty spells are treated identically (see Calvo and Dercon for more discussion on the desirability of this assumption). In the special case when $\gamma = 0$, (6.4) simply counts the number of poverty spells experienced by the individual.

The various simulations of the BCI model used in the prior section can be used to illustrate our forward-looking use of the Calvo–Dercon measures. Table 6.1 presents the $P_i^{fta}(0)$ and $P_i^{fta}(1)$ measures for the low-, medium- and

---

[15] In principle, the Carter–Barrett measure could be adjusted to account for the likelihood that some individuals will receive shocks that will knock them under the threshold.

high-skill individuals under the various simulation scenarios introduced earlier. The low-skill individual is poor all sixty periods under all scenarios, as shown by the degree zero FTA measure. The increase in the degree 1 FTA poverty gap measure under the Full Stochastic simulation reflects the impact of realized shocks.

The FTA measures for the high-skill agent shows that she escapes poverty rather quickly under all scenarios. In contrast, the degree zero FTA measure jumps from 8 to 60 for the mid-skill individual once risk is brought into the picture. As this example illustrates, the forward-looking Calvo–Dercon measure captures the chronic poverty impacts of risk that are overlooked by standard FGT measures. In addition, while not explicitly established to capture threshold effects, the Calvo–Dercon family measures are quite sensitive to their impacts.[16]

Table 6.2 similarly presents FTA measures for the stylized 100 individual economy analysed in the prior section. Results are shown for both the Non-Stochastic and the Full Stochastic simulations. While measure (6.4) is individual specific, Table 6.2 reports the simple average of the $P_i^{fta}(\gamma)$ measures across the 100 individuals in the simulation. To ease comparability with the other measures, the figures in square brackets divide the $P_i^{fta}(0)$ by the total number of periods and thus yield a measure of the fraction of time that the average individual spends below the poverty line during the course of the sixty-period simulation.

As can be seen in Table 6.2, the average value of $P_i^{fta}(0)$ when there are no economic shocks is 13, indicating that the average household was below the income poverty line 13 out of the 60 total time periods, or 22 per cent of the time. Interestingly, this figure corresponds closely to the period 60 FGT measure, as well as to the dynamic asset poverty measure. Similarly, for the stochastic simulation (in which households anticipate and are subject to economic shocks), the $P_i^{fta}(0)$ averages 28.5 poverty spells across the 100 households, indicating that households are poor roughly 48 per cent of the time. However, it should be stressed that the equivalence of the FTA figure to the Carter–Barrett CPHC measure is somewhat coincidental. The former reflects the fact that the intrinsically upwardly mobile may have poverty spells as they accumulate assets and/or recover from shocks. Similarly, the long-term chronically poor may have spells of non-poor income if they fortuitously begin life with an ample (but unsustainable) asset endowment.[17] But despite these differences from the threshold-based measure, the Calvo–Dercon FTA measures capture the intrinsic dynamics of the system and provide a more informative, forward-looking picture than does the standard FGT family of

[16] This same comment would also apply if the Calvo–Dercon measures were used to look backwards to evaluate the degree of poverty in a past realized income history.

[17] Variants on the Calvo–Dercon measures that more heavily weigh final outcomes would, however, present information that is closer in spirit to the dynamic asset poverty measures.

measures. Again it should be stressed that these forward-looking measures are in principle estimable in time 1,[18] though their accuracy depends on the stability of the underlying dynamics in the economy.

6.3.3. *Vulnerability as increased chronic poverty*

While there is debate over how best to conceptualize and measure vulnerability (compare Calvo and Dercon, 2005, with Ligon and Schechter, 2003), one natural approach would be to define vulnerability as the increase in chronic poverty that results when individuals are exposed to shocks. Linking vulnerability to increases in chronic poverty captures the sense of drastic and irreversible harm that Calvo and Dercon (2005) identify as the common thread that unites various concepts of vulnerability. In addition, the ability to define vulnerability in terms of increased chronic poverty provides a very compelling policy focus, indicating the fraction of chronic poverty that can be remedied through social protection programmes.

The far-right column in Table 6.2 defines vulnerability using both the Carter–Barrett and the Calvo–Dercon chronic poverty measures. In both cases, vulnerability is defined as the fraction of total chronic poverty revealed by the full stochastic simulation that is created by risk and shocks. That is, vulnerability is the difference between chronic poverty in the stochastic and the non-stochastic simulations, normalized by the chronic poverty in the stochastic simulation.

As can be seen in Table 6.2, nearly 60 per cent of total chronic poverty in the simulation analysis is the result of vulnerability under both the Carter–Barrett and the Calvo–Dercon measures. Social protection policies would have an enormous impact on chronic poverty in this case. This large increment in chronic poverty created by vulnerability results from the three forces discussed earlier. First, realized shocks sometimes push individuals below the income poverty line.[19] Second, increased chronic poverty also results when realized negative shocks knock individuals below the Micawber Frontier, rendering infeasible a pathway from poverty, and indeed spelling ruin in the language of Calvo and Dercon (2005) cited above. Third and finally, the prospect that ruin can occur has a discouraging effect on accumulation strategies, shifting

---

[18] They are estimable if the accumulation rule can be estimated as well as the error distribution that generates deviations between expected and actual accumulation. With those two pieces of information, a set of forward-looking projections could be generated using either stochastic or non-stochastic simulations.

[19] Note that unlike the Ligon and Schechter vulnerability measure that increases with any fluctuation in income, the vulnerability measure based on the Calvo–Dercon FTA measure has a poverty focus and only increases for fluctuations that drive individuals below the poverty line. Note that the Carter–Barrett measure will not increase for individuals pushed below the income poverty line, but who remain above the Micawber Frontier.

the Micawber Frontier beyond the reach of some individuals, driving yet additional increases in the measured (multiple equilibrium) chronic poverty.

Calculation of the vulnerability measures in Table 6.2 is feasible because the BCI model allows us to straightforwardly simulate how individuals would counterfactually behave in the absence of risk. However, the real world does not offer data on how individuals would (counterfactually) behave in the absence of risk. For example, we do not have data that could be used to directly identify what the Micawber Frontier would be in the absence of risk as we do not observe individuals behaving in the counterfactual, risk-free world. Empirical implementation of this type of vulnerability measure would therefore be far from straightforward.[20] Nonetheless, it would in principle be possible to obtain estimates of the parameters that shape behaviour and then simulate what behaviour would counterfactually be in the absence of risk. It might also be possible to take advantage of naturally occurring variation of risk (as Rosenzweig and Binswanger, 1993, do) in order to gain insight into how the Micawber Frontier shifts with risk. Significant future work will be required to empirically implement the type of vulnerability measures shown in Table 6.2.

6.4. A First Application to South Africa

The prior sections of this chapter have laid out an ambitious agenda, showing how economic theory can be used to underwrite a suite of theoretically grounded, forward-looking chronic poverty measures. This section uses data from South Africa to illustrate the use of these measures, employing the KwaZulu-Natal Income Dynamics Study (KIDS) data that cover the KwaZulu-Natal province that is home to roughly 25 per cent of South Africa's population (see Aguero et al., forthcoming, for thorough discussion of the KIDS data).

The top half of Table 6.3 displays standard FGT poverty measures for the first two rounds of the KIDS data (1993 and 1998) as reported in Carter and May (2001). As can be seen, this period was characterized by substantial downward mobility as the headcount measure of poverty rose from 27 per cent to 43 per cent, while the FGT poverty gap measure ($P(1)$) held steady at 33 per cent.[21]

---

[20] Note however that the partial impact of vulnerability can be recovered rather straightforwardly by doing an empirical analysis that is akin to the middle column of Table 6.2 (risk without shocks). Using some of the methods of Schechter, it should be possible to simulate the impact that shocks have on individuals, holding the Micawber Frontier fixed. Such information could be quite useful from the perspective of designing a social safety net.

[21] The Carter and May (2001) FGT measures are based on poverty line estimates using the household subsistence line (HSL). The HSL became unavailable after 1998 and subsequent analysis (such as that reported in Agüero, Carter, and May, forthcoming) has relied on the poverty line standard suggested by Hoogeveen and Özler (2005). Using this latter poverty line, the poverty headcount in the KIDS data rose from 52% to 57% over the 1993 to 1998 period.

147

Table 6.3. Backward- and forward-looking poverty measures for South Africa

FGT measures	
$P(0)$ in 1993	27%
$P(0)$ in 1998	43%
Carter–Barrett threshold measures	
$\tilde{P}^k(0)$ in 1998	59%
$\tilde{P}^k(1)$ in 1998	11%

These same data can be used to recover the underlying asset dynamics. In a recent paper, Adato, Carter, and May (2006) use these KIDS data to estimate the pattern of asset dynamics under the assumption that $\bar{k}(\alpha) = \bar{k}\forall\alpha$. In other words, Adato, Carter, and May assume that the Micawber Frontier is the same for all agents, irrespective of the individual's skill level. In terms of Figure 6.2, the Micawber Frontier would appear as a horizontal line under the assumptions used by Adato, Carter, and May.

As detailed in that paper, Adato, Carter, and May first estimate an asset index for each individual, and then use non-parametric regression techniques to recover the pattern of asset dynamics.[22] Interestingly, they estimate the Micawber Frontier to be at a level of assets expected to generate a living standard almost twice the poverty line. Individuals below that estimated frontier would be predicted to slide backwards over time towards a sub-poverty line standard of living, while those above it would be predicted to achieve a living standard well above the poverty line. Note also that not everyone who is observed to be poor by standard consumption measures will be predicted to be poor in the longer term. In particular, households that have assets in excess of the Frontier and are 'stochastically poor' (in the language of Carter and May, 2001) would not be predicted to be poor in the long term.

While the Adato, Carter, and May analysis rests on several strong assumptions, it does permit us to illustrate the use of asset threshold-based poverty measures. As shown in the bottom half of Table 6.3, fully 58 per cent of KIDS households were below the estimated Micawber Threshold in 1998 and are therefore expected to be chronically poor. Because of the assumption that the threshold is the same for all households, it is not possible to partition this group into the intrinsically chronically poor and the multiple equilibrium chronically poor. Nonetheless, the fact that this measure is above the 1998 backward-looking poverty headcount indicates that the underlying asset dynamics predict future increases in poverty. Put differently, the $\tilde{P}^k(0)$ measure indicates that the South African economy was not offering a

[22] The asset index includes human capital variables as well as tangible physical assets such as land and business equipment. Related methodological approaches to recovering a critical asset threshold can be found in Lybbert et al. (2004), Barrett et al. (2006), and Carter et al. (2007).

favourable environment for asset accumulation and income growth for the less well-off.

The reliability of such a prediction depends on the stability of the underlying asset dynamics, as well as on the quality of the actual estimation. The KIDS 2004 round of data indicates a decline in the standard poverty headcount, rather than further increases as would be expected based on the asset threshold-based measure (see Aguero et al. for results from the 2004 data). The predictive failure of the asset-based measure may reflect an underlying change in asset dynamics (that is, the prospects for accumulation and income growth improved dramatically between 1998 and 2004).[23] It may also reflect the simplifying assumption used by Adato, Carter, and May, that the Micawber Frontier is the same for all households. The fact that the asset poverty gap measure ($\tilde{P}^k(1)$) was a modest 11 per cent in 1998 indicates that the typically asset-poor household was not too far below the estimated frontier. Either a modest improvement in asset dynamics (or a modest overestimation of the threshold for mid-skill agents) may have led to the predictive failure of the threshold-based chronic poverty measures. Future efforts are clearly needed to help the empirical measures catch up with the sophistication of the theoretically derived measures discussed earlier.

6.5. Chronic Poverty Measurement and Policy

This chapter began with the challenge of understanding how much poverty is chronic in the sense that it would be expected to persist into the future. The microeconomic theory of asset accumulation and poverty traps suggests a way of approaching this problem and estimating future asset accumulation and income growth. This information can in turn be used as the basis for two families of theoretically grounded, forward-looking, chronic poverty measures.

While there is still much to be done to improve the chronic poverty measures put forward here, they are ultimately intended to complement, not replace, conventional, 'backward-looking' poverty measures. While the latter are meant to give us a sense of the current (or at least recent) economic status of people at the bottom of the income distribution, the former use information on patterns of asset accumulation to project forward who is likely to remain poor in the future. Together, the two classes of measures provide a more complete description of the groups for whom the economy is not well functioning.

[23] The BCI model used in the theoretical analysis here assumes that the income generation process does not change over time. In principle, the model could be modified to reflect growth in productivity and wages (or cycles of macroeconomic boom and bust). The impact on behaviour would depend on how individuals anticipated these changes.

As in any area of economics, looking forward into the future is fraught with difficulties. The information that can be gleaned from the chronic poverty measures suggested here is probably most valuable over a medium-term time horizon when the structure of the economy is relatively stable. But even within these limits, the capacity of the asset-based chronic poverty measures to provide information on the intrinsically chronically poor and the multiple equilibrium chronically poor is potentially quite valuable from a policy perspective. Moreover, while empirical calculation of the vulnerability measures discussed in section 6.3.3 is probably fraught with difficulty, the theoretical analysis put forward makes clear that vulnerability to economic shocks is potentially an important part of chronic poverty. This is especially true in economies where large numbers of agents find themselves in the multiple equilibrium category, facing a positive but finite Micawber Frontier. The theory reviewed here suggests that the provision of social protection measures will lower the Micawber Frontier for average individuals, crowding in private accumulation and rendering feasible new pathways from poverty for at least some. While there is still much to find out about whether social protection can in practice really have these twin effects on reducing chronic poverty, further efforts to more sharply conceptualize and measure chronic poverty will move us in the direction of being able to explore these ideas and pilot new social protection programmes.

Appendix 6.1: Details of Theoretical Model

This section provides additional detail on the formal model used to generate the results discussed in sections 6.2 and 6.3. For additional details, see Barrett et al. (2007).

Non-stochastic model

Under the technological specification given in section 6.1, we assume that individuals face the following infinite horizon model as they make the decision about how best to divide income ($f(a, k_t)$) every period t between consumption (c_t) and investment (i_t):

$$\max \sum_{t=1}^{\infty} \beta^{t-1} u(c_t)$$
$$\text{s.t.} \quad c_t + i_t \leq f(a, k_t)$$
$$f(a, k_t) = \max\{ak^{\gamma L}, ak^{\gamma H} - E\}$$
$$k_{t+1} = i_t + (1 - \delta)k_t$$
$$k_1 \text{ given}$$

where β is the discount factor, c_t is consumption, $u(\cdot)$ is utility function, i_t is investment and δ is depreciation rate. Note that there is neither saving nor borrowing and that the household is assumed to live forever. Solution of this problem, using the parameters given below, generates the Micawber Frontier, $\bar{k}(a)$, illustrated in Figure 6.2 in the main body of the text.

Stochastic model

Households face a number of risks. These risks can be classified as (i) asset shocks, (ii) income shocks, and (iii) marginal utility shocks. While all three types or risk are important, the analysis here focuses on the relatively simple case of asset shocks. In particular we assume that assets evolve according to the following specification:

$$k_{t+1} = \theta_t[i_t + (1 - \delta)k_t]$$

where $\theta_t \in (0, \theta^{max}]$ is the asset shock. Note that this multiplicative specification makes the magnitude of risk increase as accumulated capital stock increases.

We assume that the probability distribution of θ_t is known and that the individual decision maker allocates income between consumption and investment in order to solve the following problem:

$$\max E_1 \sum_{t=1}^{\infty} \beta^{t-1} u(c_t)$$

$$\text{s.t.} \quad c_t + i_t \le f(a, k_t)$$

$$f(a, k_t) = \max\{ak^{\gamma L}, ak^{\gamma H} - E\}$$

$$k_{t+1} = \theta_t[i_t + (1 - \delta)k_t]$$

$$k_1 \text{ given}$$

where E_1 is expectation at period 1. Solution of this problem, again using the parameters outlined below, yields the results summarized in Figure 6.3.

Parameters and other details for numerical simulation

The functional specification for the utility function $u(\cdot)$ is

$$u(c_t) = \frac{c_t^{1-\sigma} - 1}{1 - \sigma}$$

The probability density of θ_t is assumed to be:

$$\text{density of } \theta_t = \begin{cases} 0.90 \text{ if } \theta_t = 1.0 \\ 0.05 \text{ if } \theta_t = 0.9 \\ 0.03 \text{ if } \theta_t = 0.8 \\ 0.02 \text{ if } \theta_t = 0.7 \end{cases}$$

The other structural parameter values are assumed to be as follows: $\sigma = 1.5$, $\delta = 0.08$, $\beta = 0.95$, $\gamma_L = 0.3$, $\gamma_H = 0.45$, $E = 0.45$.

We discretize continuous variables k and a as follows: $k = \{0.1, 0.2, \ldots, 15.0\}$ and $a = \{0.94, 0.96, \ldots, 1.22\}$.

For the simulation of the stylized economy of 100 individuals we draw a from $N(1.08, 0.074^2)$. Parameter values of mean and variance are chosen so that ex ante proportion of low-, middle-, and high-type individuals (defined relative to the stochastic Micawber Frontier) would be 25 per cent, 50 per cent, and 25 per cent, respectively. We draw k_1 from Uniform [0.1, 10.0] and assume that k_1 and a are statistically independent from each other.

Michael R. Carter and Munenobu Ikegami

We specify the asset poverty line as the asset level that satisfies the following equation:

$$y_p = f(a, k_p).$$

where y_p is the income-based poverty line. Note that the asset poverty line depends on a and we denote it by $k_p(a)$. We assume that the income poverty line, y_p, is 1.62, the level of income that an average individual ($a = 1.12$) would produce in equilibrium using the low technology.

References

Adato, M., Carter, M. R., and May, J. (2006), 'Exploring Poverty Traps and Social Exclusion in South Africa Using Qualitative and Quantitative Data', *Journal of Development Studies*, 42(2): 226–47.

Agüero, J., Carter, M. R., and May J. (forthcoming), 'Poverty and Inequality in the First Decade of South Africa's Democracy: What can be Learnt from Panel Data?', *Journal of African Economies*.

Barrett, C. B., Carter, M. R., and Ikegami, M. (2007), 'Social Protection Policy to Overcome Poverty Traps and Aid Traps: An Asset-Based Approach', working paper.

——Marenya, P. P., McPeak, J. G., Minten, B., Murithi, F. M., Oluoch-Kosura, W., Place, F., Randrianarisoa, J. C., Rasambainarivo, J., and Wangila, J. (2006), 'Welfare Dynamics in Rural Kenya and Madagascar', *Journal of Development Studies*, 42(2): 248–77.

Buera, Francisco (2005), 'A Dynamic Model of Entrepreneurship with Borrowing Constraints', working paper, Northwestern University.

Calvo, C., and S. Dercon (2005), 'Measuring Individual Vulnerability', Oxford, Department of Economics Discussion Papers Series No. 229, March.

Carter, M. R., and Barrett, C. B. (2006), 'The Economics of Poverty Traps and Persistent Poverty: An Asset-Based Approach', *Journal of Development Studies*, 42(2): 178–99.

——and May, J. (2001), 'One Kind of Freedom: Poverty Dynamics in Post-Apartheid South Africa', *World Development*, 29(12): 1987–2006.

——Little, P., Mogues, T., and Negatu, W. (2007), 'Poverty Traps and the Long-Term Consequences of Natural Disasters in Ethiopia and Honduras', *World Development*.

Chronic Poverty Research Centre (CPRC) (2004), 'The Chronic Poverty Report 2004–05', Manchester.

Foster, J., Greer, J., and Thorbecke, E. (1984), 'A Class of Decomposable Poverty Measures', *Econometrica*, 52: 761–5.

Hoddinott, J. (2006), 'Shocks and their Consequences across and within Households in Rural Zimbabwe', *Journal of Development Studies*, 42(3): 301–21.

Hoogeveen, J. G., and Özler, B. (2005), 'Not Separate, not Equal: Poverty and Inequality in Post-Apartheid South Africa', William Davidson Institute Working Paper No. 739, Ann Arbor: University of Michigan.

Jalan, J., and Ravallion, M. (2004), 'Household Income Dynamics in Rural China', in S. Dercon (ed.), *Insurance against Poverty*, Oxford: Oxford University Press, 108–24.

Ligon, E., and Schechter, L. (2003), 'Measuring Vulnerability', *Economic Journal*, 113(486): 15–102.

Lybbert, T., Barrett, C., Desta, S., and Coppock, D. L. (2004), 'Stochastic Wealth Dynamics and Risk Management among a Poor Population', *Economic Journal*, 114(498): 750–77.

Rosenzweig, M., and Binswanger, H. (1993), 'Wealth, Weather Risk and the Composition and Profitability of Agricultural Investments', *Economic Journal*, 103(416): 56–78.

Santos, P., and Barrett, C. B. (2006), 'Heterogeneous Wealth Dynamics: On the Roles of Risk and Ability', Cornell University working paper.

Schechter, L. (2006), 'Vulnerability as a Measure of Chronic Poverty', paper presented at the Workshop on Concepts and Methods for Analysing Poverty Dynamics and Chronic Poverty, University of Manchester, 23–5 October.

Zimmerman, Fred, and Carter, Michael (2003), 'Asset Smoothing, Consumption Smoothing and the Reproduction of Inequality under Risk and Subsistence Constraints', *Journal of Development Economics*, 71(2): 233–60.

7

Poverty in Time

*Exploring Poverty Dynamics from Life History Interviews in Bangladesh**

Peter Davis

7.1. Introduction

This chapter discusses the usefulness of a life history method for analysing poverty dynamics in developing country contexts, using findings from a study in Kushtia district in Bangladesh. A high level of contextual and historical detail can be collected in life history interviews enabling the exploration of people's perceptions and understandings of the complex and dynamic realities of their lives. Life history methods uncover a number of phenomena that tend to be concealed from more usual quantitative methods. These include events with multiple causation, 'last-straw' threshold effects (events which lead to catastrophe due to a series of previous events), other cumulative trends, outcomes based on the ordering of a sequence of events, and complex interactions. Variable-based research where the household is used as the unit of analysis also produces the problem of masking events associated with household breakdown and intra-household effects. Life history approaches can help to explore these.

However in case-based research, the numbers of cases studied are usually quite small, limiting the ability to generalize across larger populations. Here a larger-than-usual number of cases are analysed and categorized, along with the patterns of crisis, coping, and opportunity that emerged. Eight main

* I would like to thank Bob Baulch, David Hulme, Andrew Shepherd, Geof Wood, and Zulfiqar Ali for helpful comments. For research assistance I am particularly indebted to Saidozamman Jewel, M. Shahidur Rahman, Rofikul Islam, Jahangir Alam, Amit Chakrabarty, and Habibur Rahman.

154

life-trajectory patterns are identified from the life histories studied and selected respondents' stories used to illustrate each pattern.

7.2. Methodological Lessons Learned

In the research outlined here, people from three towns and six villages in Kushtia district in western Bangladesh were interviewed during 1999–2001 (see Davis, 2005, 2006). A life history interview was conducted for twenty people randomly selected from each site. In addiction a profile was also constructed collecting information on household members, extended family, skills and education, religion, economic resources (income, assets, debts), household facilities, coercive power, prestige, and networks and relationships. This approach drew from the resource profile approach (Lewis and McGregor, 1992; Lawson, McGregor, and Saltmarshe, 2000; McGregor, 2004) and other livelihoods approaches (e.g. Carney, 1998), but deliberately took a power-resource-focused perspective.[1] This allowed a number of fields of power (Bourdieu, 1990) to be examined that are an important part of the informal social protection system. These include: economic resources, access to bureaucratic resources, the means of violence, social network resources, and social prestige. Household profiles were constructed before the life history interview and provided an initial platform of information allowing the life history interview to be guided towards relevant areas.

The life history interviews were in *bangla* and took 2 to 4 hours, sometimes over multiple sessions depending on the availability of respondents. As a way of visualizing the life history at the end of each interview we mapped out significant events in the history of Bangladesh on a chart. The vertical axis was used to indicate the respondent's well-being and the horizontal axis, time. Life trajectory patterns were based on the perception of a person's *obosta* (loosely 'life condition') as it changed over time, constructed by myself and the respondent. The term *obosta* was chosen because it is vague, is in common everyday usage, and roughly translates as 'life condition' which seemed to be a suitable proxy for well-being in *bangla*.

We began the interview by setting up a chronological framework of major life events and avoided general questions about overall circumstances at the initial stage of the interview. Other details could then be written onto the template referring back to these dates to triangulate data. It also helped to 'warm up' people's memories. We started the interview by working out

[1] The semi-structured interview drew from livelihoods (e.g. Carney, 1998) and resource profiles approaches (e.g. Lewis and McGregor, 1992; Lawson, McGregor, and Saltmarshe, 2000; McGregor, 2004) but extended the scope of interest beyond livelihood resources to what I called 'power-resources' drawing from Korpi (1980, 1983, 1985) and Korpi and Palme (1998), Bourdieu and Nice (1977), and Bourdieu (1986, 1990) in a more power-focused approach.

155

concrete details to do with age, marriages, births, and deaths. Very few poor people in rural Bangladesh are able to tell you their age accurately, so age was often estimated with reference to national or local events that most people remember.

If married, the respondent's date of marriage was worked out. This was followed by recording the births of children. If children's birth dates had been worked out with reference to date of marriage, it was often necessary to work back from the present to check their ages. This was followed by working out marriage dates of any married children. Dates of deaths of parents, close relatives, and children were also asked about and recorded, including children who had died around or shortly after birth.

With each marriage I asked how much dowry (*joutok*) was given and received including other wedding costs, which were often quite considerable relative to income. Often this led to discussions of loans taken out, land mortgaged, livestock sold, contributions from kin, and community collections. I explored how loans were arranged and who had organized village collections. This often revealed interesting information about patronage relations and other significant network connections. I also asked about marriages of sisters and other relatives as contributions to dowry are often also made in such situations. When others had helped, expectations of reciprocity were discussed.

Significant sicknesses were also investigated: who raised money to pay for medical care? Who devoted labour for care? And where was treatment sought? I started with the respondent's parents and grandparents, as events leading up to the death of parents often led to large expenditures and sale of assets. As with other issues, asking sweeping questions about illness yielded poor responses, but situating questions within a slowly emerging history often allowed memories to be jogged. A number of interesting issues to do with selective memory emerge, particularly when it comes to remembering episodes of ill health.[2] The structure and sequencing of the interview was important in helping to stimulate memory; it was particularly useful to map out more memorable life transitions first so that links could be explored.

I also asked about events relating to land being divided among brothers (usually), although sometimes sisters received a share. This time in life cycles often corresponded with the formation of new households and had a significant bearing on individual well-being. This then led to the history of employment and business. Attention was paid to periods of unemployment and re-employment. Who helped out during unemployment? Who helped to get another job? How were loans secured to start and maintain a business? I asked about education and work. Are children supporting the parent? I asked

---

[2] This has been a fruitful area of research among cognitive psychologists with important implications for memory-based life histories (see Becker and Mahmud, 1984; Rubin and Baddeley, 1989; Conway, 1990).

about land ownership. When was land bought and sold? Had any land been lost due to river erosion? Why was land sold? Had land been mortgaged?

Court cases were also a common cause of crisis. What were the cases over? How long had they continued? What costs were involved? Were they associated with any violence or intimidation? I asked about theft and any other forms of violent conflict including police extortion or intimidation, which seemed to be a common feature of poor people's experience.

While I was aware of the topics and issues I wanted to cover, I usually allowed the interview to follow its natural course in a conversational manner without imposing too much structure. Topics that were clearly irrelevant were ignored; unusual, significant, and interesting events were pursued in detail. After my interviewing skills had developed it was possible to cover most important issues with very little reference to the listed topics on my clipboard. By keeping the interview conversational I found that information was slowly revealed in a way that would not happen in a more formally structured interview.

At the end of the life history interview a graph was drawn with the respondent showing the various trends and the effect of crisis and opportunity episodes on well-being. The episodes were ranked from the worst crisis labelled as (C1) followed by the second (C2) and third (C3). As significant crisis episodes were identified in the course of the interview the (often complex, multifaceted, and cumulative) causes were explored, followed by the coping strategies employed during the crisis and the influence on more long-term well-being and security. When people's circumstances had improved, the main causes of these periods of opportunity were also identified (O1, O2, O3) with relevant details noted.

Once a number of crises had been identified and discussed during the life history interview, including a discussion of sources of insecurity and crisis, the range of crisis coping strategies employed during particular episodes was examined in detail. The relationship between various 'power resources' available to the individual or household was investigated, including economic assets and income, social prestige and status, access to officials and bureaucratic resources or to the means of violence, membership of organized factions or parties, and ascribed identity (gender, regional identity, etc.). The analysis of the use of these power resources aided in the understanding of the social mechanisms which led to the differentiation between highly insecure people and not-so-insecure people.

7.3. Terminology

With an explicitly dynamic focus, a number of definitions become useful. First, I used the terms 'event', 'episode', and 'trajectory' deliberately. An 'event' referred to a short discrete period of time (up to about a month) in which a crisis of single or multiple causation can occur. 'Episode' was used to describe a longer period of time (up to about a decade) which is characterized by a particular state of affairs (such as a chronic illness or a long-drawn-out court case) and within which a number of 'events' could occur. The word 'trajectory' was reserved for still longer periods of time such as a person's entire life or large part of a person's life, and could span a number of 'episodes'.

Second, I used the words 'transition', 'passage', and 'life stage', drawing from Dewilde's (2003) usage, to connect events, episodes, and trajectories to more predictable phases of a life course. A 'transition' referred to a socially defined change of state in a person's life, which is to some extent predictable and is usually abrupt. For example, this may be marriage, the death of a parent, division of paternal property, or the birth of a child. The word 'passage' was reserved for a transition, or series of transitions, which results in a new life stage. A 'life stage' is a form of identity which places people within socially constructed phases in expected life courses, such as: being a child, student, married person, parent, or elderly person. Life stages affect social roles, responsibilities, prestige, power, and household structure.

Third, in order to situate life histories within community and national contexts, I referred to groups of people in similar life stages at similar periods of national history as a 'cohort' and the periods of national history as 'eras': the 1971–4 war–famine nexus in Bangladesh is a good example of an 'era'.

7.4. Categorizing Trajectory Patterns

The following discussion is based on 90 of the 242 interviews carried out.[3] The simplest way of categorizing the trajectories of respondents is (following Lawson et al.'s 2000 groupings and the approach set out by Hulme and Shepherd, 2003) to see people in declining, level, or improving trajectories, where the variable changing is some measure of a person's well-being. In this section I attempt to build on such approaches but expand the number of trajectory types, using not only the present trajectory direction, but also the trajectory pattern observed over a longer period. I do this because much more can be learned from life trajectories than merely whether the person's condition is at present level, declining, or improving. Trajectory patterns over significant periods of time help us to piece together more interesting and complex relationships and provide better scope for improving the fit between patterns of crisis and social policy.

---

[3] The chosen interviews were those which had yielded the most comprehensive life stories and only those which I had conducted myself. The total of 242 interviews also included pilot interviews.

Table 7.1. Current trajectory direction of all respondents

	Declining	Level	Improving
Total	91	47	104
Male	43	22	54
Female	48	25	50
Jibonpur	22	7	15
Haripur	16	4	18
Gopalpur	9	12	14
Kamalpara	6	6	8
Teliapara	5	10	5
Kumarpara	6	3	12
Mirpur	8	3	9
Goshpur	9	0	11
Dukhipur	8	2	10
Rural non-remote	31	23	47
Rural remote	25	5	30
Urban	17	19	29
Hindu	8	9	12
Muslim	82	37	89

Of the 242 respondents, 91 were judged to be at present declining, 47 were level, and 104 were in improving trajectories. Overall, and in nearly all sub-categories of respondents examined in Table 7.1, the numbers of improving respondents tended to be slightly higher than the numbers of those declining.[4] This finding is compatible with the overall trend of poverty reduction in Bangladesh reported most recently by Sen and Hulme (2004). Differences in numbers of those deemed to be 'level' should not be seen as significant because the choice between seeing a trajectory as level or not was somewhat arbitrary and subjective, differing significantly between interviewers and how much detail the interview yielded. Broad variables such as religion, gender, or urban/rural, remote/non-remote location did not show significant differences in numbers of life trajectories declining or improving. What this approach does offer, however, is a high level of detail in individual stories. The challenge is then to analyse and aggregate this complex detail so that generalizations can be made and policy lessons drawn.

7.5. Using Trajectory Patterns as Heuristic Tools in Poverty Dynamics Studies

In order to analyse trajectory patterns I created a small number of categories (or fuzzy sets (Ragin, 2000)) or stylized patterns or types of life trajectory which seemed to recur in the data. Such an approach takes a preliminary step towards making generalizations over time in individual life trajectories and

[4] Village names and respondent names have all been changed to ensure anonymity.

Table 7.2. Ideal typical trajectory patterns

Trajectory direction	Trajectory pattern	Depiction	Number of cases (out of 90)
level	smooth		6
improving	smooth		3
declining	smooth		6
level	saw-smooth		17
improving	saw-tooth		17
declining	saw-tooth		14
declining	single-step		13
declining multi-step			14

across numbers of individuals. These ideal types of trajectories (or parts of a life trajectory) are represented diagrammatically in Table 7.2. The following discussion is framed using these eight trajectory categories.

A number of observations emerge as overall life trajectories were considered:

- Improvements in people's life conditions tend to happen only gradually, whereas sudden declines were much more common. People rarely win a lottery, but they can frequently and suddenly become ill, lose their land, spouse, or income.

- Crises are more likely to produce serious and sudden declines when the crisis either directly affects something constitutive of a person's well-being,[5] such as their health, or when a person has very few 'buffers' (e.g. low resilience due to previous crises, no insurance resources, few assets or savings, poor network resources). Most poor people have few buffers and are therefore more likely to translate a crisis into a serious decline in well-being.[6]

[5] See Sen (1998) for a useful discussion on the distinction between 'constitutive' and 'instrumental' determinants of well-being.

[6] See Room (2000) for a useful conceptual framework using ideas of snakes, ladders, passports, and buffers to describe a dynamic view of processes of social exclusion.

- Life trajectories and parts of life trajectories (episodes) can be categorized into a fairly small number of patterns. For example, some trajectories were marked by one big crisis that overshadowed the rest of the person's life (what I call a 'single-step decline'); others resemble more the teeth of a single action saw ('saw-tooth'), gradual improvements interspersed with more abrupt declines; others are fairly smooth all the way ('smooth'). In further research it may be useful to use categories such as these as fuzzy sets, as a way forward in bridging the qual–quant divide in studies of poverty dynamics (see Ragin, 2000).

7.6. Trajectory Direction

7.6.1. *Improving trajectories*

There were only two categories which described improvement: (i) 'improving smooth' and (ii) 'improving saw-tooth'. The lack of other patterns reflects the difference between decline and improvement in general: declines are often steep but improvements are not. Because of this, sudden single- and multi-step improvements did not appear among this sample of non-metropolitan Bangladeshis interviewed. Long-term improvements are either slow and smooth (usually for the more resource rich) or they consist of slow improvements interspersed with sudden declines, which nevertheless are not serious enough to undermine an overall upward trend. The 'improving saw-tooth' pattern which results is the most common trajectory type for poor people on an improving trajectory. An understanding of this is relevant for conceptualizing social policy interventions: if life trajectories, even among those which are improving, are interspersed with setbacks, anti-poverty policy can have two aims: to support processes which allow gradual periods of improvement to occur on the one hand, and to prevent or mitigate events which cause inevitable sudden declines on the other.

7.6.2. *Declining trajectories*

In contrast with the two forms of improvement there were four patterns of decline. Obviously in many actual cases it was difficult to decide which type (or combination of types) the idiosyncratic and complex real-world patterns corresponded most closely to. However, the distinctions are still useful for heuristic purposes because ideal types, created by abstracting out from the real-world cases, can in turn be reflected back onto real-world events and processes, as tools for further questioning and analysis.

(I) DECLINING SAW-TOOTH

It seemed to me that many trajectories of the poor people interviewed resemble the teeth of a saw. Periods of slow improvement were commonly interspersed with more sudden downward falls. When the falls outweighed the improvements an overall downward trajectory resulted. This 'declining saw-tooth' pattern has some resonance with Chambers's idea of a downward ratchet (Chambers, 1983). However, it is useful to distinguish between trajectories where there is scope for improvement between downward steps and where no scope for improvement or recovery occurs. This distinction is not so clear in the 'downward ratchet' analogy.

(II) SMOOTH DECLINE

Some trajectories decline smoothly rather than in sudden steps. Smooth decline patterns are less common and tend to appear when crisis episodes are long term (drawn-out court cases, chronic illness, underemployment) or when there is some long-term underlying or structural cause of disadvantage which precludes improvement (such as 'adverse incorporation' (Davis, 1997, 2001; Wood, 1999) within constraining or exploitative patron–client dyads).

- *Single-step decline.* Single-step declines describe a trajectory which is characterized by a crisis event (which may be of composite causation) which has an overshadowing and defining significance due to its catastrophic impact. This may be due to a relative's death, an accident or serious illness, a court case, or a catastrophic combination of adverse events (double and triple whammies) occurring at around the same time. For many poor women, their abandonment, divorce, or widowhood, if it had happened, often constituted such a defining event. Also people can be more vulnerable to such declines during transitions or passages between life stages such as the death of parents and the associated division of parental property, the beginning and end of marriages, and during or after migration.

- *Multi-step decline.* Multi-step decline was similar to a declining saw-tooth, the difference being more in terms of a small number of serious crises (2–5) with little improvement or recovery in between. The lack of recovery between crises often suggested a lack of resilience, particularly associated with more vulnerable individuals.

7.6.3. *Level trajectories*

Two categories of level trajectory appeared: what I refer to as (i) 'level saw-tooth' and (ii) 'level smooth'. These can occur at relatively high, medium, or low levels of 'life condition' (*obosta*). Saw-tooth trajectories at a fairly low level of 'life condition' are the most common type experienced by the chronically poor. For the individuals who were extremely poor, a low but 'level saw-tooth' type trajectory reflected the way that these people were barely surviving, avoiding a declining trajectory largely because there was little scope for further decline in their life condition without total destitution and death. It was usual, at this very low level, for moral-economy norms corresponding with Scott's 'subsistence ethic' to appear, which compel relatives, patrons, and neighbours to provide for these individuals in a number of ways crucial for their survival (Scott, 1976). Some of these processes, particularly those involving extended kinship relationships, have also been identified in Bangladesh by Indra and Buchignani (1997). While in their highly vulnerable states, however, these people were often beset by regular crises, for example: illness, unemployment, and various forms of violence, domination, and coercion. This suggests that low levels of informal social protection are not sufficient to prevent long-term harm.

'Level smooth' trajectories were more associated with the better off. The smooth trajectory usually reflects access to resources which effectively buffer against regular crises. For these people health problems were dealt with through relatively expensive private clinics, legal disputes resolved due to access to a number of social and economic power resources, and dowries paid for from savings and sale of assets without damaging quality of life. In addition to the better off, however, a smaller number of individuals without significant assets and low income also had fairly smooth and level trajectories. These tended to be younger respondents, sometimes married couples with young children who had not yet faced dowry problems, with their parents still relatively young and healthy, and with property not yet divided between brothers—an event which usually occurred after the death of parents. However, the level trajectories enjoyed by these poorer young people tended to be short-lived once they moved on in their life cycles when parents became old and daughters needed dowries. A smaller number of single older people were also living fairly crisis-free lives, reflected in the 'level smooth' trajectory pattern. In these cases the level smooth trajectory was due more to good fortune than to resilience or a lack of vulnerability. It occurred while elderly people were healthy, had children and neighbours caring for them, and had few responsibilities for others.

7.7. Trajectory Patterns

In the following section I draw attention to the range of trajectory patterns identified above using selected cases from actual life history interviews. The diagrams used are a distillation of information from actual life history interviews and the life trajectory diagrams drawn with respondents. For the sake

Table 7.3. Examples of causes of declining smooth patterns

Main cause	Gender	Current age
1. A combination of low household income and several chronic health problems	M	63
2. Chronic illness	M	51
3. Husband's chronic illness	F	35
4. Mother-in-law's chronic illness (TB)	F	32
5. Low income and chronic illness	M	22
6. Low income and brother's chronic illness	M	20

of clarity, only the most relevant information is included in the diagrams. Accompanying discussions are based on my interpretation of relationships and processes emerging from a much wider set of life history interviews. I use the eight trajectory types to organize the discussion.

7.7.1. Smooth trajectories

Smooth trajectories were not common. Approximately fifteen smooth trajectories (17 per cent) could be identified from the ninety most comprehensive life histories but this figure should be used with caution. Life history interviews varied greatly in the quality of information gathered, and a smooth trajectory could be erroneously drawn when an interview did not go well because there was insufficient information available to describe the ups and downs in a person's life. In interviews where a rich and accurate level of detail was recalled, a more accurate trajectory was drawn, and this tended not to be smooth. However, in some cases, the smoothness of the trajectory was not due to a lack of detail: it reflected either a period of relatively few serious crises, or sufficient resources to deal with them—particularly in the 'level smooth' and 'improving smooth' cases. In the declining smooth cases the trajectory usually reflected chronic and long-term downward pressures with few countervailing opportunities.

(I) DECLINING SMOOTH

Most cases of smooth decline in individual life condition were associated with chronic illness of the respondent, or someone close to the respondent. Table 7.3 provides examples of six cases which could clearly be identified as 'declining smooth'. For these six, it was clear that the trajectory was actually fairly smooth rather than an interview which had failed to yield adequately detailed information. A number of other cases were categorized as 'declining smooth' but, due to the paucity of information from the interviews, I had much less confidence in drawing conclusions from these.

The following case of Sukur Ali (number 1 in Table 7.3) illustrates a smoothly declining life trajectory caused mainly, but not exclusively, by the chronic health problems suffered by other members of his household.

Sukur Ali is a 63-year-old man who has worked as a village *chowkidar*, employed by the Union Parishad, since 1979. His wife Momataz is 50 and works as a day labourer in a local tobacco-processing plant. They have a 16-year-old daughter living with them in the same *ghor* (room). In addition Sukur Ali's brother eats with them but sleeps in a separate *ghor* in the same *bari* or homestead. The brother has TB and has not been able to work for the last three years. There are three separate rooms in the *bari*. Sukur Ali earns 700 Tk. per month as a *chowkidar* but is not usually paid on time. The recurring delay in wages exacerbates his dependent relationship on the Union Parishad chairman who oversees his employment.

Before 1979 Sukur Ali had worked as a rickshaw driver for twenty-nine years. When he was married in 1965 his father owned 15 *bighas*[7] (5 acres) of land. In 1962 his father became ill and over the following fifteen years (which also spanned the war of independence) they sold all of their land to pay for their father's treatment (8 *bighas* before the war and 7 after). During the 1974 famine they also sold their rickshaw to buy food. At that time also Momataz was ill with an abscess which persisted for a year. Sukur Ali's father died in 1977 after fifteen years of illness. Momataz was pregnant four times between 1974 and 1984 but all of the children died around the time of birth. In 1987 they arranged the marriage of their eldest daughter and negotiated the dowry payment of Tk. 3,000 to be paid over one year.

Figure 7.1 shows a simplified version of that drawn during the interview and attempts to clarify the relative impact of these events and episodes on Sukur Ali's well-being over time. The combination of chronic illness (father, wife, and brother) and other stresses (dowry, crop losses) produced a smoothly declining trajectory. Low and intermittent income and a denuding asset base do little to mitigate these long-term downward pressures.

In these cases the smoothness of the decline often reflects chronic problems which were met by unsustainable coping strategies. The long-term mismatch between income and expenditure was met by the sale of assets, but with each consecutive sale, the ability to cope was further weakened. The outcome of smooth decline is the result of cumulative causes where coping strategies with each setback reinforce the impact of the next event. In considering the policy implications of this pattern of decline we need to take a long-term perspective when addressing the mismatch between downward pressures and the ability to mitigate them. The prevention of denudation of coping power resources would form an important part of a social protection strategy—in this case the

---

[7] 1 *bigha* = 1/3 of an acre.

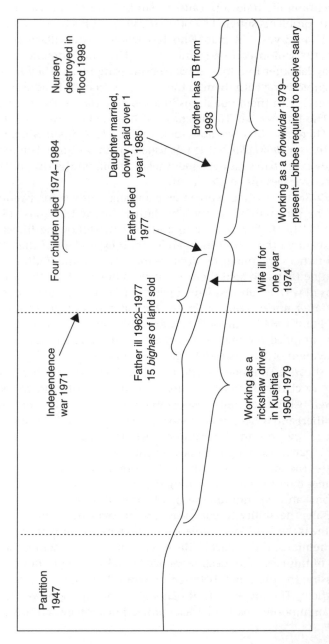

Figure 7.1. Declining smooth: Sukur Ali

sale of land—alongside the mitigation of common downward pressures such as medical problems, medical expenses, court cases, and dowries.

(II) IMPROVING SMOOTH

Only three cases of 'improving smooth' appeared among the chosen ninety life histories. In all cases the improvement in life circumstances was not so much an emergence from poverty as the gradual consolidation of already quite strong positions in communities. Smooth inclines generally reflected either an ability to cope with the inevitable vicissitudes of life by having assets, income, and other social and political power resources, or by being fortunate enough to not be visited by major setbacks. However, what often seems to be good fortune often has a structured component of being either in an advantaged position with a strong power-resource base, or occupying a less vulnerable a place in the life cycle.

One of these cases of a smooth incline is depicted in Figure 7.2. Jehangir is a 40-year-old man who had secured a long-term position as a gardener with a local Kushtia-based NGO earning approximately Tk. 3,900 per month. He also acted as a *shordar* (local labour intermediary) organizing day labour for work with the NGO in town when this was needed. This position of economic security and a strong social network allowed consolidation of an already strong position. His family owned 7 *bighas* of land of which 2 *bighas* belonged to him personally. He had not yet faced dowry costs for daughters or major medical costs for his parents and was one of five brothers, who all lived locally. His parents were also still relatively healthy. A reliable income stream, with some assets being consolidated, and a strong social network in the local area contributed to a smoothly improving trajectory.

Smooth and level trajectories were not common and were usually associated with interviews that had not gone well. A common response that poor people gave when initially asked about their situations, particularly before a relationship of trust and rapport had been established, was that their condition (*obosta*) was bad and had always been so with very little change.

One of the reasons I developed an approach based on life history interviewing was that I found that the same people produced stories which showed that their life trajectories were by no means smooth and level once time had been taken to build up trust and rapport with them and as they understood that I really was interested in the details of their lives. However, in a small number of cases, episodes of some lives reflected a fairly constant condition even after detailed histories had emerged. The problem of distinguishing between a truly smooth trajectory and a level saw-tooth highlights the difficulty of using a retrospective interviewing technique. With experience a researcher can distinguish a problematic interview from a history which really has few vicissitudes. However, problems of memory, differing perceptions of

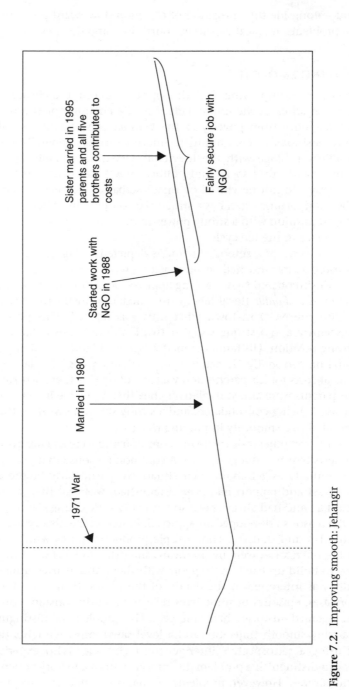

Figure 7.2. Improving smooth: Jehangir

what constituted a crisis, and varied rapport with respondents make absolute certainty difficult to achieve.

7.7.2. Saw-tooth trajectories

Trajectories which resembled the teeth of a single-action saw were the most common pattern in life trajectories and within episodes in trajectories. In these, gradual improvements were interspersed with more abrupt declines. Of what I judged to be the ninety most accurate life history interviews, forty-eight (or 53 per cent) had significant episodes following this pattern.

(I) LEVEL SAW-TOOTH

The level saw-tooth pattern was usually the reflection of a number of short-term improvements being reversed, usually suddenly, by intermittent crises, producing a long-term trend of neither improvement nor decline. In most cases the potential for long-term improvement was hampered by the common problems identified, such as dowry or illness, often coupled with a low level of resilience and low income making these full crises, rather than minor vicissitudes.

The case outlined below (and Figure 7.3) illustrates a number of common features which occurred with the level saw-tooth pattern. Improvements are possible through household members being economically active; however a number of lifecycle-related crises also occur, mostly involving illness and dowry expenses.

Fuljan is a 33-year-old woman who lives with her husband, five children (three boys and two girls), and her 66-year-old mother-in-law. Another daughter was married in 1998 and moved to her new in-laws. There were also six other households of her husband's brothers who lived in the same *bari*. Her husband worked as a loom master and earned approximately Tk. 1,200 per month and her eldest (17-year-old) son also earned about the same working with a handloom. They owned about 1.5 *kata*[8] of land where the house was built and their total assets were worth approximately Tk. 12,800. Their house was in a bad state of repair and they are looked down on in the community as 'poor' (*goreb*).

Fuljan was married at the age of 12 in 1981 after her father had died from typhoid during the famine in 1975. Both Fuljan and her husband came from poor families. In 1984 her mother-in-law (*sasuri*) became ill with a stomach ulcer and they had to pay Tk. 13,000 for medical treatment. To fund this her husband's brothers sold a handloom. In 1987 Fuljan herself became ill after a baby died before birth and Tk. 20,000 was spent on her medical treatment. In 1990 the brothers divided the family property and in the following years

---

[8] 1 *kata* = 1/60 of an acre.

their position improved. In 1998 her eldest daughter was married with a total cost of Tk. 14,000 (10,000 dowry and 4,000 costs). To raise money for this an advance was taken from an employer, Tk. 5,000 came from relatives, a goat was sold, and an NGO loan was taken out. Now with her eldest son working and contributing to the household income as well as her husband, she sees her life condition improving over the coming years.

This level saw-tooth pattern tended to be the most common type of trajectory for poor people who had maintained roughly the same level of life condition over a long period of time. Downward crises were often experienced as abrupt declines with gradual recovery between. For poor people with few coping resources, shocks tended to be converted more directly into a decline in well-being with more likelihood of a cumulative decline.

(II) DECLINING SAW-TOOTH

The declining saw-tooth trajectory has much in common with the multi-step decline pattern discussed later and it is often difficult to distinguish between the two. However, it is useful to have two separate categories to distinguish trajectories declining without much recovery between downward steps (multi-step decline) from those where some recovery occurs but with further crises nevertheless outweighing the improvements. As can be seen in the cases considered below most real-life trajectories are a mix of the various ideal types.

The case of Amir Hossain below illustrates the saw-tooth pattern in an overall declining trajectory (Figure 7.4). His trajectory is beset with the common crises such as illnesses, but times of improvement were also identified: land was bought using a gift from in-laws and a new business was started. However, the larger crises—a brother's death in an accident and his mother's illness and death—outweighed the improvements, producing an overall downward trend.

Since this pattern is the most common type for those who decline into poverty, or from poverty into further destitution, a better understanding of the long-term dynamics of patterns of decline within individual and household life cycles is crucial for the better formulation of protective and preventive social protection strategies. It is also particularly important in the planning of formal social protection to seek a synergistic combination of formal and informal strategies.

(III) IMPROVING SAW-TOOTH

Improving trajectories of the saw-tooth pattern are the most common trajectory of poor people when they are emerging from poverty. Table 7.4 shows the main reasons for improvement in a sample of people with life trajectories of this type. These highlight a number of important explanations for an improved trajectory even while people were beset by intermittent crises.

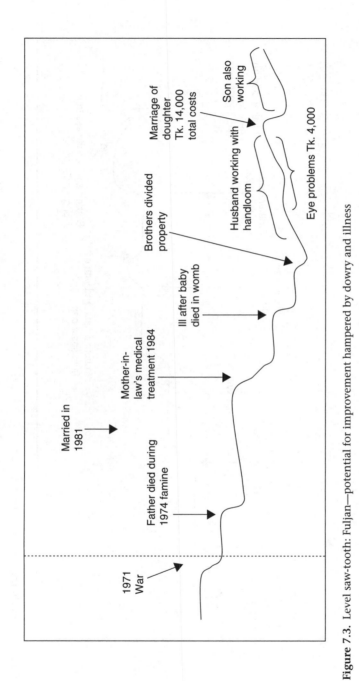

Figure 7.3. Level saw-tooth: Fuljan—potential for improvement hampered by dowry and illness

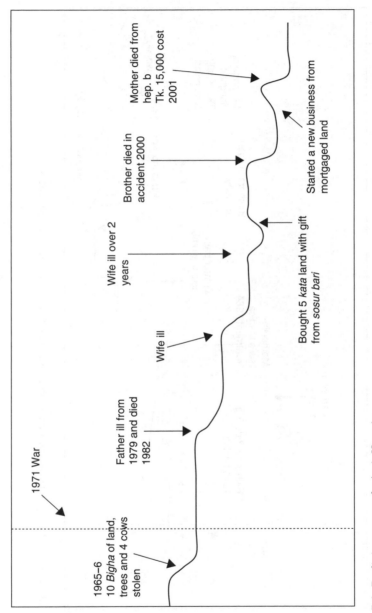

Figure 7.4. Declining saw-tooth: Amir Hossain

Table 7.4. Reasons for improvement in saw-tooth trajectories

Age	Sex	Main reason(s) for an improved trajectory
20	F	Sufficient regular work for husband with handloom, driving a *van gari*, and agricultural day labour
26	M	Started a new business benefiting from: receipt of dowry, NGO loan in wife's name, and illegal electricity connection
29	M	Permanent job with an NGO
30	M	Division of property between brothers, regular income from handloom
35	F	Two sons begin working and a *van gari* was bought using an informal loan *(howlat)*
35	M	Used an informal loan to open a tea shop in the *bazar*, and wife started working
39	M	Loans taken out from relatives and an NGO and a new business was started
40	F	Son starting to earn income
42	F	Son starting to earn income, daughters all married
42	F	Son starting to earn income
42	M	Successful farming, hard work, and entrepreneurial use of other's mortgaged land
49	M	Regular income from agriculture, handloom, son's dowry, and son beginning to work
55	M	Regular income from agriculture and a number of sons working
56	M	Continued small but regular income as a school teacher

Most improvements were associated with the achievement of a steady income stream by a member, or members, of the household which provided a buffer for intermittent crises. The lifecycle transition of sons beginning to work and contributing to the household was particularly important, especially for the women interviewed and especially for women who had lost a husband. The ability to establish or consolidate small businesses using either informal or NGO loans was also very important. In other cases, benefits for some people had costs attached for others. For example, the receipt of dowry money for men was commonly used to start businesses, while the costs to the bride's family often produced a crisis. Also, in some cases the division of property among brothers led to benefits for some but with a decline for others who had benefited in the past from property being held in common.

Even though Table 7.4 shows that work-related activities of household members are an important part of emergence from poverty, we should be careful not to neglect other less visible aspects of this emergence. The absence of crisis involves both upward opportunities and the lack of, or mitigation of, downward pressures. What *could have* happened if something else was absent will obviously not feature as strongly as what *did* happen.

The danger is that a superficial reading of stories of emergence from poverty due to work-related activities can lead to policy priorities based solely around promoting income generation—as is the case with the microfinance-dominated poverty-reduction model which has existed for the last two decades in Bangladesh. However, emergence from poverty has two sides: slow upward episodes of opportunity interspersed with sudden, downward crisis-causing events. The prevention or mitigation of downward crises can also help convert declining saw-tooth trajectories into improving ones, but

Peter Davis

Table 7.5. Examples of causes of single-step decline patterns

Nature of crisis	Gender	Age
1. Husband poisoned on a train, became paralysed, and was ill for 10 years. Business, house, trees, sold to pay for husband's medical care before his death.	F	45
2. Husband died when he fell from a tree	F	38
3. Husband died from an undiagnosed chest infection	F	37
4. Illness and death of husband from asthma leading to survival by begging	F	50
5. Court case fought over disputed land for 5 years. Other land sold to pay for the case. When the case was lost her husband died from a heart attack leaving the household landless and destitute	F	60
6. Father died leaving no money	F	46
7. Husband attacked by a rival gang in a village dispute. Tk. 15,000 treatment costs followed by death from injuries sustained in the attack 8 months later.	F	55
8. Abandonment by husband. Kushtia textile mill closed leading to loss of husband's job (alongside 1,000 other workers) which led to her husband abandoning her.	F	45
9. Tk 30,000 medical costs before death of father raised by the sale of 2 *bighas* of land. Now works as a landless day labourer.	M	27
10. Eye lost in an accident with a rice-husking machine.	M	44
11. Land and property lost by theft and forcible occupation.	M	60
12. Combination of illness of mother and costs associated with marriage of sister.	M	33
13. Illness of child at the same time as division of property between brothers.	M	29

because they prevent what *could have* happened, they can be overlooked when tales of emergence are favoured in development literature. When stories of success have disproportionate coverage, social protection measures can be neglected. In the Bangladesh case the mitigation of the negative impacts due to illness (particularly of the elderly), dowry costs, social conflict, marriage breakdown, and household dissolution all need to be kept as social protection priorities. Improvement is 'caused' by both upward drivers and the removal of downward ones.

Figure 7.5 helps to contextualize improving saw-tooth patterns within longer trajectories. It shows an initial declining trajectory for a woman due mainly to a failed marriage. Improvement began with a second marriage and a son's contribution to household income, offsetting ongoing expenses for a parent's medical care.

7.7.3. *Step trajectories*

(I) SINGLE-STEP DECLINE

Single-step declines tended to occur when a serious single or composite crisis event led to deterioration in life condition, which was usually irreversible and catastrophic (Table 7.5). Distinguishing between composite single-step declines and multi-step declines is a little arbitrary, particularly if inaccuracies in memory recall conflate events which were in fact separated by months or even years. This commonly occurs when the events recalled were several years or decades in the past.

174

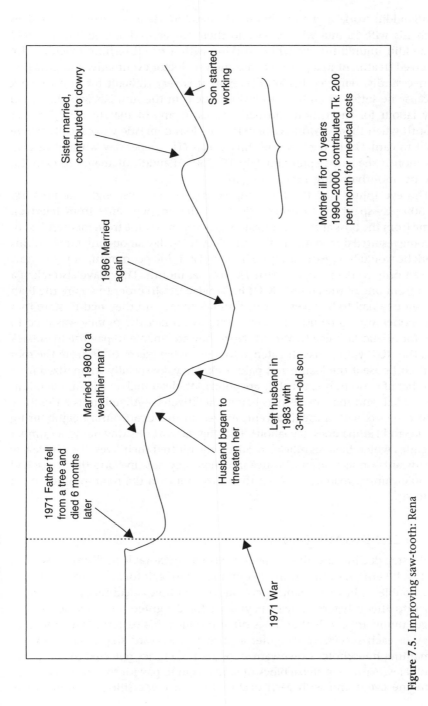

Figure 7.5. Improving saw-tooth: Rena

1971 Father fell from a tree and died 6 months later

Married 1980 to a wealthier man

Husband began to threaten her

Left husband in 1983 with 3-month-old son

1986 Married again

Sister married, contributed to dowry

Son started working

Mother ill for 10 years 1990–2000, contributed Tk. 200 per month for medical costs

1971 War

Allauddin works as a day labourer (Figure 7.6). He is 44 years old. He lives with his wife Fatima who is 35 and their 15-year-old son Ruhul. In 1993 Allauddin injured his eye while working with a rice-threshing machine. He received treatment in a private clinic and the doctor eventually, and probably unnecessarily, removed his left eye. Now it is very difficult for him to work because he suffers from bad headaches if he is in the sun. His wife does road day labour for the Union Parishad and earns approximately Tk. 1,200 per month when there is work. Otherwise she does domestic work locally where she can earn Tk. 18 per day and three meals (Tk. 35 per day without meals). Per month she earns approximately Tk. 260. Allauddin manages to earn Tk. 400 per month driving a cycle *van gari*.

The eye injury had the following consequences: over eight months Tk. 13,500 was spent on treatment. Some of this money came from relatives, some from the boss at the local tobacco *godown*, and some from loans. A loss of income resulted due to Allauddin's inability to do day labour any more. In this work he would have earned approximately Tk. 1,700 per month; however now he can only work enough to earn Tk. 400 per month. They have also taken a loan from one of the largest NGOs in Bangladesh. In order to secure the loan the money had to be taken out in Fatima's name and they had to state that the money was to be used to buy a *van gari*. In fact the money was used to pay for Allauddin's eye treatment. Now they are unable to pay the loan back and the NGO worker has threatened to remove ten pieces of tin from the roof of their house if the loan is not paid back. They are socially stigmatized for a number of reasons: because they are poor, have defaulted on a loan, Allauddin is disabled, and they are seen as being uncultivated—Allauddin is a rickshaw driver, speaks with a rough accent, moved to the area from a neighbouring *thana*, and Fatima does day labour. This stigma works its way out in a number of guises which have significantly adversely affected their lives: they have few significant connections in the area in which they now live and they have had trouble gaining road access from their own home to the road in order to get to town.

(II) DECLINING MULTI-STEP

Multi-step declines are often experienced as an inexorable decline in resources and well-being resulting from a combination of reinforcing adverse events. The double and triple whammy episodes of multiple or cumulative causation fall into this category. Dowry payments for daughters in households with larger numbers of girls than boys often produce this pattern. With the marriage of each successive daughter a further downward step is taken by the remaining household. Downward steps are sometimes reflected in successive land sales. With each step a block of land is sold to pay for the costs associated with the event and with each decline in land ownership the resilience of

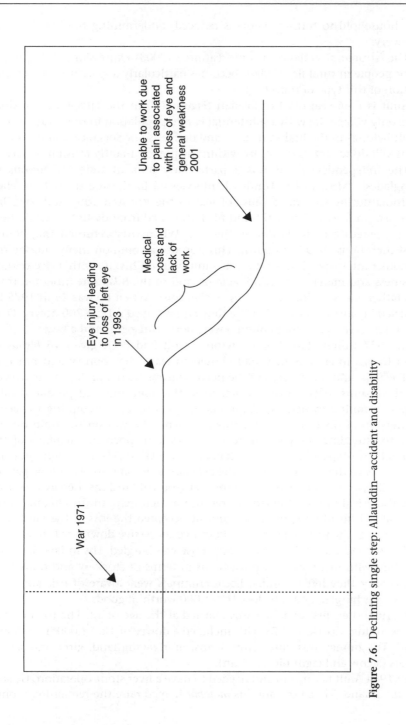

Figure 7.6. Declining single step: Allauddin—accident and disability

War 1971

Eye injury leading to loss of left eye in 1993

Medical costs and lack of work

Unable to work due to pain associated with loss of eye and general weakness 2001

the household to further events is reduced, undermining the likelihood of recovery.

The 'structural violence' (to use Farmer's (2003) expression) facing many poor people in rural Bangladesh becomes particularly apparent in the examination of this type of trajectory.

Amit is a 46-year-old Hindu man (Figure 7.7) in the village of Gopalpur (the only village site with a substantial Hindu population in the study). While Amit belongs to the Brahmin caste, and derives some social capital from this, he is still disadvantaged socially within the predominantly Muslim society.

The independence war was a particularly difficult time for Hindus in Bangladesh. Most of the Hindus I interviewed in Kushtia district travelled to India during the war because of fear of the Pakistan army and so-called *rajakars*. Amit was 22 in 1971 and his father died from dysentery while they were sheltering in India during the war. When they returned they found that their house had been burnt. This was also a common theme among the Hindus I interviewed. After the war Amit built up his life with a rice-trading business and managed to add 9 *kata* of land to the 8 *kata* he inherited from his father. He was also able to buy twelve cows. When he was 26 in 1975 he married Jayanti who was 14 at the time and received a Tk. 1,200 dowry. Over the next eleven years four children were born, three girls and a boy.

In 1977 things started going wrong. Amit had been given 16 *bighas* of land by his in-laws as they had chosen to leave the country and move to India. This land was located in the neighbouring district of Rajbari. However, local Muslims in the area had occupied the land and had produced false papers claiming ownership. Amit started a court case attempting to secure ownership of his in-laws' land. However, while he was on the train on the way to attending the court hearing he was kidnapped by members of the group he was opposing. The case had cost him Tk. 17,750 in various fees and payments to the advocate (*ukil*), the assistant advocate, the *hajira* for papers, the police, and various witnesses. Another group of Muslims then assisted him but also asked him for the land in return for their help. In the circumstances he realized his life was in danger and he accepted the loss of the land. This episode was the first of a series of about five successive downward steps.

The second was in 1983 when his house was burgled. His in-laws had also left him with many of their possessions in terms of crockery and household items after they left for India. Local criminals were aware of this and their house was burgled and they lost Tk. 21,000 worth of goods.

In 1990 their first daughter was married at the age of 13. The total cost of the wedding was Tk. 27,775. This included a dowry of Tk. 14,000 in cash and gold. The money was raised from loans, mortgaging land, gifts, and sale of assets (a cow and eight pieces of tin).

In 1994 Amit became ill and needed to have a liver stone operation. He sold 4 *kata* of land (Tk. 6,000) and his *matobar* helped raise the remaining money

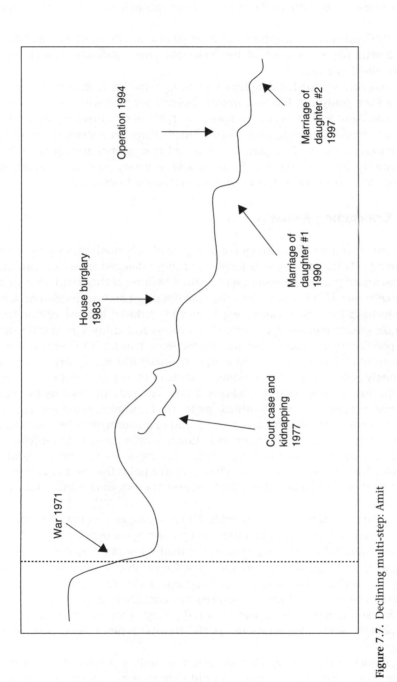

Figure 7.7. Decliming multi-step: Amit

War 1971

House burglary 1983

Operation 1994

Marriage of daughter #2 1997

Marriage of daughter #1 1990

Court case and kidnapping 1977

in the community with a collection. Without this help he said he would have died.

In 1997 his second daughter was married at a total cost of Tk. 28,000. To raise this money a cow was sold, two NGO loans were taken out, and Tk. 5,000 was received in gifts.

He has one unmarried daughter remaining. His son is now working as a helper for a goldsmith but he currently doesn't get paid while he is learning the trade. Amit and his wife earn about Tk. 1,700 per month from agriculture (3 *kata*), conducting *puja*, and making small items. As a Brahmin from the prestigious *thakur gosti* he performs *puja* and is respected among the Hindu community. However, outside this small and relatively powerless community he does not have wide influence or power resources to draw from.

7.8. Concluding Remarks

There are a number of advantages of using life history methodology in studies of poverty dynamics. A much longer and more detailed interview can take place without boring the respondent, mainly because of the fascination we all have with our life histories when they are discussed and depicted. The sense of objectification which can be experienced is reduced because respondents can take greater control of the interview process and enjoy a greater freedom of expression than in more structured interviews. This leads to better communication of contextual detail and a more nuanced historical story which can accurately reflect people's own understanding of their experiences.

A life history approach also allows a different type of analysis to occur. Lifecycle patterns can be identified, patterns of complex causation emerge, and individual episodes of crisis, coping, and opportunity can be seen within the interrelated and wider context of national, community, and family trajectories. It allows patterns to emerge of diminishing or accumulating resources and socially structured behaviour. These patterns point the researcher towards the underlying social structures that support the informal social protection system.

Life history interviews also provide a rich source of contextually situated (spatially and temporally) qualitative data providing the opportunity to bridge the qual–quant divide through the use of medium-n case-based research and categorical data analysis techniques (see Ragin, 2000). Such an approach allows a reflexive interchange between conceptual theory and substantive data analysis. The use of trajectory categories can contribute to poverty dynamics research and enhance its impact on social policy—particularly social protection policies. Such categorizations can also be used as heuristic tools to inform policy.

A broader range of research approaches, including combinations of qualitative and quantitative methods, would help inform a range of protective, promotional, and redistributional social policies, aimed at enhancing and complementing informal forms of social protection, and taking into account the changing (structured and structuring) profiles of risk and coping that poor people face over their life cycles. This leads to a rethinking of social protection based on an understanding of dynamic risk profiles and their underlying social structures. Interventions need to complement existing informal and formal means of coping and be sensitive to lifecycle stages and transitions when people are most vulnerable.

The present research uncovers the harsh and long-term impact of a number of categories of crisis in a fresh way. These include: illness, dowry, underemployment and low income, court cases, business failure, crop loss, divorce, household breakdown, violence, conflict, and crime. Our understanding of the causes and consequences of these can only be improved if they are viewed from within a life course perspective. The different vantage point taken addresses many of the blind spots of other methods and provides a complement to the existing suite of research approaches already informing social policy in development contexts.

References

Becker, S., and Mahmud, S. (1984), *A Validation Study of Backward and Forward Pregnancy Histories in Matlab, Bangladesh*, Voorburg: International Statistical Institute.

Bourdieu, P. (1986), 'The Forms of Capital', in J. G. Richardson (ed.), *Handbook of Theory and Research for the Sociology of Education*, New York: Greenwood Press, 241–58.

——(1990), *The Logic of Practice*, Cambridge: Polity.

——and Nice, R. (1977), *Outline of a Theory of Practice*, Cambridge: Cambridge University Press.

Carney, D. (ed.) (1998), *Sustainable Rural Livelihoods: What Contribution Can We Make?*, London: Department for International Development.

Chambers, R. (1983), *Rural Development: Putting the Last First*, London: Longman.

Conway, M. A. (1990), *Autobiographical Memory: An Introduction*, Philadelphia: Open University Press.

Davis, P. (1997), 'Social Exclusion in Bangladesh: New Problematic or Eurocentric Imposition?', M.Sc. dissertation, School of Social Sciences, University of Bath.

——(2001), 'Rethinking the Welfare Regime Approach: The Case of Bangladesh', *Global Social Policy*, 1: 79–107.

——(2005), 'Power-Resources and Social Policy in Bangladesh: A Life-History Perspective', Ph.D. thesis, Department of Economics and International Development, University of Bath.

——(2006), 'Poverty in Time: Exploring Poverty Dynamics from Life History Interviews in Bangladesh', CPRC Working Paper No. 69, Chronic Poverty Research Centre.

Dewilde, C. (2003), 'A Life-Course Perspective on Social Exclusion and Poverty', *British Journal of Sociology*, 54(1): 109–28.

Farmer, P. (2003), *Pathologies of Power: Health, Human Rights, and the New War on the Poor*, Berkeley and Los Angeles: University of California Press.

Hulme, D., and Shepherd, A. (2003), 'Conceptualizing Chronic Poverty', *World Development*, 31: 403–23.

Indra, D. M., and Buchignani, N. (1997), 'Rural Landlessness, Extended Entitlements and Inter-household Relations in South Asia: A Bangladesh Case', *Journal of Peasant Studies*, 24: 25–64.

Korpi, W. (1980), 'Social Policy and Distributional Conflict in the Capitalist Democracies: A Preliminary Comparative Framework', *West European Politics*, 3: 296–316.

—— (1983), *The Democratic Class Struggle*, London: Routledge.

—— (1985), 'Power Resources Approach vs. Action and Conflict: On Causal and Intentional Explanation in the Study of Power', *Sociological Theory*, 3: 31–45.

—— and Palme, J. (1998), 'The Paradox of Redistribution and Strategies of Equality: Welfare State Institutions, Inequality, and Poverty in the Western Countries', *American Sociological Review*, 63: 661–87.

Lawson, C. W., McGregor, J. A., and Saltmarshe, D. K. (2000), 'Surviving and Thriving: Differentiation in a Peri-urban Community in Northern Albania', *World Development*, 28: 1499–514.

Lewis, D., and McGregor, J. A. (1992), *Change and Impoverishment in Albania: A Report for Oxfam*, Bath: Centre for Development Studies, University of Bath.

McGregor, J. A. (2004), *Researching Well-being: Communicating between the Needs of Policy Makers and the Needs of People*, ESRC Research Group on Well-being in Developing Countries, University of Bath.

Miller, R. L. (1999), *Researching Life Stories and Family Histories*, Thousand Oaks, Calif.: Sage.

Ragin, C. (2000), *Fuzzy-Set Social Science*, Chicago: University of Chicago Press.

—— Shulman, D., Weinberg, A., and Gran, B. (2003), 'Complexity, Generality and Qualitative Comparative Analysis', *Field Methods*, 15: 323–40.

Room, G. (2000), 'Trajectories of Social Exclusion: The Wider Context', in D. Gordon and P. Townsend (eds.), *Breadline Europe: The Measurement of Poverty*, Bristol: Policy Press, 407–39.

Rubin, D. C., and Baddeley, A. D. (1989), 'Telescoping is not Time Compression: A Model of the Dating of Autobiographical Events', *Memory and Cognition*, 17: 653–61.

Scott, J. C. (1976), *The Moral Economy of the Peasant: Rebellion and Subsistence in Southeast Asia*, New Haven: Yale University Press.

Sen, A. (1998), 'Social Exclusion: A Critical Assessment of the Concept and its Relevance', *Asian Development Bank*, 49.

Sen, B., and Hulme, D. (2004), 'Chronic Poverty in Bangladesh: Tales of Ascent, Descent, Marginality and Persistence', Bangladesh Institute of Development Studies, Dhaka, and Chronic Poverty Research Centre, Institute for Development Policy and Management, University of Manchester.

Wood, G. D. (1999), 'Adverse Incorporation: Another Dark Side of Social Capital', paper presented to DfID/World Bank meeting on WDR 2000, Eynsham Hall, February.

—— (2003), 'Staying Secure, Staying Poor: The "Faustian Bargain"', *World Development*, 31: 455–71.

8

Subjective Assessments, Participatory Methods, and Poverty Dynamics

The Stages of Progress Method

Anirudh Krishna

8.1. Studying Poverty in Dynamic Contexts: The Need for New Methods

Despite decades of studying poverty, it is still not possible to say how many people were born poor in any country and how many others have become poor within their lifetimes. Available poverty knowledge also does not tell us how many formerly poor people have escaped from poverty in any country. Because it is not possible to identify those who have escaped from poverty, it becomes hard to compare them with those who have not. Thus, it becomes hard to fathom why only *some* (but not other) poor individuals succeeded in moving out of poverty.

Poverty has to be studied in dynamic context; otherwise the reasons for escape are not properly known. Different reasons operate in diverse regional contexts, and guessing these reasons is hardly enough. For policy to have an impact upon poverty, reasons for escape must be known; they must form the targets of policy. However, relatively little has been done so far to study these reasons as they operate within specific regional and local contexts.

New methods of studying poverty have been developed over the past few years that are helping to build better micro-foundations for poverty knowledge. I present below one of these new methods, developed with colleagues in five countries where poverty is a significant problem.

8.2. The Stages of Progress Method

The first Stages of Progress study was undertaken in the summer of 2002 in Rajasthan, India. I went into field research in April of that year, looking to understand why some but not other poor households had been able to escape from poverty. What had they experienced that others had not? Did education make the difference in most cases, or was is it an increase in productivity, or better market returns, or new opportunities, or fewer children?

How many people, not previously poor, had fallen into poverty within the same time period? What reasons had operated to bring about their downfalls?

I started looking within a group of rural communities in Rajasthan, the part of the world that I know best in terms of sensibilities and aspirations. But I had little idea about how I would go about this study. I knew that having a panel of data for two time periods would help, but it would take unbearably long to assemble: a gap of seven or eight years, at least, is required for having a panel capable of supporting effective comparisons over time (Walker and Ryan, 1990). I went ahead hoping to uncover through innovation on the ground a quicker and equally productive methodology yielding reliable and useful results. It took six months of field research, including four months experiencing nothing but failure, before a potentially workable methodology started taking shape.

These initial formulations, implemented in the first Rajasthan study (Krishna, 2003, 2004), were successively improved upon in additional studies, undertaken with research partners and community groups in other parts of India and later in Kenya, Uganda, Peru, and North Carolina, USA. These research partners—notably Patti Kristjanson in the Kenya studies and the Peru study; Mahesh Kapila, Mahendra Porwal, Sharad Pathak, and Virpal Singh in the three India studies; Dan Lumonya in Uganda; Judith Kuan in Peru; Milissa Markiewicz in Uganda and in North Carolina, together with Leslie Boney, Christina Gibson, and students at Duke University—have contributed in different ways to the present state of development of this methodology. I am equally indebted to the thousands of individuals whom we interviewed individually and in community groups, who gave freely of their time.

In each separate region we conducted investigations in the local language, thus different teams of investigators were selected and trained separately in each region. Up to three teams operated in tandem after training in each region. Typically, each team was composed of two facilitators and between four and six investigators, equally male and female. These facilitators are mostly college graduates, while the investigators have usually eight to ten years of school education.

Because so much depends upon the quality of interviewing—and upon combining carefully results derived separately from individual interviews and community groups—training is a very important aspect of this methodology.

Training for a period of ten days was built in at the start of this exercise in each study site. Following three days of classroom discussions and simulation, the study teams would go out to conduct practical exercises with the methodology, first in one set of communities, then, following feedback and discussions, in a second set of communities.[1] I remained with the study teams for additional periods of up to two weeks, working with them and watching them as they worked, and developing in discussion with them further refinements to these methods. As practised today, the methodology has seven successive steps, followed in order each time a study is conducted within any community.

Step 1. Assembling a representative community group. A male and a female community group were convened separately in each community. We took particular care to ensure that all members of the village community, particularly poorer and lower-status ones, were represented at these meetings. In some cases, where women let men do all the talking in mixed groups, a separate meeting was convened for women of the community.

Step 2. We presented our objectives, introducing ourselves as researchers. It needed to be made clear that there would be no benefits or losses from speaking freely and frankly to us. We were not implementing any development project or 'selecting beneficiaries'. Making this clear would help remove, we hoped, any incentive someone had to misrepresent himself or some other person as being poor.

Step 3. Describing 'poverty' collectively. Community groups in each village were asked to delineate the locally applicable stages of progress that poor households typically follow on their pathways out of poverty. 'What does a household in your community typically do', we asked the assembled community members, 'when it climbs out gradually from a state of acute poverty?' 'Which assets or capacities are acquired first? Which expenditures are the very first ones to be made?' 'Food,' was the answer invariably in every single village. Which expenditures follow immediately after? 'Some clothes,' we were told almost invariably. As more money flows in incrementally, what does this household do in the third stage, in the fourth stage, and so on? Lively discussions ensued among villagers in these community groups, but the answers that they provided, particularly about the first few stages of progress, were relatively invariant across all communities of each region studied.

After crossing which stage is a household no longer considered poor, we asked the assembled community members, after drawing up the progression of stages? The placement of this poverty cut-off and the nature of the initial stages (i.e. those below the poverty cut-off) differed somewhat across

---

[1] A detailed manual developed for these trainings can be downloaded free of charge from the website: <www.pubpol.duke.edu/krishna>.

Table 8.1. Stages of progress and the poverty cut-off

Stage	Peru (Cajamarca and Puno)	Western Kenya	Uganda (West and Central)	Andhra Pradesh, India	Gujarat, India	Rajasthan, India
1.	Food	Food	Food	Food	Food	Food
2.	Clothing	Clothing	Clothing	House repairs	Clothing	Primary education
3.	House repairs	House repairs	Primary education	Debt payments	Primary education	Clothing
4.	Purchase small animals	Primary education	House repairs	Clothing	Debt payments	Debt payments
			----------	-----------		--------------
5.	Primary education	Small animals			House repair/roof	

6.	Purchase small plot of land				Renting a small tract of land to farm as sharecropper	
	----------				--------------	

Note: The dotted line corresponds to the poverty cut-off in each case. Households advancing past this threshold are no longer considered poor, either by themselves or by their neighbours.

communities belonging to the different regions studied. However, remarkably similar understandings exist across diverse communities within each particular region. Across regions as well, there were considerable similarities in terms of these understandings of poverty, as Table 8.1 shows.

It was community members and not researchers who defined these stages of progress. The similarity in stages is more remarkable for this reason.

Notice the progression in stages as households gradually make their way out of poverty. In villages of Rajasthan, India, for example, the first four stages are food, primary education for children, clothing, and debt repayment. The poverty cut-off is drawn immediately after the fourth stage. In Andhra Pradesh villages, similarly, the poverty cut-off is drawn immediately after the fourth stage. Three of these first four stages are similar between Rajasthan and Andhra Pradesh villages, but instead of primary education, reported in Rajasthan villages, another stage, corresponding to minor house repairs, was reported among the first four stages in villages of Andhra Pradesh. Across countries, as well, there is considerable similarity across stages, but there also significant differences, reflecting diverse lifestyles and aspirations.

Later stages of progress beyond the first few are not reported in Table 8.1, and these stages included, for example, digging an irrigation well on one's own land, purchasing larger animals, particularly cattle, starting a small retail business, constructing a new house, purchasing jewellery, acquiring radios, fans, and tape recorders, and so on. These are, however, discretionary expenses, and depending upon the taste of a household's members, purchasing a radio or a tape recorder can precede or come after acquiring ornaments. There was, consequently, more variation in the ordering of these later stages in different villages.

The first few stages of progress are not so discretionary: they are both physically and socially obligatory. Physical needs—for food, for clothing, for protection from the elements—combine with considerations of social recognition to constitute the definition of poverty that is prevalent within these communities.[2] It is a commonly known and widely agreed-upon understanding of poverty, and this everyday understanding of poverty is much more real for these villagers than any definition that is proposed from the outside.

These locally constructed understandings of poverty constitute the criteria within these communities for identifying who is poor. They also constitute a threshold or an objective that defines the goals and the strategies of poor people: what people do in order to deal with poverty depends on what they understand to be the defining features of this state.

Villagers participating in community groups developed these criteria among themselves, and they used these well-understood and commonly known criteria to classify which households are poor at the present time and which households were poor twenty-five years ago. We chose to work in most regions with a period of twenty-five years because it corresponds roughly to one generation in time. Households' strategies are made in terms of generational time horizons. In addition to asking about twenty-five years ago, however, we also enquired about an interim period of eight to ten years ago.

Step 4. Treating households of today as the unit of analysis, enquiring about households' poverty status today and twenty-five years ago. In this step a complete list of all households in each village was prepared. Referring to the shared understanding of poverty developed in the previous step, the assembled community groups identified each household's status at the present time, for twenty-five years ago, and also for an intervening period, eight to ten years ago.[3]

---

[2] Social recognition matters as much as economic conditions in defining the shared understandings of poverty within these (and other) communities. For instance, in Gujarat, the fifth stage, fixing leaky roofs, usually entails an expenditure that does not in most cases exceed an amount larger than Rs. 400–500 (about $10), and it is a one-time expense, not often incurred year after year. Even as it is a relatively modest expense, however, its critical significance is in terms of status and recognition: people who are not poor in this region do not have leaky roofs. Similarly, the sixth stage reported in Gujarat villages—renting small tracts of agricultural land on a sharecropping basis—also has a distinct social significance that is related to the prevalence of debt bondage in this region. Possessing to rent even a small tract of land helps elevate the social status of a household above those who currently are or might later become bonded debtors in the village. It does not necessarily imply any considerable increase in net income.

[3] In order to denote the earlier periods clearly, we made reference to some significant event that is commonly known. For instance, in India, we referred to the national emergency of 1975-7, which is clearly remembered particularly by older villagers. In Kenya, similarly, we referred to the year of President Kenyatta's demise.

Households of today formed the unit of analysis for this exercise. Household composition has been relatively stable in all communities studied: relatively few households, less than 2 per cent in all, have either migrated in or migrated out permanently. Individual members of households, particularly younger males, have left these communities in search of work, but very few members have left permanently, and fewer still have left permanently along with their families.

Step 5. Assigning households to particular categories. After ascertaining their poverty status for the present time and for twenty-five years ago (or ten years ago), each household was assigned to one of four separate categories:

Category A. Poor then and poor now   (*Remained poor*);

Category B. Poor then but not poor now   (*Escaped poverty*);

Category C. Not poor then but poor now   (*Became poor*); and

Category D. Not poor then and not poor now   (*Remained not poor*).[4]

Step 6. Enquiring about reasons for escape and reasons for descent in respect of a random sample of households. We took a random sample of about 30 per cent of all households within each category, and we enquired in detail from the assembled community groups about causes and contributory factors associated with each selected household's trajectory over the past twenty-five years.

Step 7. Following up by interviewing household members. Reasons indicated by the community groups for each selected household were cross-checked separately through individual interviews with members of the household concerned. At least two members of each household were interviewed separately in their homes. Multiple sources of information were thus consulted for ascertaining reasons associated with the trajectories of each selected household.

It took a team of six to eight individuals three to four days on average to complete these enquiries in one rural community (which has on average about 150 households). These were not standard eight-hour days, but it was an enjoyable learning experience for me and for my colleagues.

8.3. Brief Synthesis of Results

Significant proportions of households have escaped poverty over the last twenty-five years. During the same period, large numbers of households have also fallen into poverty (Table 8.2).

Such simultaneous up-and-down movements have occurred in every one of more than 200 communities that we studied. Achieving poverty reduction

---

[4] A residual category, E, was also defined, and households that could not be classified otherwise because of lack of information were assigned to this category. Very few households, less than half of 1% in all, were placed within Category E.

Table 8.2. Trends in poverty dynamics over twenty-five years (%)

	Escaped poverty	Became poor	Change in poverty
Rajasthan (35 villages)	11	8	3
Gujarat (36 villages)	9	6	3
Andhra (36 villages)	14	12	2
W. Kenya (20 villages)	18	19	−1
Uganda (36 villages)	24	15	9
Peru (20 communities)	17	8	9
North Carolina (13 communities, 10 years)	23	12	11

goals will require taking action aimed at helping poor people escape poverty—but it will also call for actions that stem the flow of people into poverty.

Depending upon the region studied, between 6 per cent and 19 per cent of *all* households have fallen into poverty over the period examined. These households were not poor at the start of the study period, but by the end of this period they had joined the ranks of the poor.

The newly impoverished constitute a significant subgroup within each region. In the thirty-five Rajasthan villages, for example, almost *one-third* of those who are currently poor were not born poor; they have become poor within their lifetimes.

Introducing a separate focus on falling into poverty is an important contribution of studies that used the Stages of Progress method. Very large numbers of households are falling into poverty everywhere. Yet, very few policies are directed specifically toward reducing these frequent (and often needless) descents. As discussed below, a separate set of policies will be required specifically to curb descents into poverty. Understanding the reasons for descent will help give shape to appropriate policies.

8.3.1. *Reasons for descents*

Descents into poverty occur generally (though not always) in a gradual and cumulative fashion, and not from one moment to the next. No single reason is usually associated with falling into poverty; multiple linked factors propel most descents. Tackling these major factors should lead to large reductions in the incidence and probability of descent. Important local-level factors of descent included, in descending order of frequency, health and health-related expenses, death of a major income earner, disability, marriage and new household-related expenses, funeral-related expenses, high interest private debt (in India), land division, and land exhaustion (Table 8.3).

Healthcare is overwhelmingly the single most important reason for households descending into poverty in every region studied. Ill health and health-related expenses were mentioned as important reasons associated with nearly

Table 8.3. Principal reasons for falling into poverty (% of descending households)

Reasons	Rajasthan, India n = 364	Gujarat, India n = 189	Western Kenya n = 172	Andhra, India n = 335	Uganda: Central and Western n = 202	Peru: Puno and Cajamarca n = 252
Poor health and health-related expenses	60	88	74	74	71	67
Marriage/dowry/new household-related expenses	31	68		69	18	29
Funeral-related expenses	34	49	64	28	15	11
High-interest private debt	72	52		60		
Drought/irrigation failure/crop disease	18			44	19	11
Unproductive land/land exhaustion			38		8	

60 per cent of all descents recorded in villages of Rajasthan, India, with 74 per cent of all descents examined in Andhra Pradesh, India, and with as many as 88 per cent of all descents studied in villages of Gujarat, India. In communities of Kenya, Uganda, and Peru that we studied, respectively 74 per cent, 71 per cent, and 67 per cent of all descents were associated with ill health and health-related expenses.

Not only does ill health reduce the earning capacity of a household's members; in the absence of affordable and easy-to-access healthcare facilities, it also adds considerably to the household's burden of expenditure, thereby striking a double blow, which quite often results in tragedy. The human body is often poor people's main productive asset, an indivisible and, in most cases, an uninsured asset, which unlike most other assets can flip or slide from being an asset to being a liability.[5] The resulting dependence of survivors, including orphans, upon other households contributed further to descent in many cases.

Funeral expenses, especially expensive death feasts, were associated with a high proportion of descending households in communities studied in Kenya (64 per cent), Rajasthan (34 per cent), Gujarat (49 per cent), Andhra Pradesh (28 per cent), and Peru (11 per cent). Marriage-related expenses were very important in all three states studied in India. They were also cited as an important factor in communities of Peru, affecting younger couples in particular. Over a twenty-five-year period ending in 2004, marriage and new household-related expenses were associated with 29 per cent of all cases of households falling into poverty in these forty Peruvian communities.

[5] I thank Robert Chambers for suggesting this formulation.

Land-related factors, including crop disease, land exhaustion, drought, and irrigation failure, were also associated with a significant number of descents, particularly in some regions. In communities of western and central Uganda this set of factors was associated with 39 per cent of all observed descents and in communities of western Kenya with 38 per cent of all descents. Other reasons for descent included the loss of a job resulting from retrenchment, sacking, or retirement.

Drunkenness and laziness, sometimes thought to be important causes of poverty among the poor, were found to be relatively insignificant reasons. In all the communities investigated, these factors were associated with no more than 5 per cent of all descents.[6]

High-interest private debt is highly prevalent as a factor contributing to descents in the three Indian states. Villagers deal with high healthcare expenses and with expenses on marriages and death feasts by taking out high-interest loans from private moneylenders, paying rates of interest as high as 10 per cent *per month*. The high burden of debt that results helps push households deeper into poverty.

Drought and irrigation failure constituted another important reason for descent. However, the effect of this factor, as of many other factors reviewed above, varies considerably across different parts of a region and country.

These reasons for descent are different everywhere from the reasons that have helped take poor households out of poverty. This essential *asymmetry* between escaping poverty and falling into poverty will require simultaneously mounting two parallel sets of poverty policies, as discussed below.

8.3.2. *Reasons for escapes*

Income diversification has been the most important pathway out of poverty in all areas studied (Table 8.4). Poor rural households diversified their livelihood and income sources through two broad means: on-farm—through pursuing new crop- and/or livestock-related strategies; and off-farm—through local petty trade, small businesses, and, most importantly, through casual or temporary employment within the informal sector in a city. Diversification of income sources was related to 70 per cent of all escapes observed in communities of Rajasthan, India, 78 per cent of those observed in communities of western Kenya, 69 per cent in Peru, and 54 per cent in Uganda.

In general, growth of private sector employment has not been the principal or even a very prominent reason for escaping poverty. Even in Gujarat, India,

---

[6] There might have been a few more households that hid this information successfully from us, but I doubt that there are very many households of this type. In community groups especially, villagers were hardly shy in talking about another person's slothfulness or penchant for drink, and gently probed, household members also came forth to speak frankly about these aspects.

Table 8.4. Principal reasons for escaping poverty (% of escaping households)

Reasons	Rajasthan, India n = 499	Gujarat, India n = 285	Western Kenya n = 172	Andhra, India n = 348	Uganda: Central and Western n = 398	Peru: Puno and Cajamarca n = 324
Diversification of income	70	35	78	51	54	69
Private sector employment	7	32	61	7	9	19
Public sector employment	11	39	13	11	6	10
Government assistance/NGO scheme	8	6		7		4
Irrigation	27	29		25		

where economic growth rates have averaged 9 per cent over many years, only about one-third of those who escaped from poverty could do so on account of acquiring a regular job in the private sector (Krishna et al., 2005).

Growth in agriculture—related particularly to irrigation and land improvement—has been more important as a reason for escape from poverty.[7] Improvements in productivity as well as diversification into cash crops were quite important in both regions of Uganda, where first coffee, then vanilla, were grown. Cash crop diversification was also important in western Kenya and in the Cajamarca region of Peru. Over one-quarter of all escaping households in each of the three Indian states benefited from large-scale irrigation schemes or from small-scale irrigation activities on their lands.

While most children are going to school in these communities, education has hardly always amounted to an escape out of poverty. Information and connections matter in addition to education, and the lucky few who have found a job or business opportunities in the city have been assisted—usually with information and sometimes also with a contact or two—by an uncle or cousin established for many years in a city-based occupation.

It is disheartening that government as well as non-governmental assistance and programmes are not contributing substantially to households' movements out of poverty. Perhaps these programmes are not well spread out over all communities; perhaps lack of reach is made worse by lack of knowledge about reasons to target.

Different trends and different causes operate in different regions and localities, and pinpointed rather than blanket solutions need to be devised and

---

[7] Ravallion and Datt (1996) show that 84.5% of the recent significant poverty reduction in India was due to growth in the agricultural sector. See Timmer (1997) and Mellor (1999) for cross-country comparisons yielding a similar conclusion.

implemented. Disaggregated enquiries are important for this reason. Without knowing what reasons are most prominent for escape and for descent in a particular locality, appropriate interventions cannot be identified.

The Stages of Progress methodology helps critically with such locality-specific identification of reasons for escape and descent. Building on a rich history of participatory approaches (including Salmen, 1987; Chambers, 1997; Narayan et al., 2000), this methodology is rigorous but relatively simple to apply.

8.4. Subjective Assessments in Relation to Panel Studies

Panel datasets have been used traditionally to examine households' and individuals' movements into and out of poverty. Panel data on households' consumption levels at two different points in time are very helpful for comparing changes in monetary poverty among households. Because they utilize a standardized definition of poverty, it might be thought that they deliver more precise numbers for escape and descent. But these numbers are precise only in the terms of their definition. Other definitions are more valid and precise for other observers; the poor themselves do not use dollar-a-day.

Depending upon the questions that some study is intended to address, different methods are more appropriate and different definitions more useful to follow.[8] Stages of Progress is a preferable method to use in situations where data for a prior period are simply not available, or as is often the case, particularly in developing countries, where available data are hard to access, unclear, or not rigorously obtained. In such situations, a panel dataset might take unbearably long to assemble, and other methodologies, including Stages of Progress, may be preferred.

It is also better to use Stages (or some other method like it) in situations where it is important to identify household-level reasons. With a notable few exceptions, including Sen (2003), panel data studies have not identified reasons for escape and reasons for descent at the household level. In doing so, they have missed out upon households' strategies for dealing with poverty, thereby de-linking the understanding of poverty dynamics from individuals' own efforts.

In order to understand households' strategies it helps to accept the definitions by which these strategies get defined. Adopting a place-bound and local understanding of poverty is better for this purpose.

---

[8] Different understandings of poverty coexist, and whose reality we adopt influences the results that we obtain.People identified as being poor according to standardized monetary measures do not always consider themselves poor in their own terms (Jodha, 1988; Chambers, 1997; Franco and Saith, 2003; Laderchi, Saith, and Stewart, 2003; McGee, 2004).

Third, because Stages is easy to apply, enjoyable in practice,[9] and its logic is intuitively clear, it can help community groups assist with the analyses that are undertaken. Applying this methodology and uncovering the reasons for escape and descent helps to provide the rationale for selecting particular investments over others.

Combining different methods will be important to understand different facets of poverty. New and reliable methods must be developed that can uncover more facets of poverty knowledge (O'Connor, 2001).

8.5. Comparability and Reliability

How reliable are the data from Stages of Progress? Recall can be quite imperfect for an earlier period, and oral evidence may be faulty, incomplete, or deliberately skewed. In order to deal with these possible sources of weakness, several precautions have been built in, many as a result of experience.

To begin with, the methodology retraces *large* steps that are better remembered compared to finer distinctions. Each movement upward along the Stages of Progress represents a significant improvement in material and social status. People remember, for instance, whether their household possessed a motorcycle or a radio set at the time when Kenyatta passed away; they can recall clearly whether they lived in a mud or a brick house while growing up, and whether they could afford to send their children to school. By seeking recall data in terms of these clear, conspicuous, and sizeable referents, the Stages of Progress method adds reliability to recall. Members of particular households remember quite well where they were located along this clearly understood hierarchy of Stages, and these recollections are verified by others who have lived together with them for long periods of time.

One of the risks associated with subjective enquiries—which arises when people think back to some mythical golden age: 'everything was better in the past'—gets limited because communities think in terms of distinct Stages (and not in terms of better or worse). These stages are visible to all in the community, so community members are able to say which households are at each stage and where they were in previous time periods.

---

[9] Wilson Nindo, who has implemented Stages of Progress in more than 40 Kenyan communities, had the following to say when I interviewed him in Nairobi (21 May 2006): 'I like Stages of Progress because this study is never boring. Communities' enthusiasm [for it] keeps your own enthusiasm going...Communities have given you two–three things [names for Stages]. You ask them "OK, which among them comes first?" Doing the stages is the most challenging bit of this methodology. If you are not careful, you'll just be making a list, a wish list, not the Stages of Progress. You ask and probe a bit more. If you don't make them compare, they will just be adding items, not always in a [sequential] flow. If you don't take care, you get confusion. Working with them is important. You work with them to come up with a sequence acceptable to them [not to you].'

Table 8.5. Stages of Progress and asset ownership
(thirty-six communities in Uganda)

Household's stage at the present time	Average number of household assets (out of 10)
1	2.46
2	3.08
3	3.58
4	4.08
5	4.94
6	5.24
7	5.55
8	5.71
9	6.42
10	6.72
11	7.31
12	8.01

Triangulation of all data collected helps to further verify recall. Information about each household is obtained separately at both the community and the household level. Discrepancies, when found, bring forth repeat interviews; community groups and the household verify each other's account.

Corroboration with more 'objective' evidence was found by comparing stages with asset holdings for households. Table 8.5 presents evidence in this regard from the study conducted in thirty-six villages of Uganda (Krishna et al., 2006a). Households were asked about ownership in respect of ten different types of assets, including animals, radios, household furniture, and so on. Table 8.5 shows that a monotonically increasing relationship exists between a household's ownership of assets and the stage at which they were placed.

Communities' gradations and rankings point in the same directions as the grading schemes that 'we' (i.e. the experts and outsiders, in Robert Chambers's sense of the word) would prefer to employ, corresponding to 'our' preferred definitions of poverty. We found in other studies that some other visible characteristics of material status—e.g. housing type and cattle ownership— also align neatly (though hardly perfectly) with a household's position on the Stages of Progress. How well any household is doing in terms of material achievement at the present time is thus reflected quite well by the stage recorded for it in the current period.

But what about stage as recorded for a previous period? Does it also accord quite well with what it actually was at that time?

In order to convert from this hypothetical question to one that could actually be answered using the available evidence, I conducted a study in 2004 in the same group of sixty-one villages in Rajasthan, India, where I had undertaken a previous study seven years before. I found households' Stages

Table 8.6. Stages (as recalled) vs. assets actually possessed seven years ago (sixty-one communities of Rajasthan, India)

Stage in 1997 (as recalled in 2004)	Assets actually possessed in 1997			
	Land (*bighas*)	Large animals	Small animals	Kaccha (mud) house
Very poor (Stage 1–3)	3.6	1.8	2.8	86%
Poor (Stage 4–5)	5.5	2.5	3.7	77%
Middle (Stage 6–8)	8.1	3.1	5.1	51%
Better-off (Stage 9+)	10.6	4.3	3.1	22%

of Progress for 1997 (as recalled in the community meetings of 2004) to be closely correlated with the number of assets possessed by them seven years ago (as recorded in the survey conducted in 1997). Table 8.6 presents these figures.

Objective data from a more distant past are not readily or abundantly available (if they were, we would never have needed to develop any such methodology). I knew of only instance—others may know more—of written records from twenty-five years ago, records which stated, in this instance, the amount of land ownership of every household in some of the villages that we had studied. By checking these land records for an earlier period it is theoretically possible to map stages (as recalled) against landholdings actually possessed twenty-five years ago. In practice, this task is both complicated and arduous. It can also be considerably expensive, especially if it is delegated to someone else who is qualified. Backtracking land ownership records requires manually locating, collating, and compiling diverse handwritten registers, which are most often not available at a single physical location. It also requires matching present-day households with the individuals whose names were recorded in the land registers of twenty-five years ago (and in cases where the household concerned has experienced subdivision, it also requires calculating the share in the prior land holding of the household recorded at the present time). Finding a match with land records for villages studied in Rajasthan was simply not possible given the resources available. Instead, I selected a random sample of feasible size, picking twenty-five households at random from among all those who have fallen into poverty in five villages, also randomly selected, in two districts of Rajasthan. With generous assistance provided by the administration of Udaipur district, land ownership for these twenty-five households was tracked backward over twenty-five years.

This examination of land records showed that of these twenty-five households, all of which suffered descents into poverty, twenty-two households (88 per cent) had simultaneously lost all or part of the land they had owned twenty-five years ago. About half of these households had lost *all* of their lands. The rest had to part with significant chunks of their holdings.[10]

Observing this close match between land records and Stages data helped justify the effort required to obtain this information. But I was not too surprised upon learning of these facts. The villagers whom I had met and interviewed had shared generously of their knowledge, and what I had learned from these discussions, I felt instinctively, was true.

It helped to have local area residents working as the interviewers for these studies. I have learned at my cost not to speak much at these community meetings. Many questions cannot reasonably be asked by outsiders, but speaking about misfortunes with ones who know and can empathize is easier and, as I observed, also cathartic in some cases.

The interface between researcher and respondent is critical for this method to work well. This is why intensive training is built in at the start of every such exercise.

8.6. Limitations and Planned Developments

Some limitations will need to be addressed as this methodology is extended further. Some other limitations will not be easily overcome. I outline below what I currently know about these limitations. I welcome comments and suggestions about dealing with these limitations better and also about other limitations that I may have failed to spot.

First, the methodology needs to deal better with intra-household differences, particularly those based on gender.[11] Second, it will need to be adapted for dealing better with newly formed communities, particularly those located in large urban centres. To some extent, the study undertaken in North Carolina helped develop amendments in the methods appropriate for studying urban areas. Because 'poverty' is less easily discussed publicly here than in the other countries we had studied, and because communities are less stable here, the Stages of Progress methodology needed to be modified for North Carolina. Relatively more reliance was placed upon household interviews. While the stages themselves were ascertained in community meetings, households' rankings and reasons were elicited mostly through household interviews (Krishna et al., 2006c). This procedure helped us to go forward with the process of enquiry, but it compromised to some extent the triangulation

---

[10] The detailed results, not provided here for lack of space, are available on request from the author.

[11] In our 36-village study in Gujarat, we interviewed members of a random sample of 133 female-headed households, finding that 74% have remained poor over twenty-five years, and another 15% have become poor during this time, making a total of almost 90% poor in 2003.

and verification that was possible.[12] Further refinements have been made for an ongoing study in Kenya, where communities in Nairobi and Mombasa are being studied along with several others.

Applying Stages in a community setting helps abate to a considerable extent the danger of stigmatization. By categorizing people as occupying a particular Stage (1–13) or belonging within some particular category (A–D), we have no need to refer to some individual as 'poor' or 'rich'. Tracy Rhoney, an enthusiastic and well-regarded community organizer in Burke County, North Carolina, explained to me in her unforgettable accent: 'Honey, it's almost like asking a woman about her dress size: Are you a five or a four? Are you Stage 5, or are you Stage 4? It's that simple.' She was right in this regard; people who attended these North Carolina community meetings spoke freely about their own positions along the Stages of Progress. They were wary and close-mouthed, however, when someone else's situation was discussed.

Another danger for community-based studies is that of elite capture. In the Stages process, we make clear at the very start of community discussions that no tangible benefits will be given out by us to anybody. This reduces the incentives that people might have to fabricate or distort the facts, but the danger of elite domination is not fully averted nevertheless. We have maintained some balance in the composition of the community group. In India, for instance, we did not commence formal discussion until lower and upper castes were both present. We also learned techniques for rotating community respondents and isolating domineering speakers by taking them aside for separate interviewing. One other part of the Stages process helped to reduce the impact of elite domination: all facts ascertained in the community meeting were separately verified in privately held household interviews. To the extent the fear of elites does not also extend into private spaces, imbalances arising in the community group were ironed out at this point in the study process.

Another potential weakness, common to all longitudinal studies, arises on account of the changing compositions of communities and households. Households twenty or even ten years hence will not be the same as the households of today. Some new households will be set up by young adults, and some others will not be in the same place when a later study is conducted. Because households do not remain the same over time, some simplifying assumptions have to be made in longitudinal studies. Panel data studies consider households in the starting year of the study. They compare these households over time, neglecting all households newly arisen. This neglect does not, however, detract from the purpose of these studies, which is to understand and trace

---

[12] It was comforting to observe that asset ownership continued to be closely related to Stages.

households' trajectories over time. The Stages of Progress method involves an equal though opposite neglect. By considering households at the end of this period, this method neglects all households that have faded away during the period. We have found in a few locations where we enquired about this disappearance that it was undergone by roughly equal numbers of very rich and very poor households, with members of both groups leaving to try their luck in some city. By studying households that exist at the present time, we could elicit, particularly in the case of younger households, the difference between some individual's inherited and acquired status: did a person who was born to poverty remain poor at the end of the period, or did she or he manage to escape from poverty? Is another person who was part of a non-poor household ten years ago still non-poor, or has she, regrettably, fallen into poverty during this time? Compiling these trajectories—of stability and of change—helped us to assess the overall situation of poverty over time. More important, learning about the reasons for change in each individual case helped to identify chains of events associated with escaping or falling into poverty.

It needs to be mentioned that the reasons for escape and descent identified in these studies are all micro-level and proximate, as experienced by households and individuals. More distant and macro-level reasons operating on account of national policies and international economic conditions are not directly identified using the Stages of Progress methodology; thus combining these micro-level analyses together with macro-level examination of policies and structures will help fill out a more complete picture. It would be useful to undertake such a synthetic micro–macro study.

It would also be interesting to undertake a study that combines monetary measures of poverty together with community-based ones. In future work I intend to undertake such comparisons. It would be useful to consider the extent to which these different measures—and perhaps also a third one, based on an asset-ownership index—offer the same or a different identification of poverty.

No single method is ever adequate, I feel, for studying poverty in all its complexities and dimensions. Different combinations of methods work better for different ends. Which method or methods one elects to adopt must be guided by the nature of questions that are addressed. For instance, Stages is not useful for making cross-country (and in some cases, even cross-regional) comparisons. Because somewhat different poverty lines are identified in different countries, cross-country comparisons are not precise using this method.[13]

Stages of Progress is also not very useful for looking at dimensions of poverty other than material ones. Communities' rankings of households are enquired

---

[13] Although, according to Reddy and Pogge (2002) and Wade (2004), comparability problems are also severe when some standardized metric is used.

after in terms related to *material* poverty. Other dimensions of poverty, including social exclusion and political disempowerment, are not reflected within these assessments.

Combinations of methods for studying poverty will be required to fill important gaps in poverty knowledge. Different methods are variously suited for studying different facets. No one true method or definition of poverty exists or can exist. Adopting a problem-solving approach is better than striving for purity of technique.

References

Barrett, C., and Clay, D. (2003), 'How Accurate is Food-for-Work Self-Targeting in the Presence of Imperfect Factor Markets? Evidence from Ethiopia', *Journal of Development Studies*, 39(5): 152–80.

—— and Maxwell, D. (2005), *Food Aid after Fifty Years: Recasting its Role*, New York: Routledge.

—— Reardon, T., and Webb, P. (2001), 'Non-Farm Diversification and Household Livelihood Strategies in Rural Africa: Concepts, Dynamics, and Policy Implications', *Food Policy*, 26: 315–31.

Carter, M., and Barrett, C. (2006), 'The Economics of Poverty Traps and Persistent Poverty: An Asset-Based Approach', *Journal of Development Studies*, 42(2): 178–99.

Chambers, R. (1988), 'Poverty in India: Concepts, Research and Reality', Discussion Paper 241, Brighton: Institute of Development Studies.

—— (1997), *Whose Reality Counts? Putting the First Last*, London: Intermediary Technology Publications.

Franco, S., and Saith, R. (2003), 'Different Conceptions of Poverty: An Empirical Investigation and Policy Implications', available at <www.wider.unu.edu/conference/conference-2003-2/conference%202003-2-papers/papers-pdf/Franco%20270503.pdf>.

Hulme, D., and Shepherd, A. (2003), 'Conceptualizing Chronic Poverty', *World Development*, 31(3): 403–24.

Jodha, N. (1988), 'Poverty Debate in India: A Minority View', *Economic and Political Weekly*, November: 2421–8.

Krishna, A. (2003), 'Falling into Poverty: The Other Side of Poverty Reduction', *Economic and Political Weekly* (Bombay), 8 February.

—— (2004), 'Escaping Poverty and Becoming Poor: Who Gains, Who Loses, and Why?', *World Development*, 32(1): 121–36.

—— (2006). 'Pathways out of and into Poverty in 36 Villages of Andhra Pradesh, India', *World Development*, 34(2): 271–88.

—— Kristjanson, P., Radeny, M., and Nindo, W. (2004), 'Escaping Poverty and Becoming Poor in 20 Kenyan Villages', *Journal of Human Development*, 5(2): 211–26.

—— Kapila, M., Porwal, M., and Singh, V. (2005), 'Why Growth is not Enough: Household Poverty Dynamics in Northeast Gujarat, India', *Journal of Development Studies*, 41(7): 1163–92.

——Lumonya, D., Markiewicz, M., Mugumya, F., Kafuko, A., and Wegoye, J. (2006a), 'Escaping Poverty and Becoming Poor in 36 Villages of Central and Western Uganda', Journal of Development Studies, 42(2): 346–70.

——Kristjanson, P., Kuan, J., Quilca, G., Radeny, M., and Sanchez-Urrelo, A. (2006b), 'Fixing the Hole in the Bucket: Household Poverty Dynamics in Forty Communities of the Peruvian Andes', Development and Change, 37(5): 997–1021.

——Gibson-Davis, C., Clasen, L., Markiewicz, M., and Perez, N. (2006c), 'Escaping Poverty and Becoming Poor in Thirteen Communities of Rural North Carolina', working paper, Sanford Institute of Public Policy, Duke University. Available at <www.pubpol.duke.edu/krishna>.

Laderchi, C., Saith, R., and Stewart, F. (2003), 'Does it Matter that We Don't Agree on the Definition of Poverty? A Comparison of Four Approaches', Queen Elizabeth House (QEH) Working Paper Series 107, Oxford: QEH.

McGee, R. (2004), 'Constructing Poverty Trends in Uganda: A Multidisciplinary Perspective', Development and Change, 35(3): 499–523.

Mellor, J. W. (1999), 'Pro-Poor Growth: The Relation between Growth in Agriculture and Poverty Reduction', report prepared for USAID, Washington.

Narayan, D., Patel, R., Schafft, K., Rademacher, A., and Koch-Schulte, S. (2000), Voices of the Poor: Can Anyone Hear Us?, New York: Oxford University Press.

O'Connor, A. (2001), Poverty Knowledge: Social Science, Social Policy, and the Poor in 20th Century U.S. History, Princeton: Princeton University Press.

Ravallion, M., and Datt, G. (1996), 'How Important to India's Poor is the Sectoral Composition of Economic Growth?', World Bank Economic Review, 10(1): 1–25.

Reddy, S., and Pogge, T. W. (2002), 'How Not To Count the Poor', <www.socialanalysis.org>.

Salmen, L. (1987), Listen to the People: Participant–Observer Evaluation of Development Projects, New York: Oxford University Press.

Sen, B. (2003), 'Drivers of Escape and Descent: Changing Household Fortunes in Rural Bangladesh', World Development, 31(3): 513–34.

Timmer, P. C. (1997), 'How Well do the Poor Connect to the Growth Process?', CAER Discussion Paper No. 178, Cambridge, Mass.: Harvard Institute for International Development.

Van Schendel, W. (1981), Peasant Mobility: The Odds of Life in Rural Bangladesh, Assen: Van Gorcum.

Wade, R. H. (2004), 'Is Globalization Reducing Poverty and Inequality?', World Development, 32(4): 567–89.

Walker, T. S., and Ryan, J. G. (1990), Village and Household Economies in India's Semi-Arid Tropics, Baltimore: Johns Hopkins University Press.

Part III

Explanatory Frameworks for Understanding Poverty Dynamics

Part III

Explanatory Frameworks for
Understanding Poverty Dynamics

9

Bringing Politics Back into Poverty Analysis

Why Understanding of Social Relations Matters More for Policy on Chronic Poverty than Measurement

John Harriss

Poverty becomes what has been measured and is available for analysis.

(Robert Chambers)

[It is] a matter of a knowledge base that, however unintentionally, has opened itself to conservative interpretation by locating the crux of the poverty problem in the characteristics of the poor.

(Alice O'Connor)

9.1. Reconceptualizing Poverty: The Story so Far

My first epigraph comes from a paper written by Robert Chambers for the World Bank in Delhi twenty years ago, with the title 'Poverty in India: Concepts, Research and Reality' (Chambers, 1988), which contributed to rethinking on the concept and the nature of poverty in the 1990s (shown up in the differences between *WDR 1990* and *WDR 2000*). Chambers argued that there are two possible starting points for understanding poverty and ways of reducing it: with the perceptions of professionals—social scientists and development practitioners—or with the perceptions of poor people themselves. His paper compares these two sets of perceptions. The professionals define poverty in terms of deprivation and 'the poor' are those who are in various ways deprived. But in practice the professionals have concerned themselves with those aspects of deprivation that are most readily measured— flows of income or consumption—and a huge amount of intellectual energy and resources has gone, and continues to go, into poverty research which is concerned with refining these measures (involving a chain of assumptions). But as Chambers says, the poverty line—which is what so much research has been about defining—is not concerned with wealth or material possessions, nor with aspects of deprivation relating to access to water, shelter, health services, education, or transport, nor with debt, dependence, isolation, migration, vulnerability, powerlessness, physical weakness or disability, high mortality, or short life expectancy; nor with social disadvantage, status, or self-respect (1988, p. 3). Many possible aspects of deprivation are left out of conventional poverty measurement, therefore—and thus it was that Chambers argued that poverty has come to be equated with what can most readily be measured. When it comes to action too, he thought, professionals also tend to focus on poverty defined in terms of lack of income, and perhaps physical weakness and isolation, rather than on those aspects of poverty that have to do with vulnerability and powerlessness, perhaps because 'Members of elite groups...find [these] less threatening aspects of deprivation to measure and tackle' (1992, p. 10).

Chambers contrasts this 'professional' way of thinking about poverty with the concepts of the poor themselves, as these have been interpreted ethnographically. He shows that if 'we' (professional outsiders) take account of poor people's own concepts and concerns then we should give much greater weight to qualitative social and psychological aspects of well-being. He summed up by arguing that we should think about poverty in terms of different dimensions that are all relevant to poor people themselves. Incomes and consumption do matter (he labels this dimension 'survival'), but so do net assets and security[1] (labelled 'security'), and beyond even security there is the dimension of independence and self-respect ('self-respect').

These arguments contributed to recognition of the multidimensional character of poverty, and of not allowing it to be understood simply in terms of the flows that are most easily measured. They also helped to bring much more sharply into focus the importance of taking account of the perceptions and understandings of poor people themselves—recognition of which led in the next decade to that major programme of participatory research undertaken by the World Bank that gave rise in the end to celebrated publications on the 'Voices of the Poor'. These adumbrated parts of Chambers's original argument—reflected in the list of chapters that discuss the ten dimensions of powerlessness and ill-being that emerged from the study, and in the summing up 'call to action' in the volume *Crying out for Change* (Narayan et al.,

---

[1] At about the same time that Chambers was writing, analyses of the ways in which people respond to the stress of drought and famine showed, of course, that in these circumstances they may choose to forgo consumption in order to maintain assets, striving to balance out immediate survival and longer-run security: see e.g. de Waal (1989).

2000). The chapter headings in the book recall Chambers's earlier listing of different dimensions of deprivation or poverty (quoted above) rather closely. The results of the 'Voices' research, however, display the same features that characterize the literature on the measurement of poverty: causes and effects are muddled up, and the characteristics of individuals, or of households, that are associated/correlated with poverty are represented as causal. There is no analysis of the structures and relationships that give rise to the effects that are taken to define poverty.

This is also the principal limitation of Chambers's analysis of the conceptualization of poverty, and of poverty research: in his account of it poverty remains a characteristic of individuals or of households (it is individuals or households that lack incomes, security, and self-respect) and the effects of poverty are sometimes represented as causes. Still, his paper does show that 'poverty' is a construct, and that it is construed in different ways by different actors; he does begin to recognize that these constructions are profoundly political—in the passing remark about those ideas of poverty that maybe suit the interests of elites; and there is more than a suggestion there that conventional poverty analysis rests on a mistaken view of 'science' that elevates measurement and disregards contextualization. The last is a point to which I return later in this chapter. The other points that I have raised here have been taken up by several other writers in the more recent literature of poverty, perhaps notably by Maia Green and David Hulme (Green, 2005; Green and Hulme, 2005). The core of their arguments is that through the way in which it is conceptualized in mainstream research, poverty is not seen as the consequence of social relations or of the categories through which people classify and act upon the social world. Notably the way in which poverty is conceptualized separates it from the social processes of the accumulation and distribution of wealth, which depoliticizes it—and depoliticization is of course a profoundly political intellectual act. Poverty is then treated as a kind of social aberration rather than as an aspect of the ways in which the modern state and a market society function.

What has been going on in mainstream poverty research in the time since Chambers wrote his seminal critique? How much has research been changed by the changing ideas that Chambers's paper exemplifies? In practice, though there has been more exploration of alternative approaches, a great deal of intellectual effort has continued to be expended on poverty measurement, and on the related analysis of 'poverty dynamics' by comparison of the characteristics of individuals or households that have remained poor (in the sense of being below the conventionally defined poverty line) over time, or that have moved into or out of poverty. The focus of poverty research in the World Bank, for notable instance, remains—according to the information given on the Bank's website—on measurement, relying still on the headcount measure, and based on nationally representative income and/or expenditure surveys. There is also work going on dealing with risk and vulnerability, and aspects of social exclusion, but it appears to be somewhat peripheral to the main thrusts of World Bank poverty research.

Another vein in recent research that departs significantly from the main-stream work of World Bank researchers is that of the asset-based approach developed by Christopher Barrett, Michael Carter, and their associates (see the special issue of the *Journal of Development Studies*, February 2006). This is based on the persuasive view that

flow measures tend to be more subject to considerable measurement error than stock variables, even in well-run surveys, because they can only rarely be directly observed and verified. Moreover, productive assets are the durable inputs used to generate income . . . Understanding the dynamics of assets is thus fundamental to understanding persistent poverty and longer-term socio-economic dynamics.

(Barrett, Carter, and Little, 2006, p. 169)

The asset-based approach—which in fact recalls in some respects work done in the 1970s on differentiation and class formation in agrarian economies (a point discussed later)—has come up with impressive results, drawing on longitudinal data of both qualitative and quantitative kinds,[2] that show up the factors influencing movements into and out of poverty and highlight the existence of poverty traps. The possession of assets, whether of land, labour, livestock, human, or social capital, greatly influences the capacities of individuals and households to withstand shocks, such as drought or—as is shown very often to be of particular significance—episodes of ill health (reflecting the fact of the particular dependence of the very poor on their own bodies). Greater attention is paid in this work to structural determinants of poverty but it is a moot point whether it has much to say about 'the dynamics of those underlying structural positions'—as Barrett, Carter, and Little claim in their introduction to the special issue (2006, p. 169)—as opposed to treating precipitating causes of movements into or out of persistent poverty.

I will come back to the asset-based approach later in this chapter but turn now to examine two country cases in which a lot of effort has gone into poverty analysis on the lines suggested by the World Bank poverty research programme: Vietnam and India. I aim to point up difficulties that derive from the model of knowledge that underlies the poverty research industry.

---

[2] The way in which this work has sought very deliberately to build links between quantitative and qualitative research in the way suggested in the *Conversations between Economists and Anthropologists*, orchestrated by Pranab Bardhan (1989), is very welcome, though in some cases the use of qualitative cases studies is only to provide descriptive support to arguments drawn from quantitative analysis.

9.2. Questioning the Mainstream Model of Poverty Knowledge

Vietnam is widely regarded as a success story of economic liberalization (see, for instance, *The Economist*, 5–11 August 2006). Economic reform and integration into the global economy are held to have brought about growth that has been remarkably pro-poor (Klump and Bonschab, 2004). Indeed, according to data from the Vietnam Household Living Standards Surveys (VHLSS) poverty fell by one-third between 2002 and 2004, which scarcely seems credible. The Vietnam story depends on analysis of the Vietnam Living Standards Surveys of 1992–3 and 1997–8, and then of the two rounds of the VHLSS. Though sample designs and sample sizes in these surveys have changed they are held to provide comparable results and they are widely used and widely respected. Yet Pincus and Sender (2006) have recently shown that there are serious problems with the design of these surveys that are likely to have resulted in underestimation of the total numbers of very poor people in Vietnam. These authors do not deny that rapid growth in Vietnam has improved living standards for many, but they show that there are strong grounds for believing that there are many more very poor people in the country than are represented in the surveys on which poverty measurements are based. It is particularly those who migrate for wage work who are likely to have been missed, and Pincus and Sender argue that 'the failure to capture migrants in surveys that aim to measure living standards in a rapidly urbanising country in which the structure of the labour force is experiencing profound change leads to questions concerning the *intent*, representativeness and accuracy of the surveys' (2006, p. 7, emphasis added). Migrants are excluded because the sampling frame consists only of the official lists of registered households in communes and urban wards of Vietnam, who must have lived in the enumeration area for at least six months. The problem is compounded by the fact that these lists of registered households are anyway often outdated. The resulting exclusion of mobile people reflects the precarious legal position of migrants in Vietnam where the *ho khau* system of registration of households, designed to control migration to cities, makes it difficult for people to migrate legally. The two authors show by means of comparison of VHLSS data with the evidence of surveys conducted by the Statistics Office of Ho Chi Minh City that the former excludes quite large numbers of young migrants; and that VHLSS population estimates and census figures don't match up, especially for those aged 20–9. Yet in an experimental survey conducted in rural areas of Hanoi and four neighbouring provinces Pincus and Sender found that they were able easily to identify relatively large numbers of 'illegal' migrants, in spite of the blocking tactics in some cases of local administrators, and they show that such migrants—not all of whom, by any means, are poor—have very diverse characteristics. The survey still makes it clear that 'large numbers of desperately poor people are living in geographical areas that conventional analysis has classified as "non-poor" ', and that 'It seems likely that VHLSS has mis-estimated poverty by excluding a large number of very poor and vulnerable households' (2006, p. 40). Pincus and Sender further make the point that it is difficult to square claims from the living standards surveys regarding the rapid decrease in the incidence of income poverty with anthropometric data or with data on child malnutrition.

Analysis of the 'determinants' of poverty in Vietnam, based on the living standards surveys—it is rather analysis of the characteristics of those who are shown as still being poor—highlights geographical factors (Klump and Bonschab, 2004, for example, refer to emerging regional imbalances in Vietnam), and those of household size, ethnicity, and educational attainment (the 'usual suspects'); and this analysis has led through to policy recommendations in the *Comprehensive Poverty Reduction and Growth Strategy* that is Vietnam's PRSP. Poverty reduction is expected to be driven in future by private sector development, especially of household enterprises; and it will be assisted by better targeting to ensure that poor people get access to basic services, by the provision of infrastructure for poor and remote communes, and by giving ethnic minorities greater voice in the design of anti-poverty programmes. Pincus and Sender argue that what is striking about these 'standard policy recommendations' is what is omitted. The emphasis is on household enterprise, when

Studies from a range of developing countries show that the most secure route out of poverty for the majority of the poor is access to regular waged employment [the argument is spelled out in Sender, 2003; but the point is also made in a recent study of poverty reduction in Bangladesh, in which it is argued that it has been waged employment in the rural non-farm sector rather than self-employment that has been associated with poverty reduction: Sen et al., 2004]. Although the standard recommendations cite job creation as a major objective, no attempt is made to account for labour market dynamics, the determinants of the growth of unskilled wage employment and real wages. (2006, p. 22)

It is very odd indeed, as Pincus and Sender say, that in a country like Vietnam where so much emphasis is placed on urbanization and the development of labour-intensive industries, poverty rates should be calculated based on data 'that systematically exclude migrants to cities and industrial areas' (2006, p. 41). It is not that the significance of migration has not previously been recognized (it is discussed for instance by Klump and Bonschab, 2004), and the two authors argue that 'It is inexcusable that the poverty analyses for Vietnam should make no reference to the fact that the VHLSS sample is limited to long-term, legally registered households' (2006, p. 41). It is for this reason that they see deliberate *intent* on the part of poverty analysts in the World Bank and the government to paint a particular picture of poverty reduction in the country.

This may be going too far, but it is easy to understand how one narrative of change, attractive to those persuaded by theoretical arguments in favour of particular policies, comes to drive the construction and interpretation of data.

Just how politically charged the apparently scientific task of counting the poor can become is shown up very starkly in what Deaton and Kozel (2004) refer to as 'the Great Indian Poverty Debate'. This is the debate over the impact of India's liberalizing economic reforms, initiated in 1991, on the incidence of poverty. Different perceptions have become highly politicized in circumstances in which the gap in terms of the measure of average consumption derived from the National Accounts, on the one hand, and from the results, on the other, of the regular household income and expenditure surveys run by the National Sample Survey Organization has grown wider, and the reporting periods used in the sample surveys for different categories of consumption have been changed. One set of changes in reporting periods in an experiment conducted by the NSSO increased estimates of per capita incomes by 15–18 per cent, thus halving the numbers of the poor. Those who are supportive of the economic reforms prefer one interpretation of inconsistent datasets, while the critics of reform prefer another. Deaton and others have attempted a considered reconciliation of the data, but the debate as a whole shows just how sensitive measures of poverty are to statistical problems and the different ways in which these problems are addressed. It also exemplifies Chambers's point that 'poverty becomes what has been measured'. Even if there were not the particular technical problems that have arisen because of changes in the design of the sample surveys in the 1990s, so that successive rounds of the NSS are not easily compared with each other, it would still be the case that the measurement of trends in the incidence of poverty is highly sensitive to judgements made in a whole string of assumptions.

What puzzles many observers of Indian development is what the economic processes are that can have brought about the kind of reduction in income poverty that is claimed by some. How can it be that poverty has declined as much as some maintain when, as is widely recognized, India has been experiencing high rates of growth but without the creation of many regular jobs—'jobless growth', as it is described—and when the agricultural economy over much of the country is reasonably understood as being in a state of crisis? The problem is brought out in studies of employment and poverty trends in the city of Ahmedabad, once known as 'the Manchester of India'. In the last twenty years of the last century as many as 100,000 'good jobs' were lost in the cotton textile industry, and there has been extensive casualization of employment—as has happened very widely. Ethnographic research shows that in these circumstances households have very often become more dependent upon women's work for their survival. This has posed a serious threat to the dignity and the self-esteem of men, who have reacted in ways that may have harmful social and political consequences (an important theme that I cannot pursue here). There are scholars, however, who argue that the evidence from Ahmedabad shows that the policy of flexibilizing labour markets—which leads to casualization of labour—is working, because there has been (in the 1990s) substantial growth in employment, a rise in the level of real wages, and greater participation of both men and women in the labour process. Such positive conclusions from the analysis of National Sample Survey data (by the Deshpandes, by Dutta and Batley, and by Kundu) conflict with those from the ethnographic research of Jan Breman (2001). This shows that the increased vulnerability of households has led to the greater involvement of dependent members of families, both women and children, in work, and that while workers may have 'regular' jobs in the dynamic sectors of the urban economy such as power loom units, diamond ateliers, and garment workshops, they can be dismissed at any time and do not enjoy the social provisions that have historically accompanied 'formal sector' employment. Breman further points out, on the basis of survey evidence, that underemployment and low pay are extensive and that the percentage of the population living in slum areas almost doubled between 1981 and 1996–7. These differing views of what is going on in Ahmedabad reflect precisely the point made by Kanbur in his comparable observations of the radical differences that exist in perceptions of poverty trends in Ghana (2002): both the 'optimists' and the 'pessimists' can in a sense be 'right' because they are looking at different things. The optimists may be right. Employment in Ahmedabad may have increased. But what about the quality of that employment, asks Breman? If more people's livelihoods are more vulnerable, doesn't this connote deterioration in levels of well-being, even if real wages have risen? Doesn't it mean that they are more likely to enter into relations of dependence on particular patrons, with negative implications for their self-respect and psychological well-being?

9.3. Going against 'Normal Science' and Making Social Science Matter

Reflection upon these examples of the kinds of difficulties that arise in poverty measurement—difficulties that are ontological as well as practical problems of methodology—points to the underlying problem with the whole model of knowledge on which conventional poverty analysis rests. It is the model of what we may call 'normal science' which aims at developing explanatory and predictive theory of universal application, based on generalization from empirical observation. This is a model that has worked well in the natural sciences which have been characterized by the cumulation of knowledge as well as by shifting paradigms. It is quite clear, I believe, that the social sciences have not done nearly so well as the natural sciences in developing explanatory and predictive theory of universal application (there are few lawlike generalizations that can be made about human behaviour). Neither have they done very well in cumulating knowledge, while they are characterized—as Bent Flyvberg has put it—not so much by paradigm shifts as by style changes: 'it is not a case of evolution [in the social sciences] but more of fashion' (Flyvberg, 2001, p. 30). And there are powerful reasons for this difference which have to do essentially with the nature of the phenomena with which social scientists deal—the actions/behaviour of self-reflecting human beings— while the background conditions of the natural sciences are physical facts. In social science the object of analysis is a subject, whereas the objects of research in the natural sciences don't talk back. Of course studies of science have shown that there is no radical distinction between the natural and the social sciences,[3] and hermeneutics is now recognized as applying to natural science too—but it can still be demonstrated that the natural sciences are relatively cumulative and predictive, and the social sciences not. This has been a source of considerable anxiety for many social scientists—reflected in my own experience, in regard to poverty research, in the 'Conversations between anthropologists and economists' set up by Pranab Bardhan (Bardhan, 1989). In these conversations some argued tenaciously that it must be possible to establish 'the facts' about poverty and to develop predictive theory of universal application, whereas others (not all of them anthropologists) argued that knowledge about poverty must always be context dependent. Now there is even greater fear amongst many social scientists of a descent to relativism, which the currents of postmodernism over the last two decades have served to intensify.

Flyvberg's argument in *Making Social Science Matter: Why Social Inquiry Fails and How it can Succeed again* (2001) is that social scientists set themselves an impossible task in seeking to emulate the natural sciences. The crux of the difficulty for the social sciences is that human beings are 'skilful'—referring essentially to the ability of human beings to make judgements, and change their ways of thinking and of behaving. Human skills go well beyond following rules; they are context dependent. The kind of theory that is developed in 'normal science', on the other hand, depends on freedom from context and the existence of rules (see Flyvberg's summary of his arguments, 2001, p. 47). The social sciences, however, have distinctive strengths in areas where

[3] This is brought out eloquently in Stephen Jay Gould's history of geology in *Time's Arrow, Time's Cycle* (1987), which shows how archetypal differences between scholars in terms of their conceptions of time and history led to very different theories about the 'facts' of geology.

the natural sciences are weak—precisely in dealing with reflexive analysis and discussion of values and interests. Such analysis is necessarily context dependent; but recognizing the centrality of context does not mean descending into relativism.

Flyvberg's aim is 'to help to restore social science to its classical position [based on Aristotelian concepts] as a practical intellectual activity aimed at clarifying the problems, risks and possibilities we face as humans and societies, and at contributing to social and political praxis' (2001, p. 4). On the face of it this is probably not a radically different ambition from that of those like the poverty measurers who seek to pursue social-science-as-normal-science. But the latter work with a model of knowledge which implies that scientific analysis can establish, for example, whether or not policy changes in India in the 1990s have led to a reduction in poverty, and that policy making can be an exercise in rational problem solving. Flyvberg's view, however, of what sort of knowledge is possible about people and societies is that it is interpretative, and dialogical. In social-science-as-normal-science the key task is taken to be the making of deductions and discovering of general principles across large samples, and detailed case study research is often regarded as unproductive (as it was by some of the economists at the 'Conversations' conference to which I referred earlier). If we recognize the context dependence of human action, however, then the kind of concrete, context-dependent knowledge that may be derived from careful case study research is seen as being 'more valuable than the vain search for predictive theories and universals' (Flyvberg, 2001, p. 72). Interestingly, a very similar conclusion is reached by two economists in a recent review of theory and of empirical research on economic growth. Kenny and Williams argue that 'the social world is more causally complex than the natural world' and that 'events rarely, if ever, have a single cause, but are rather the result of a conjuncture of several factors or conditions [so particular historical analysis is essential]' (2001, p. 13); and they conclude that 'more energy should be directed toward understanding the complex and varied inner workings of actual economies rather than trying to assimilate them into abstract universal models' (2001, p. 16).

The approach to research that Flyvberg advocates, therefore, is to address real-world problems of particular societies, probably using a case study methodology, in an interactive and engaged way (not to be equated, however, with 'action research') and to be ready to use a good deal of bricolage in drawing on the work of other professional social scientists—doing 'what works' to address the key underlying questions: (i) where are we going?; (ii) who gains, and who loses, by what mechanisms of power?; (iii) is this desirable?; (iv) what should be done? Let me come back to this approach later in this chapter when I outline a different approach to poverty research from the currently prevalent fashion.

9.4. Poverty Research and the 'Anti-politics Machine'

There are very strong similarities between the history of poverty research and (less clearly so, perhaps) policy practice in the context of international development, and that of 'poverty knowledge' in the United States, as this has been analysed by Alice O'Connor (2001)—and I find it quite striking that O'Connor's suggestions about 'what is to be done' in poverty research are closely comparable with Flyvberg's general propositions for 'making social science matter'. O'Connor's argument starts with the observations that 'The idea that scientific knowledge holds the key to solving social problems has long been an article of faith in American liberalism [and that] Nowhere is this more apparent than when it comes to solving the "poverty problem"' (2001, p. 3). As I have suggested earlier, the international poverty research industry, too, rests on the same article of faith—that scientific knowledge holds the key to solving the poverty problem. O'Connor shows that although early work on poverty in the United States linked it with unemployment, low wages, labour exploitation, and political disenfranchisement—'and more generally [with] the social disruptions associated with large-scale urbanization and industrial capitalism' (2001, p. 18) (note the similarity to Pincus and Sender's arguments about contemporary Vietnam)—it was quite soon turned away from these matters of political economy. Latterly this has been associated with the influence of research foundations and government agencies, which have provided large amounts of funding for poverty research, and have been able to set the agenda. They have required that research should be 'policy relevant', 'scientific', and free from ideology—but in all the work that they have financed poverty has never been defined as anything other than an *individual* condition. Poverty knowledge rests on an ethos of scientific neutrality, but it is very clearly distinguished by what it is not:

[C]ontemporary poverty knowledge does not define itself as an enquiry into the political economy and culture of late Twentieth Century capitalism; it is knowledge about the characteristics and behaviour, and, especially in recent years, about the welfare status of the poor. Nor does it much countenance knowledge honed in direct action or everyday experience . . . [which] kind of knowledge does not translate into measurable variables that are the common currency of 'objective', 'scientific' and hence authoritative poverty research. (2001, p. 4)

The technically very sophisticated survey research on poverty that has been carried on has by now built up a very accurate statistical portrait of poverty in America, but the results of the interactions between politicians and policy makers, research foundations, and researchers have been to ensure that poverty is seen as the failure of individuals or of the welfare system 'rather than of an economy in which middle- and working-class as well as officially poor Americans faced diminishing opportunities' (2001, p. 241).

Very similar features characterize poverty knowledge in the international context as well. Here too early studies of poverty—such as Dadabhai Naoroji's *Poverty and Un-British Rule in India* (1901) which sought explanation for endemic poverty in India in the political economy of colonialism—were concerned with the structural conditions that caused the effects of poverty, but the poverty research industry that became established in the 1970s has turned to analysis primarily of the characteristics of the poor and of the correlates of poverty. Studies of the causes of poverty, or latterly of 'poverty dynamics', establish correlations between the characteristics of individuals and households and poverty—generally understood in terms of flows of consumption. Such studies have tended to highlight much the same broad set of factors: features of households (high dependency ratios; female headship; ill health of members); assets (holding few productive assets); education (illiteracy); nature of occupations (lack of regular waged employment amongst household members whether resident or working elsewhere); sometimes factors having to do with ethnicity and/or geography (e.g. being a 'tribal'/indigenous person in a remote area)—and the significance of crises or of other idiosyncratic factors which in turn highlights the general problem of the lack of insurance. What international poverty research has *not* done very much has been to explain how and why these factors have the effects they do, in the context of an analysis of the political economy of the locality and of the state. Poverty research does not usually address the processes of accumulation in contemporary capitalism and evades the problems of the distribution of economic resources and of political power, apparently offering technical solutions to the problem in a way that is not threatening to the elites who benefit from existing structures and relationships. The current mantra about the role of 'private business' in growth and—it is hoped—in 'pro-poor growth' and the achievement of the Millennium Development Goals is only one, particularly egregious instance of how language matters. International poverty research, too, aims to be 'objective' and 'scientific' and—Chambers's paper and the later 'Voices of the Poor' work notwithstanding—has not much countenanced knowledge deriving from direct action or everyday experience. Just as it is striking that in the United States the problems of the poor have not been connected with the economics of rising inequality but rather have been 'centred squarely on issues framed as "family values"' (O'Connor, 2001, p. 10), so it is striking that in Vietnam, for instance, contemporary poverty knowledge should ignore the everyday experience which teaches that the industrializing, urbanizing economy draws in large numbers of migrant workers who are likely to be missed out in a sampling frame drawn from lists of only registered households. As O'Connor says in the second of the epigraphs to this chapter, poverty knowledge in the United States has opened itself to conservative interpretation. Poverty knowledge in the international context, too, opens itself to conservative interpretation, at least in the sense that by reducing the problem of poverty to the characteristics of individuals, abstracted from class and other power relationships—note the language of 'private business' rather than of 'capitalism'—it has the effect of depoliticizing it. The poverty research industry constitutes a part of what James Ferguson (1990) memorably described as 'the anti-politics machine'.

Alice O'Connor concludes her history of poverty knowledge in the United States by arguing that this knowledge needs to be reconstructed, and she suggests five important steps towards this reconstruction:

1. Shifting from explanation of individual deprivation to explanation of inequalities in the distribution of power, wealth, and opportunity;
2. Recognizing that studying poverty is not to be equated with 'studying the poor';
3. Getting away from the research industry model;
4. Challenging the privilege attached to hypothesis-testing models of enquiry;
5. Recognizing that the ideas of value-free social science and of finding scientific 'cures' for social problems are chimeras.

The last three of these points correspond very closely with Flyvberg's general critique of the attempt to establish social-science-as-normal-science, and all are entirely apposite in the case of international poverty research. Very significant amounts of money and of intellectual resources continue to be poured into surveys like the Vietnam Household Living Standards Survey, for the production of poverty headcounts based on detailed expenditure surveys that are prone to enormous errors—think, for instance of the impact on poverty estimates for India of changing reporting periods. To what end? They can never provide definitive answers to a question like 'what has been the impact on well-being/ill-being of liberalizing economic reforms?', and they actually provide very little information on the causes of poverty. Insofar as it is important to monitor trends in income and its distribution then there may be simpler and cheaper methods, such as collecting visually confirmed data on the consumer durables owned by households, or collecting information on the education of all household members. There is a growing body of research showing that the ranking of households by these means is not significantly different from that obtained by collecting information on household income per capita (work by Filmer and Pritchett, 1998; Sahn and Stifel, 2000; Stifel and Christiaensen, 2006; all cited by Pincus and Sender, 2006). And how many more studies are needed to test hypotheses on poverty dynamics using data obtained from living standards surveys? Such studies have often tended to confirm what Pincus and Sender reasonably describe as more or less 'standard' policy recommendations deriving from demographic and geographic explanations that downplay the role of class formation and factors such as gender discrimination in the labour market.

9.5. Refocusing Poverty Research

Rather than devoting international poverty research to the refinement of measurement (in the way that happened years before in poverty research in the United States) and to hypothesis testing aimed at establishing predictive theory, it will be more productive to redirect research so as give greater attention to the analysis of the social processes, structures, and relationships that give rise to poverty—recognizing that the creation and re-creation of poverty is inherent within the dynamics of capitalism (Harriss-White, 2006). Such research will often be based on strategically selected case studies, in which researchers build up familiarity with social practice in particular contexts (as Hulme and Shepherd suggest is likely to be necessary in analysing chronic/persistent poverty: 2003)—and desirably will help people themselves to question the relations of knowledge and power that give rise to poverty (though it is clearly essential in this case that this is done responsibly so that poor people are not left to be victims of reprisals at the hands of the power holders).

Within current poverty research some of the most interesting work is that around the assets-based approach. It is quite striking, however, that this recalls in significant respects a much earlier vein of research on differentiation and class formation in rural societies. Assets researchers construct indices of assets and then identify thresholds—such as the 'asset poverty line' used by Adato, Carter, and May, 'defined as the level of assets needed to generate an expected living standard equal to the poverty line' (Adato, Carter, and May, 2006, p. 230). This is similar to the procedure adopted by scholars who sought to study peasant differentiation (see for example Harriss, 1982a). Recent work, encouraged by development agencies, on 'livelihood diversification' is also anticipated in the differentiation literature—which was concerned with the portfolios of livelihood activities of peasants in different presumptive classes, and drew attention to the importance of rural non-farm activity at an early stage (see e.g. Harriss, 1985; Bhaduri et al., 1986). Indeed, the analysis of processes of differentiation in rural societies in some respects went beyond the livelihoods approach that has found such favour with development agencies. The latter 'is less (well) able to grasp the external influences on [the] disparate components ["of income that rural people have to pull together in order to make a living of sorts" and] the extent to which rural dwellers are embedded in regional and transnational economies' (Green and Hulme, 2005, p. 868). Precisely these 'external influences' are brought into the analysis of the

reproduction of households in the context of the development of capitalism—
for example by Deere and de Janvry (1979).

The point of drawing attention to the ways in which some aspects of contemporary poverty analysis are anticipated in this older literature is because
this literature has certain strengths that are less apparent in contemporary
assets-based approaches. These do help to identify structural determinants of
poverty and they are 'dynamic' insofar as they show how households move
in and out of poverty. But their dynamic analysis remains quite descriptive,
and though they are sometimes concerned with social relationships (as in
the work on social capital and social exclusion by Adato, Carter, and May,
2006), they do not address questions of political economy, nor do very much
to link up local patterns with wider processes of capitalist accumulation (see
also Green and Hulme, 2005, p. 9 of web copy). This is attempted in the
older literature on the political economy of agrarian change. For instance,
the work on African rural economies of Henry Bernstein and others shows
how places for petty commodity production are continually destroyed and
re-created with the development of capitalism, and his analysis of the 'simple
reproduction squeeze' to which such producers may be subject places them
into relation with other classes: it is a relational analysis, showing how poverty
is reproduced under capitalism to the benefit of owners mainly of money capital (see e.g. Bernstein, 1977, 1990). The analysis has the qualities that Green
and Hulme look for in the concept of chronic poverty, identifying 'those in
society who have minimal or no prospects for economic and social mobility
and are structurally constrained by the social relations which produce poverty
effects' (2005, p. 9 of web copy). Work of this kind has some of the features,
at least, of the sort of social science advocated by Flyvberg.

To give a further, more detailed example: analysis of what was labelled
'semi-feudalism' in West Bengal has been concerned with the relationships
that give rise to poverty rather than with measurement (though it also came
up with convenient measures of assets). This is a context in which the large
majority of rural people who own very small holdings of land, or whose livelihoods are based upon agricultural and other forms of casual labour, depend
upon their relationships with the small class of larger land holders who are
themselves subordinate to the overarching power of the numerically tiny but
economically overwhelmingly preponderant group of rice millers. Household
reproduction in this context is described in village studies from the 1950s
(Bhattacharjee et al., 1958), and was analysed and modelled by Amit Bhaduri
some years later (Bhaduri, 1973). He shows how relationships of dependence
(and the 'compulsive involvement' in markets, or 'forced commerce', that it
entails[4]) ensure that the class of larger land holders comes to control most of

[4] I refer here to the comparable arguments of Krishna Bharadwaj (1985) on 'compulsive involvement' in markets, and of Amit Bhaduri (1986) on 'forced commerce'. Both

the product of the region through rents from sharecropping and interest on loans for subsistence and for production, so that they are then able to earn speculative profits from trading in rice. He then sought to show, more controversially, how in these circumstances the larger land holders would have no incentive to invest in productivity-raising technology, because this could relax the dependence upon them of the small producers—but in the present context what is significant about this work is the way in which it shows how processes of accumulation bring about the reproduction of poverty. The wealth of some is causally linked to the crushing poverty of others.[5] Some years later I showed how, in spite of changes in the rural economy that followed from the modest land reforms that had been brought about by the then recently elected Left Front government of West Bengal, the reproduction of households depended upon the same mechanisms (Harriss, 1982b). This analysis also showed how a variety of non-crop agriculture-based activities, and some non-farm activities, were involved in the survival of 'poor peasant' and agricultural labour households ('livelihoods analysis', according to the more recent terminology). Work by Barbara Harriss(-White) on the paddy and rice trade (1983), conducted at the same time in the early 1980s, showed how legislation enacted to ensure rice supplies to Calcutta underpinned the overarching power of the rice millers, on whose capital the entire rural economy ultimately rested. Connections were made, therefore, with wider processes of capitalist accumulation, and the whole body of literature and the analysis it develops shows how poverty is reproduced through these processes. More recent work has shown how agrarian reform in West Bengal, the institution of panchayats and (in some instances) political mobilization of agricultural labour, have been instrumental in relaxing the conditions of 'semi-feudalism' and in bringing about higher levels of agricultural productivity and the reduction of income poverty—with the development of rural capitalism (see Harriss, 2006, for a short review of literature). The widely attested relative success of the state of West Bengal in reducing poverty (see Besley, Burgess, and Esteve-Volart, 2004) has come about significantly as a result of structural reforms and innovations rather than through programmes focused on 'the poor'.

Considerations of space preclude the development of further examples of research that shows how relationships that arise in the context of the development of capitalism influence the reproduction of poverty. The commentary above on the work of Pincus and Sender on Vietnam refers to their emphasis

are concerned with the implications of the ways in which the commercialization of rural economies takes place, in circumstances in which there are big disparities in entitlements.

[5] As Maureen Mackintosh has put it in a critical commentary on the nature of markets, 'profits of a few thrive in conditions of uncertainty, inequality and the vulnerability of those who sell their labour power, and of most consumers' (Mackintosh, 1990, p. 50).

on labour markets and how they work. Another example of research that traces the links between the operations of labour markets and poverty is in work by Gillian Hart in Indonesia (Hart, 1986), and later by Jonathan Pincus (1996). In all of this it is extremely important to bring gender relations into the analysis—as, for instance, Ann Whitehead shows in relation to West African societies (e.g. 1981), and Bina Agarwal in regard to South Asia (e.g. 1994).

9.6. Conclusion

I have argued here that mainstream research on poverty in international development suffers from the same flaws as those that Alice O'Connor brings out in her analysis of 'poverty knowledge' with regard to the United States— and for similar reasons. O'Connor refers to the role of research-funding agencies in bringing about a preoccupation with measurement that has abstracted poverty from its context in the way in which a particular capitalist economy is functioning, and to the mistaken appeal to 'scientific neutrality' as the means of justifying this. She then shows how this kind of poverty knowledge has suited conservative interests. The same conclusions can reasonably be drawn in regard to international development—and they substantially explain the persisting dominance of 'measurement approaches' in spite of the strength of critiques, like that of Robert Chambers, that were developed more than twenty years ago. Poverty knowledge exemplifies the kind of social science that is critiqued powerfully by Bent Flyvberg, and there is reason for taking seriously his arguments about building 'social science that matters'—arguments that converge with O'Connor's on the reconstruction of knowledge about poverty. These are worth recalling here: shifting from explanation of individual deprivation to explanation of inequalities in the distribution of power, wealth, and opportunity; recognizing that studying poverty is not to be equated with 'studying the poor'; getting away from the research industry model; challenging the privilege attached to hypothesis-testing models of enquiry; recognizing that the ideas of value-free social science and of finding scientific 'cures' for social problems are chimeras. Though the 'assets-approach' in the recent literature has brought some advances it too fails to examine the social and political-economic relationships that bring about the effect of poverty. I have argued that the earlier and now largely disregarded literature on the development of capitalism in rural economies (discouraged, of course, by what O'Connor refers to as the 'research industry') does develop the analysis of these relationships—which is so strikingly lacking in mainstream research on poverty in international development. It is a literature, it is true, that is concerned very much with 'process' rather than with 'output' (following one of the distinctions between anthropological and economics-based approaches recently made by Bardhan and Ray, 2006)—but this seems more likely to be conducive to practical action (including 'policy') to address the causes of poverty.

References

Adato, M., Carter, M., and May, J. (2006), 'Exploring Poverty Traps and Social Exclusion in South Africa Using Qualitative and Quantitative Data', *Journal of Development Studies*, 42(2): 226–47.

Agarwal, B. (1994), *A Field of One's Own: Gender and Land Rights in South Asia*, Cambridge: Cambridge University Press.

Bardhan, P. (1989), *Conversations between Economists and Anthropologists: Methodological Issues in Measuring Economic Change in Rural India*, Delhi: Oxford University Press.

—— and Ray, I. (2006), 'Methodological Approaches to the Question of the Commons', *Economic Development and Cultural Change*, 54: 3.

Barrett, C., Carter, M., and Little, P. (eds.) (2006), *Understanding and Reducing Persistent Poverty in Africa*, Special Issue of the *Journal of Development Studies*, 42(2); and these authors' 'Introduction', pp. 167–77.

Bernstein, H. (1977), 'Notes on Capital and Peasantry', *Review of African Political Economy* 10: 60–73.

—— (1990), 'Taking the Part of Peasants?', in H. Bernstein et al. (eds.), *The Food Question: Profits versus People?*, London: Earthscan.

Besley, T., Burgess, R., and Esteve-Volart, B. (2004), 'Operationalising Pro-Poor Growth: India Case Study', Department of Economics, London School of Economics.

Bhaduri, A. (1973), 'A Study in Agricultural Backwardness under Semi-Feudalism', *Economic Journal*, 83(329): 120–37.

—— (1986), 'Forced Commerce and Agrarian Growth', *World Development*, 14(2): 267–72.

—— et al. (1986), 'Persistence and Polarization: A Study in the Dynamics of Agrarian Contradiction', *Journal of Peasant Studies*, 13(3): 82–9.

Bharadwaj, K. (1985), 'A View on Commercialization in Indian Agriculture and the Development of Capitalism', *Journal of Peasant Studies*, 12(4): 7–25.

Bhattacharjee, J. P., and associates (1958), *Sahajapur, West Bengal: Socio-economic Study of a Village*, Santiniketan: Agro-Economic Research Centre for East India, Visva Bharati University.

Breman, J. (2001), 'An Informalised Labour System: End of Labour Market Dualism', *Economic and Political Weekly*, Review of Labour, 29 December.

Chambers, R. (1988), 'Poverty in India: Concepts Measurement and Reality', IDS Working Paper (repr. in B. Harriss et al. (eds.), *Poverty in India: Research and Policy*, Delhi: Oxford University Press, 1992).

Deaton, A., and Kozel, V. (2004), 'Data and Dogma: The Great Indian Poverty Debate', World Bank.

Deere, C., and Janvry, A. de (1979), 'A Conceptual Framework for the Analysis of Peasants', *American Journal of Agricultural Economics*, 61(4): 601–11.

Ferguson, J. (1990), *The Anti-Politics Machine: 'Development', Depoliticisation and Bureaucratic Power in Lesotho*, Cambridge: Cambridge University Press.

Flyvberg, B. (2001), *Making Social Science Matter: Why Social Inquiry Fails and How it can Succeed again*, Cambridge: Cambridge University Press.

Gould, S. J. (1987), *Time's Arrow, Time's Cycle: Myth and Metaphor in the Discovery of Geological Time*, Cambridge, Mass.: Harvard University Press.

Green, M. (2005), 'Representing Poverty and Attacking Representations: Some Anthropological Perspectives on Poverty and Development', Global Poverty Research Group, Working Paper No. 9.

—— and Hulme, D. (2005), 'From Correlates and Characteristics to Causes: Thinking about Poverty from a Chronic Poverty Perspective', *World Development*, 33(6): 867–79.

Harriss, B. (1983), 'Paddy and Rice Marketing in a Bengal District', *Cressida Transactions*, 2.

Harriss, J. (1982a), *Capitalism and Peasant Farming: Agrarian Structure and Ideology in Northern Tamil Nadu*, Bombay: Oxford University Press.

—— (1982b), 'Making out on Limited Resources: or, What Happened to Semi-Feudalism in a West Bengal District', *Ecoscience: Cressida Transactions*, 2(1–2): 16–76 (repr. in part in J. Harriss, *Power Matters: Essays on Institutions, Politics and Society in India*, Delhi: Oxford University Press, 2006).

—— (1985), 'What Happened to the Green Revolution in South India? Economic Trends, Household Mobility, and the Politics of an Awkward Class', Discussion Paper No. 175, School of Development Studies, University of East Anglia.

—— (2006), 'Postscript on Agrarian Reform and Agricultural Development in West Bengal', in *Power Matters: Essays on Institutions, Politics and Society in India*, Delhi: Oxford University Press.

Harriss-White, B. (2006), 'Poverty and Capitalism', *Economic and Political Weekly*, 41(13): 1243–6.

Hart, G. (1986), *Power, Labor and Livelihoods*, Berkeley and Los Angeles: University of California Press.

Hulme, D., and Shepherd, A. (2003), 'Conceptualising Chronic Poverty', *World Development*, 31(3): 403–24.

Kanbur, R. (2002), Introduction to the special section on Cross-Disciplinary Approaches in International Development, *World Development*, 30(3): 477–86.

Kenny, C., and Williams, D. (2001), 'What Do We Know about Economic Growth? Or, Why Don't We Know Very Much', *World Development*, 29(1): 1–22.

Klump, R., and Bonschab, T. (2004), *Operationalizing Pro-Poor Growth: A Country Case Study on Vietnam*, AFD, BMZ, DFID, and the World Bank.

Mackintosh, M. (1990), 'Abstract Markets and Real Needs', in H. Bernstein, B. Crow, M. Mackintosh, and C. Martin (eds.), *The Food Question: Profits versus People?*, London: Earthscan.

Narayan, D., et al. (2000), *Voices of the Poor: Crying Out for Change*, New York: Oxford University Press for the World Bank.

O'Connor, A. (2001), *Poverty Knowledge: Social Science, Social Policy and the Poor in Twentieth Century US History*, Princeton: Princeton University Press.

Pincus, J. (1996), *Class, Power and Agrarian Change: Land and Labour in Rural West Java*, Houndmills: Macmillan.

223

Pincus, J., and Sender, J. (2006), 'Quantifying Poverty in Vietnam: Who Counts?', paper presented at the Annual Meeting of the Association of Asian Studies, San Francisco.

Sen, B., et al. (2004), *Operationalising Pro-Poor Growth: Country Case Study on Bangladesh*, AFD, BMZ, DFID, and the World Bank.

Sender, J. (2003), 'Rural Poverty and Gender: Analytical Frameworks and Policy Proposals', in H.-J. Chang (ed.), *Rethinking Development Economics*, London: Anthem Press.

de Waal, A. (1989), *Famine That Kills: Darfur, Sudan, 1984–5*, Oxford: Oxford University Press.

Whitehead, A. (1981), ' "I'm hungry, mum": The Politics of Domestic Budgeting in Northeast Ghana', in K. Young, C. Wolkovitz, and R. McCullagh (eds.), *Of Marriage and the Market*, London: CSE Books.

10

Poverty Measurement Blues

*Beyond 'Q-squared' Approaches to Understanding Chronic Poverty in South Africa** *

Andries du Toit

> We don't want complicated stories. What we need is a number. One number, if possible. One indicator that tells us where the poor and vulnerable are. That's what we need.
>
> (Member of the Regional Vulnerability Assessment Committee
> (RVAC) for Botswana at an October 2004 planning meeting
> of the Southern African Vulnerability Initiative)

10.1. Introduction

Discussions about the limits of econometric approaches to understanding poverty are often framed as if the central differences are those between quantitative and qualitative *method* and as if the key issue up for discussion is the best way of 'integrating' them (see e.g. Kanbur, 2002; Hulme and Shepherd, 2003; Kanbur and Shaffer, 2007; Shepherd, 2007). This chapter argues that it is necessary to go further. It considers the difficulties that arise out of the domination of development studies and poverty research by what is here called the 'econometric imaginary': an approach that frames questions of social understanding as essentially questions of measurement. But, although the limitations of the econometric imaginary clearly illustrate the need for qualitative modes of research and understanding, I argue here that more is

* This chapter is based on research funded by the Chronic Poverty Research Centre (see <www.chronicpoverty.org>). An earlier version was presented to the First International Conference on Qualitative Inquiry (see <www.qi2005.org>). Many thanks to those who saw and commented on these early drafts, including Tony Addison, Philippa Bevan, Colleen Crawford Cousins, David Hulme, Uma Kothari, and Jeremy Seekings.

needed than various methods of combining or 'integrating' qualitative and quantitative approaches, as if these are traditions that can be connected to one another without themselves being transformed or affected; or as if they proceed from a set of underlying assumptions that can seamlessly merge. Some of the differences that are often named in references to the split between qualitative and quantitative go deeper than method or even epistemology. What matters are also the larger explanatory metanarratives: the paradigms, theoretical frameworks, and underlying ontological assumptions about the nature of poverty, society, social knowledge, and judgement that guide the process of 'integration'. Meeting this challenge may also require us to consider the ways in which applied social science research in the twenty-first century is shaped by the architectures of power and knowledge in modern states and donor institutions. In South Africa these limitations, I argue, are part of a fertile yet hazardous terrain for engagement and contestation by critical scholars and researchers.

These threads of argument are hung from the rather humble edifice of a consideration of some years of 'chronic poverty' research conducted in South Africa (see Aliber, 2001; Arnall et al., 2004 De Swardt, 2004a,b; du Toit, 2004, 2005; De Swardt et al., 2005; du Toit, Skuse, and Cousins, 2007). In the first place, I argue that dominant approaches to the conceptualization of chronic poverty are undermined by their reliance on a mystificatory theoretical metanarrative that tries to imbue poverty judgements with a spurious aura of objectivity, and by the fact that they direct attention away from structural aspects of persistent poverty. Second, I argue that if the analysis of structural poverty is to avoid either reductionism or a vitiating abstraction we need to come to grips with the extent to which the structural configurations of poverty are relational and socially meaningful: shaped through and through by the complexities of culture, identity, discursive practice, and agency. Third, I propose that this implies that more is needed than the simple addition of qualitative data to existing measurement-based accounts: instead, critical theory allows a reimagining and reframing of the way in which inequality and poverty are conceptualized in the first place. The chapter closes with a consideration of some of the obstacles and limitations in the way of an attempt to bring these alternative ways of imagining poverty into the mainstream of applied poverty work in South Africa.

10.2. Imagining and Understanding Chronic Poverty

10.2.1. *Conceptualizing and measuring chronic poverty*

Our research on persistent poverty in South Africa is essentially framed by the organizing concept of *chronic* poverty. This is often given a fairly broad meaning—in the work of the Chronic Poverty Research Centre, for instance, it refers *inter alia* to poverty of long duration, the poverty of those who are poor for most of their lives and 'transmit their poverty' (*sic*) to subsequent generations, to the situation of those caught in poverty traps, and to those who number among the 'hard-to-reach poor', etc. (see e.g. Hulme and Shepherd, 2003; CPRC, 2004). Ultimately, however, chronic poverty is usually understood in its canonical econometric sense, where it is defined in contradistinction to *transitory* poverty. Though the econometric analysis of chronic poverty is possible on the basis of 'static' indicators that are robust to change over time (e.g. Chauduri and Ravallion, 1994; see also McKay and Lawson, 2003), a preferred strategy—indeed the litmus test by which other strategies are evaluated—is to aggregate static snapshots in a way that might allow a composite 'moving' picture to emerge. A typical approach is to run a panel dataset and to use a poverty line (most commonly monetary in nature) to develop a dichotomous indicator which is then used to divide the individuals in the population in each wave of the panel study into two groups—usually 'the poor' and 'the non-poor'. Those who move above (or dip below) the poverty line are held to have 'escaped poverty' (or to have 'entered' it); those who are counted as poor in every wave of the survey, or who on average remain below the poverty line, are counted as the 'chronically poor' (see Bane and Ellwood, 1986; Baulch, 1996; Baulch and Masset, 2003). This approach dominates the ways in which 'the chronic poor' are identified: although other ways of approaching persistent poverty exist they are often treated simply as complementary.

In this chapter I argue that important as the distinction between chronic and transitory poverty can be, it is also very limited, focusing attention away from other matters critical to the understanding of persistent poverty. It is also tied up with some deeply problematic—indeed, thoroughly mystificatory— underlying metanarratives about poverty itself, what it is and how it can be scientifically known. To go beyond the limitations of the econometric concept of *chronic* poverty, then, it is necessary to engage with the ways in which the econometric imaginary dominant in applied social science frames the concept of poverty itself.

10.2.2. *Some chronic problems with poverty measurement*

Let us begin this engagement by considering the practices of 'poverty measurement' upon which the definition of chronic poverty—and the identification of 'the chronic poor'—depend. These involve two key operations. First, they require the identification of an indicator which stands as a proxy for the state of poverty; and, second, they require the division of a 'population' into two groups on the basis of this indicator.

These operations raise three key difficulties. First, poverty judgements—judgements as to whether someone is poor, and about what it is that constitutes their poverty—are ordinarily moral and political judgements: they derive their import and are invested with significance and consequence by virtue of being embedded in and drawing on a rich and diverse current of overlapping and divergent underlying moral, philosophical, social, and religious discourses about (*inter alia*) the nature of society, the identity of its members, the nature of the obligations and claims that membership enables, and the relationships between material lack, human suffering, and the claims of solidarity. Any judgement about whether or not a particular person is poor—or about what the 'essentials of life' are, the lack of which constitutes poverty—is always a political judgement, and is as such almost always contested (Noble, Ratcliffe, and Wright, 2004). Furthermore, poverty judgements are always made *by* particular social actors acting in a particular strategic context and are therefore always part of some larger social and political agenda.

This has important implications. It means, *inter alia*, that 'poverty' as a concept in political and social discourse is an inherently messy notion—one that cannot simply and without loss be reduced to any one of its sometimes contradictory and competing underlying threads. This is not a bad thing: indeed, some of the power and importance of poverty as a concept in debates about social justice, policy, and legitimacy in the present global order probably lies precisely in its protean many-facetedness and its breadth of potential meaning, which render it available for mobilization in a diversity of contexts and allow it to be used to problematize and focus on a wide range of social issues and phenomena.

But this also means that there is no objective, uncontroversial, value-free, and unitary concept of poverty directly available for transparent operationalization by 'social science'. Scholarly and applied research about poverty cannot disregard this. The claims to truth, resources, time, and attention made by 'poverty experts' are dependent—even parasitic—upon these broader and essentially contested pre-existing political and moral metanarratives. Trying to impart a spurious cut-and-dried 'objective' scientificity to poverty measurement is not to make it rigorous, but to mystify it.

This is not simply an abstract point. Consider the role played by poverty lines in the attempt to make poverty judgements rigorous and objective. Evidently this immediately raises the issue of just where the poverty line should be set (for a South African discussion see e.g. Leibbrandt and Woolard, 2001). Some have developed interesting approaches that attempt to ground this decision in local consensus(es) about 'socially accepted necessities' (Noble, Ratcliffe and Wright, 2004), but quite often (see e.g. Baulch and Masset, 2003) this decision seems to be informed by the assumption that value judgements can be avoided altogether and that it is possible to develop a 'scientific' standard based on some 'objective' reality (e.g. dietary needs, caloric intake requirements, and the like). Almost inevitably this leads not to an uncontroversial but to a punishingly *conservative* poverty line—one in which only those who are at risk of starvation or malnutrition will ever really formally count as poor—and a situation where, paradoxically, there is widespread poverty above the poverty line.

Second, one important consequence of the inherently political and moral character of poverty judgements is that they ordinarily, 'in the wild', involve a wide space for nuance and indeterminacy. It is part of the *logic* of the concept of poverty that we can speak of someone as being, for example, 'not very poor', 'almost poor', or (in South Africa, for example) 'poor—for a white person'. The econometric habit of dividing 'populations' into 'poor' and 'non'-poor—a distinction absolutely central to the way in which chronic poverty is distinguished from transitory—involves a misrecognition of this essential feature. Though some have attempted to recognize the space for indeterminacy in poverty judgements, e.g. by using fuzzy set theory (Qizilbash, 2002), these involve a doomed attempt to shoehorn them into a binary, two-tailed form.[1]

Third, poverty judgements are complex, theory-rich, and layered *interpretations*—not simply of one aspect of a person or group's existence (how much they earn, for instance) but of complex and dynamic states of well-being or suffering. Though those states of being typically involve aspects of deprivation, some of which may be quantifiable, these are moments in a complex non-linear interactive process—'transient elements in the moving now', as Bevan (2004, p. 28) puts it—a process in which they figure both as momentary outcomes of complex interactions and as determinants of further interactions. What is central in understanding people's prospects and situation is not any particular aspect of deprivation but how all the facets of their existence and experience come together in a complex and always historically situated way to produce a state of lack, powerlessness, suffering, or need which can then (always in a particular context, always within the framework of meanings of a particular political or moral discourse, and always by particular people with their agendas and interests) be called poverty. This is why poverty is not just a contested concept, but an *essentially* contested one.

Econometric definitions of poverty on the other hand are, as Bevan (2004) has pointed out, measurement based, relying on the interpretation of 'indicators' which in turn are created through abstracting and isolating particular elements of people's overall situation from the broader context in which they exist and assigning meanings to these in their own right. This kind of abstraction is a tricky enterprise at the best of times, in which a lot depends on

---

[1] This is because, *contra* Qizilbash and the fuzzy set theorists, saying 'someone is to some extent part of the group of the poor' is *not* the same as saying 'someone is part of the group of the to-some-extent poor'. The later Wittgenstein had a lot to say about this.

the ability to use those indicators in an informed way—and it is particularly difficult when used to flag a condition such as 'poverty', which is highly complex, comprising a number of different determinants, mechanisms, and long-term trajectories. In practice what this approach comes down to is that the definition of poverty is essentially collapsed into its indicator—and the indicator then taken for the condition it tries to measure: a circular operation that directs attention away from the complex underlying causal dynamics that link particular aspects of deprivation with the social experience of lack disempowerment, need, and suffering.

10.2.3. *Capabilities and multidimensionality*

The problems pointed out here apply most trenchantly—and most obviously—to that most familiar of 'poverty indicators': income or expenditure measured at household level. One approach that attempts to transcend some of the limitations of this approach involves a focus, deriving from the work of Amartya Sen, on 'multidimensional' poverty and on people's 'capabilities'. Sen famously argued that the study of poverty should focus, not on attempting to measure income and expenditure, but on the underlying capabilities without which it is not possible to live a fully human life (e.g. Nussbaum, 1999; Sen, 1999). This offers the potential for an account of poverty that is alive to the complex and time-bound dynamics of deprivation, suffering, and need. But though the capabilities approach has fundamentally challenged some of the underlying assumptions of welfare economics its implications have only been followed through in limited ways. Sen's framework is notoriously hard to operationalize (see e.g. Martinetti, 2000), and many attempts at operationalization have fallen foul of similar problems to those described in the previous section. Typically, attempts to put it into practice have involved identifying various capabilities (e.g. health, nutrition, education, political participation), matching these to quantifiable indicators (longevity, anthropometric measurements, school enrolments, democratic institutions), and then trying to assess whether people are deprived or not according to these criteria (see e.g. Klasen, 2000; UNDP, 2002; Barrientos, 2003; Qizilbash, 2003; McGillivray, 2003). This can shed valuable additional light on the extent and nature of poverty, making visible aspects of deprivation not discernible from a monetary perspective alone—but ultimately the *underlying* problem has not been transcended, and sometimes leads to approaches that just seem to miss the point. McGillivray (2003), for instance, has endeavoured to use correlations between 'non-economic dimensions of well-being' (life expectancy, adult literacy, gross school enrolment) to empirically identify 'the variation not accounted for by income per capita', and then take this variation as an 'aggregate measure of non-economic well-being'—assuming, in other words, that there is some abstract thing called 'non-economic well-being' which all these indicators partly measure. Another, less extreme example is again Baulch and Masset (2003), who understand the idea that 'monetary and non-monetary indicators of poverty tell different stories about chronic poverty' to mean that there are 'different subgroups' of the chronic poor, or even different kinds of chronic poverty (e.g. 'nutritional poverty', 'chronic education poverty'—Baulch and Masset, 2003, pp. 449, 450).

Aside from the conceptual difficulties involved in describing capability deprivation in this way (how can hunger, for example, be described as 'non-economic'?) this approach produces intractable problems when used to try to identify 'the chronic poor' on the basis of panel studies. Are 'the chronic poor' *only* those who show up as deprived *every* time along *every* dimension measured? If we do not wish to adopt such a rigorous criterion, should we disaggregate 'the chronic poor' into 'the chronic monetary poor', 'the chronically malnourished', and so on? And how are we to understand the difference between those who are deprived in 'only one' dimension and those who suffer multiple forms of deprivation? (Is someone who is educationally deprived, chronically sick, and food insecure three times as poor as someone who is just food insecure? Is someone who is deprived in two 'dimensions' as poor as someone who is deprived in two others?) These may seem like silly questions, but they are precisely the ones that arise in any attempt to develop an aggregate multidimensional poverty score, or to rank poor people—activities that are routine in econometric approaches to poverty (see e.g. Atkinson, 2003; Bourguignon and Chakravarty, 2003).

Surely all this misses Sen's point. The relationship between human capabilities and the 'full human life' that they enable is complex and dynamic. To treat the absence of a particular capability, or the lack of access to the resources required for it, as an 'indicator' of 'poverty' is to reify it and to miss its significance. Those who lack education are not suffering from 'education poverty'; and those who have poor health are not 'the health poor'. This is to do violence to words. They are caught in a *process* of lack, deprivation, or suffering which may (or may not!) lead to a severe impairment of their social and economic agency and functioning in the world—and the different dimensions of their deprivation reflect the diverse material roots and determinants of that state. It may well be that those who are deprived in more dimensions than one are less likely to escape poverty—but this depends on the local structural context and the actual, empirical ways in which different aspects of deprivation play into and feed into one another. The significance of a variation, for example, in literacy or access to water lies not in the fact that they are 'indicators' or transparent reflections of 'non-economic well-being' (whatever that is!), but in their implications and consequences for *what people can do*—which are in the first place always shaped by a dynamic and complex interplay; and which are irreducibly different and therefore non-substitutable.

More to the point, all these difficulties undermine the ability of poverty researchers to achieve what is, after all, their avowed aim, which is to develop a more disaggregated picture of 'the poor', and in particular to highlight the existence of 'the chronic poor', imagined as a distinct subgroup, systematically different from 'the transitory poor' in significant and policy relevant ways (Hulme and Shepherd, 2003). Given the shaky ground underneath the notion that a poverty line marks any really significant discontinuity in people's ability to make a living, such a claim seems dubious indeed. Surely it is true that those who show up under a poverty line in repeated measurements are worse off, in a general sense, than those who do not. But does it mean anything more? It does not in itself constitute an argument that they are a socially distinct group; indeed, depending on where the poverty line is drawn, those with stable incomes (above *and* below the 'poverty' line) may have more in common with one another than with those whose incomes are highly variable.

10.3. From Chronic to Structural Poverty

10.3.1. *Vulnerability, agency, and structural poverty*

The above arguments seem to indicate that if we want to identify 'the chronic poor' and understand what keeps them poor, measurement-based approaches, then, offer only a slippery grasp. This, of course, is *not* to say that measurement is irrelevant. The problem arises when we think that what we are measuring is not income (or any other variable that we can construct as an 'indicator') but *poverty itself*; when we believe that a distinction based on an (inevitably arbitrary, conventional, formal) threshold genuinely can be said to divide 'the poor' from 'the non-poor'; and when this one marker is used as the critical and paradigmatic criterion by which 'the chronic poor' are distinguished from all the rest and imagined to constitute a distinct population with its own special policy needs. A different approach is to recognize that many of those who show up as 'transitorily poor' in a panel study may still be held to be chronically poor if their *underlying* situation—the way they are structurally inserted in society—means that they are unlikely to get out of poverty in the long run. Such an approach requires an engagement with the *causal* dynamics and processes that drive and shape livelihood careers. Understanding who is likely to sink into poverty, who is likely to stay out of it for long periods of time, and who is able to make the investments required to ensure that a subsequent generation gets out (and *stays* out) of it requires not only the post hoc tracking of actual welfare over time, but also an assessment of the underlying factors that shape their likely welfare. This means that the study of chronic poverty—and the identification of the chronically poor—is inseparable from the study of *structural* poverty and *vulnerability*.

Development economics and econometrics are not disciplines well geared towards understanding the structural configurations of vulnerability. Sen's approach and the currently popular 'livelihoods framework' at least orient enquiry towards an exploration of the material systems that underlie poverty and well-being—but even these offer scant guidance, partly because they offer very abstract and decontextualized ways of thinking about the particular ways in which individuals and groups are situated in society.

10.3.2. *From 'distributions' to relationships*

Here, it may be instructive to look at one of the more innovative attempts in South African poverty scholarship to use econometric analysis to develop an assessment, not simply of whether or not people are poor, but of their underlying 'structural poverty': Carter and May's (2001) analysis of the KwaZulu-Natal Income Dynamics Study panel dataset (see also Carter and Barrett, 2005). Their analysis goes well beyond the limitations explored above, partly because it uses a component analysis to explore the underlying aspects of people's livelihood situation. Rather than simply look at income, expenditure, or capability deprivation, Carter and Barrett look at the assets (land, human capital, financial wealth, social claims, and grain stocks) upon which households rely to generate their income and argue that households whose assets fall below the level required to generate an income equal to the poverty line are 'structurally poor' even though a windfall may cause them to show up above the income poverty line during a particular measurement. They further postulate that though some people may suffer *transitory* structural poverty (in other words, 'structural poverty' from which it is possible to escape by accumulating sufficient assets) there may be a 'Micawber Threshold'—a level of asset deprivation so severe as to render escape through accumulation impossible.

This is an important corrective to the 'structure blindness' of definitions of chronic poverty that rely entirely on poverty spells—but it begs an important question. Although the notion of 'the steady level of well-being' a household 'can expect' based on a particular level of assets or asset combination is a useful fiction—one that can be adopted to great effect in the kinds of thought experiments that econometric approaches are so good at—a fiction it to some extent remains. Any attempt to 'derive' an expected income level from an assessment of a given household's asset base will be dogged by uncertainty—particularly if we want to start including notions like 'social capital' in that asset base. Although there *is* a link between the assets over which someone disposes and the income one may expect them to generate from it, that link is not linear and is mediated in complex ways by a host of other often non-quantifiable factors.

This is something not well recognized in the econometric approach to poverty and social understanding. For all the innovativeness of their approach May, Carter, and Barrett still see inequality *statistically*: as a matter of *distribution*. But as important as access to assets and resources are the social power relations that govern this access within 'households' and in society more broadly. This is where the seductive language of 'household assets', 'social capital', and 'human capital' becomes dangerously misleading. For one thing, households are not natural units but small, open systems (Bevan, pers. comm.) that are internally contested, that change and re-form over time—and whose access to resources are powerfully mediated by networks and connections that extend outside the supposed household boundaries, so that there is often not a very clear line between household members and non-members (Spiegel, Watson, and Wilkinson, 1996; Russel, 2004; Ross, 2005; du Toit, Skuse, and Cousins, 2007). For another, 'social capital' is not a quantifiable resource, like a seed bank or a herd of cattle, which exists in greater or lesser amounts and which can be cashed or converted into other forms of capital in predictable ways. Rather, it is a (theoretically contested) term for a wide range of variously structured human *relationships*—kinship networks, friendships, affiliation to formal and informal bodies, patron–client relationships, political alliances—that can be used to make claims and counter-claims (Meagher, 2005; du Toit and Neves, 2006; du Toit, Skuse, and Cousins, 2007). And these, crucially, are 'meaning-ful' relationships: in other words, relationships that are what they are partly because of the way they are shaped by discursive practices, underlying ideologies, moral metanarratives, and cultural paradigms that come together to form a more or less consensual or contested 'moral economy' (Thompson, 1964; Scott, 1985) that defines them and that specifies which expectations can legitimately be based upon them.

A consideration of the different social landscapes explored as part of PLAAS's ongoing poverty research in South Africa (see the map in Figure 10.1) highlights how these complex webs of relationship and power work in very different ways in different contexts. On the commercial fruit farms of Ceres, for instance, one very important form of 'social capital' is constituted by the patron–client relationships between the coloured workers who work on deciduous fruit farms and the white people who manage and own them (du Toit, 2004). These relationships are shaped by discourses and practices of paternalism that took shape in the course of a century and a half of slavery and that adapted and mutated into new forms in the course of a century and a half more of capitalist modernization (du Toit, 1993, 1998; Ewert and Hamman, 1999; du Toit and Ewert, 2005). Paternalist discourse sets in place an underlying 'moral community' between black workers and white owners that is highly racialized and hierarchical; which also allows for the formulation of

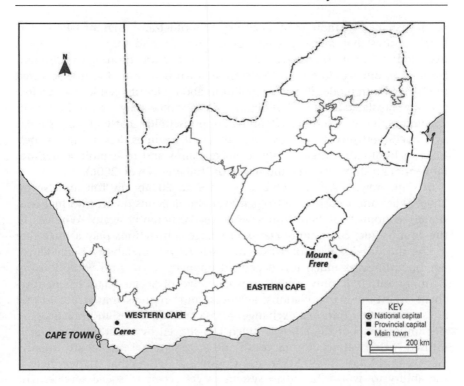

Figure 10.1. PLAAS and CPRC's research sites in South Africa (map by John Hall)

claims for resources and protection dependent on personal histories of loyalty and service, and which requires a complex politics of moral suasion, hidden resistance, and subtle negotiation beneath the façade of racial deference. This racialized ideology shapes relationships among white and black, between African and coloured, and among the powerful and the powerless even off the farms (du Toit, 2004). People with highly similar levels of 'asset endowment', as the livelihood framework (or Carter and May) would describe them, will have wildly different fortunes depending on their ability to negotiate these relationships and to secure their interests.

In Mount Frere in the remote Eastern Cape, 'social capital' is also central— but here what matter are complex traditional networks of kinship, clan membership, village history, and patronage shaped by local history; and the ways in which these have adapted and mutated in response to modernization and change (du Toit, Skuse, and Cousins, 2007; Skuse and Cousins, 2007a). 'Social capital' exists nowhere but in a vast, complex, relational economy involving deeply embedded and socially coded practices of reciprocity within and between 'stretched' households (Spiegel, Watson, and Wilkinson, 1996): extensive trade in goods, services, favours, labour, and sometimes even money, shaped by more than a century of conflict and migrant labour. The local cultures that shape this relational economy and that define people's expectations about themselves and one another are thoroughly different from those one would find in Ceres: though Xhosa culture has not persisted unchanged into modernity, local traditions about identity gender and *isidima* (loosely translated as 'status' or dignity), for instance, play a powerful role in shaping aspirations and behaviour. Again, households that look very similar in a livelihood survey can have very different fortunes depending on their links to local elites, their ability to make claims and to exploit sometimes tangential kinship networks and so on (du Toit and Neves, 2006).

In Cape Town's African suburbs (de Swardt, 2004b; du Toit and Neves, 2006; Skuse and Cousins, 2007b) survival also depends on an informal relational economy, but here things work very differently again. Whereas in the countryside, community clan and village connections play a huge role in the practices of reciprocal exchange whereby vulnerability is mediated, neighbourliness is much less depended upon in town. And while kinship is important, it is only one of a wide range of social relations, patron–client arrangements, affiliations, alliances, and enmities that structure and are structured by informal exchange. Xhosa cultural forms and practices are still important, but the ethos is much less shaped by traditionalism and is infused with a valorization of youth and an assertive, street-smart urbanity (Sagner and Mtati, 1999; Skuse and Cousins, 2007b). What matters here is the ability to 'work' the urban system to get access to social services; the ability to juggle debts and obligations and the 'politics of intimacy' in the dance of the relational economy; the ability (crucially) to manage risk and violence; and the ability to interface effectively with the still white-dominated formal economy. The ability to insert oneself in complex local development processes; the ability to claim membership of particular sub-communities and interest groups; one's history of belonging in Khayelitsha and the alliances and allegiances thus formed: all have a major impact on the resources one can mobilize.

In all three of these contexts, the local logic of 'social capital' leads to the identification of very different groups of vulnerable people. In Mount Frere, for instance, women and girl children bear the brunt of the impact of gender roles that assign to them most of the responsibility for care work and household reproduction (du Toit and Neves, 2006; du Toit, Skuse, and Cousins, 2007). At the same time, those gender roles have given them, after more than a century of migrant labour, a very real centrality in the networks of civil society, while young men are no longer as able to use migrancy as a path to full adult manhood, and are in some ways much more peripheral to village politics and society (Banks, 2005). A different vulnerable group is comprised by older people who end up being the heads of HIV/AIDS-affected households. In urban Cape Town, it is young women and female household heads who are particularly at risk, partly because gender roles dictate that they should be dependent on men; and they often lack either the social or the material resources that allow them to accumulate social capital. And in Ceres, African men *and* women are disadvantaged by a racialized local culture that constructs them as outsiders (du Toit, 2005).

Clearly an attempt to deduce 'expected incomes' from 'asset combinations' by running regressions on household survey data stands a poor chance of uncovering any of this complexity. The point is not merely that there is plenty that does not show up in the radar of any particular dataset. It is also that the incorporation of these additional factors involves, not merely their addition to an existing analysis of correlations, but the development of a *critical* and *theoretical* account of power, ideology, culture, and inequality in these contexts. The thumbnail sketches provided above derive from an analysis informed by a family of (Geertzian *and* Foucauldian; agent centred *and* structuralist) theoretical frameworks very different from the econometric one—a theoretical imaginary that emphasizes the role of structure, agency, antagonism, and social change, and according to which the perspectives and stated experiences of various social actors are not taken simply at face value but are seen as complex social creations, shaped by social power relations and in turn impacting upon them. This has crucial implications for the prospects of building more robust accounts of the nature of structural and chronic poverty.

10.4. Poverty Measurement and the Government of Poverty

10.4.1. *Beyond Q-squared*

In one sense, of course, none of the above arguments is very new. Arguments about the limitations of purely quantitative research are probably as old as 'quantitative social science' itself and have recently become commonplace again even within the development mainstream (see e.g. Kanbur, 2002; Kanbur and Shaffer, 2007). This is undoubtedly a good thing: forays into 'q-squared' attempts to integrate qualitative and quantitative work can clearly add to the rigour, depth, reach, and accuracy of poverty research (see e.g. Adato, Lund, and Mhlongo, 2007). At the same time, this recognition is often quite circumspect and the integration between 'qualitative' and 'quantitative' often takes place in restricted ways. The recognition of the limitations of econometric analysis usually takes quite a limited form—being confined, for instance, to the idea that it is enough for econometric analysis to be supplemented, corrected, or added to in some way by 'qualitative' research. For writers like Thorbecke, for instance, qualitative data seem to be understood as being equivalent to doing some PRAs—and the role of qualitative data seems to be limited to generating hypotheses that can be quantitatively tested (Thorbecke, 2004; see also Parker and Kozel, 2007; Hargreaves, et al., 2007). Others admit of a wider range of methods and highlight a number of different ways in which qualitative and quantitative work can illustrate, confirm, refute, enrich, and illuminate one another (Carvalho and White, 1997; see also Adato, Lund, and Mhlongo 2007; Howe and McKay, 2007; Jha, Rao, and Woolcock, 2007; London, Schwartz, and Scott, 2007; Place, Adato, and Hebinck, 2007; Rew, Khan, and Rew, 2007). On the whole, however, 'qualitative data' has been seen to have an essentially supplementary and illustrative role in accounts of poverty still essentially shaped by the econometric imaginary. The tensions produced by the underlying differences in epistemological approach and normative theory that exist between 'qualitative approaches' and econometric research are only rarely noted within this literature (Kanbur and Shaffer, 2007; see also Rew, Khan, and Rew, 2007; for a more searching and critical account, see Bevan, 2004). Even more problematically, 'qualitative data' themselves are all too often still understood, very simplistically, as if they are transparently meaningful in themselves, and as if what emerges from PRAs, life histories, focus groups, and the like can be taken at face value—and even quantitatively analysed (Hargreaves et al., 2007; Parker and Kozel, 2007), without an engagement with the need to interpret these as textual artefacts, themselves the products of conflicts, antagonisms, and other encounters that are shaped by social power relations and concrete social interests.

There is a danger, therefore, that attempts to assert the value of qualitative research can simply take us back to a new positivism, in which slightly more methodologically diverse research strategies (household surveys plus focus group interviews; panel datasets plus life histories; econometric regressions plus PRAs) figure within accounts of society and social change essentially still caught within the ahistorical, power-blind, technicist, and rational-choice imaginary of econometric analysis and mainstream development economics (see e.g. Kothari, 2001). What the calls for 'integration' ignore is that the real issue is not *whether* we need to connect qualitative and quantitative research—obviously we do—but that any attempt at integration is always theory rich, dependent on underlying narratives about the nature of society, agency, power, poverty, and social change.

Two observations issues arise out of this point. The first is that this theoretical poverty is not necessary. If the purpose is indeed to understand chronic (and therefore structural) poverty, and to understand how social relations shape people's chances of getting into or out of poverty, then the field of social science and critical social theory offers rich resources. A veritable academic industry exists in which the links between power, agency, culture, identity, and history are explored and which offers fertile space for reflective and incisive accounts of the ways in which these are linked to the distribution of resources in society.

The second is that, in spite of this promise, these critical traditions are to a large extent marginalized in the field of development research and poverty studies, relegated to a fairly well-defined circuit of institutions and journals which development economists and poverty scholars seem to feel they can safely ignore. In South Africa, for instance, there is a rich legacy of critical debate and research dating from the 1980s and 1990s on the relationships between capital accumulation, identity, ideology, social change, and inequality—a legacy that has been radicalized and extended more recently, in the work of institutions such as WISER, into searching reflections on postcoloniality, racism, and identity. Yet at the same time it is possible for scholars who to all intents and purposes are clearly deeply committed to social justice and the eradication of inequality and poverty to produce an account of labour market vulnerability and poverty in South Africa that reads as if the 'revisionist' debates of the 1980s never took place and as if the liberal orthodoxy of the 1960s and 1970s was never subjected to critique (Bhorat, et al., 2001; for a discussion, see du Toit, 2005).

10.4.2. *Power, knowledge, and the government of poverty*

What scope is there for this state of affairs to be addressed and for applied social science in general (and policy-oriented poverty research in particular) to become more sensitive to the need for—and the power of—critical and agent-centred accounts of structural poverty and the prospects for getting out of it? Recently, the author (see du Toit, 2005) has to some extent attempted to name and problematize the marginalization described here, which is all too often seen as the natural order of things.

One of the most prominent *stated* reasons for the failure of critical social theory to seriously challenge the hegemony of the econometric imaginary is that there is no clearly hegemonic 'critical theory' approach even within the margins. In contrast to the disciplines of economics and econometrics, where debates and discussions are underpinned by a widely shared and hegemonic framework setting the boundaries of a generally accepted 'normal science' (and also in contrast to the field of development studies, which lacks its own rigour but is thoroughly governed by the changing orthodoxies and frameworks adopted by leading donor institutions), critical social theory and anthropology have since the mid-1980s been characterized by a flowering of increasingly divergent and sometimes competing explanatory paradigms and ontologies, subdisciplines and specialities: post-colonial, gender, and cultural studies, social constructionism, critical realism, post-structuralist theory and discourse analysis, actor network theory, global value chain analysis, convention theory, to name but a few—with no specific approach decisively succeeding in establishing itself as central or dominant.

Norman Long has argued that, rather than being seen as fragmentation and crisis, this diversity should be recognized as a fundamental condition of social enquiry and welcomed as an opportunity for innovation (Long, 1992). Nevertheless, this diversity means that there is no single generally accepted 'qualitative' or 'non-positivist' or 'post-foundational' approach. Calls by economists for examples of generally accepted (or 'best practice') ways in which social theory can help them understand chronic poverty unfortunately have to be met by the answer that there is no master paradigm. Any attempt to 'operationalize' the insights of qualitative sociology and critical social theory has to be partial and local, and will require the case-by-case theoretical concepts and approaches that can help illuminate particular problems.

But this is of course only part of the story, for the demand for 'normal science' in social research—for powerful, uncontroversial, and replicable methodologies and schemata that can be used to produce reliable, policy-relevant knowledge about poverty—has its own political economy. Paradoxically many of the most problematic features of poverty measurement described in previous pages are precisely those that make it attractive to governments and donor institutions. Some of the features of econometric approaches to defining chronic poverty that I have criticized above arise to some extent out of the underlying logic of the social technologies of knowledge and power which make poverty measurement necessary and possible as an enterprise in the first place. Poverty measurement has a complex history, but a very important role in this history has been played by what we might call the historical project of the 'government of poverty'. The need for universal measurements and easily replicable indicators is linked to the project of constituting poverty as an object of management and government—as something whose presence in society needs to be recognized in ways that render it subject to regulation and which can contain and limit its potential as a radically disruptive political problematic.

As such, the discipline of poverty measurement is caught on the horns of a dilemma, a double bind that arises out of the 'optics' of modern government described by James C. Scott (Scott, 1998; but see also Foucault, 1987). This way of looking at poverty is partly driven by the need to make society 'legible' in a regular, homogeneous, and universalizing way. In order to be useful for the process of government and planning at all, technologies of measurement and assessment have to be developed that can be formalized and routinized, and which can be de-linked from the complexity and intransparency of local context. Economies of scale in government, in decision making, in judgement and assessment require the development of embodied techniques of knowing and decision making that can be 'ported' from one context to another, that make it possible to compare one individual (or household or region) with another against a homogeneous, calibrated scale, that allow them to be ranked, that can inform decisions about the allocation of resources—and that allow all of these operations to be done in the shadow of the authority of 'science': *apparently* free of bias, objective, and incontrovertible.

The problem, as Scott points out, arises when this process of abstraction and decontextualization leads not to legibility but to misreading: when, for example, imposing the template of monoculture on forestry management destroys the underlying ecological base of biodiversity on which the forest depends, or when *dirigiste* city planners misunderstand the local dynamics that make neighbourhoods liveable and attractive (Scott, 1998). In such cases the preference for certain kinds of information—information that is readily quantifiable and standardized, that abstracts from local complexity and appears to sidestep intransparency—leads not to an accurate grasp of the dynamics of a situation, but to distorted and misleading accounts that miss crucial dynamics.

The question is, what follows from the recognition of these distortions and misunderstandings? What scope is there for what Scott called *metís*—for more flexible forms of knowledge that allow for an understanding of some of these complex dynamics and which are by their very nature more provisional, more embodied and localized, more connected with specific histories and relationships, more value laden and political? What scope is there for 'the state' and donor agencies to graduate from the 'short-cut' methodologies of quantitative surveys and PRAs (Rew, Khan, and Rew, 2007) and to learn other ways of seeing and imagining poverty and vulnerability?

The struggle is an uphill one, if recent attempts to build governmental capacity to understand food insecurity and vulnerability in South Africa are anything to go by. A case study of the development of a Food Insecurity and Vulnerability Information and Mapping System (FIVIMS) for the 'social cluster' of departments in South Africa shows that, in spite of the recognition of the role of local history, power relations, and in spite of the acknowledgement of the importance of practical local knowledge embedded in institutions on the ground, very little could be done to shift the perception on the part of the officials involved that ultimately, what was *practical* was a GIS-based system that would provide information about 'indicators' of 'structural vulnerability' in unambiguous, mappable, quantifiable terms. This institutional inertia seemed to be produced partly by what one could call the mystique of quantitative data—a wholly misplaced faith in what one could learn from the quantitative data that are available for use in a GIS-based system—but partly also by underlying totalizing narratives about the place of 'integrated planning and implementation' and centralized knowledge in the exercise of state power (du Toit, Vogel, and Drimie, 2005). Asking governments and donor institutions to make space for critical accounts of social change—accounts that are more sensitive to the nature and dynamics of power relations—seems inevitably to come up against the limitations that arise out of the present-day logic of forms of power-knowledge and modes of governmentality that seek to de-link claims to authority from knowledge from locality, and that depend on technologies for decontextualizing and homogenizing social and political space (for a broader discussion see Kothari, 2005).

10.5. Conclusion

What, then, is the scope for 'decolonizing' methodologies that are so clearly linked to formations of power and knowledge deeply shaped by their links to postcolonial (and still imperial!) forms of governance and governmentality? In the long run, there is only one way of finding out: by actually trying to contest homogenizing positivist narratives by developing powerful and convincing counter-hegemonic accounts. In South Africa, at least, it is possible to imagine that the terms of this engagement do not run only one way. Rather than being the stage for a seamless 'ordering of dissent' (Kothari, 2005) in which the institutions of globalized corporate power are always and inevitably able to contain criticism by incorporating it, the field of applied social science research in South Africa seems to embody a fruitful, if hazardous, terrain for engagement. Given the urgency of addressing persistent poverty in South Africa and the recognition by the ruling party that modernizing narratives about trickle-down are not working (see Mbeki, 2003), there is a wide scope for critical scholars to interrupt and to problematize the apparent self-evidence of normalizing metanarratives about growth, modernity, security, and the like. It is part of both the fertility and the hazard of this terrain that all such interventions needs must be themselves situated and informed by an awareness of their own dependency on and inevitable complicity with a history steeped in conflict and suffering.

References

Adato, M., Lund, F., and Mhlongo, P. (2007), 'Methodological Innovations in Research on the Dynamics of Poverty: A Longitudinal Study in Kwazulu-Natal, South Africa', *World Development*, 35(2): 247–63.

Aliber, M. (2001), 'Study of the Incidence and Nature of Chronic Poverty and Development Policy in South Africa: An Overview', Chronic Poverty Research Centre Background Paper 3, Manchester: CPRC.

Arnall, A., Furtado, J., Ghazoul, J., and de Swardt, C. (2004), 'Perceptions of Informal Safety Nets: A Case Study from a South African Informal Settlement', *Development Southern Africa*, 21(30): 443–60.

Atkinson, A. B. (2003), 'Multidimensional Deprivation: Contrasting Social Welfare and Counting Approaches', *Journal of Economic Inequality*, 1: 51–65.

Bane, M. J., and Ellwood, D. T. (1986), 'Slipping into and out of Poverty: The Dynamics of Spells', *Journal of Human Resources*, 21(1): 1–23.

Banks, L. (2005), 'On Family Farms and Commodity Groups: Rural Livelihoods, House-holds and Development Policy in the Eastern Cape', *Social Dynamics*, 31(1): 157–81.

Barrientos, A. (2003), *Non-Contributory Pensions and the Well-Being of Older People: Evidence on Multi-dimensional Deprivation from Brazil and South Africa*, mimeo, Institute for Development Policy and Management,Manchester, UK: University of Manchester.

Baulch, B. (1996), 'Neglected Trade-Offs in Poverty Measurement', *IDS Bulletin*, 27(1): 36–42.

—— and McCulloch, N. (1998), 'Being Poor and Becoming Poor: Poverty Status and Poverty Transitions in Rural Pakistan', IDS Working Paper No. 79, Brighton: Institute of Development Studies.

—— and Masset, E. (2003), 'Do Monetary and Non-Monetary Indicators Tell the Same Story about Chronic Poverty? A Study of Vietnam in the 1990s', *World Development*, 31(3): 441–54.

Bevan, P. (2004), 'Exploring the Structured Dynamics of Chronic Poverty: A Sociological Approach', WeD Working Paper 06, Bath: Well-Being in Developing Countries ESRC research group, University of Bath.

Bhorat, H., Leibbrandt, M., Maziya, M., van der Bergh, S., and Woolard, I. (eds.) (2001), *Fighting Poverty: Labour Markets and Inequality in South Africa*, Cape Town: UCT Press.

Bourguignon, F., and Chakravarty, S. R. (2003), 'The Measurement of Multidimensional Poverty', *Journal of Economic Inequality*, 1: 25–49.

Carter, M., and Barrett, C. (2005), 'The Economics of Poverty Traps and Persistent Poverty: An Asset-Based Approach', unpublished typescript, Basis CRSP. See <http://www.cfnpp.cornell.edu/images/wp178.pdf>.

—— and May, J. (2001), 'One Kind of Freedom: Poverty Dynamics in Post-Apartheid South Africa', *World Development*, 29(12): 1987–2006.

Carvalho, S., and White, H. (1997), 'Combining the Quantitative and Qualitative Approaches to Poverty Measurement and Analysis: The Practice and the Potential', World Bank Technical Paper No. 366, Washington: World Bank.

Chaudhuri, S., and Ravallion, M. (1994), 'How Well Do Static Indicators Identify the Chronically Poor?', *Journal of Public Economics*, 53: 367–94.

Chronic Poverty Research Centre (CPRC) (2004), *The Chronic Poverty Report 2004–05*, Manchester: Chronic Poverty Research Centre.

Cichello, P. L., Fields, G. S., and Leibbrandt, M. (2003), *Earnings and Employment Dynamics for Africans in Post-apartheid South Africa: A Panel Study of KwaZulu-Natal*, Development Policy Research Unit, May, Working Paper No. 03/77, Cape Town: DPRU.

De Swardt, C. (2004a), 'Chronic Poverty and the Basic Income Grant', Chronic Poverty and Development Policy Working Paper No. 2, Bellville: Programme for Land and Agrarian Studies.

—— (2004b), 'Cape Town's African Poor: Chronic Poverty and Development Policy', Working Paper No. 3, Bellville: Programme for Land and African Studies.

—— Puoane, T., Chopra, M., and du Toit, A. (2005), 'Urban Poverty in Cape Town', *Environment and Urbanization*, 17(2): 101–11.

Du Toit, A. (1993), 'The Micropolitics of Paternalism: Discourses of Management and Resistance on Western Cape Fruit and Wine Farms', *Journal of Southern African Studies*,

19(3): 314–36.

—— (1998), 'The Fruits of Modernity: Law, Power and Paternalism in Western Cape Fruit and Wine Farms', in A. Norval and D. Howarth (eds.), *South Africa in Transition: New Theoretical Perspectives*, London: Macmillan, 149–64.

—— (2004), 'Forgotten by the Highway: Globalization and Chronic Poverty in Ceres', CPRC Working Paper No. 49, Bellville: PLAAS, CPRC, and CSSR.

—— (2005), 'The Sociology of Chronic and Structural Poverty in South Africa: Challenges for Action and Research', CPRC Working Paper No. 56, Bellville: PLAAS, CPRC, and CSSR.

—— and Ewert, J. (2005), 'A Deepening Divide in the Countryside: Restructuring and Rural Livelihoods in the South African Wine Industry', *Journal of Southern African Studies*, 31(2): 315–32.

—— and Neves, D. (2006), 'Vulnerability and Social Protection at the Margins of the Formal Economy: Case Studies from Khayelitsha and the Eastern Cape', report for National Department of Treasury, unpublished typescript, Bellville: PLAAS, CPRC, and USAID.

—— Skuse, A., and Cousins, T. (2007), 'The Political Economy of Social Capital: Chronic Poverty, Remoteness and Gender in the Rural Eastern Cape', *Social Identities*, 13(4): 523–42.

—— Vogel, C., and Drimie, S. (2005), 'Institutional Arrangements and Utilization of FIVIMS-ZA', unpublished typescript, Pretoria; FIVIMS-ZA.

Ewert, J., and Hamman, J. (1999), 'Why Paternalism Survives: Globalisation, Democratisation and Labour on South African Wine Farms', *Sociologia Ruralis*, 39(2): 202–21.

Foucault, M. (1987), *Discipline and Punish: The Birth of the Prison*, Harmondsworth: Penguin.

Hargreaves, J. R., Morison, L. A., Gear, J. S. S., Makhubele, M. B., Porter, J. D. H., Busa, J., Watts, C., Kim, J. C., and Pronyk, P. M. (2007), ' "Hearing the Voices of the Poor": Assigning Poverty Lines on the Basis of Local Perceptions of Poverty. A Quantitative Analysis of Qualitative Data from Participatory Wealth Ranking in Rural South Africa', *World Development*, 35(2): 212–29.

Howe, G., and McKay, A. (2007), 'Combining Quantitative and Qualitative Methods in Assessing Chronic Poverty: The Case of Rwanda', *World Development*, 35(2): 197–211.

Hulme, D., and Shepherd, A. (2003), 'Conceptualizing Chronic Poverty', *World Development*, 31(3): 403–24.

Jha, S., Rao, V., and Woolcock, M. (2007), 'Governance in the Gullies: Democratic Responsiveness and Leadership in Delhi's Slums', *World Development*, 35(2): 230–46.

Kanbur, R. (2002), 'Economics, Social Science and Development', *World Development*, 30(3): 477–86.

—— and Shaffer, P. (2007), 'Epistemology, Normative Theory and Poverty Analysis: Implications for Q-Squared in Practice', *World Development*, 35(2): 183–96.

Klasen, S. (2000), 'Measuring Poverty and Deprivation in South Africa', *Review of Income and Wealth*, 46(1): pp. 33–58.

Kothari, U. (2001), 'Power, Knowledge and Social Control in Participatory Development', in B. Cooke and U. Kothari (eds.), *Participation the New Tyranny*, London: Zed, 139–52.

—— (2005), 'Authority and Expertise: The Professionalisation of International Development and the Ordering of Dissent', *Antipode*, 37(3): 425–46.

Kritzinger, A., and Barrientos, S. W. (2004), 'Squaring the Circle: Global Production and the Informalization of Work in South African Fruit Exports', *Journal of International Development*, 16: 81–92.

Leibbrandt, M., and Woolard, I. (2001), 'Measuring Poverty in South Africa', in H. Bhorat, M. Leibbrandt, M. Maziya, S. van der Bergh, and Ingrid Woolard (eds.), *Fighting Poverty: Labour Markets and Inequality in South Africa*, Cape Town: UCT Press.

London, A. S., Schwartz, S., and Scott, E. K. (2007), 'Combining Quantitative and Qualitative Data in Welfare Policy Evaluations in the United States', *World Development*, 35(2): 342–53.

Long, N. (1992), 'From Paradigm Lost to Paradigm Regained: The Case for an Actor Oriented Sociology of Development', in N. Long and A. Long (eds.), *Battlefields of Knowledge: The Interlocking of Theory and Research in Social Theory and Development*, Wageningen: Wageningen Agricultural University, 17–42.

McCulloch, N., and Baulch, B. (1999), 'Distinguishing the Chronically from the Transitorily Poor: Evidence from Pakistan', Working Paper No. 97, Brighton: Institute of Development Studies.

McGillivray, M. (2003), 'Capturing Non-Economic Dimensions of Human Well-Being', UNI-WIDER *Conference on Poverty, Inequality and Well-Being*, United Nations World Institute for Development Economics Research, Helsinki, Finland, 30–31 May 2003.

McKay, A., and Lawson, D. (2003), 'Assessing the Extent and Nature of Chronic Poverty in Low Income Countries: Issues and Evidence', *World Development*, 31(3): 425–40.

Martinetti, E. C. (2000), 'A Multidimensional Assessment of Well-Being Based on Sen's Functioning Approach', *Revista internazionale di scienze sociali*, 2.

Mbeki T. (2003), 'Letter from the President', <http://www.anc.org.za/ancdocs/anctoday/2003/at33.htm#preslet>.

Meagher, K. (2005), 'Social Capital or Analytical Liability? Social Networks and African Informal Economies', *Global Networks*, 5(3): 217–38.

Noble, M., Ratcliffe, A., and Wright, G. (2004), 'Conceptualising, Defining and Measuring Poverty in South Africa: An Argument for a Consensual Approach', Oxford: CASASP.

Nussbaum, M. (1999), 'Women and Equality: The Capabilities Approach', *International Labour Review*, 138(3): 227–45.

Parker, B., and Kozel, V. (2007), 'Understanding Poverty and Vulnerability in India's Uttar Pradesh and Bihar: A Q-Squared Approach', *World Development*, 35(2): 296–311.

Place, F., Adato, M., and Hebinck, P. (2007), 'Understanding Rural Poverty and Investment in Agriculture: An Assessment of Integrated Quantitative and Qualitative Research in Western Kenya', *World Development*, 35(2): 312–25.

Qizilbash, M. (2002), 'A Note on the Measurement of Poverty and Vulnerability in the South African Context', *Journal of International Development*, 14: 757–72.

—— (2004), 'On the Arbitrariness and Robustness of Multi-dimensional Poverty Rankings', WIDER Research Paper No. 2004/37, Helsinki: World Institute for Development Economics Research, United Nations University.

Ravallion, M. (1996), 'Issues in Measuring and Modelling Poverty', *Economic Journal*, 106: 1328–43.

Rew, A., Khan, S., and Rew, M. (2007), ' "P^3 > Q^2" in Northern Orissa: An Example of Integrating "Combined Methods" (Q^2) through a "Platform for Probing Poverties"

(P3)', *World Development*, 35(2): 281–95.

Ross, F. C. (2005), 'Urban Development and Social Contingency: A Case Study of Urban Relocation in the Western Cape, South Africa', *Africa Today*, 51(4): 19–31.

Russel, M. (2004), 'Understanding Black Households in Southern Africa: The African Kinship and Western Nuclear Family Systems', CSSR Working Paper No. 67, Cape Town: CSSR.

Sagner, A., and Mtati, R. (1999), 'Politics of Pension Sharing in Urban South Africa', *Aging and Society*, 19: 393–416.

Scott, J. C. (1985), *Weapons of the Weak: Everyday Forms of Peasant Resistance*, New Haven: Yale University Press.

—— (1998), *Seeing Like a State: How Certain Schemes to Improve the Human Condition have Failed*, New Haven: Yale University Press.

Sen, A. (1999), *Development as Freedom*, Oxford: Oxford University Press.

Shepherd, A. (2007), 'Understanding and Explaining Chronic Poverty: An Evolving Framework for Phase III of CPRC's Research', Working Paper 80, Manchester: IDPM/Chronic Poverty Research Centre.

Skuse, A., and Cousins, T. (2007a), 'Managing Distance: The Social Dynamics of Rural Telecommunications Access and Use in the Eastern Cape, South Africa', unpublished typescript submitted to *Journal of African and Asian Studies*, (42): 185–207.

—— —— (2007b), 'Getting Connected: The Social Dynamics of Urban Telecommunications Use in Khayelitsha, Cape Town', *New Media and Society*, Sage Publications.

Spiegel, A., Watson, V., and Wilkinson, P. (1996), 'Domestic Diversity and Fluidity among Some African Households in Greater Cape Town', *Social Dynamics*, 22(1): 7–30.

—— —— —— (1999), 'Speaking Truth to Power: Some Problems Using Ethnographic Methods to Influence the Formulation of Housing Policy in South Africa', in A. Cheater (ed.), *The Anthropology of Power: Empowerment and Disempowerment in Changing Structures*, London: Routledge, 175–90.

Thompson, E. P. (1964), *The Making of the English Working Class*, Harmondsworth: Penguin.

Thorbecke, E. (2004), 'Conceptual and Measurement Issues in Poverty Analysis', WIDER Discussion Paper No. 2004/04, Helsinki: World Institute for Development Economics Research and United Nations University.

Qizilbas, M. (2004), On the Arbitariness and Robustness of Multi-dimensional Poverty Rankings'. WIDER Research Paper No. 2004/37. (Helsinki: World Institute for Devolpment Economics Research, United Nations University).

United Nations Development Program (UNDP) (2002), *Human Development Report*, New York: Oxford University Press.

11

When Endowments and Opportunities Don't Match

Understanding Chronic Poverty

S. R. Osmani

11.1. Introduction

Recent attempts to understand the causes of chronic poverty have centred largely on the concept of poverty trap. In this perspective, the main focus is on the paucity of initial wealth or endowments, which under certain plausible conditions can create a trap from which a poor person will find it hard to escape without help from outside. While acknowledging the value of insights gained from this perspective, this chapter proposes to draw attention to a different perspective that can also prove useful in both understanding the causes of chronic poverty and looking for its solution. Instead of focusing on the level or the magnitude of endowments possessed by the poor, this new perspective focuses on the structure or composition of endowments. The crucial insight offered by this perspective is that chronic poverty can arise not just from a low level of endowments but also from a mismatch between the structure of endowments possessed by the poor and the structure of opportunities open to them. This chapter is an attempt to elaborate on this insight and to draw out some of its implications.

Section 11.2 sets the scene by offering a formal characterization of chronic poverty, and in the process it also tries to clarify the distinction between chronic and transitory poverty more precisely compared to the usual way this distinction is drawn in the literature. Section 11.3 constitutes the core of the chapter in which the new perspective is introduced and its implications are analysed. First, the point is made that chronic poverty can exist even without a poverty trap. Next, an attempt is made to examine the genesis of chronic poverty, in which the idea of a mismatch between endowments and opportunities plays an important role. Finally, the relationship between economic growth and chronic poverty is discussed in the light of the notion of structural mismatch discussed earlier. Section 11.4 offers some brief concluding observations.

11.2. Characterization of Chronic Poverty

Chronic poverty is essentially a dynamic concept—the idea of a time dimension is inherent in it. And yet the standard literature on chronic poverty seldom brings out the time dimension explicitly. For how long does a person have to be poor in order to be counted as chronically poor? This would seem to be a natural question to ask but is rarely asked. A particular strand of the literature, which equates the concept of chronic poverty with that of poverty trap, implicitly assumes an indefinitely long time span. The very concept of trap implies that a person will never escape poverty unless some exogenous event helps her to break out of the trap. Suppose, however, that there is no such trap for some poor person, so that under the prevailing circumstances she should be able to break out of poverty, given sufficient time. But she only has a finite lifespan and an even shorter working life. So even if she could in theory escape poverty given sufficient time, in reality she may never do so because the time required could be longer than she can reasonably expect to live or be fit enough to work. For all practical purposes, she too should be counted as chronically poor even though she may not be caught in a trap from which there is no endogenous escape route. The concept of chronic poverty must, therefore, explicitly incorporate the idea of a lifespan—strictly speaking, the span of working life.[1]

Yet another essential feature of the concept of chronic poverty is the recognition that income is subject to stochastic variation. This feature is of course duly recognized in the standard literature; indeed it is with reference to such variation that chronic poverty is generally distinguished from transitory poverty. I would argue, however, that the manner in which this distinction is generally made is not rigorous enough. Typically, a person is said to suffer from transitory poverty if her income sometimes falls below the poverty line and sometimes rises above the poverty line, whereas a chronically poor person is said to be one whose income is always below the poverty line. The basic idea behind this way of looking at the distinction is sound enough, but the way it is formulated lacks rigour. Consider, for example, a person whose income occasionally rises above the poverty line but remains below it most of the

---

[1] Throughout this chapter, we shall focus exclusively on the so-called 'working poor', leaving out poor people outside the labour force—such as the very young or very old or disabled people—for whom the problem of poverty is qualitatively different in nature, and calls for a rather different kind of analysis.

time. It seems reasonable to argue that such a person should be counted as chronically poor for all practical purposes, but the standard definition doesn't allow it.

In defence of the standard procedure, one could argue that if a person's income goes above the poverty line from time to time, she is probably living pretty close to the poverty line even if staying below it most of the time. That's possible, and if true this may disqualify her from being classified as extremely poor or ultra-poor in some sense but not from being classified as chronically poor. It's important to keep the concepts of extreme poverty and chronic poverty separate. Extreme poverty relates to the notion of depth or intensity of deprivation, whereas chronic poverty relates to the duration of deprivation. In the real world, there may be considerable overlap between the two concepts—many of the chronically poor people may be found to be extremely poor as well. But for analytical purposes the two concepts must be kept distinct, allowing for the possibility that some people suffering from chronic poverty (in terms of duration) may be only moderately poor (in terms of intensity).

By combining the two features—namely time dimension of deprivation and stochastic variation of income—it is now possible to formalize the notion of chronic poverty. Let the income of a person at any point in time t be denoted by Y_t, which depends on two sets of factors:

- A set of observable individual-specific variables such as age, gender, assets, education, skills, etc. and observable household-level variables such as the number of dependants, the size of household labour force, etc. We call it the endowment set of the individual and denote it by D_t.

- A set of observable variables exogenous to the individual and the household. These could be village-level or community-level or national-level or even global-level variables that affect the income of the person one way or the other. Denote this set by X_t.

Some of the endowments (D) may be time invariant (e.g. gender), others may have a deterministic time trend (e.g. age), and yet others may be amenable to choice on the part of the individual (e.g. physical assets, skills, etc.). The endowments that are amenable to choice will in general depend upon three sets of factors: the value of all the D variables in the preceding time period (D_{t-1}), income of the preceding period (Y_{t-1}), and the set of exogenous factors (X_t).

Then the income generation process over time can be described by the following recursive system of dynamic equations:

$$Y_t = F(D_t, X_t) + e_t \tag{11.1}$$

$$D_t = G(Y_{t-1}, D_{t-1}, X_t) + \varepsilon_t \tag{11.2}$$

where G is a vector of functions—with one function for each element of D_t—and e_t and ε_t are random error terms, with all the classical properties of white noise.

It is through these error terms that stochastic variation is introduced in the income generation process.

Because of stochastic variation people may move into or out of poverty from time to time, and even a chronically poor person may occasionally rise above the poverty line, but what distinguishes her from the transitorily poor is that more often than not she would be expected to remain below the poverty line. The expression 'more often than not' is obviously rather vague, but there are several possible ways of making it precise. One simple way of doing so is to think in terms of expected income $E(Y_t)$. If the time path of expected income is such that it always stays below the poverty line (Z), then we would expect a person's actual income to be below the poverty line more often than not. That's the approach we take below in order to define chronic poverty.

Let τ denote the point in time at which the existence of chronic poverty is being assessed and T denote the end-point of a person's working life. If the exogenous variables obtaining at time τ were to remain unchanged over the remainder of a person's working life—denoted by the interval $[\tau, T]$—then the income generation process can be expressed as:

$$Y_t = F(D_t, X_\tau) + e_t; \quad \text{for all} \quad t \in [\tau, T] \tag{11.3}$$

$$D_t = G(Y_{t-1}, D_{t-1}, X_\tau) + \varepsilon_t \quad \text{for all} \quad t \in [\tau, T] \tag{11.4}$$

Note that taking expectation of income Y_t, conditional on D_t and X_τ, would eliminate the stochastic variation arising from different realizations of e_t, but it would still retain an element of stochastic variation arising from ε_t, which would operate through D_t. In order to eliminate that element of variation, so as to arrive at the essence of chronic poverty, we will have to work with expectation of D_t rather than particular realizations of D_t. In other words, we shall have to think in terms of expectation of income conditional on X_τ and the expectation of D_t.

Let $D_t^* = E(D_t)$. Then the criterion by which we can identify the chronically poor is the time path of $E(Y_t|D_t^*, X_\tau)$. The formal definition of chronic poverty can now be given as follows.

Definition: A person is chronically poor if $E(Y_t|D_t^*, X_\tau) < Z$, for all $t \in [\tau, T]$, where Z is the poverty line income, τ denotes the point in time at which the existence of chronic poverty is being assessed, and T is the end-point of a person's working life.

The time path of chronic poverty according to this definition is shown in Figure 11.1.[2] To see exactly what this definition entails, recall that D_t^*

---

[2] The time path has been drawn as upward rising on the assumption that a rational person will try to accumulate some capital—either physical or human or both—to the extent

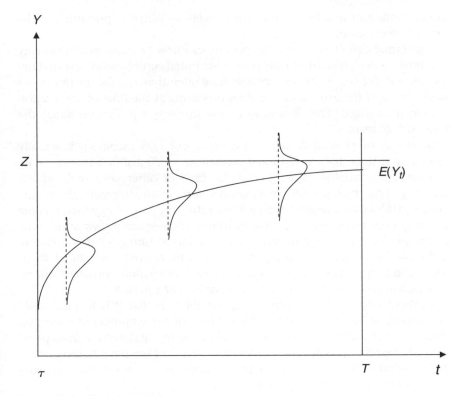

Figure 11.1. Chronic poverty

contains two types of variables. There are some over which a person has no control, such as gender and age; these can be seen as part of a person's initial conditions. There are other variables over which she does have a degree of control such as accumulation of different types of assets and skills, size of the household, labour force participation, and so on. The time paths of the latter group of variables are determined by the person herself, presumably operating within some kind of optimizing decision framework under the constraints imposed by the initial conditions of Y and D and the status of exogenous variables X prevailing at the time of observation (τ). Thus considering both types of variables, the evolution of D_t^* as a whole can be seen to depend on the initial conditions (including preferences which guide the optimization process) and the state of the exogenous variables prevailing at the time of observation. This in turn implies that the evolution of the time path of the conditional expectation of income $E(Y_t|D_t^*, X_\tau)$ also depends solely on the

permitted by her resources and in line with her subjective rate of time preference, which will enable her to earn higher income over time.

initial conditions and the state of the exogenous variables prevailing at the time of observation.

The formal definition of chronic poverty can now be translated informally as follows. A person is chronically poor if her initial conditions ensure that her income will fall below the poverty line more often than not for the rest of her working life, if the exogenous variables prevailing at the time of observation remain unchanged. This definition clearly involves a prediction about the time path of income.

However, the prediction involved is not about how income will actually change over time. It's a conditional prediction which assumes that the state of exogenous variables prevailing at the time of observation will remain unchanged for the remainder of a person's working life. In reality, the exogenous variables may change, which will alter the time path of expected income and may even ensure that a person identified as chronically poor at the time of observation will escape poverty at some point in future. Chronic poverty is thus not a statement about a person's actual future, but a statement about the income dynamics that the current state of exogenous variables can be expected to generate given the initial conditions of a person.

A salient feature of the definition given above is that it is forward looking instead of being backward looking. Much of the empirical literature on chronic poverty adopts a backward-looking view, trying to discern from panel data what kind of people have remained stuck below the poverty level over a given period of time. For policy purposes, however, it is the forward-looking view that must be of primary interest.

For the sake of completeness, we may now define transitory poverty in a manner analogous to chronic poverty. Transitory poverty refers to a situation where the time path of (conditional) expected income always stays above the poverty line but sufficiently close to it that the actual income would fall below the poverty line fairly frequently (but not most of the time), if the exogenous factors remained unchanged. In Figure 11.2, this case is demonstrated by the line TP, in contrast to chronic poverty, which is shown by the line CP.

It should be apparent that this way of defining the transitory poor involves a certain degree of ambiguity while trying to distinguish them from the non-poor. After all, the non-poor too would have a time path of (conditional) expected income that always stays above the poverty line and if the (conditional) density function of income has a sufficiently long tail at the lower end then they too might slip into poverty from time to time. The main difference with the transitory poor would be that they would have a higher time path of expected income and would slip below the poverty line less frequently. That makes the difference one of degree rather than of different kinds of dynamics. The resulting ambiguity would, however, seem to be inherent in the concepts

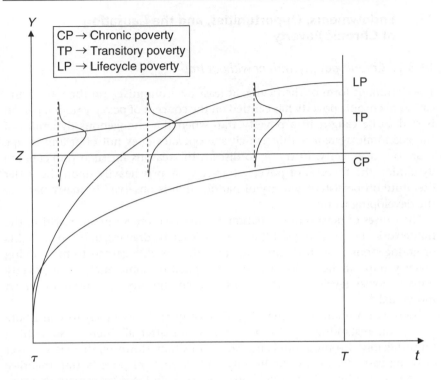

Figure 11.2. Varieties of poverty

themselves—perhaps the difference between the transitory poor and the non-poor is essentially one of degree rather than of substance.

Finally, it may be noted that the approach adopted here brings into light a rather different kind of poverty that is often lost sight of in the discussion on chronic versus transitory poverty. Consider the time path of (conditional) expected income denoted by the line LP in Figure 11.2. This line is neither always below the poverty line nor always above; instead it is below the poverty line for some part of working life and above it for the rest. Obviously, it does not fit in the category of either chronic or transitory poverty, and it is certainly not the time-path of a non-poor person either. This is the case of lifecycle poverty. A person may experience poverty in the early part of life when the resources at her disposal, such as assets, skills, experience, and labour force within the household, are not adequate to yield a sufficiently high income to live above the poverty line. However, over time as some or all of these resources increase through the process of accumulation and learning-by-doing, the same person may be able to escape poverty in the mature years of her working life.

11.3. Endowments, Opportunities, and the Causation of Chronic Poverty

11.3.1. *Chronic poverty with or without trap*

The dominant form of theorizing, at least by economists, on the nature and causes of chronic poverty has centred on the concept of poverty trap. A person is said to be caught in a poverty trap when the endogenous dynamics of the economic system within which she operates does not offer any escape route out of poverty. In trying to discern the reasons for such trap-creating dynamics, the theories of poverty trap have drawn heavily upon the wider literature on persistent poverty of nations that is observed in many parts of the developing world.

The causes of persistent stagnation are analysed predominantly within the framework of poverty traps at the national level, by drawing upon the insights of endogenous growth theory.[3] In turn, the insights gained from studying poverty traps at the national level are applied by some analysts to poverty traps at lower levels—e.g. the levels of a community, a household, or an individual.[4]

There is no doubt that the idea of poverty trap has much to contribute to our understanding of chronic poverty, for after all there is something unmistakably chronic about being caught in a trap. However, there is a danger of being carried away by the novelty and elegance of poverty trap theories, derived in part from the novelty and elegance of endogenous growth theories, and to be lulled into thinking that poverty trap is all there is to chronic poverty. As shown below, chronic poverty can exist even without a poverty trap.

In the framework developed in the preceding section, the idea of a poverty trap is best captured by a time path of expected income that either hits a ceiling that lies below the poverty line or approaches it asymptotically. Formally, a poverty trap exists, if

$$E(Y_t|D_t^*, X_\tau) \leq W \leq Z, \qquad \text{for all } t \geq \tau \qquad (11.5)$$

where W is an asymptote that is no higher than the poverty line income Z and τ is the point in time at which the observation is being made.

Time paths A and B in Figure 11.3 represent this case. In A the conditional expected income path actually hits the ceiling below the poverty line and in B it approaches the ceiling asymptotically. Obviously, if the dynamics generated by the combination of a person's initial endowments and exogenous factors

---

[3] For a recent and comprehensive account of this literature, see Azariadis and Stachurski (2005).

[4] See, for example, Barrett (2003); Barrett and Swallow (2003); Carter and Barrett (2005); Bowles, Durlauf, and Hoff (2006).

lead to time paths of expected income like these, then the person is caught in a poverty trap from which there is no escape unless there is some favourable change in the exogenous factors. Chronic poverty follows inevitably from such a trap.

The special feature of such a trap is that the persistence of chronic poverty becomes independent of the length of the working life or even the lifespan of a person. No matter how long a person lives and keeps on working, there is no way out of poverty, even with all the assets and skills she might accumulate along the way. In the asymptotic case, the accumulation of assets and skills will allow her to raise her income indefinitely, but it will do so at such a sharply diminishing rate that despite an ever-increasing income she will not be able to escape poverty—even if she were to live forever. This is chronic poverty with a vengeance!

There is, however, a milder version of chronic poverty. In this case, either there is no ceiling to the time path of expected income or if there is such a ceiling then it lies above the poverty line. In other words, there is no poverty trap, and yet a person may live the life of a chronically poor and die as one, only because the time path does not rise above the poverty line during her lifetime. The time paths C and D in Figure 11.3 represent this case.

There is a simple reason why this type of chronic poverty can exist. It is that people have a finite life. Even if the dynamics of the income generation process were such that it would some day take the expected income above the poverty line, a person may simply not live long enough to see that day. Chronic poverty would be the outcome. In their preoccupation with poverty traps, most analysts have failed to take adequate notice of this type of non-trap chronic poverty that has to do with the finiteness of human life. Perhaps the reason for this neglect lies in the fact that the literature on poverty traps at individual and household levels has drawn inspiration from the wider literature on persistent poverty at the level of the nation state or large communities, where the idea of an infinite lifespan has more salience.

In any given context, the set of chronic poor may be made up of both types of people—those who are caught in a trap and those who are not. The relative importance of the two types of chronic poverty is an empirical matter. On purely theoretical grounds, there is no reason for thinking that one type or the other will dominate. More importantly, as we argue below, for policy purposes this distinction does not really matter—what matters is the nature of the constraints she faces, which could be similar for those who are in a trap and for those who are not.

11.3.2. *Causes of chronic poverty: macro versus structural constraint*

Chronic poverty is a characteristic of the time path of expected income generated by the constrained choices made by individuals at each point in time

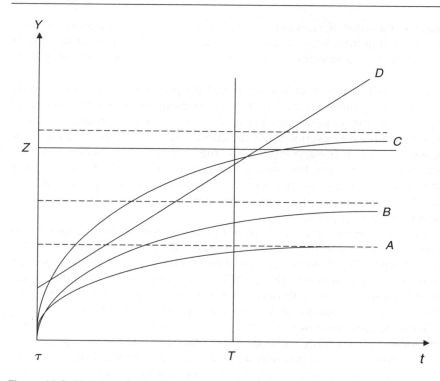

Figure 11.3. Varieties of chronic poverty

as to how to allocate their income between consumption and accumulation of assets of various types (including human capital), given the constraints of initial conditions and exogenous factors. The nature of the emerging time path depends on the evolution of two sets of factors, namely (a) the portfolio of assets—i.e. the quality and quantity of various types of physical, natural, and human capital—a person can employ and (b) rates of return on different types of assets. The evolution of the portfolio of assets will itself depend, however, on the rates of return earned (or expected to be earned) on the assets because these rates will determine both the ability and incentives of a person to invest in different types of assets.

Therefore, the future income stream would depend essentially on the evolution of the rates of return, as determined by individual choices made under the constraints imposed by the initial portfolio of assets and the exogenous factors. In other words, the time path of (conditional) expected income, which determines whether or not a person will be chronically poor, is primarily a function of the current and future rates of return on different types of assets. If a person is chronically poor it must be because these rates of return are very low. This is true regardless of whether the person is caught in a poverty trap or not.

The varieties of constraints that may depress the rates of return can be usefully classified into two groups—namely macro-level constraint and structural constraint—leading to two different types of chronic poverty. One way of seeing this distinction is to draw an analogy with the typology of unemployment. The distinction I wish to make here is analogous to the one between Keynesian or demand-deficient unemployment and structural unemployment. Keynesian unemployment arises from deficiency of aggregate demand at the macroeconomic level, which imposes an overall limit to how much employment can be sustained by the economy. Structural unemployment, by contrast, emerges not from the existence of an overall macroeconomic limit to employment but from mismatch between the supply side and demand side of the labour market. The mismatch consists in the fact that some workers may not possess the kinds of skills demanded by the changing structure of an economy: as a result, they fail to get employed.

The distinction I have in mind—between the types of chronic poverty caused by macro-level versus structural constraints—has something in common with these notions of overall limit and structural mismatch. There is one major difference, however. The overall limit in the present context originates not so much from deficient aggregate demand, which is essentially a short-run phenomenon, as from the limitations of market size, which can be a longer-term constraint. What is relevant here is the famous insight of Adam Smith that division of labour is limited by the size of the market.

The macro constraint, in the form of the size of the market, can be an important limiting factor on the rates of return. For instance, if the size of the overall market is small, then there will be limited opportunities for wage employment, resulting in low wages. In the case of self-employed poor, if the market in which they sell their products is small in size, any attempt to earn higher income by expanding the scale of operation may be subject to rapidly diminishing returns, because in a small market more can be sold only by lowering the price. This will result in perennially low rates of return. If these rates happen to be lower than either the subjective rate of time preference or the rate of interest at which a person is able to borrow, new investments will not be made and the scale of production will not rise. Poverty will become chronic.

Striking evidence of how market limitations can prevent the poor people from escaping poverty has been found by studies on microfinance, for example. An early evaluation of the *Grameen* Bank found that as the scale of operation expanded the rate of return fell rapidly (Hossain, 1984). Many subsequent studies have found that quite often poor borrowers would not opt for borrowing at a higher scale even if the opportunity was offered to them, presumably because they were concerned about the falling rate of return. This implies that so long as the limitation of market size remains a serious problem the time path of expected income will not rise enough to enable the poor to escape poverty altogether.

The limitation of market size is like an envelope that sets a limit to how far individuals can go in their effort to improve their lot even if they have the means to advance further, and it is all-embracing in nature in the sense that it affects everyone although perhaps not equally. As the market size becomes bigger, the envelope is pushed forward, thereby expanding the opportunity set of everyone.

Structural constraint differs from the macro constraint of market limitation in two ways. First, it affects specific groups of people rather than economic actors in general. Second, the constraint arises not from the overall lack of opportunities but from a mismatch between the structure of opportunities that become available and the structure of endowments possessed by a specific individual.

An example can be given from the field of microfinance again. Studies on microfinance have found that even successful credit programmes fail consistently to serve one group of the poor—namely landless wage labourers. In principle, the opportunities for microfinance are open to the landless wage labourers as well; in fact the *Grameen* Bank model was specifically designed to cater to the needs of the landless and near-landless people. The problem, however, is that wage labourers are unable to take advantage of the opportunities opened up by microfinance. The opportunities that are created are in the nature of self-employment—mainly in trading, but to a smaller extent in handicrafts and farming as well. This may help those who already have past experience in self-employment and have, through that experience, accumulated some human capital specific to their fields. The landless wage labourers, who have no such experience, do not possess this particular type of human capital. Since the structure of their endowments does not match the structure of expanding opportunities, they remain outside the reach of microfinance programmes.[5]

The problem of mismatch between endowments and opportunities is actually quite a pervasive one and manifests itself in many different ways. In a different context, this has been described as the 'integrability' problem (Osmani, 2006). The idea is that as the economy grows and the overall economic opportunities expand, some people may find it difficult to integrate with the growth process since the structure of their endowments does not match the structure of opportunities that are being opened up. The mismatch can occur for a variety of reasons—some of them have to do with the nature of

---

[5] Both the market limitation aspect and the structural mismatch aspect of the impediments to poverty reduction in the context of microfinance have been discussed in Osmani (1989).

technology, some with economic organization, and some with deeply rooted social and cultural practices.

An example of limited integrability arising from the mismatch between the skills demanded by an expanding economy and the skills possessed by the poor is offered by the recent attempts at economic liberalization by some Latin American countries. As these countries have tried to open up their economies, they have found that, unlike the countries in East and South-East Asia which had opened up their economies earlier, their comparative advantage does not lie in the activities that are intensive in relatively unskilled labour. The emergence of the poor and populous countries such as China and India on the global scene has prevented Latin America from being competitive in these types of products. Instead, they have found their comparative advantage in activities involving technologies that use relatively more skilled labour (Wood, 1997). The opening up of these economies has, therefore, led predictably to an expansion of these skill-intensive activities, but the poorest segments of the society have benefited rather little from this expansion so far, as they do not possess the skills that are needed by the expanding sectors.[6] For them, the structure of endowments does not match the structure of opportunities.

Many of the disadvantages suffered by women in the economic sphere can also be seen as a mismatch between endowments and opportunities when gender is seen as an invariant endowment of a person. Culturally determined phenomena such as gendered stereotyping of occupations, time constraint imposed on women by the burden of combining productive and reproductive activities, and discrimination in various spheres of life render the integrability problem especially severe for poor women.[7] For instance, where poverty is concentrated mostly among women, and yet the types of jobs for which demand rises are culturally defined as men's jobs, poor women would benefit little from overall expansion of opportunities. This problem is especially acute in much of Africa, where crop production has acquired a gendered pattern— with many cash crops being identified as men's crops and subsistence food crops being identified as women's crops. As some of these countries move toward greater liberalization of trade and commercialization of agriculture, employment potential in the cash crop sector may receive a boost, but to the extent that gendered pattern of crop production remains a constraint, poor women will find it hard to take advantage of the new opportunities. The overall economy may expand but many rural women will still remain chronically poor because the structure of their endowments does not match the structure of opportunities.

[6] The resulting phenomenon of widening wage differentials between skilled and unskilled workers has been analysed, among others, by Behrman, Birdsall, and Székely (2000).

[7] The specific disadvantages faced by poor women are discussed, among others, by DAW/ UN (1999, 2001) and World Bank (2001).

It may be useful at this point to explore the relevance of the macro and structural constraints discussed above for the insights gained from the poverty trap literature. The essential feature of poverty traps is the existence of thresholds in the rates of return to assets. The thresholds have the important property that diminishing rates of return become increasing rates once the threshold is crossed. As more assets are accumulated, diminishing returns might set in again, but this may not be a problem because there may exist yet another threshold at a higher level after which increasing rates of return can be enjoyed again. Those among the poor who can cross the initial thresholds move out of poverty riding on the back of increasing returns; those who can't, remain caught in a poverty trap.

The important question is why some people fail to cross the thresholds. The answer lies in a combination of several factors. First, the livelihood strategies that would enable someone to enjoy the increasing rates of return beyond a threshold usually involve some entry barrier, typically requiring lumpy investments. Second, those who are below the threshold to begin with do not earn a sufficiently high rate of return to be able to accumulate the capital necessary to overcome the entry barrier. Third, the poor people are sufficiently credit constrained not to be able to borrow the required capital. The combination of these three factors together ensures that those who start off below the initial thresholds are condemned to remain below the threshold—caught in a poverty trap.

Our discussion on macro and structural constraints is relevant to this story of poverty trap at several levels. First, once the notion of structural constraint is grasped, it becomes clear that the entry barrier to livelihood strategies offering increasing returns does not have to consist only in lumpy investments. It may arise simply from a mismatch between the structure of endowments and the structure of opportunities. If lumpy investment happens to be the barrier, then the root of the problem appears to lie in 'inadequate' assets in a quantitative sense—a person doesn't have enough assets to make the necessary investment. But if the mismatch creates the barrier, then the focus must fall not on the size or magnitude of endowments but on their structure or composition. For example, when a poor woman in Africa fails to make the transition from low-paying food crop production to high-paying cash crops, the barrier lies in the endowment of gender in the context of a society that has evolved a gendered pattern of crop production. Gender rather than lumpy investment acts as the entry barrier here. If lumpy investment were the problem, it could in principle be solved either by transfer of assets or by innovations in the credit market. But when gender is the problem, the remedy involves an altogether different kind of social action. The implication of all this is that the analytical underpinning of the concept of poverty trap needs to be extended far beyond the constraint of lumpy investment so as to consider structural constraints of various kinds if the concept is to make sense of chronic poverty more generally.

Second, the poverty trap literature recognizes that there is nothing inexorable about the low and diminishing rates of return below the threshold and that appropriate changes in exogenous factors can lead to an improvement, even to an extent that escape from the poverty trap might become possible, but exactly how this might happen is not clearly explained. A little reflection will show that what keeps the rates of return low and diminishing below the threshold is nothing other than either the macro constraint or the structural constraint discussed earlier. Softening of whichever happens to be the binding constraint in a particular context will help raise the threshold and thereby create the possibility of escape from poverty. Investigation of these constraints and identification of the binding constraint in specific contexts should, therefore, form an integral part of any enquiry into poverty traps.

Third, once it is understood that it is either the macro constraint or the structural constraint that lies behind the poverty trap, it also becomes clear that there is nothing special about poverty traps as an explanation of chronic poverty. These same constraints are also at the root of the non-trap type of income trajectories that fail to take a poor person above the poverty line during her working life even though at some distant future they might have done so if the person had lived long enough. In other words, there is no fundamental difference in the causal stories behind the trajectories A and B in Figure 11.3. Trajectory A leads to a trap while trajectory B doesn't, but both of them make a person chronically poor for much the same reasons. Therefore, especially from this point of view it doesn't really matter whether a chronically poor person is caught in a trap or not. The much more important distinction relates to the causality of chronic poverty, namely whether it is the macro constraint or the structural constraint that is binding in a specific context, because as discussed below this will have a crucial bearing on the choice of policy response.

11.3.3. *Economic growth and chronic poverty*

The relationship between growth and poverty has been much discussed in recent times. There is an increasing recognition that while growth by itself may not be sufficient to bring about a rapid reduction of poverty, high and sustained growth is at least necessary for sustained poverty reduction. However, when it comes to chronic poverty, as distinct from poverty in general, there is sometimes a presumption that economic growth may not be of much help. Indeed, the whole research agenda on chronic poverty seems to be based on the premiss that there is something very special about this type of poverty that at least weakens, if not nullifies, the potency of growth as a remedy. The increasingly common tendency to identify chronic poverty with poverty trap makes that presumption even stronger.

The analysis presented in this chapter suggests, however, that growth is not necessarily impotent in reducing chronic poverty. Much depends on the causation behind the genesis of chronic poverty. The distinction made above between the macro constraint and structural constraint is especially relevant here. The impact of growth on chronic poverty would depend crucially on which of the two happens to be the binding constraint in a specific context.

First consider the case where the macro-level limitation of market size is the binding constraint—the envelope of opportunities available in the economic system is simply too crushing to allow most people to earn a high enough rate of return to whatever endowments they possess. For wage earners, it would mean fewer employment opportunities and low levels of wages; for the self-employed people, it would mean low rates of return in their respective lines of production. With determined individual effort, or with a bit of luck, a few people may still be able to break out of poverty, but so long as the market size continues to act as the binding constraint, there will be an overall limit on how many can break out.

It might be tempting to argue that the limitation of market size need not be taken to be invariant to individual efforts to move out of poverty. Since the overall economy is the sum of individual actors in the economy, it might be argued that if everyone tried to raise the scale of production and improve productivity at the same time, then the market size itself would expand. But there is a problem here, identified more than half a century ago by the likes of Rosentein-Rodan and Ragnar Nurkse and analysed more rigorously in recent times by the likes of Murphy, Shleifer, and Vishny (1989) and others. Because of externalities, individuals would try to expand production only if they were confident that others would do so but not otherwise, and since the market mechanism by itself does not offer this assurance, everyone might end up not expanding enough. The problem is one of coordination failure that keeps the overall market small.

This is a case of poverty trap at the macro level. Several other sources of poverty trap at the macro (national) and meso (sub-regional or community) levels have been identified by recent research (Azariadis and Stachurski, 2005; Bowles, Durlauf, and Hoff, 2006). We now know that for a variety of reasons constraints to expansion can be created above the level of individuals that may not be easily broken by individual effort alone. These reasons include not just market failure but also institutional failures of various kinds.

Higher-level poverty traps can be a major cause of chronic poverty at the individual level, whether or not individual poverty itself takes the form of a trap (i.e. regardless of whether the trajectory of expected income takes route *A* or route *B* in Figure 11.3). We have argued before that in order to explain chronic poverty it is not essential to invoke the notion of poverty trap at the individual level, but we wish to emphasize now that poverty traps at higher levels may have a very big role to play in explaining chronic poverty at individual level. Empirically, this is more likely to be true for countries that are experiencing very sluggish growth and have pervasive chronic poverty at the same time.

In such cases, the main solution to chronic poverty can only be found by stimulating overall growth of the economy, by somehow neutralizing the forces that have been responsible for creating poverty traps at the macro and meso levels. As faster growth helps expand the market and pushes up the envelope of opportunities, those suffering from chronic poverty would find it easier to earn a higher rate of return on their endowments. In the process, they might be able to push up the trajectory of expected income rapidly enough to take it beyond the poverty line during their lifetime.

Matters are very different, however, if structural mismatch happens to be the binding constraint. Growth is still relevant here, but what matters in this case is not so much the rate of growth as the 'pattern of growth', by which we mean the combination of certain characteristics of the growth process, such as the sectoral pattern of growth, geographical distribution of growth, factor bias in the choice of technology, and so on, which together determine how the expanded opportunities offered by growth would affect different individuals and social groups. While the rate of growth has to do with expansion of opportunities as a whole, the pattern of growth has to do with the distribution of those opportunities. Obviously, when the main reason for chronic poverty lies in the mismatch between endowments and opportunities, what matters more is the distribution of opportunities rather than expansion of opportunities in general. In this case, chronic poverty will be dented only by a pattern of growth that alters the structure of opportunities in a way that reduces the problem of mismatch, i.e. brings the structure of opportunities in line with the structure of endowments of the chronically poor people.

Clearly, solving the problem of chronic poverty that stems from structural mismatch is a much more difficult proposition than dealing with chronic poverty that arises from the macro-level market constraint. For a start, it requires detailed knowledge of the nature of structural mismatch, which may be different for different groups of the chronically poor. More importantly, it requires a policy regime that is consciously designed to guide the growth process in a way that aligns the structure of opportunities more in conformity with the structure of endowments of the chronically poor. This is no simple task, but if pro-poor growth is to mean anything, this is what it must mean.

Actually, dealing with the problem of structural mismatch is even more demanding than what the preceding analysis suggests. There are two ends of the mismatch—opportunity is at one end and endowment is at the other. The pattern of growth operates at the end of opportunities, but there may be situations where acting on opportunities alone would not suffice; actions might be needed at the endowment end as well. Indeed, acting at the endowment end may sometimes be the more cost-effective and durable method of tackling the problem of chronic poverty that stems from structural mismatch. Such actions would include targeted interventions of various kinds, such as redistribution of assets, special programmes for enhancing the human capital of specific groups of people, removing various kinds of entry barriers that certain groups of people might face while trying to access markets and government services, and so on. In general, the removal of structural mismatch would call for a two-pronged strategy of engendering an appropriate pattern of growth on the one hand and adopting the right kind of targeted interventions on the other.

11.4. Concluding Observations

This chapter has tried to offer a new perspective on the phenomenon of chronic poverty based on the notion of a mismatch between the structure of endowments possessed by the poor and the structure of opportunities open to them. This perspective has been examined by taking as the point of departure the current focus on poverty traps as the predominant analytical framework for understanding chronic poverty. While acknowledging the value of insights offered by the poverty trap approach, the chapter has argued the case for going beyond it, at least in two ways. First, it has been noted that chronic poverty can exist with or without a trap, and more importantly that for policy purposes it does not really matter whether a chronically poor person is caught in a trap or not. Second, in searching for causes of chronic poverty, the focus should be broadened from the level or magnitude of endowments, on which the poverty trap literature mainly concentrates, to include the structure or composition of endowments as well, to which the new perspective draws attention.

In the latter context, two broad types of causal forces have been identified, described as the macro constraint and the structural constraint. The macro constraint refers to the possibility that limitations of a small market may keep many people chronically poor by forcing down the rates of return on their endowments. The structural constraint refers to the problem created by a mismatch between the structure of endowments and the structure of opportunities. We have argued that the structural mismatch can be an important reason for the existence of chronic poverty, because the effect of a mismatch is to force down the rates of return on endowments.

The relative importance of the two types of constraints may vary in different contexts. When the macro constraint is binding, rapid rate of growth may help reduce chronic poverty quite satisfactorily. However, if the structural constraint is binding, then rapid growth by itself won't be of much help. What would matter more is the pattern of growth—in particular, whether the pattern of growth is such that it aligns the structure of opportunities for the poor more in conformity with their structure of endowments. In order to achieve this alignment better, the pursuit of an appropriate pattern of growth will have to be supplemented by targeted interventions so as to alter the structure of endowments.

References

Azariadis, C., and Stachurski, J. (2005), 'Poverty Traps', in P. Aghion and S. Durlauf (eds.), *Handbook of Economic Growth*, Amsterdam: North Holland.

Barrett, C. B. (2003), 'Rural Poverty Dynamics: Development Policy Implications', paper presented at the 25th International Conference of Agricultural Economists, Durban.

—— and Swallow, B. M. (2003), 'Fractal Poverty Traps', mimeo, Department of Applied Economics and Management, Cornell University.

Behrman, J. R., Birdsall, N., and Székely, M. (2000), 'Economic Reform and Wage Differentials in Latin America', Research Working Paper No. 435, Washington: Inter-American Development Bank.

Bowles, S., Durlauf, S., and Hoff, K. (2006), *Poverty Traps*, Princeton: Princeton University Press.

Carter, M. R., and Barrett, C. B. (2005), 'The Economics of Poverty Traps and Persistent Poverty: An Asset-Based Approach', mimeo, University of Wisconsin and Cornell University.

DAW/UN (1999), *1999 World Survey on the Role of Women in Development: Globalization, Gender and Work*, New York: United Nations, Division for the Advancement of Women, Department of Economic and Social Affairs.

—— (2001), 'The Situation of Rural Women within the Context of Globalization', report of the Expert Group Meeting held in Ulaabbaatar, Mongolia, 4–8 June, New York: United Nations, Division for the Advancement of Women, Department of Economic and Social Affairs.

Hossain, M. (1984), *Credit for the Rural Poor: The Experience of Grameen Bank in Bangladesh*, Research Monograph No. 4, Dhaka: Bangladesh Institute of Development Studies.

Murphy, K. M., Shleifer, A., and Vishny, R. W. (1989), 'Industrialization and the Big Push', *Journal of Political Economy*, 97: 1003–26.

Osmani, S. R. (1989), 'Limits to the Alleviation of Poverty through Non-Farm Credit', *Bangladesh Development Studies*, 17(4): 1–18.

Osmani, S. R. (2006), 'Exploring the Employment Nexus: The Analytics of Pro-Poor Growth', in R. Islam (ed.), *Fighting Poverty: The Development-Employment Link*, Boulder, Colo.: Lynne Rienner.

Wood, A. (1997), 'Openness and Wage Inequality in Developing Countries: The Latin American Challenge to East Asian Wisdom', *World Bank Economic Review*, 11(1): 33–57.

World Bank (2001), *Engendering Development: Through Gender Equality in Rights, Resources and Voice*, Washington: World Bank.

12

Investments, Bequests, and Public Policy

*Intergenerational Transfers and the
Escape from Poverty*

Agnes R. Quisumbing

12.1. Introduction

While intergenerationally transmitted poverty is the most enduring form of
poverty (Hulme, Moore, and Shepherd, 2001), we know much more about
factors governing the transfer of wealth, than the transmission of poverty.
This chapter focuses more narrowly on factors that impede the transfer of
human and physical capital (assets), forms of wealth for which we have
more empirical evidence. Section 12.2 uses a conceptual framework of wealth
transfers to highlight barriers the poor may face in transferring wealth to
the next generation. Section 12.3 illustrates various aspects of the conceptual
framework using empirical evidence from developing countries, focusing on:
(1) the role of credit constraints in preventing optimal investments in human
capital and asset transfers; (2) the role of gender differences in schooling and
assets in perpetuating unequal lifetime incomes; and (3) the role of the marriage market and assortative matching in perpetuating asset inequality across
families and across generations. Section 12.4 examines the scope for public
policy in relieving constraints to the poor in accumulation and transferring
wealth to the next generation.

12.2. A Conceptual Framework for Understanding Intergenerational Transfers and the Intergenerational Transmission of Poverty[1]

12.2.1. *Introduction*

Most intergenerational transfers take place within the family.[2] Families, often but not always parents, take decisions about the resources to be provided to their children to enable them to grow, learn, socialize, and eventually become adult members of society.[3] Most of the decisions taken while children are young are related to investment in human capital. As children marry and form their own households, decisions are taken regarding transfers of assets that enable them to form a new productive and social unit. Finally, as parents age and die, children make decisions regarding old age support and the transfer of remaining assets to children.

A basic analytical framework for understanding intergenerational transfers to children has four building blocks:

1. Parents care about the well-being of their children, though parental concern may vary across children.

2. Parents take into account the extent to which investments will make both their children and themselves better off in the future when choosing to invest in their children.

3. Parents' ability to undertake investments in their children is constrained by the resources—money and time—available to them, the prices they face, and their ability to trade off present versus future resources.

4. Parents may disagree about these decisions, hence the ability of an individual parent to determine household decisions will also affect these investments.

These building blocks can be summarized as 'preferences', 'returns', 'constraints', and 'bargaining'.[4]

---

[1] This conceptual framework is very similar to that in Hoddinott and Quisumbing (2003). For a more extensive discussion of intergenerational transfers, see Behrman (1997).

[2] The term 'family' designates a group of individuals related by marriage and consanguinity, which is different from the term 'household', which is a group of individuals living together and sharing the same food budget or cooked meals.

[3] Moore (2001) has argued that poverty can also be transmitted through 'public' spheres of community, market, and state. Since this chapter aims to provide both a conceptual framework and empirical evidence, its focus is on the family, since the bulk of empirical evidence deals with familial transfers.

[4] Note that while we describe this framework in terms of parental decisions, not all children live with their parents. This framework applies equally to cases where children live with other relatives or foster carers or where the extended family is the decision maker regarding transfers to children.

The mirror image of this framework shows how 'stumbling blocks' can prevent the intergenerational transfer of wealth:

1. Parents may care about the welfare of their children, but unequal preferences may lead to their favouring some children over others.

2. Parents may perceive that 'returns' to investing in children are low, owing to high child mortality, few opportunities in the labour market, or that returns to investing in some children may be lower than in others.

3. Parents may have limited resources, find the costs of investing in children too high, and are constrained by their ability to trade off present for future resources, which may be critical when they face adverse shocks.

4. Parents may exercise their bargaining power in ways that may not be conducive to the transfer of wealth to their children, or to some of their children.

Most economic analyses of intergenerational transfers encompass elements (1) to (3), and this framework, called a general parental consensus model by Behrman (1997), places few restrictions on the allocation of human resource investments and transfers to and among children. Two special cases of this model, the wealth model (Becker and Tomes, 1976, 1979; Becker, 1991) and the separable earnings-transfers (SET) model of Behrman, Pollak, and Taubman (1982), make stronger assumptions. Both models take the total resources that parents allocate to children as given, assume that parents make human capital investment decisions for children, and find that under imperfect capital markets, parents are not necessarily able to equalize the market rate of return on investments to the market rate of interest on financial assets.

More recent analyses of intergenerational transfers have taken into account the possibility that parents may not have equal preferences to transfer resources to children. Inspired by collective models of household behaviour (see Haddad, Hoddinott, and Alderman, 1997, for a review), these studies have examined the differential impact of parental resources on the allocation of resources within the household. Behrman (1997) and Strauss and Thomas (1995, 1998) review this growing evidence. Bargaining between parents, as suggested by (4) above, will therefore affect the eventual allocation of transfers among members of the household.

12.2.2. Preferences

We assume that parents are altruistic; that is, they care about the well-being of their children both now and in the future. But while parents care about their children, it does not necessarily follow that parents care equally about all their children, or that all children are treated equally. Accordingly, parental preferences may affect investments in children through two pathways. One pathway reflects the extent to which parents have equal concern for the well-being of their children; the second reflects the child outcomes that are of concern to parents.

Parents with 'equal concern' for all children are parents who value a given improvement in the well-being of any child equally. But not all parents' preferences can be described as equal concern. For example, in parts of South Asia where boys are valued more highly than girls (Miller, 1981; Sen, 1990) parents exhibit unequal concern since they value an improvement in a boy's well-being more highly than an equal improvement in a girl's well-being. A child's birth order also comes into play, interacting with the child's gender as well as family size, which is intimately linked with the stage of the parents' life cycle. First-born or low birth-order children may have parents who are less experienced with child rearing, but later-born children have to share parental resources with more siblings. Indeed, siblings may compete for scarce parental resources, with male siblings often favoured; Garg and Morduch (1998) and Morduch (2000) present evidence of this in rural Ghana. Children may thus end up doing better if their siblings are sisters, since in many societies, they have a smaller claim on parental resources, or, as in the case of Taiwan, older sisters may contribute to school fees for younger children (Parish and Willis, 1993).[5]

The outcomes that parents value also influence the form of investments made in children. In the wealth model of transfers (Becker and Tomes, 1976; Becker, 1991), human resource investments in children are both socially efficient (Pareto optimal) and privately efficient (wealth maximizing). That is, altruistic parents will invest in the human capital of each child until the expected rate of return on each such human capital investment equals the market rate of interest. Each child need not receive the same wealth-maximizing level of human capital, owing to differences in children's ability to benefit from these investments. These differences might reflect innate child characteristics—for example, some children may be more 'educable' (in the sense of being able to do well academically) than others—or may reflect societal norms and constraints—for example, where there is gender discrimination in the labour market. Optimal distribution amongst offspring is then obtained via transfers of money and other assets to offset earnings differences.

However, this model results in efficient human levels of human resource investments only if parents devote enough resources to their children that there are positive transfers to at least one of them (Behrman, Pollak, and Taubman, 1995), which may be unlikely in a poor developing country. Credit

---

[5] Parents may also exhibit greater concern for children with closer genetic links, as the literature on orphans and child fostering suggests (e.g. Case, Lin, and McLanahan, 2000).

constraints may also prevent parents from investing optimally in their children's human capital. Behrman, Pollak, and Taubman (1982, 1995) suggest that when parents cannot fully compensate for unequal investments, their investments in children will reflect a trade-off between equitable outcomes and the maximization of expected incomes of all children.

12.2.3. *Returns*

The discussion in the previous section described 'returns' in terms of future earnings either in the labour market or working on one's own account in agriculture or in a non-agricultural enterprise. Where individuals' characteristics such as health and education matter in terms of the type of partner a child marries—the idea that there is 'assortative matching'—there may be additional returns in the sense that children will enter into a 'better' marriage. This conveys benefits not only to the child, but also to the parents where such marriages represent an alliance of families, not individuals. Parents may transfer wealth strategically to their children at the time of marriage to ensure a better match.

In making these investments, parents might also be considering their own future well-being. As they age, they will increasingly require assistance from their adult children. The knowledge that such assistance may be needed partly motivates their choice to have children and make investments in them, the 'old age security' motive for fertility (Leibenstein, 1957, 1975). Such a motive reflects two forms of market imperfections: in capital markets (Cigno, 1991) and in the market for services such as care for the elderly and companionship (Cox, 1987).

Intergenerational transfers provide children with the financial means of caring for their elderly parents but also make children more independent of their parents. To ensure that they are not abandoned in their old age, parents may invest in the socialization of their children to ensure that such transfers do take place (Cigno, 1991).[6] If potential returns in terms of transfers and care giving are less from daughters in societies where girls 'marry out', parents may be less inclined to invest in daughters, even if they may care equally for the welfare of daughters and sons.

Children may also provide an insurance function. In the absence of well-developed formal private sector insurance markets and governmental safety nets, insurance arrangements with family members may dominate because information is likely to be better for family members than for others.[7] For such insurance to be effective, different family members need to be subjected to risks of different shocks that are not too highly positively correlated (Stark

---

[6] Alternatively, parents may make future transfers to children, such as bequests, contingent on the provision of attention, assistance, and companionship.

[7] For a developed-country example, see Altonji, Hayashi, and Kotlikoff (1992).

and Levhari, 1982). Geographical distances tend to lessen the extent of positive correlations among many of these shocks. For this reason, migration of family members and exogamous marriages both have the potential to increase insurance possibilities. For example, Rosenzweig and Stark (1989) provide evidence of the role of marriage in consumption smoothing in India while de La Brière et al. (2002) find that female migrants to the United States increase remittances in response to loss of work due to illness of their parents in the Dominican Republic.

12.2.4. Constraints

Time and budget constraints are obvious factors that may limit the ability of parents to transfer resources to their children. Budget constraints reflect both decisions made by the household as well as exogenous factors. Decisions to work rather than undertake child care, to engage in wage work or agriculture or some form of own-business activity—and decisions regarding the amount of time spent in these activities—will influence household income. These decisions will be affected by household characteristics including education and assets such as land and capital goods. At the same time, returns to time spent in different types of work and the price of goods purchased by the household are typically beyond the control of the household. Wages in the labour market, prices for agricultural commodities, even the exchange rate, will affect household incomes. Budget constraints will also depend on the number, age, and other characteristics of other family members.

Because some transfers to children are 'lumpy', e.g. assets, credit constraints may have a particularly important role in parental strategies to invest in children. For example, parents will typically have to save to purchase assets that can be transferred to children, if they want to transfer more than the stock of assets they themselves inherited. Even in the case of schooling, a less lumpy investment, credit constraints matter. Becker and Tomes (1986) show that, in the presence of credit constraints, parents may not be able to equate the expected rate of return on each such human capital investment to the market rate of interest. The actual amount invested in each child will then be a function of parental income. If parental incomes are derived from past human capital investments and assets, and if children's lifetime incomes are derived from returns to their attained human capital, the presence of credit constraints provides a pathway by which parental assets can influence children's lifetime incomes and poverty status.

12.2.5. Bargaining

The above framework implicitly assumes that parents or other decision makers are in agreement regarding investments made in children and that they are willing to pool their resources in order to undertake these investments. Alderman et al. (1995) and Haddad, Hoddinott, and Alderman (1997) describe this as a 'unitary model' because it assumes that parents act 'as one'. However, it is possible that parents disagree on the nature and the allocation of these investments across children. Where this is true, the ability of individual parents to impose their preferences—their bargaining power—also plays a role.

Bargaining power is affected by four sets of determinants: (1) control over resources, such as assets; (2) influences that can be used to influence the bargaining process; (3) mobilization of interpersonal networks; and (4) basic attitudinal attributes. Economic analysis of bargaining power has tended to focus on economic resources exogenous to labour supply as a major determinant of bargaining power. The threat of withdrawing both oneself and one's assets from the household grants the owner of those assets some power over household resources. These threats are credible if supported by community norms or divorce laws; see, for example, Thomas, Contreras, and Frankenberg (2002) for Indonesia.

Factors that can influence the bargaining process include legal rights, skills and knowledge, the capacity to acquire information, education, and bargaining skills. Some of these influences are external to the individual (for example, legal rights), but many of them are highly correlated with human capital or education. In some instances, domestic violence can be used to extract resources from spouses or their families, as in the case of dowry-related violence in India (Rao, 1997; Bloch and Rao, 2002). Individuals can also mobilize personal networks to improve their bargaining power. Membership in organizations, access to kin and other social networks, and 'social capital' may positively influence a person's power to affect household decisions. Last, basic attitudinal attributes that affect bargaining power include self-esteem, self-confidence, and emotional satisfaction.[8]

A variety of proxies for bargaining power have been used in the economics literature, including: (1) shares of income earned by women (Hoddinott and Haddad, 1995); (2) unearned income (Schultz, 1990; Thomas, 1990); (3) current assets (Doss, 1999); (4) inherited assets (Quisumbing, 1994); (5) assets at marriage (Thomas, Contreras, and Frankenberg, 2002); and (6) the public provision of resources to specific household members (Lundberg, Pollak, and Wales, 1997). All of these measures capture some dimension of bargaining strength, but only the relatively uncommon natural experiments related to public provision of resources are likely to be entirely exogenous to individual

---

[8] While the economic literature has not dealt extensively with this issue, part of the success of group-based credit programmes such as the *Grameen* Bank has been attributed to its group-based empowerment approach. Many NGOs have explicit empowerment objectives that go beyond economic means to include legal awareness, political participation, and use of contraception (Schuler, Hashemi, and Riley, 1997).

and household decisions.[9] Regardless of the specific measure used, most of these studies indicate that resources controlled by men and women significantly affect the allocation of resources to children.

For example, Thomas (1994) finds that in Brazil, Ghana, and the United States, maternal education has a larger impact on the health of girls than on boys, with the reverse holding true for paternal education. He suggests that because girls (boys) substitute for activities performed by mothers (fathers), women (men) have an incentive to invest in girls (boys). By contrast, Haddad and Hoddinott (1994) find that in rural Côte d'Ivoire, increases in the share of household income accruing to adult women improve height given age for pre-school boys relative to girls. They argue that if women desire an equitable distribution of health amongst all children, and given that boys at very young ages are relatively less biologically robust, they will favour boys relative to girls. Second, elderly Ivorian women typically co-reside with at least one of their male offspring. Hence, the need for assistance in old age encourages women to skew relatively more resources under their control towards male offspring. Quisumbing and Maluccio (2003) find that while women's assets at marriage are reflected in higher expenditure shares for education in Bangladesh and South Africa, these allocations do not benefit boys and girls equally.[10] In Bangladesh, fathers' schooling has a negative effect on girls' schooling for both 6–10-year-olds and 11–15-year-olds; but fathers' and mothers' assets do not have differential effects on daughters relative to sons. In South Africa it is the opposite: fathers' schooling has a positive effect on girls' schooling while mothers' assets brought to marriage have a negative effect on girls. In Ethiopia, Quisumbing and Maluccio (2003) find that mothers with more assets invest preferentially in boys. Thus, in all three countries, the pattern is consistent with patterns of old age support, and thus

[9] For example, labour income is problematic because it reflects time allocation and labour force participation decisions that may have been the *result* of previous bargaining. Non-labour income, on the other hand, is more likely to be exogenous, though the assumption that it is independent of labour market decisions may not be true if a substantial portion comes from, for example, pensions, unemployment benefits, or earnings from accumulated assets. Current asset holdings are likely to be affected by asset accumulation decisions made during the marriage. Inherited assets are less likely to be influenced by decisions within marriage, particularly those inherited before the union, but remain vulnerable to other potential 'endogeneity' problems. Inheritances could be correlated with individual unobservable characteristics, such as tastes or human capital investments in the individual, and these characteristics in turn influence the outcomes under study (Strauss and Thomas, 1995). Also, they may be endogenous to the marriage as a result of marriage market selection (Foster, 1998). Assets brought to marriage, while not affected by decisions made within the marriage, are susceptible to the same potential endogeneity problems as inheritances.

[10] In examining the impact of father's and mother's resources on allocations among sons and daughters within a family, it is important to control for unobserved family-level characteristics that may affect allocations between boys and girls. The appropriate analysis therefore involves family fixed-effects analysis, with the sample of families being restricted to those with more than one child, with at least one of either sex.

may reflect the impact of both potential returns and parental preferences. In contrast, in matrilineal Sumatra, Indonesia, mothers with more paddy land invest preferentially in sons' education, while better-educated fathers invest in their daughters' schooling. Mothers with more paddy land may invest less in their daughters' education since their land will traditionally be bequeathed to daughters, whereas fathers, who normally engage in other non-farm activities in addition to cultivating their wife's family land, may benefit from having better-trained daughters.

12.2.6. *Summary*

This conceptual framework has identified possible barriers that the poor may face in making wealth transfers to children. Parents may have different preferences regarding the child in which to invest resources; when resources are scarce, these trade-offs become more stark. Expected returns in labour markets, in marriage markets, and in terms of support to parents in their old age, may lead parents to invest differentially in sons versus daughters. Lastly, differences in the relative bargaining power of individual household members may reinforce patterns of discrimination embedded in parental preferences.

12.3. Empirical Evidence on Intergenerational Transfers, Lifetime Incomes, and Inequality

12.3.1. *The impact of credit constraints on intergenerational transfers*

Abundant empirical evidence shows that, in the presence of credit constraints, parental resources—household income and socio-economic status—affect investments in children's human capital. Evidence that household income is associated with increased years of completed schooling comes from countries as diverse as Malaysia (King and Lillard, 1987), Brazil (Levison, 1991), Indonesia (Deolalikar, 1993), and Peru (King and Bellew, 1991). In sub-Saharan Africa, the education of the household head has a positive and significant effect on school enrolment, attendance, and completion (Lloyd and Blanc, 1996). Enrolment rates are 26 to 39 percentage points lower for household heads without schooling compared to household heads who have seven or more years of schooling.

We know less about the effects of parental resources on asset transfers. Not surprisingly, the available evidence shows that parents with lower levels of initial assets are less able to make larger asset transfers to children. This may arise due to credit constraints—poorer parents are less able to self-finance asset accumulation and eventual transfer of assets to children.

An alternative way of examining the impact of credit constraints is to examine what happens when households experience income shocks. A large literature on consumption smoothing (e.g. Hall and Mishkin, 1982; Altonji and Siow, 1987; Zeldes, 1989; Townsend, 1994) shows that if credit markets are perfect, households should be able to smooth consumption against idiosyncratic shocks. However, village-level insurance mechanisms are usually less able to smooth the impact of aggregate shocks. But poor households typically do not have the same access to the same consumption-smoothing opportunities enjoyed by the rich, such as borrowing and remittances (Skoufias and Quisumbing, 2005). In the poorest households of urban Brazil, loss of earnings by the household head has adverse consequences on child time in school and grade advancement (Neri et al., 2000), with children more likely to be working as a consequence. In rural India, households withdraw their children from school when experiencing shortfalls in crop income (Jacoby and Skoufias, 1997).

There is relatively little evidence on impacts of credit constraints on intergenerational transfers of assets because of longitudinal data linking parental credit constraint to asset transfers to children is scarce. Recent empirical evidence from a longitudinal study in Bukidnon, Philippines, however, suggests that the effects of credit constraints persist to the next generation (Quisumbing, 2006). Parents who were credit constrained in the past (approximately twenty years ago) have lower levels of land and non-land assets in 2003, made significantly lower transfers of land and non-land assets to children, and have significantly lower levels of consumption expenditure per adult equivalent in 2003 compared to those who were unconstrained. Children whose parents were credit constrained in the past also have significantly lower levels of land and non-land assets, and significantly lower levels of consumption per adult equivalent. Related work by Gilligan (2006) on children's adult height and educational attainment confirms that parental credit constraints have an adverse impact on children's human capital. Individuals who spent their childhood in households that were credit constrained have significantly lower adult height and lower educational attainment than those whose households were unconstrained.

12.3.2. The impact of the intra-household distribution of transfers on lifetime incomes

Differences in the type and amount of wealth transferred by gender could also result in differences in lifetime incomes of men and women. Intergenerational transfers do not necessarily penalize women: whether the bestowal of different types of assets to sons and daughters sets one on a permanently lower income path depends critically on the social, cultural, and labour market environment. Quisumbing, Estudillo, and Otsuka (2004) address this issue in the Philippines, Sumatra, and Ghana. In the Philippines, which is characterized by bilateral kinship and inheritance, sons inherited more land, but daughters achieve higher educational attainment.[11] In matrilineal Sumatra, land inheritance has traditionally favoured women, although men have higher schooling attainments. With the introduction of agroforestry and the expansion of public schooling, respectively, sons are increasingly inheriting land that is suited to agroforestry, and the gender gap in schooling has narrowed. Finally, in Ghana, which has uterine matrilineal inheritance,[12] daughters are disadvantaged in both land transfers and schooling investments, although wives are increasingly receiving 'gifts' of land with strong private property rights from their husbands, if they help the husband establish a cocoa farm.

Quisumbing, Estudillo, and Otsuka (2004) estimated the impact of changing the distribution of land and education between sons and daughters on lifetime incomes, based on estimated coefficients of the effect of farm land and schooling on household incomes. In the Philippines, the smaller farm income of daughters due to smaller areas of inherited paddy land is almost exactly compensated by their larger non-farm incomes due to their higher schooling attainments. In the Sumatra sites, sons' and daughters' incomes are largely equalized, reflecting the rough equality of agricultural land inheritance and the equal level of schooling between sons and daughters. In the case of Ghana, however, women's income is significantly lower than men's. Such a persistent and significant income gap can be attributed largely to social discrimination against females in land transfers and schooling, even if the gap is decreasing through time. The authors conclude that in relatively egalitarian societies, such as the Philippines and Sumatra, lifetime incomes will tend to be equalized. Lifetime incomes will be systematically lower for women in societies where social discrimination against women persists.

It is difficult to generalize beyond these three countries because the patrilineal inheritance system is probably more dominant in the developing world as a whole. In the case of the three inheritance systems discussed above, women have both interests in and influence on land inheritance decisions, but are often excluded from land inheritance decisions in patrilineal communities. Micro-level studies in South Asia show significant pro-male bias in patrilineal societies: women have less access to land (Agarwal, 1994), tend to receive

---

[11] In societies with bilateral kinship and inheritance, individuals consider both their father's and mother's relatives as kin, and can inherit property from both their father and mother.

[12] Traditionally, Akan households in this region have practised uterine matrilineal inheritance, in which land is transferred from the deceased man to his brother or nephew (sister's son) in accordance with the decision of the extended family or matriclan. The preferred order of inheritance if a man dies intestate is first, his uterine brother; second, if there is no uterine brother, the son of a uterine sister. The third option is one of the sons of the deceased mother's sister (Awusabo-Asare, 1990). The type of matrilineal kinship system in Ghana is different from that in Sumatra, where property passes directly along the female line, from grandmothers, to mothers, to daughters.

significantly less schooling than men (Meier and Rauch, 2000, p. 267), and receive significantly less food intake and provision of medical care (Haddad et al., 1996). Moreover, whether land inheritance and schooling can be close substitutes depends crucially on the ability of educated women to realize returns to schooling in non-farm jobs. Even if women have a higher probability of participating in the non-farm labour market (as in the Philippines), they may not have equal opportunities for advancement and may have to confront sexual harassment and violence in the workplace. Moreover, if land bestows social status, power, and access to credit that education does not provide, the above calculations of economic returns may miss out on important non-measured social and economic returns (Floro, 2006).

12.3.3. *Assets at marriage and the marriage market*[13]

(I) ASSORTATIVE MATCHING

The above discussion has assumed that returns to parental investments are realized by individuals, not by couples. However, marriage is one of the most important occasions for intergenerational transfers in many agrarian settings. First, it typically marks the onset not only of a new household but also of a new production unit, e.g. a family farm. Assets brought to marriage determine the start-up capital of this new enterprise. Second, assets brought to marriage play a paramount role in shaping the lifetime prosperity of newly formed households. Assortative matching between spouses—the rich marry the rich, the poor marry the poor—not only increases inequality, it also reduces social mobility due to intergenerational transfers of assets at marriage.[14]

Assortative matching is of interest to policy makers because of its effect on inequality, both within and among households. Fafchamps and Quisumbing (2005a) find that, to a large extent, the formation of new couples in rural Ethiopia is characterized by assortative matching. There is also substantial inequality in assets brought to marriage, with a Gini coefficient for all combined assets of 0.621. The high correlation between parental wealth and wealth at marriage also suggests relatively low intergenerational mobility. However, the correlation between assets at marriage and current assets is lower, indicating either that couples continue to accumulate assets over their married life, that bequests counteract some of the initial asset inequality at marriage, or that public redistribution policies (particularly the redistribution

---

[13] This draws heavily from Fafchamps and Quisumbing (forthcoming).

[14] There is ample empirical evidence in support of the assortative matching hypothesis (Montgomery and Trussell, 1986; Fafchamps and Quisumbing, forthcoming). Recent evidence also suggests that assortative matching on human capital attributes has increased relative to sorting based on parental wealth and physical capital (Fafchamps and Quisumbing, 2005a; Quisumbing and Hallman, 2006).

of land by Peasant Associations) have had an impact on current inequality. Combined with high inequality in assets brought to marriage, the pairing of prospective brides and grooms based on human capital favours the reproduction of rural inequality over time. This result is consistent with studies of earnings inequality elsewhere: Hyslop (2001), for instance, shows that in the United States assortative matching contributes over one-quarter of the level of permanent inequality, and 23 per cent of the increase in inequality between 1979 and 1985.

(II) ASSETS AT MARRIAGE AND IMPACTS ON THE NEXT GENERATION

In many developing countries, parents and the extended family are involved in the decision to marry. Since assets brought to marriage in large part come from the parents of the bride and groom, bequest considerations come into play as well. The empirical evidence strongly indicates that sons and daughters are not treated equally (Strauss and Thomas, 1995; Behrman, 1997). As indicated above, the extent of gender inequality in asset inheritance nevertheless varies across cultures, depending on the form of kinship and inheritance (Quisumbing, Estudillo, and Otsuka, 2004). In many societies, marriage is also the occasion for large transfers of wealth between the family of the bride and that of the groom. Brideprice refers to the case when assets are transferred from the groom's family to the bride's; when assets flow from the bride's family to the groom's, it is called a dowry. Others define dowry as a large transfer made to the daughter at the time of her marriage, regardless of whether it is controlled by her or by the groom's family (Botticini and Siow, 2003).[15]

There are several explanations for the presence of dowry and brideprice, including marriage market clearing, intergenerational transfers, and strategic motivations, that is, manipulation of marriage outcomes.[16] Regardless of the functions of dowry and brideprice, what is probably most important for the intergenerational transmission of poverty is the extent of gender differences in total assets brought to marriage, and the impact of these differences on investments in the next generation. In most societies for which we have data on assets at marriage, men bring more physical and human capital to marriage than women (Quisumbing and Maluccio, 2003; Quisumbing and Hallman, 2006).[17] An analysis of trends in schooling, age, and assets at marriage in

[15] There may also be other kinds of transfers, such as contributions to the cost of the wedding ceremony itself. These are relatively small compared to the value of assets ultimately transferred to the bride and groom.

[16] See Goody (1973) for the classic anthropological treatment, Botticini and Siow (2003) and Fafchamps and Quisumbing (forthcoming) for reviews of the economic literature.

[17] Most of these data come from the International Food Policy Research Institute's research programme on Strengthening Development Policy through Gender and Intrahousehold Analysis, and are publicly available from <www.ifpri.org>.

279

six developing countries shows that in all six countries, years of schooling at marriage have increased for husbands and wives (Quisumbing and Hallman, 2006). In four out of six countries, grooms also seem to be bringing more physical assets to marriage. Over time, however, in three out of six countries, husband–wife gaps in schooling attainment at marriage have decreased—pointing to an equalization of human capital at marriage. Nevertheless, the distribution of assets at marriage continues to favour husbands. In three out of six countries, the husband–wife asset difference has not changed through time—and therefore continues to favour husbands—and has even increased in the two Latin American countries. Finally, transfers at marriage are increasingly favouring men in Bangladesh, while the gap in transfers at marriage is decreasing in South Africa.

The reduction of husband–wife gaps in age and schooling indicates a potential improvement in the balance of power within the family, but asset ownership continues to favour husbands. Persistent differences in assets in favour of men have important implications for household well-being and the welfare of future generations, given recent findings that increasing women's status and control of assets has favourable effects on child nutrition and education (Quisumbing and Maluccio, 2003; Smith et al., 2003).

12.4. Implications for Public Policy

The above discussion has highlighted aspects of the process of intergenerational transfers, as well as the constraints that parents face in making those transfers. Strategies to break the intergenerational cycle of poverty should include those that enable the poor to accumulate assets over time and preserve their asset base in the face of unexpected shocks, as well as those that enable them to transfer wealth to the next generation in an efficient and equitable manner.

12.4.1. *Enabling the poor to accumulate assets over time*

For the poor to transfer assets to the next generation, they have to be able to accumulate a stock of assets that exceeds the value of their lifetime consumption. Strengthening property rights will be important: in many societies, the poor do not have legal rights to land or other forms of property. Without recognized property rights, it is difficult to make investments to sustain and improve one's asset base or to obtain access to formal financial markets, which typically require collateral. Governments should consider mechanisms to reduce initial costs for acquiring capital, which are usually prohibitively high for the poor. These include 'sweat equity' (contributing labour to asset-creation schemes), or group guarantees as collateral substitutes (as in the

Grameen Bank's microfinance programmes). Groups also offer the opportunity to invest in social capital, although the acquisition of social capital is not costless, requiring investment of time and, sometimes, financial resources. Other approaches may help the poor accumulate assets for which initial costs are not prohibitively high (such as livestock), and use such initial asset accumulation as a springboard for accumulating larger assets. Governments (or private institutions) may also need to look into providing a whole spectrum of financial services that enable the poor to save (especially if there are positive shocks) and draw down on savings, if necessary, rather than liquidate assets in case of negative shocks.

12.4.2. *Providing mechanisms to maintain the poor's asset base in case of negative shocks*

Evidence from life histories (see Davis, 2005, for Bangladesh) suggests that asset accumulation is gradual and incremental, but shocks such as death and illness can lead to a rapid depletion of assets. Safety nets that enable the poor to smooth consumption—ranging from publicly provided health insurance, credit-cum-insurance schemes, as well as food-for-work—may protect the poor from temporary shocks that could otherwise lead to a permanent depletion of asset stocks. Studies of emergency assistance after droughts and floods in Ethiopia and Bangladesh, for example, indicate that well-targeted food assistance enabled poor households to attain pre-disaster levels of consumption and to restore their asset base (Gilligan and Hoddinott, 2005; Quisumbing, 2006).

12.4.3. *Enabling the poor to invest in the next generation's human capital*

As economies urbanize and non-agricultural employment grows, investment in the next generation's human capital will increasingly become the most important type of intergenerational transfer for the poor. Scholarship programmes targeted to the poor and conditional cash or food transfers to increase school and clinic attendance can reduce the effective price of education to the poor. While these can be targeted to increase schooling of children, regardless of gender (see Ahmed and del Ninno, 2002, on Bangladesh's Food for Education programme), they often yield larger impacts on girls' education, and can also provide greater incentives to girls. Other approaches that have shown promise both for reaching the poor as well as promoting gender equality in education are: (1) reducing prices and increasing physical access to services; (2) improving the design of service delivery; and (3) investing in time-saving infrastructure (World Bank, 2001).

12.4.4. *Enabling the poor to continue investing in human capital even if they are credit constrained or if shocks occur*

Credit constraints prevent the poor from investing optimally in human capital. Conditional cash transfers not only provide income transfers to the poor, but may provide a safety net to prevent them from withdrawing children from school in case of shocks. De Janvry et al. (2006) provide evidence from PROGRESA in Mexico; Gitter (2005) provides similar evidence for Nicaragua. The Red de Proteccion Social, the Nicaraguan conditional cash transfer programme, helped to substantially increase school enrolments especially for credit-constrained households that experienced an economic shock.

12.4.5. *Enabling the poor to transfer assets to the next generation through legally sanctioned, transparent, and equitable mechanisms*

The reform of property rights systems and the legal framework is crucial to enabling the poor to transfer assets to the next generation. If property rights are weak and are contested, assets may not be transferable across generations. Oftentimes, statutory and customary law may not be consistent. Transparency of inheritance law may be a prerequisite for enabling the poor to assert their claims in court. Moreover, poor claimants often do not have the resources or legal know-how to assert their property rights, and in developing countries, formal legal systems may well be biased against them. Assuring claims to common property across generations may also be critical to ensuring sustainable natural resource management.

The difficulty of ensuring equity in intergenerational transfers is well illustrated by persistent gender disparities in inheritance, particularly land inheritance. Gender disparities in the inheritance of natural and physical capital persist partly because the legal framework supports property rights systems that are biased against women (Gopal, 2001). Thus, legal reform is necessary to change statutory laws to strengthen women's entitlements, and to increase the enforceability of their claims over natural and physical assets. Land titling is often mentioned as a solution to gender disparities in land rights. However, land titling is feasible only if land rights are sufficiently individualized, and many programmes have failed largely due to premature implementation. If titling programmes are implemented, they must pay special attention to the gender issue. If men are traditionally owners of land, land titling may strengthen their land rights at women's expense. To be fair, men and women should be equally qualified to acquire land titles, or titles could be awarded jointly to men and women.

Women should be able not only to hold a title to land but also to inherit land. In many traditional societies, women may be left without property if their husbands die without leaving a will. In Ghana, widows' property rights were strengthened with the promulgation of the Intestate Succession Law (PNDCL 111) in 1985, which provides for the following division of the farm: three-sixteenths to the surviving spouse, nine-sixteenths to the surviving children, one-eighth to the surviving parent, and one-eighth in accordance with customary inheritance law (Awusabo-Asare, 1990; Quisumbing et al., 2001). However, the effectiveness of legal reforms also depends on women's knowledge of the provisions of the law and their ability to enforce their claims in court. While improving women's land rights is conducive to both increased gender equity and production efficiency, it is not enough. Transferring ownership of land to women is unlikely to raise productivity if access to and use of other inputs remains unequal.

The gender issue in asset inheritance is important not only because of equity considerations, but also because it has important implications for the transfer of wealth to the next generation. In the face of the HIV/AIDS epidemic in sub-Saharan Africa, widows may be forced to leave their husband's village upon his death and therefore have no control over land and other assets used jointly. In some cultures, 'widow inheritance', in which a woman is expected to marry the brother of the deceased, is the only way she can retain rights to her husband's land. However, such practices place women at even greater risk of acquiring the disease (Drimie, 2003; Strickland, 2004; Gillespie and Kadiyala, 2005). Increasing evidence has also shown that assets controlled by women often result in increased investments in the next generation's health, nutrition, and schooling (Quisumbing and Maluccio, 2003; Smith et al., 2003). Preventing the intergenerational transmission of poverty may require a two-pronged solution of making opportunities to acquire and transfer asset more equitable across households, as well as reducing inequality in the control of resources within the household.

References

Agarwal, Bina (1994), *A Field of One's Own: Gender and Land Rights in South Asia*, Cambridge: Cambridge University Press.

Ahmed, A. U., and Ninno, C. del (2002), 'Food for Education Program in Bangladesh: An Evaluation of its Impact on Educational Attainment and Food Security', Food Consumption and Nutrition Division Discussion Paper No. 138, Washington: International Food Policy Research Institute.

Alderman, Harold, Chiappori, PierreAndre, Haddad, Lawrence, Hoddinott, John, and Kanbur, Ravi (1995), 'Unitary Versus Collective Models of the Household: Time to Shift the Burden of Proof?', *World Bank Research Observer*, 10: 1–19.

Altonji, J., Hayashi, F., and Kotlikoff, L. (1992), 'Is the Extended Family Altruistically Linked? New Tests Based on Micro Data', *American Economic Review*, 82(5): 1177–98.

——and Siow, A. (1987), 'Testing the Response of Consumption to Income Changes with (Noisy) Panel Data', *Quarterly Journal of Economics*, 102: 293–328.

Awusabo-Asare, K. (1990), 'Matriliny and the New Intestate Succession Law of Ghana', *Canadian Journal of African Studies*, 24(1): 1–16.

Becker, G. S. (1974), 'A Theory of Social Interactions', *Journal of Political Economy*, 82(6): 1063–93.

—— (1991), *A Treatise on the Family*, 2nd edn., Cambridge, Mass.: Harvard University Press.

—— and Tomes, N. (1976), 'Child Endowments and the Quantity and Quality of Children', *Journal of Political Economy*, 84: S143–62.

———— (1979), 'An Equilibrium Theory of the Distribution of Income and Intergenerational Mobility', *Journal of Political Economy*, 87(6): 1153–89.

———— (1986), 'Human Capital and the Rise and Fall of Families', *Journal of Labor Economics*, 4: S1–S39.

Behrman, Jere R. (1997), 'Intrahousehold Distribution and the Family', in Mark R. Rosenzweig and Oded Stark (eds.), *Handbook of Population and Family Economics*, Amsterdam: NorthHolland Publishing Company, 107–68.

—— Pollak, R., and Taubman, P. (1982), 'Parental Preferences and Provision for Progeny', *Journal of Political Economy*, 90: 52–73.

———— (1995), 'The Wealth Model: Efficiency in Education and Equity in the Family', in J. Behrman, R. Pollak, and P. Taubman, *From Parent to Child: Intrahousehold Allocations and Intergenerational Relations in the United States*, Chicago: University of Chicago Press.

Bloch, F., and Rao, V. (2002), 'Terror as a Bargaining Instrument: A Case Study of Dowry Violence in Rural India', *American Economic Review*, 92(4): 1029–43.

Botticini, M., and Siow, A. (2003), 'Why Dowries?', *American Economic Review*, 93(4): 1385–98.

Case, A., Lin, I.-F., and McLanahan, S. (2000), 'How Hungry is the Selfish Gene?', *Economic Journal*, 110(466): 781–804.

Cigno, A. (1991), *Economics of the Family*, Oxford: Oxford University Press.

Cox, D. (1987), 'Motives for Private Income Transfers', *Journal of Political Economy*, 95: 508–46.

Davis, P. (2005), 'Power-Resources and Social Policy in Bangladesh: A Life-History Perspective', D.Phil. thesis, University of Bath.

Deolalikar, A. (1993), 'Gender Differences in the Returns to Schooling and in School Enrollment Rates in Indonesia', *Journal of Human Resources*, 28(4): 899–932.

Doss, C. R. (1999), 'Intrahousehold Resource Allocation in Ghana: The Impact of the Distribution of Asset Ownership within the Household', in G. H. Peters and J. von Braun (eds.), *Food Security, Diversification and Resource Management: Refocusing the Role of Agriculture?*, Aldershot: Dartmouth Publishing.

Drimie, S. (2003), 'HIV/AIDS and Land: Case Studies from Kenya, Lesotho, and South Africa', *Development Southern Africa*, 20(5): 647–58.

Fafchamps, M., and Quisumbing, A. R. (2005a), 'Marriage, Bequest, and Assortative Matching in Rural Ethiopia', *Economic Development and Cultural Change*, 53(2): 347–80.

———— (2005b), 'Assets at Marriage in Rural Ethiopia', *Journal of Development Economics*, 77(1): 1–25.

———— (forthcoming), 'Household Formation and Marriage Markets', in T. P. Schultz and J. A. Strauss (eds.), *Handbook of Development Economics*.

Floro, M. S. (2006), review of Agnes R. Quisumbing, Jonna P. Estudillo, and Keijiro Otsuka, *Land and Schooling: Transferring Wealth across Generations*, Baltimore: Johns Hopkins University Press, 2004, *Feminist Economics*, January/April: 307–12.

Foster, A. D. (1998), 'Marriage Market Selection and Human Capital Allocations in Rural Bangladesh', mimeo.

Garg, A., and Morduch, J. (1998), 'Sibling Rivalry and the Gender Gap: Evidence from Child Health Outcomes in Ghana', *Journal of Population Economics*, 11(4): 471–93.

Gillespie, S., and Kadiyala, S. (2005), *HIV/AIDS and Food and Nutrition Security: From Evidence to Action*, Food Policy Review No. 7, Washington: International Food Policy Research Institute.

Gilligan, D. (2006), 'Credit Constraints, Childhood Nutritional Status, and Adult Nutrition Outcomes', unpublished manuscript, International Food Policy Research Institute, Washington.

——and Hoddinott, J. (2005), 'The Impact of Food Aid on Consumption and Asset Levels in Rural Ethiopia', unpublished manuscript, International Food Policy Research Institute, Washington.

Gitter, S. (2005), 'Conditional Cash Transfers, Credit, Shocks, and Education: An Impact Evaluation of Nicaragua's RPS', unpublished paper, Department of Agricultural and Applied Economics, University of Wisconsin-Madison.

Goody, J. R. (1973), 'Bridewealth and Dowry in Asia and Eurasia', in J. Goody and S. J. Tambiah, *Bridewealth and Dowry*, Cambridge: Cambridge University Press.

Gopal, G. (2001), 'Law and Legal Reform', in A. R. Quisumbing and R. S. Meinzen-Dick (eds.), *Empowering Women to Achieve Food Security*, 2020 FOCUS 6, Washington: International Food Policy Research Institute.

Haddad, Lawrence, and Hoddinott, John (1994), 'Women's Income and Boy–Girl Anthropometric Status in the Côte d'Ivoire', *World Development*, 22(4): 543–54.

————and Alderman, Harold (eds.) (1997), *Intrahousehold Resource Allocation: Methods, Models, and Policy*, Baltimore: Johns Hopkins University Press for the International Food Policy Research Institute.

——Pena, Christine, Nishida, Chizuru, Quisumbing, Agnes R., and Slack, Alison (1996), 'Food Security and Nutrition Implications of Intrahousehold Bias: A Review of Literature', Food Consumption and Nutrition Division Discussion Paper No. 19, Washington: International Food Policy Research Institute.

Hall, R. E., and Mishkin, F. S. (1982), 'The Sensitivity of Consumption to Transitory Income: Estimates from Panel Data on Households', *Econometrica*, 50: 461–81.

Hoddinott, J., and Haddad, L. (1995), 'Does Female Income Share Influence Household Expenditures? Evidence from Côte d'Ivoire', *Oxford Bulletin of Economics and Statistics*, 57: 77–95.

——and Quisumbing, A. R. (2003), 'Investing in Children and Youth for Poverty Reduction', unpublished manuscript, Washington: International Food Policy Research Institute.

Hulme, D., Moore, K., and Shepherd, A. (2001), 'Chronic Poverty: Meanings and Analytical Frameworks', CPRC Working Paper No. 2.

Hyslop, D. (2001), 'Rising US Earnings Inequality and Family Labor Supply: The Covariance Structure of Intrafamily Earnings', *American Economic Review*, 91(4): 755–77.

Jacoby, H., and Skoufias, E. (1997), 'Risk, Financial Markets, and Human Capital in a Developing Country', *Review of Economic Studies*, 64(3): 311–35.

Janvry, A. de, Finan, F., Sadoulet, E., and Vakis, R. (2006), 'Can Conditional Cash Transfers Serve as Safety Nets in Keeping Children in School and from Working When Exposed to Shocks?', *Journal of Development Economics*, 79: 349–73.

King, E., and Bellew, R. (1991), 'Gains in the Education of Peruvian Women, 1940–1980', in B. Herz and S. Khandkher (eds.), *Women's Work, Education, and Family Welfare in Peru*, World Bank Discussion Paper No. 116, Washington: World Bank.

——and Lillard, L. A. (1987), 'Education Policy and Schooling Attainment in Malaysia and the Philippines', *Economics of Education Review*, 6: 67–181.

La Brière, B. de, Sadoulet, E., Janvry, A. de, and Lambert, S. (2002), 'The Roles of Destination, Gender and Household Composition in Explaining Remittances: An Analysis for the Dominican Sierra', *Journal of Development Economics*, 68: 309–28.

Leibenstein, H. (1957), *Economic Backwardness and Economic Growth*, New York: Wiley.

——(1975), 'The Economic Theory of Fertility Decline', *Quarterly Journal of Economics*, 89: 1–31.

Levison, D. (1991), 'Children's Labor Force Activity and Schooling in Brazil', Ph.D. dissertation, University of Michigan.

Lloyd, C. B., and Blanc, Ann K. (1996), 'Children's Schooling in Sub-Saharan Africa: The Role of Fathers, Mothers and Others', *Population and Development Review*, 22(2): 265–98.

Lundberg, S., Pollak, R., and Wales, T. J. (1997), 'Do Husbands and Wives Pool their Resources? Evidence from the United Kingdom Child Benefit', *Journal of Human Resources*, 32: 463–80.

Meier, Gerald, and Rauch, James R. (2000), *Leading Issues in Economic Development*, 7th edn., Oxford: Oxford University Press.

Mensch, Barbara S., and Lloyd, Cynthia B. (1998), 'Gender Differences in the Schooling Experiences of Adolescents in Low-Income Countries: The Case of Kenya', *Studies in Family Planning*, 29(2): 167–84.

Miller, B. (1981), *The Endangered Sex: Neglect of Female Children in Rural North India*, Ithaca, NY: Cornell University Press.

——(1997), *The Endangered Sex: Neglect of Female Children in Rural North India*, Delhi: Oxford University Press.

Montgomery, M., and Trussell, J. (1986), 'Models of Marital Status and Childbearing', *Handbook of Labor Economics*, vol. i, Amsterdam: Elsevier Science, 928–56.

Moore, K. (2001), 'Frameworks for Understanding the Inter-generational Transmission of Poverty and Well Being in Developing Countries', CPRC Working Paper No. 8, Manchester: IDPM/Chronic Poverty Research Centre (CPRC).

Morduch, Jonathan (2000), 'Sibling Rivalry in Africa', *American Economic Review*, 90(2): 405–9.

Neri, M. C., Gustafsson-Wright, E., Sedlacek, G., da Costa, D. R., and Carvalho, A. P. (2000), 'Microeconomic Instability and Children's Human Capital Accumulation: The Effects of Idiosyncratic Shocks to Father's Income on Child Labor, School Drop-Outs and Repetition Rates in Brazil', *Ensaios econômicos da EPGE*, 394, Rio de Janeiro: Escola de Pós-Graduação em Economia.

Parish, W., and Willis, R. (1993), 'Daughters, Education, and Family Budgets: Taiwan Experiences', *Journal of Human Resources*, 28(4): 962–98.

Psacharopoulos, George (1994), 'Returns to Investment in Education: A Global Update', *World Development*, 22(9): 1325–44.

Quisumbing, A. R. (1994), 'Intergenerational Transfers in Philippine Rice Villages: Gender Differences in Traditional Inheritance Customs', *Journal of Development Economics*, 43(2): 167–95.

——(2005), 'A Drop in the Bucket? The Impact of Food Aid after the 1998 Floods in Bangladesh', unpublished paper.

——(2006), 'The Long-Term Impact of Credit Constraints on Assets, Intergenerational Transfers, and Consumption: Evidence from the Rural Philippines', unpublished paper, Washington: International Food Policy Research Institute.

——Estudillo, Jonna P., and Otsuka, Keijiro (2004), *Land and Schooling: Transferring Wealth across Generations*, Baltimore: Johns Hopkins University Press for the International Food Policy Research Institute.

——and Hallman, K. (2006), 'Marriage in Transition: Evidence on Age, Education, and Assets from Six Developing Countries', in Cynthia B. Lloyd, Jere R. Behrman, Nelly P. Stromquist, and Barney Cohen (eds.), *The Changing Transitions to Adulthood in Developing Countries: Selected Studies*, Panel on Transitions to Adulthood in Developing Countries, Committee on Population, Division of Behavioral and Social Sciences and Education, Washington: National Academies Press.

——and Maluccio, J. A. (2003), 'Resources at Marriage and Intrahousehold Allocation: Evidence from Bangladesh, Ethiopia, Indonesia, and South Africa', *Oxford Bulletin of Economics and Statistics*, 65(3): 283–328.

——Payongayong, E., Aidoo, J. B., and Otsuka, K. (2001), 'Women's Land Rights in the Transition to Individualized Ownership: Implications for the Management of Tree Resources in Western Ghana', *Economic Development and Cultural Change*, 50(1): 157–82.

Rao, V. (1997), 'Wife-Beating in Rural South India: A Qualitative and Econometric Analysis', *Social Science and Medicine*, 44(8): 1169–80.

Rosenzweig, M. R., and Stark, O. (1989), 'Consumption Smoothing, Migration, and Marriage: Evidence from Rural India', *Journal of Political Economy*, 97(4): 905–26.

Schuler, S. R., Hashemi, S. M., and Riley, A. P. (1997), Men's Violence against Women in Rural Bangladesh: Undermined or Exacerbated by Microcredit Programs?', paper presented at the 1997 Annual Meetings of the Population Association of America, Washington, March.

Schultz, T. P. (1990), 'Testing the Neoclassical Model of Family Labor Supply and Fertility', *Journal of Human Resources*, 25(4): 599–634.

Sen, A. (1990), 'More than 100 Million Women are Missing', *New York Review of Books*, 37: 61–6.

Skoufias, E., and Quisumbing, A. R. (2005), 'Consumption Insurance and Vulnerability to Poverty: A Synthesis of the Evidence from Bangladesh, Ethiopia, Mali, Mexico and Russia', *European Journal of Development Research*, 17(1): 24–58.

Smith, L. C., Ramakrishnan, U., Haddad, L., Martorell, R., and Ndiaye, A. (2003), 'The Importance of Women's Status for Child Nutrition in Developing Countries', Research Report No. 133, Washington: International Food Policy Research Institute.

Stark, O., and Levhari, D. (1982), 'On Migration and Risk in LDCs', *Economic Development and Cultural Change*, 31(1): 191–6.

Strauss, John, and Thomas, Duncan (1995), 'Human Resources: Empirical Modeling of Household and Family Decisions', in Jere R. Behrman and T. N. Srinivasan (eds.), *Handbook of Development Economics*, vol. iii/a, Amsterdam: NorthHolland Publishing Company, 1883–2024.

——— (1998), 'Health, Nutrition, and Economic Development', *Journal of Economic Literature*, 36(2): 766–817.

Strickland, R. (2004), 'To Have and to Hold: Women's Property and Inheritance Rights in the Context of the HIV/AIDS in Sub-Saharan Africa', International Center for Research on Women Working Paper.

Thomas, D. (1990), 'Intrahousehold Resource Allocation: An Inferential Approach', *Journal of Human Resources*, 25(4): 635–64.

—— (1994), 'Like Father, Like Son; Like Mother, Like Daughter: Parental Resources and Child Height', *Journal of Human Resources*, 29(4): 950–89.

—— Contreras, D., and Frankenberg, E. (2002), 'Distribution of Power within the Household and Child Health', mimeo, RAND, Santa Monica, Calif.

Townsend, R. (1994), 'Risk and Insurance in Village India', *Econometrica*, 62: 539–91.

World Bank (2001), *Engendering Development through Gender Equality in Rights, Resources, and Voice*, World Bank Policy Research Report, Washington.

Zeldes, S. P. (1989), 'Consumption and Liquidity Constraints: An Empirical Investigation', *Journal of Political Economy*, 97: 305–46.

13

Questioning the Power of Resilience

Are Children up to the Task of Disrupting the
Transmission of Poverty?

Jo Boyden and Elizabeth Cooper

13.1. Introduction

Scholars have long been interested in learning how human beings react to adversity, and human responses to phenomena such as family separation, poverty, and armed conflict, categorized as adversities in and of themselves, or as inducing risk exposure to adversity, are now the subject of several major bodies of literature globally. Risk and resilience have been judged powerful conceptual and analytical tools in this work and are invoked by researchers in a range of disciplines. Historically, the notion of resilience first entered the health sciences from applied physics and engineering, where it signifies the ability of materials to 'bounce back' from stress and resume their original shape or condition. In medicine the term characterized the recovery of patients from physical traumas such as surgery or accidents. Somewhat later, it was adopted into psychological and social research to indicate an individual's capacity to recover from, adapt to, and/or remain strong in the face of adversity. This literature tends to ascribe the concept of resilience to three kinds of phenomena: (a) good outcomes despite high-risk status; (b) sustained competence under threat; and (c) recovery from trauma (Masten, Best, and Garmezy, 1990; Masten, 1994).

Given that adversity and risk are enduring features of human existence, the resilience concept has special appeal for scholars: the promise of research on resilience being the discovery of those factors that enable individuals to triumph over catastrophe. Unsurprisingly, the popularity of this concept in research has led to a remarkable proliferation in popular

Western media, 'trade' literature (Boyden and Myers, forthcoming), and contemporary development discourse and practice (Christian Children's Fund, 2002–6; International Rescue Committee, 2002–7; World Health Organization, 2006). Much of the trade literature and development discourse, and much of the research that informs it, focuses on children. In research with the young, the concept of resilience is used largely as a means of exploring what is predetermined and what is pliant in the child. Hence, children's resilience is located at the nexus of the nature–nurture dialectic, or as Rutter (2002) pointedly corrects, at the interplay of these two influences.

Applied to childhood poverty, poverty over the life course, and the intergenerational transmission of poverty, the resilience of boys and girls may be considered as serving as a conceptual and analytical tool for examining the ways in which young humans are able to overcome the negative outcomes of poverty and prevent its transfer within families, households, and communities. However, research shows that, as a general rule, children are more susceptible to the effects of poverty than are adults, especially during infancy and in terms of physical impacts. It is not merely by chance that many of the more robust global indicators of poverty— low birth weight, infant and under-5 mortality, for example—relate to the survival and well-being of children. And child and maternal nutrition and health status are cited as critical in determining the irreversibility of poverty transfers (Smith, 2006, p. 5). Children's relative vulnerability is due both to processes of maturation in young humans and configurations of power and dependence within society, especially bearing in mind their need for security, nurturance, and teaching through to (and beyond) puberty.

Evidence of high rates of infant and child mortality and morbidity in poor communities throughout the world as well as observations of enduring poverty and cumulative effects of poverty over the life course and subsequent generations would seem to fly in the face of any assertion of childhood resilience against poverty. Yet, narratives of children's resilience have from the beginning of the concept's popular adoption by social scientists been interwoven with narratives of childhood poverty. To ascertain whether resilience is an article of ideological faith or in fact a cross-culturally evident feature of young human lives, this chapter reviews the advances and persistent challenges in realizing a credible and useful definition of resilience in the social sciences as a basis for considering specific associations between children and resilience in the context of chronic poverty. Its purpose is to explore what, if anything, studies of resilience in children can tell us about the life course and intergenerational transmission of poverty and its effects.

13.2. The Development and Application of Resilience in 'Risk' Research

The most systematic and influential research on risk, resilience, and coping has been conducted in the United States and Europe in the fields of human development and social work. Early psychological and social studies of children focused far less on competence and strength than on pathology and were motivated by concerns of parents, welfare professionals, and public institutions about behavioural problems in the young such as school failure, crime, and suicide (Fraser, 2004). One of the aims of this research was to identify forces in children's lives that increase risks for such behaviours and to establish how policy might prevent or reduce these risks. Theoretical and empirical advances were soon made in understanding that a variety of social problems appeared to be influenced by a common set of multiple risk factors (Barton, 2005). Acknowledgement of the recurrence of social and behavioural problems in successive generations motivated an emphasis on intergenerational influences on conduct. Emphasizing children's psycho-emotional and social dependence on adults, there was a particular focus on the values, condition, and circumstances of parents and carers. Harsh or neglectful parenting behaviour, together with parental mental illness, unemployment, and recurrent ill health, early and single parenthood, family separation, and divorce were among the many phenomena highlighted as significant.

Even though research long ago established a clear link between a range of stressors and behavioural problems in the young, the accumulated evidence that some individuals appear to thrive despite sharing the characteristics and conditions of those with problems (e.g. Rutter, 1985; Anthony, 1987; Werner and Smith, 2001) led eventually to a shift in scholarly interest. These 'successful' individuals were deemed to be resilient, and discovering the factors that enhance their resilience became a prominent line of enquiry.

In this research context risk is defined in terms of statistical probabilities of susceptibility to negative outcomes. Hence the focus on resilience is trained on those factors that moderate outcomes and impacts. These moderating factors are variables that influence the potency and direction of the association between cause and effect, thereby strengthening or weakening the effects of stressors on children. Those factors that exacerbate susceptibility to negative effects are often termed risk or vulnerability factors while those factors that mitigate negative effects are generally described as protective factors or protective processes (Luthar, 2006). Coping is another term associated with both risk and resilience, and usually denotes struggling or dealing with difficulties. Although coping may imply some degree of success in managing adversity, it does not normally indicate positive adaptation in the same way as protective factors leading to overall resilience.

Appreciating that the effects of adversity on human development are highly influenced by both individual and collective processes, there has been a significant concern with identifying different mechanisms operating at different levels—individual, familial, communal, institutional, and so on—and how they correlate with and reinforce one another. Some risk and protective factors are characterized as internal; they result from the unique combination of characteristics that make up an individual, such as temperament, intelligence, or physical health. Thus, ethnographic research conducted in Brazilian shanties by anthropologist Nancy Scheper-Hughes (1992) found that, through higher levels of alertness and social interaction, some infants are able to attract greater attention from carers than others, with significant effects on the levels of care they receive and hence on their survival in the context of poverty. Others are external or ecological; that is, they are the outcome of environmental factors, such as social and material conditions, which affect an individual's healthy development and well-being. The significance of the interplay between internal and external factors is bound to how each is transmitted and options for responses.

Developmental psychologist Suniya Luthar concludes her synthesis of resilience research with the evaluation that 'Resilience rests, fundamentally, on relationships' (Luthar, 2006, p. 780). By relationships, Luthar is explicitly referring to social relationships between human beings:

During the childhood years, early relationships with primary caregivers affect several emerging psychological attributes and influence the negotiation of major developmental tasks; resolution of these tasks, in turn, affects the likelihood of success at future tasks. Accordingly, serious disruptions in the early relationships with caregivers—in the form of physical, sexual, or emotional abuse—strongly impair the chances of resilient adaptation later in life. Whereas some maltreated children will obviously do better in life than others, the likelihood of sustained competence, without corrective, ameliorative relationship experiences, remains compromised at best. On the positive side, strong relationships with those in one's proximal circle serve vital protective processes, for children as well as for adults.   (Luthar, 2006, p. 780)

As resilience and competence have risen to the fore in research, so social workers and other 'helping' professionals (e.g. Saleebey, 1997) have sought to establish models of practice that emphasize clients' strengths rather than their problems or deficits. In this sense, it can be understood that the conceptual genealogy of resilience hints at an ideological bias. In other words, one way of framing the sudden popularity of the notion of resilience is to acknowledge its purposeful contrast with the vulnerability discourse, much in the same way that the assets discourse in poverty studies provided a counter to the deficit-focused model that emphasizes needs (Narayan et al., 2000). Applied to children, this change in approach reflects a decidedly political orientation in its recognition of the young as competent social agents rather than inherently vulnerable beings that are wholly dependent on others for their survival and development.

With recent advances in the study of the human genome, genetic researchers have begun to contribute to the conceptualization of human resilience. These advances have expanded the boundaries of research on human development, giving rise to studies of the activities of specific genes and their potential effects. Scientists have pursued research that indicates correlations between certain genes and psychological traits, including those involving attitudes or social behaviour (linking genetic effects to probabilities of divorce, religiosity, and parenting styles, for instance; Rutter, 2002). While such associations have been critiqued among their disciplinary peers for being overly reductionist, there is acceptance of the idea that all behaviours are affected in some way by genetics (Rutter, 2002; Curtis and Cicchetti, 2003). In other words, it would seem that resilience is at least partly heritable, with protective processes operating through both genetic and environmental effects, the test being the ability 'to find out how these genetic effects are mediated because, obviously, they are most unlikely to operate directly on the social behaviour as observed' (Rutter, 2002, p. 3).

As yet, there have been few studies examining genetic contributors to resilient functioning (Curtis and Cicchetti, 2003), although genetic inheritance has been hypothesized as an 'obvious place' to investigate human resilience based on the truism that individuals differ in both genetic make-up and their responses to the same environmental stimuli (Hampton, 2006, p. 1756). As Thomas Insel of the US National Institute of Mental Health justifies the convergence of genetic and resilience research: 'To not exploit the power of modern genomics would really be a mistake in a field in which we start by saying that this is about individual variation' (ibid.). A 2006 conference sponsored by the New York Academy of Sciences and Brown Medical School that focused on Resilience in Children advertised the potential of the 'new biology' of resilience as offering 'an unprecedented understanding of processes of development in atypically and typically developing children and will have profound implications for preventive intervention programs' (New York Academy of Sciences, 2006).

Some progress has been reported in studying the combined effects of genetic variants and environmental factors. For example, a study of maltreated children with a particular variation of a specific gene found that these children were more likely to develop antisocial problems than those without this variation and similarly that depression after childhood maltreatment was more common among individuals with the same type of variation of a different gene than individuals without this variation (Hampton, 2006, referencing Caspi et al., 2002). Research into how genetic and environmental factors interact and how these interactions can affect individuals has also been recognized as providing new plausible interpretations. For instance, a team at the US

National Institute of Child Health and Human Development that studied the different behavioural tendencies (high and low levels of aggression) of monkeys found that monkeys with the same genetic variation both experienced different genetic effects (in serotonin metabolism rates) and demonstrated different behavioural tendencies (in aggression levels) according to whether they were mother- or peer-reared. These findings can be interpreted in two different ways: either an environmental influence ('good' mothering) buffers the potential deleterious effect of a certain genetic variation; or, a particular genetic variation can protect an individual in a potentially deleterious environment (absence of 'good' mothering). As the study's lead scientist Stephen Suomi reflects on the implications of the latter interpretation: 'If you use the argument that good genes are protecting against bad environments, that's nice if you have good genes, but it's a little tough to change your genetic background' (Hampton, 2006, p. 1759).

Thus we see different branches of resilience research extending in different directions according to disciplinary interests: those scientists propounding the potential of the 'new biology' are attempting to become more precise in understanding how genetic and environmental influences interact, whereas social scientists focus their attention at the complexities of how individuals socially engage with the world as part of their survival. These are both valuable pursuits, particularly for their recognition of dynamic and interactive processes in people's lives. Yet, it is at the convergence of these different levels of analysis that the most promising new insights may be located. Recent findings from biological research indicate that social and psychological experiences exert actions on the brain which can modify gene expression and brain structure, function and organization, which in turn can lead to the initiation and continuation of behavioural changes (Curtis and Cicchetti, 2003; Hampton, 2006). As such, all stages of feedback loops, i.e. the cyclical interaction of social experiences and biological effects, require integrated analysis. The work of those few people who seek to translate findings from each domain of research so that they might converge to inform more holistic and long-term definitions of problems, risk and protective factors, and ultimately the potential for positive adaptation at the locus of the individual who is negotiating her or his environment may prove supremely valuable for informing what can be contributed to support people in adversity.

13.3. Some Problems with Applying Resilience in Poverty Research

The vast majority of the popular and scholarly literature on resilience represents the phenomenon as though it embodied scientifically proven principles that can be applied to positive effect in the lives of those living in adversity.

Yet, in spite of the appeal of resilience as a tool in the struggle to 'inoculate' children against hazards of many kinds and prevent the transmission of susceptibilities across generations, research in this area is beset with conceptual and analytical problems. Here we examine a few of the major difficulties.

One of the more fundamental limitations of the resilience research has to do with its origin in particular domains of psychology, social work, and other human sciences. This disciplinary legacy has led to an inordinate focus first on the individual as the unit of observation and second on intra-psychic functioning and individual behaviour as the object of analysis. Such foci are sustained at the expense of broader structural and collective considerations that make a crucial difference to human experiences of adversity. The distortion in perspective becomes apparent when one considers the extent to which chronic poverty and intergenerational poverty transmission are in fact shaped by overwhelming structural forces, as in the cases of institutionalized labour and property market discrimination against people of a particular caste or ethnic status. While the agentive role of the individual cannot be denied, such structural forces can become deeply embedded within society, entrenching poverty and related distress in many generations of a population.

At a more practical level, the emphasis on individual functioning and the harnessing of individual resources to overcome adversity depoliticizes the project of poverty reduction. Attention is diverted away from the state and other actors with the power and moral responsibility to intervene and bring about change, with populations living in poverty being charged with using their own resources to support themselves through crisis. Hence we find major players in the field of poverty reduction adopting a default position which individualizes that which should, in fact, involve structural or collective effort for change in most circumstances. Thus, even the World Bank can be found promoting the resilience concept, as evidenced by a paper it produced on early childhood development: 'Parents and other caregivers can promote resilience in their children by positively responding to situations and by teaching children how to respond' (World Bank, n.d.). Resilience researcher Michael Ungar articulates the reasons for concern: 'The discourse of resilience can be (has been?) co-opted by proponents of a neo-conservative agenda that argues if one person can survive and thrive, then shouldn't the responsibility for success be on all individuals within populations at risk to do likewise?' (2005b, p. xvi; bracketed content in original).[1]

The multi- and interdisciplinary nature of resilience research is another major challenge to this field and is one that undermines the achievement of a coherent conceptual and theoretical framework that can be applied to

---

[1] The concerns outlined above resonate in important ways with the long-standing debate in which the concept of 'the culture of poverty' as a predisposition to fatalism or laziness was proposed in explanations of the causes of and solutions to poverty.

practice. Scholarly debates have yet to produce clarity on the definition, locus, determinants, mediating, and moderating factors and outcomes of resilience. The lack of conceptual and theoretical coherence is evident even with the core constructs of this field. We have stated that in psychological and social theories, the effects of resilience are revealed only in their interaction with risk, and it is therefore apparent that the concept cannot have meaning without a pre-existing understanding of risk. Clearly, then, the starting point for defining and identifying resilience is knowledge of the 'problem'. But in practice defining a problem for an individual or a society incurs normative judgements; what is 'bad' is predicated on values, interests, and assumptions.

Indeed, the 'problem' of poverty itself continues to be redefined according to paradigmatic shifts and methodological innovations, especially as the long-cherished premise that poverty can be ascertained according to unidimensional measures is increasingly contested and countered. Multidimensional definitions of poverty are now being advocated and accepted, thereby gradually moving away from definitions resting solely on income or consumption shortfall (e.g. the World Bank's demarcation of US$1/day for the poverty line, which still dominates much poverty-related policy). Development researchers and practitioners have encouraged the employment of more contextually specific definitions of poverty in which the social and political rather than, or as well as, the economic dimensions of the phenomenon are stressed. These analyses commonly give prominence to emic perspectives, which are often divergent and which emphasize that even if consensus on the definition of poverty is reached it is not always characterized or experienced as a problem (Graham and Pettinato, 2005; Hulme and McKay, 2005). Certainly, children's poverty has a long and contentious history of problem definition (Feeny and Boyden, 2003; Gordon et al., 2005).

Such mutations in the course of problem conceptualization obviously complicate the establishment of a baseline of risk, from which to evaluate what resilience to that problem may look like. If resilience manifests positive adaptation despite exposure to a problem then what constitutes positive adaptation also requires definition. This clearly implicates the same challenges as problem definition, given that positive adaptation is difficult to claim as universally and objectively knowable. The proliferation of research and theory concerning well-being definitions is testament to the difficulties in validating factors associated with both objective and subjective perceptions of quality of life across contexts (Camfield and McGregor, 2005). Most current resilience researchers justify presenting only very general indicators of positive adaptation as sensitivity to contextual specificity. For instance, Luthar posits that the concept of resilience is most salient with the concept of social competence, or the effective performance in developmental tasks appropriate for people 'of a given age, society or context, and historical time' (Luthar, 2006, p. 751).

Even if the general domains of well-being turn out to be broadly universal, specific factors and specific competencies will inevitably prevail in different contexts according to socio-cultural patterning. Scholars in psychology and anthropology (for example, Goodnow, 1990; Rogoff, 1990; Cole, 1996) who follow the socio-cultural approach to human development first expounded by Lev Vygotsky (Vygotsky, 1978) would have no difficulty with such a proposition for they maintain that all psychological phenomena, including perceptions of risk and resilience, are highly dependent on context. It is their contention (Rogoff, 1990) that, consciously or not, caregivers and other mentors structure children's learning to support the acquisition of the knowledge, skills, and experience needed to function successfully in their particular environment. Since each environment contains unique socio-cultural and material features and challenges, this is an enduring source of cognitive, psychological and social diversity in the young, with clear implications for variation in 'positive' or 'resilient' behaviour.

Since values, interests, and perspectives influence judgements of what is 'good', this raises the possibility that outside researchers may not share that same understanding about positive adaptation as the individuals whose behaviour they are analysing. To add further to this complexity, responses may function as positive adaptations in immediate circumstances but generate other negative outcomes in different circumstances (in the future, in other environments). Research among children of depressed mothers in the United States, for instance, showed that boys and girls who adopt a caretaker role at first appeared to be responding well. However, susceptibility to problems such as depression and anxiety were later observed (Luthar, 2006, citing Hammen, 2003; and Hetherington and Elmore, 2003). Indeed, the response in such cases has been characterized as 'false maturity', hinting at the masking of problems beneath the surface of outward behaviours. In relation to poverty or other experiences of marginalization, the theory of false consciousness, if valid, suggests that people's perceptions of how they are doing 'can easily be swayed by mental conditioning or adaptive expectations' (Sen, 1999, p. 62). Hence, it is important to appreciate that even while resilience traits imply the ability to overcome adversity, such traits need not necessarily manifest in behaviours that are generally understood as positive adaptation. For example, resilience against the adversities of war may entail responses such as emotional numbing or hyper-vigilance which can have the effect of reducing the capability of affected individuals to empathize and interact positively with others (Dawes, 2000).

Only after ideas of the problem and the resilient response are established is it possible to begin identification of associated risk and protective factors, a task which Luthar describes as 'the central objective of resilience researchers' (Luthar, 2006, p. 743). Thus, risk and protective factors are defined in relation to problem or positive adaptation definitions. Findings from a study of child labour in Vietnam illustrate this point. Child labour is prevalent among those Vietnamese households likely to have higher borrowing costs, that are further from schools, and whose adult members experienced negative returns to their own education (Beegle, Dehejia, and Gatti, 2005). Five years subsequent to child labour experiences, researchers find significant negative impacts on educational enrolment and attainment, but also substantially higher earnings for those (young) adults who worked as children. The study also showed no significant effects of child labour on individuals' health. Forecast estimates of earnings from the age of 30 onward, however, indicate that forgone earnings attributable to lost schooling exceed any earnings gain associated with child labour, and that the net present discounted value of child labour is positive for discount rates of 11.5 per cent or higher. The researchers interpret their results to show that in the medium run (i.e. over a five- to ten-year horizon) there are important economic benefits to child labour that offset its opportunity cost (lower school attainment) for households. However, over a longer horizon the returns to education increase, with more-educated individuals experiencing increased wage growth, and the returns to work experience decrease. As this study's findings demonstrate, if the problem is defined as household earnings in the next five to ten years then child labour could be regarded as a protective factor against poverty (particularly since no health problems were noted). On the other hand, if the problem is defined as the earning potential of individuals twenty to thirty years hence, child labour may be a vulnerability factor for future poverty.

In studies of poverty, the power of subjective valuation in confounding interpretations of ill-being and well-being, risk and resilience, is often illustrated through comparison of the social and psychological effects of relative versus absolute poverty (Camfield and McGregor, 2005). Surprisingly perhaps, subjective perceptions of life satisfaction or happiness are seldom found to correlate in an obvious way with 'objective' assessments of people's material circumstances. Subjective interpretations of adversity by those affected, however, make a significant difference to resilience and well-being since the meaning of experience is a crucial moderator of its effect. Thus, relative poverty commonly has far more deleterious effect on psychological, emotional, and social well-being than does absolute poverty. Such findings are likely to reflect the fact that material lack is perceived as far more debilitating when associated with stigma, social exclusion, and denigration.[2] Therefore, it follows that judging whether a phenomenon such as child labour is a

---

[2] In rural Bolivia, for example, despite knowing full well that chronic shortages of water have a significant effect on livelihoods and on the survival and health of humans and livestock, children highlighted above all the humiliation of being unable to wash and therefore being labelled smelly, dirty, and poor (Boyden et al., 2003). These children acknowledged that one of the worst consequences of being thought of as 'poor' is the associated shame, social exclusion, and humiliation by peers.

risk or protective factor remains contentious and the debate is probably only resolvable according to careful attention to specific contexts' local values in relation to this activity and perhaps even individuals' particular situations. This kind of complexity points to the danger of approaches to well-being and resilience that 'fragment people's accounts of their experience or reduce them to a single indicator' (Camfield and McGregor, 2005, p. 197).

13.4. Assessing the Role of Children's Resilience in Preventing Poverty Transmission

Researchers have often sought to investigate life course and intergenerational aspects of transmission as a means of explaining how poverty becomes a chronic condition within families and communities (Harper, Marcus, and Moore, 2003; Hulme and Shepherd, 2003; Smith and Moore, 2006; Bird, 2007). In assessing the potential of resilient individuals to disrupt poverty transmission, the question remains as to how deterministic these transmissions are.

In making a case about a potential relationship between children's resilience and the obstruction of poverty transmission, the first step would need to be acknowledgement that children inherit rather than create their poverty. The understanding that children do not of their own making cause their poverty implies the intergenerational transmission of poverty from parents to children, which in turn reflects a view of poverty as dynamic (Green and Hulme, 2005). Insofar as inheritance of poverty is the concern, this highlights the mediated nature of childhood experience, in which poverty (and other adversities) may impact both directly on the child, but also indirectly through stress or disruption to care arrangements, family networks, community, and other environmental support systems. This emphasis on the inseparability of the well-being of boys and girls from the settings, systems of relationships, and cultural processes within which they are raised resonates strongly with the key tenets of resilience research.

Such a conceptualization brings to the fore the capital of households, parents, carers, and other adults with a significant role in children's lives. In accordance with this paradigm, Hulme and Shepherd (2003) present a list of poverty-related capital that can be transmitted from 'parent' to 'child' through various means. They include items of financial, material, and environmental capital (e.g. land, physical assets, debt), human capital (e.g. survival strategies, disease), and social, cultural, and political capital (e.g. norms of entitlement, value systems, access to key decision makers). Different modes of transmission are recognized for the different forms of capital, such as inheritance (both the physical inheritance of goods and genetic inheritance), investment (of time and capital in care, education, and health), and socialization (ibid.). One of the more robust correlations to emerge in research of this nature is between mother's education attainment, child survival, and children's eventual education attainment, with implications for opportunity and well-being (Harper, 2004).

But, while it would seem to make a lot of sense to think about poverty as being inherited by children through deprivations of various forms of capital that are conveyed via different means, pinning down the mechanisms of intergenerational transfer of non-material forms of capital is not so straightforward. For example, in the case of resilience in individuals, we are not necessarily talking about observable goods in the way of financial, material, and environmental capital but, as defined by Hulme and Shepherd (2003), various forms of human, social, cultural, and political capital; these manifest in far more intangible variables such as traits, competencies, values, self-perceptions, and the like. It is hard to imagine precisely how these kinds of variables can be measured concretely as acting against poverty transmission across generations. Further, whereas it is possible to conceive of highly developed skills in problem solving and lateral thinking as encouraging entrepreneurial actions that lead in turn to capital accumulation, some other competencies, even whilst manifesting significant positive adaptation to adversity, may appear to have only tenuous connection with poverty eradication.

In emphasizing the mother–child dyad, or systems of relationships based in the nuclear family or household, as the locus of transmission of non-material forms of capital, poverty research shares with much of the resilience research some significant assumptions that may not in practice be valid. Thus, for such transfers to work they must somehow be embedded in a mix of genetic heritability and environmental influences related to physical proximity and underpinned by ties of affect, mentoring, and role modelling. This kind of thinking seems to take for granted the family structures and relationships through which transmission occurs, as well as the care arrangements made for young children. As it happens, family structures and relationships— especially nuclear family structures and relationships—may well be quite marginal to intergenerational transmissions of non-material forms of capital and resilience traits in the many parts of the world where alternative family forms and care arrangements prevail. Practices like child labour migration, exchange, and fosterage, or shared caretaking by extended kin and neighbours and sibling caretaking including in child-headed households, would seem likely to result in multiple and diffuse emotional and social attachments across a range of relationships and reduced interaction and allegiance between parents and children (Mann, 2001). Hence, the power of intergenerational transmission between parent(s) or household and child may be much diluted in such situations. Indeed, current research is challenging assumptions about the foundational role of family in children's development (Harris, 1998), highlighting the influence of peers, school, neighbourhood networks, and the like as well as the development of domain-specific behaviours. This research raises important questions concerning the efficacy of the concept of intergenerational transfers of non-material forms of capital.

Turning to lifespan or life course transmission of poverty, we find a different set of research challenges. The thinking in this area rests on extensive evidence provided by health sciences and developmental psychology that childhood experience and children's development and well-being are foundational in shaping individual life trajectories. In other words, how children respond to their poverty will probably have major ramifications for adaptation and functioning in adulthood; such transmission being expressed in diverse domains, including physical health, social skills, emotions, values, and conduct. In scrutinizing the health and developmental psychology literature, then, we find a proclivity for emphasizing the timeliness of children's resilience which is what distinguishes the resilience of the young from that of adults. This timeliness boils down to the idea that children have developmental pathways or, in other words, behaviours that manifest in a systematic or orderly fashion, with behaviours at later stages in the sequence characterizing those in the earlier stages but progressing to more exaggerated forms. Early childhood is theorized as especially critical in building lifelong attributes, including resilience competencies and/or vulnerability traits (Compas, Gerhardt, and Hinden, 1995; Kelley et al., 1997). This is both because developmental patterns established at this stage will probably be reproduced later on in the lifespan and also because this early phase of life is characterized by accelerated processes of developmental change that are in turn associated with heightened receptiveness to environmental stimuli.

Certainly the concept of developmental pathways is attractive for those interested in studying the possibility of building and sustaining in children resilience against poverty, the most obvious convergence of ideas and understanding in this respect being around time sensitivity. This notion builds on the evidence that there are important 'sensitive periods' for some developmental processes and potentials (Yaqub, 2002; Dawes and Donald, 2005) during which the stimulation that a child receives has a lasting effect on specific domains of development. Resilience theorists also predicate their approach on recognition of time sensitivity: 'there is broad consensus that in working with at-risk groups, it is far more prudent to promote the development of resilient functioning early in the course of development rather than to implement treatments to repair disorders once they have been crystallized' (Luthar, 2006, p. 739).

In poverty research, deprivation during sensitive periods has been correlated with later poverty in life and linked to intergenerational transmissions of poverty (Harper, 2004). Studies concerning various aspects of foetal, neonatal, infant, and child development have indicated the likelihood that different human motor and mental developments have time-sensitive receptivity to environmental factors. For instance, correlations have been observed between maternal malnutrition during pregnancy (for example iron deficiency anaemia) and low birth weight in infants, lowered resistance to infection, inhibited growth and cognitive development, and chronic diseases in later life (WHO, 2006). And prenatal and infant protein-energy under-nutrition has been causally linked to later impairment of intellectual function-ing (Alderman, Hoddinott, and Kinsey, 2001). Findings on nutrition, physical health, and education in particular make a compelling case for time-sensitive or age-appropriate strategies and interventions to assist children in mastering key developmental tasks and thereby prevent potentially irreversible harm to their future well-being, for once these developmental 'sensitive periods' have passed, opportunities to avoid permanent damage can diminish and even disappear (Moore, 2004, citing Gordon et al., 2003).

Even if the idea of developmental pathways has some practical signifi-cance for understanding how to bolster children against adversity, the con-cept does require further interrogation. The obvious question arising from a hypothesized connection between children's resilience and pathways is: how accessible are these pathways? First, are there universal pathways, for example in terms of self-esteem, self-efficacy, or emotional stability? Or are pathways more effectively conceptualized according to specific contexts (as with Sen's freedoms to realize competencies, for example, or with Rogoff's and anthropological views of socialization as training in cultural competencies)? And second, on a more methodological line of enquiry, does resilience create pathways or are the foundations of pathways required before children can mobilize their resilient potential to embark on their transformative journeys? On a more critical note, the concept conjures up a rather static model of human development in which the life course for adults seems to be largely predetermined according to patterns laid down in childhood. Proponents of transactional theory on the other hand have elaborated a far more dynamic perspective in which child-context interactions are seen to contribute dif-ferently to development at different points in the life cycle, such trans-actions leading to a continuous modification of developmental trajectories (Sameroff, 1975; Dawes and Donald, 2005). As Dawes and Donald highlight, this view 'challenges the idea that what is established early in development always has lasting or permanent effects' (2005, p. 14), and recognizes 'the complex interplay between genetic endowment and contextual influences across the lifespan' (ibid. 15).

Time sensitivity is obviously a concern for addressing many potential effects and causations of poverty (especially malnutrition), and this can necessarily mean targeting children who experience poverty, or may be susceptible to poverty given environmental factors. Nevertheless, recognition of the hetero-geneity of both contexts and children is crucial, as is retaining an understand-ing of poverty that does not reduce its characterization to biological effects

(Hastrup, 1993; Green and Hulme, 2005). As we have indicated, psychological, emotional, and social well-being are more complex states to ascertain than biological health and are far less likely to be subject to mechanistic cause and effect relations. Even while biological causal mechanisms are better understood, or at least more easily empirically verifiable, than social causal mechanisms, it is important to notice that these biological relationships are based on environmental influences rather than genetic influences. Thus our cognitive map of intergenerational transmission is at the present time extremely restricted to the site of the individual's body and does not stretch very far either internally into her or his genetic make-up or externally out to her or his roles and relationships in the social world.

The impossibility of observing resilience directly or of identifying precise causal relations and the complexity of identifying contributory effects of interacting and cumulative factors means that it makes most sense to speak in probabilities. Incertitude of causal relationships in human development and conduct remains, since the correlation between various inputs (for example, mother's education) and outputs (for instance, child's health or education attainment) are derived from large sets of socio-economic variables that cover many different parental and community characteristics (Yaqub, 2001). Thus, direct pathways are not identifiable (nor assumed to exist) and understanding of how different inputs and conditions interact remains complicated. And herein lies one of the most profound problems for resilience research, as Barton observes:

The sheer multiplicity of potential risk and protective factors and the possible relationships among them (reciprocal, conditional, etc) places strains on the most complex multivariate, quantitative models. When one introduces time as a variable—that is, that certain processes may apply only at certain times, have lagged effects, or both—another layer of complexity emerges. (Barton, 2005, p. 142)

13.5. Conclusion

At the outset of this chapter we assigned ourselves the task of questioning whether studies of resilience are useful for research and practice concerning children's poverty and the life course and intergenerational transmission of poverty. Based on our review of the increasing exercise of the resilience concept in various fields of research, we conclude that it has not yet been demonstrated as a valid analytical tool for poverty research. In short, we find that so far resilience has achieved neither a sufficiently functional definition nor a credible theory by which to identify its existence. Confident of unearthing direct cause and effect relations, much of the resilience research has been framed in positivist and mechanistic modes. But this kind of reasoning has been confounded by reality, leading some scholars to argue that we are in practice dealing with a multivariate phenomenon that is subject to highly complex moderating forces which in each individual combine uniquely to influence the outcomes and impacts of adversity in countless ways. To insist upon recognizing this multivariate phenomenon as 'resilience' runs the risk of generating a concept that by attempting to mean everything ends up meaning nothing of analytical value.

Efforts to improve understanding of the causes and effects of children's poverty and the intergenerational transmission of poverty would be better served by relinquishing the metaphor of resilience while retaining the focus on particular factors that moderate and mediate poverty experiences and outcomes. It seems supremely naive to expect that any absolute 'resilience process' could be identified given the infinite contingencies of the interplay between multiple factors. A more fruitful approach is to explicitly value and investigate these contingencies and how they play out in human development (broadly conceptualized). To do so means to invest in research that attends to the interactions of genetic and environmental influences as well as to how structural influences translate in people's everyday lives. The key challenge will be to retain the understanding that despite the empirical findings of chronic and intergenerational poverty, poverty is always experienced as dynamic. This dynamism is the challenge that spurs us on.

References

Alderman, H., Hoddinott, J., and Kinsey, B. (2001), *Long Term Consequences of Early Childhood Malnutrition*, Washington: World Bank.

Anthony, E. J. (1987), 'Risk, Vulnerability, and Resilience: An Overview', in E. J. Anthony and B. J. Cohler (eds.), *The Invulnerable Child*, New York: Guildford Press, 3–48.

Barton, W. (2005), 'Methodological Challenges in the Study of Resilience', in M. Ungar (ed.), *Handbook for Working with Children and Youth: Pathways to Resilience across Cultures and Contexts*, Thousand Oaks, Calif.: Sage Publications, 135–48.

Beegle, K., Dehejia, R., and Gatti, R. (2005), 'Why Should We Care about Child Labor? The Education, Labor Market, and Health Consequences of Child Labor', World Bank Policy Research Working Paper No. 3479.

Bird, K. (2007), 'The Intergenerational Transmission of Poverty: An Overview', CPRC Working Paper No. 99, Manchester: Chronic Poverty Research Centre. Available at: <http://www.chronicpoverty.org/pdfs/99Bird.pdf>.

Boyden, J. (2003), 'Children under Fire: Challenging Assumptions about Children's Resilience', *Children, Youth and Environments*, 13(1).

——and Mann, G. (2005), 'Children's Risk, Resilience, and Coping in Extreme Situations', in M. Ungar (ed.), *Handbook for Working with Children and Youth: Pathways to Resilience across Cultures and Contexts*, Thousand Oaks, Calif.: Sage Publications.

——and Myers, W. (forthcoming), 'Using the Idea of Resilience'.

——Eyber, C., Feeny, T., and Scott, C. (2003), *Children and Poverty: Experiences and Perceptions from Belarus, Bolivia, India, Kenya and Sierra Leone*, Richmond, Va.: Children's Christian Fund.

Camfield, L., and McGregor, A. (2005), 'Resilience and Well-Being in Developing Countries', in M. Ungar (ed.), *Handbook for Working with Children and Youth: Pathways to Resilience across Cultures and Contexts*, Thousand Oaks, Calif.: Sage Publications, 189–209.

Caspi, A., McClay, J., Moffitt, T. E., Mill, J., et al. (2002), 'Role of Genotype in the Cycle of Violence in Maltreated Children', *Science*, 297(5582): 851–4.

Christian Children's Fund (2002–2), 'Building Resilience in Angolan Children and Communities', Angola: USAID Displaced Children and Orphans Fund.

Clark, D., and Hulme, D. (2005), 'Towards a Integrated Framework for Understanding the Breadth, Depth and Duration of Poverty', GPRG Working Paper No. 20, retrieved 7 August 2006, from <http://www.gprg.org/pubs/workingpapers/pdfs/gprg-wps-020.pdf>.

Cole, M. (1992), 'Culture in Development', in M. Bornstein and M. Lamb (eds.), *Human Development: An Advanced Textbook*, Hillside, NJ: Erlbaum.

——(1996), 'Culture and Cognitive Development: From Cross-Cultural Comparisons to Model Systems of Cultural Mediation', in A. Healy, S. Kosslyn, and R. Shiffrin (eds.), *Essays in Honor of William K. Estes*, Hillsdale, NJ: Lawrence Erlbaum Associates, Inc, 279–306.

Compas, B., Gerhardt, C., and Hinden, B. (1995), 'Adolescent Development: Pathways and Processes of Risk and Resilience', *Annual Review of Psychology*, 46: 265–93.

Curtis, J., and Cicchetti, D. (2003), 'Moving Research on Resilience into the 21st Century: Theoretical and Methodological Considerations in Examining the Biological Contributors to Resilience', *Development and Psychopathology*, 15: 773–810.

Dawes, A. (1992), 'Psychological Discourse about Political Violence and its Effects on Children', in *Mental Health of Refugee Children Exposed to Violent Environments*, Oxford: Refugee Studies Centre, University of Oxford.

——(2000), *Cultural Diversity and Childhood Adversity: Implications for Community Level Interventions with Children in Difficult Circumstances*, Children in Adversity: Ways to Reinforce the Coping Ability and Resilience of Children in Situations of Hardship, Oxford University.

——and Donald, D. (2005), *Improving Children's Chances: Developmental Theory and Effective Interventions in Community Contexts*, Richmond, Va.: Christian Children's Fund.

Feeny, T., and Boyden, J. (2003), 'Children and Poverty: A Review of Contemporary Literature and Thought on Children and Poverty', Children and Poverty Series, Part I, Richmond: Christian Children's Fund. Available at: <www.christianchildrensfund.org/uploadedFiles/Publications/7659_Poverty%20Pt%201.pdf>.

Fraser, M. W. (ed.) (2004), *Risk and Resilience in Childhood: An Ecological Perspective*, 2nd edn., Washington: NASW Press.

Goodnow, J. (1990), 'The Socialization of Cognition: What's Involved', in R. A. S. J. W. Stigler and G. Herdt (eds.), *Cultural Psychology: Essays on Comparative Human Development*, Cambridge: Cambridge University Press.

Gordon, D., Nandy, S., Pantazis, C., Pemberton, S., and Townsend, P. (2003), *Child Poverty in the Developing World*, Bristol: Policy Press.

Gordon, D., Irving, M., Nandy, S., and Townsend, P. (2005), *Multidimensional Measures of Child Poverty*, International Conference on the Many Dimensions of Poverty, Brasilia.

Graham, C., and Pettinato, S. (2005), 'Subjective Well-Being and Objective Measures: Insecurity and Inequality in Emerging Markets', *Measuring Empowerment: Cross Disciplinary Perspectives*, Washington: World Bank.

Green, M., and Hulme, D. (2005), 'From Correlates and Characteristics to Causes: Thinking about Poverty from a Chronic Poverty Perspective', *World Development*, 33(6): 867–79.

Hammen, C. (2003), 'Risk and Protective Factors in Children of Depressed Parents', in S. Luthar (ed.), *Resilience and Vulnerability: Adaptation in the Context of Childhood Adversitie*, New York: Cambridge University Press, 50–75.

Hampton, T. (2006), 'Researchers Seek Roots of Resilience in Children', *Journal of the American Medical Association*, 295(15): 1756–60.

Harper, C. (2002), 'Recent Approaches to Understanding Policy and Action for Eradicating Childhood Poverty', *Journal of International Development*, 14: 1075–9.

—— (2004), 'Escaping Poverty Cycles', *inFocus*: 3–4.

—— Marcus, R., and Moore, K. (2003), 'Enduring Poverty and the Conditions of Childhood: Lifecourse and Intergenerational Poverty Transmissions', *World Development*, 31(3): 535–54.

Harris, J. (1998), *The Nurture Assumption: Why Children Turn out the Way They Do*, New York: Touchstone.

Hastrup, K. (1993), 'Hunger and the Hardness of Facts', *Man*, 28(4): 727–39.

Healthlink Worldwide (2006), *Building Children's Resilience in a Supportive Environment: Reflecting on Opportunities for Memory Work in HIV Responses*, London: Healthlink Worldwide.

Hetherington, E., and Elmore, A. (2003), 'Risk and Resilience in Children Coping with their Parents' Divorce and Remarriage', in S. Luthar (ed.), *Resilience and Vulnerability: Adaptation in the Context of Childhood Adversities*, New York: Cambridge University Press, 182–212.

Hulme, D., and McKay, A. (2005), 'Identifying and Measuring Chronic Poverty: Beyond Monetary Measures', International Conference on the Many Dimensions of Poverty, Brasilia.

—— —— (2006), 'Identifying and Measuring Chronic Poverty: Beyond Monetary Measures', CPRC-IIPA Working Paper No. 30, New Delhi: Indian Institute of Public Administration. Available at: <www.chronicpoverty.org/pdfs/IIPA-CPRC2005 Seminar/Hulme_Mckay(BeyondMonetary)Final.pdf>.

—— and Shepherd, A. (2003), 'Conceptualizing Chronic Poverty', *World Development*, 31(3): 403–23.

International Institute for Child Rights and Development (n.d.), 'Supporting Children's Development, Children's Rights, Children's Participation and Vulnerable Children Following the Tsunami', retrieved 21 July 2006, from <http://web.uvic.ca/iicrd/proj_war-affected.html#tsunami>.

International Rescue Committee (2002–7), 'Community Resilience and Dialogue', Uganda: International Rescue Committee.

Kelley, B., Loeber, R., Keenan, K., and DeLamatre, M. (1997), 'Developmental Pathways in Boys' Disruptive and Delinquent Behavior', *Juvenile Justice Bulletin*, December.

Luthar, S. (2006), 'Resilience in Development: A Synthesis across Five Decades', in D. J. C. D. Cicchetti (ed.), *Developmental Psychopathology: Risk, Disorder, and Adaptation*, New York: Wiley, 740–95.

McConnell Gladstone, B., Boydell, K. M., and McKeever, P. (2006), 'Recasting Research into Children's Experiences of Parental Mental Illness: Beyond Risk and Resilience', *Social Science and Medicine*, 62(10): 2540–50.

Mann, G. (2001), *Networks of Support: A Literature Review of Care Issues for Separated Children*, Stockholm: Save the Children Sweden.

Masten, A. S. (1994), 'Resilience in Individual Development: Successful Adaptation despite Risk and Adversity', in M. C. Wang and G. W. Gordon (eds.), *Educational Resilience in Inner-City America*, Hillsdale, NJ: Lawrence Erlbaum Associates, Inc.

—— Best, K., and Garmezy, N. (1990), 'Resilience and Development: Contributions from the Study of Children Who Overcome Adversity', *Development and Psychopathology*, 2: 425–44.

Moore, K. (2004), *Chronic, Life-Course and Intergenerational Poverty, and South-East Asian Youth*, UN Workshop on Youth Poverty in South-East Asia, Yogyakarta.

Narayan, D., Chambers, R., Shah, M., and Petesch, P. (2000), *Voices of the Poor: Crying out for Change*, New York: Oxford University Press for the World Bank.

New York Academy of Sciences (2006), 'Resilience in Children: Preliminary Program'.

Noble, K., Tottenham, N., and Casey, B. J. (2005), 'Neuroscience Perspectives on Disparities in School Readiness and Cognitive Achievement', *Future of Children*, 15(1): 71–89.

Rogoff, B. (1990), *Apprenticeship in Thinking: Cognitive Development in Social Context*, Oxford: Oxford University Press.

Rutter, M. (1985), 'Resilience in the Face of Adversity: Protective Factors and Resistance to Psychiatric Disorder', *British Journal of Psychiatry*, 147: 598–611.

—— (2002), 'Nature, Nurture, and Development: From Evangelism through Science toward Policy and Practice', *Child Development*, 73(1): 1–21.

Saleebey, D. (ed.) (1997), *The Strengths Perspective in Social Work Practice*, 2nd edn., White Plains, NY: Longman.

Sameroff, A. J. (1975), 'Transactional Models in Early Social Relations', *Human Development*, 18: 65–79.

Save the Children UK (2005), *Inheriting Extreme Poverty: Household Aspirations, Community Attitudes and Childhood in Northern Bangladesh*, London: Save the Children UK.

Scheper-Hughes, N. (1992), *Death without Weeping : The Violence of Everyday Life in Brazil*, Berkeley and Los Angeles: University of California Press.

Sen, A. (1999), *Development as Freedom*, Oxford: Oxford University Press.

Smith, B., with Moore, K. (2006), 'Intergenerational Transmission of Poverty in Sub-Saharan Africa: A Select Annotated Bibliography with Special Reference to Irreversabilities Associated with Poor Nutrition, Health and Education', CPRC Working Paper No. 59, CPRC Annotated Bibliography No. 3, Manchester: Chronic Poverty Research Centre. Available at: <www.chronicpoverty.org/pdfs/59Smith_(Moore).pdf>.

Ungar, M. (2004), 'A Constructionist Discourse on Resilience', *Youth and Society*, 35(3): 341–65.

Ungar, M. (2005a), *Summary Support of IRP Research Forum II Proceedings*, International Resilience Project Research Forum II: Pathways to Resilience, Halifax: International Resilience Project.

—— (2005b), 'Introduction: Resilience across Cultures and Contexts', in M. Ungar (ed.), *Handbook for Working with Children and Youth: Pathways to Resilience across Cultures and Contexts*, Thousand Oaks, Calif.: Sage Publications.

Vygotsky, L. S. (1978), *Mind and Society: The Development of Higher Mental Processes*, Cambridge, Mass.: Harvard University Press.

Werner, E., and Smith, R. (2001), *Journeys from Childhood to Midlife: Risk, Resilience and Recovery*, Ithaca, NY: Cornell University Press.

World Bank (n.d.), 'Early Childhood Development', retrieved 21 July 2006, from <http://web.worldbank.org/WBSITE/EXTERNAL/TOPICS/EXTEDUCATION/EXTECD/ 0,,contentMDK:20216720~menuPK:524408~pagePK:148956~piPK:216618~theSitePK: 344939,00.html>.

World Health Organization (2006), *Standards for Maternal and Neonatal Care*, Geneva: World Health Organization.

Yaqub, S. (2001), *At What Age Does Poverty Damage Most? Exploring a Hypothesis about 'Timetabling Error' in Antipoverty*, Justice and Poverty: Examining Sen's Capability Approach, Cambridge: University of Cambridge.

—— (2002), ' "Poor Children Grow into Poor Adults": Harmful Mechanisms or Over-Deterministic Theory?', *Journal of International Development*, 14: 1081–93.

14

The Social Distribution of Sanctioned Harm

Thinking through Chronic Poverty, Durable Poverty, and Destitution

Maia Green

14.1. Introduction

This chapter presents an anthropological take on the concept of chronic poverty. An anthropological approach places social construction at the centre of enquiry, considering how concepts come to inform the practice of those who are the subjects of study and the classificatory practices through which analysis is conducted. This reflexivity differentiates anthropology from other social sciences. Anthropological perspectives on the constitution of development categories not only provide a qualitative understanding of the social processes through which such classificatory systems come to have salience (Green, 2007). In exposing how the social is constituted as a category of organization and analysis, anthropology sheds light on the delineations of the social in other social sciences and hence on the explanatory limits of what is represented as social analysis (Green, 2006).

Chronic poverty is defined in the development literature as a state of deprivation of income, consumption, or capacities lasting more than five years. Economistic conceptions of chronic poverty, whether based on income or consumption measures, are based on normative theories about growth and market engagement as the means through which escape from poverty is possible, except for the chronically poor. The paradigm attempts to identify the exceptions to the growth rule, that is to isolate and explain why some agents fail to escape poverty. As such when framed in terms of economics the chronic poverty concept relies ultimately on neo-liberal characterizations of agency and markets. Apparently alternative propositions of what chronic poverty entails from the human development perspective are similarly removed from actual social situations. Such approaches do not describe the effects of contemporary institutional constellations on social outcomes but instead infer the social impacts of a range of assumed deprivations on abstract potentialities. Neither approach has the capacity to apprehend the social constitution of poverty; that is, not merely as an effect of deprivation of income or entitlements but as the outcome of a system of social relationships.

The limitations of the chronic poverty concept are explained by its origins in confronting core assumptions about the relation between economic development and poverty reduction as conjoined temporal outcomes along the depth versus duration axis. Perhaps paradoxically, although chronic poverty theorists have opted for *time* as a key analytical tool, their approach has focused on duration rather than process (cf. Bevan, 2003). This has implications for analytical reach. Approaches to chronic poverty have tended to be classificatory, rather than dynamic, concentrating on attributes associated with poverty as a state or, where based on panel data, comparing states across time periods. Focus on attributes rather than process creates the chronically poor as a category of analysis. But, because this category is not one through which societies and economies are organized on the ground, it cannot enhance social analysis, that is, our understanding of how societies, inequalities, and economies are made to work together in various places and times. Chronic poverty as a category may correspond to some local conditions, but it is not a local category of organization.

The concept of poverty from which chronic poverty derives is, however, an important category in the conceptual ordering of international development and of the wider global social imaginary in which this is embedded. Current constitutions of poverty which rest on implicit arguments about economic growth and the agency of households as maximizing actors in market-oriented economies are constitutive of modern social imaginaries, depending as they do on its categories of ordering—the economy as abstracted from political order, the public sphere, and the disembedding of the person as an individual property holder from wider structures of kinship and society (Habermas, 1989, p. 29; Taylor, 2004, p. 17). Much of the change which development seeks to achieve is ultimately concerned with effecting the alignment between social order and social imaginary, between social institutions and social forms (cf. Rabinow, 1995). Policy work, in government and development, is an explicit instance of institutional reordering. Policy makers and analysts use concepts and categories to represent the worlds which they seek to change, and resource transfers to effect the institutional transitions through which these may be realized (Green, 2007). The importance of significant categories and key words in policy discourses derives not only from the condensation of meanings and associations which they embody, but from their situation as nodes in the social orders which those policies seek to effect. Although policy constructs claim to be empirically grounded and evidence based, they are also fundamentally theoretical. Consequently, how poverty is theorized, that is imagined and represented, matters because it can inform how social relations are envisioned and the kinds of social orders which are thinkable and potentially brought into being through policy (cf. Fraser, 1993, pp. 8–9).

The concept of chronic poverty can pose challenging questions if informed by social analysis which interrogates the social processes through which some people stay poor. Insights from theories of destitution are useful here because they highlight the institutional nexus of social relations which ensure that certain people, rather than others, are likely to experience the effects of poverty for an extended time. The concept of destitution corresponds closely to indigenous and local understandings of extreme deprivation, which emphasize depth and duration combined. Second, destitution understood as an outcome of social exclusion acknowledges its social basis as a moral shift in the performance of categorical entitlements within a social system. Finally, apprehending destitution as a social status rather than an economic condition frees us from implicit assumptions about the necessity of economic engagement as the means to escape poverty traps. Combining findings from analyses of destitution with the problematic of chronic poverty leads to a proposed emphasis on *durable* poverty as the effect of particular constellations of unequal social relations, that is as an outcome of the ways in which societies are organized (after Tilly, 1998, pp. 5–6).

14.2. Time and Traps

Chronic poverty is as yet a rather unspecified concept within the emerging field of poverty studies. Intentionally conceived to confront development representations of poverty as a temporary state which people move in and out of, chronic poverty is defined as the condition of poverty persisting for more than five years, but which is commonly associated with far longer deprivations across multiple indicators. Chronic poverty affects those individuals and their families who will remain below a certain threshold from year to year, and generation to generation (Hulme and Shepherd, 2003; Hulme and McKay, 2006; Shepherd, 2006). This finding is critically important for development thinking about how the problem of poverty is to be addressed. The resilience of poverty, its immovability, provides concrete evidence that arguments about economic growth automatically benefiting the poor are deeply flawed.

The tenacity of poverty raises difficult questions about its durability: the extent to which social institutions perpetuate the relations of exclusion and allocation which ensure that certain individuals and their families will remain poor (Green and Hulme, 2005; Harriss, 2006). Because the concept of chronic poverty is so recent these questions are yet to be adequately addressed within the chronic poverty paradigm. Although implicit theory is embedded within the concept, namely its situation in relation to theories about the effects of growth, the main utility of chronic poverty is to capture those individuals and households with similar attributes in order to aggregate them into a development category as a potential object of policy. In practice, chronic poverty as a conceptual instrument in development studies is restricted at present to framing. Chronic poverty as a frame which captures the individuals and households whose conditions remain unchanged for five years or longer applies duration to poverty descriptors. In selecting duration over depth of poverty, that is the intensity and extent of deprivation, chronic poverty claims not to be so much concerned with differentiating between categories of the poor as to identify those most at risk of remaining poor across generations.[1] The durable poor are in any case often severely poor (Hulme and McKay, 2006). The longer individuals or households remain in poverty the less chance they have of getting out of it. The durability of poverty affects individuals whether poverty is conceptualized in terms of income/consumption axes or across human development criteria. Absence of assets, resources, capitals, or entitlements impacts on income, consumption, and potentialities over time.

Absence of growth or stasis does not challenge dominant poverty paradigms but reinforces them, necessitating the creation of a sub-paradigm to account for the phenomenon of households and economies which are seemingly impervious to growth. The chronic poverty paradigm, as an adjunct to mainstream theories of poverty, reiterates rather than replaces the theories about society and economy which structure poverty thinking. Chronic poverty as a concept is situated within this paradigm in which growth is assumed to inhere in the human condition as economic man (the gendering is intentional given assumptions about household headship and the enduring problematic of female-headed households) strives to achieve 'development'. Associated with the negative effects of poverty but without the escape route offered through growth, chronic poverty, like some inherited disorder, is intergenerationally transmitted (Moore, 2001; Hulme and Shepherd, 2003). From this perspective, persistent poverty becomes a pathological condition to be isolated and exposed. Biological metaphors are applied to the multitude affected, who become a mass, a demographic (cf. Fanon, 1967, p. 19; Hardt and Negri, 2000). The children of chronically poor parents are likely to be chronically poor themselves, confined within a transgenerational poverty trap that runs vertically and horizontally, across time and space (Harper, Marcus, and Moore, 2003; Green and Hulme, 2005).

The ultimate effects of transgenerational or long-term poverty traps are empirically uncertain. If the notion of trajectories of growth lifting all boats

---

[1] See Devereux on chronic poverty and destitution for an account of why depth matters.

is as much a fallacy as that of hard work being rewarded or of 'sustainable rural livelihoods', the opposite equally applies. Just as 'getting out of poverty' does not necessarily mean that one gets very far from the poverty line, staying poor does not necessarily mean that the poor become poorer, although some people will progressively lose assets to the point where they struggle to subsist. Of these, however, only a small minority risk sliding into absolute impoverishment and destitution. If poverty here appears as a relatively static condition in both directions this perhaps tells us less about the trajectories of people so classified than about the representational effects of poverty within development studies and within economics, that is as a state and a condition not so much of relative differentiation but of positionality in relation to an analytical boundary, the conceptual barrier separating the poor from the non-poor. Poverty thinking has prioritized this boundary and the means of traversing it over the subdivisions on either side. This is because poverty discourse has consistently situated itself within normative arguments about 'getting out of' poverty and because poverty reduction as a boundary shifted provides a visible object of public intervention (Sen, 1981, p. 157; O'Connor, 2001, p. 14; Devereux, 2003, p. 5). Poverty represented as deprivation below a common level, whether of income or consumption, focuses attention on the possibility of crossing the line and hence of the range of policy prescriptions which can facilitate this movement.

Where poverty is understood in income and consumption terms, the prescriptions logically focus on increasing income, not necessarily directly but through assumed relationships between increase in the overall economy and the incomes of individuals and households (Escobar, 1995, pp. 63–75). Where poverty is understood in human development terms to connote a state in which social agents are deprived of their potentiality to achieve a series of moral conditions and abstract freedoms, the emphasis is on the unspecified range of social and regulative regimes which could ensure that individuals achieve their capabilities.[2] If the former conceptualization of poverty rests on implicit assumptions about market engagement and increases in productivity as much as value as the means through which growth can be achieved, the latter depends on implicit assumptions about the latency of enabling institutions through which individual capabilities could be realized (Gore, 1993). As such, although both conceptualizations of poverty claim to be empirically grounded in research findings and so on, what is actually accessed through such conceptual tools is simply that which can be quantified and hence captured within their respective frames. Both rest on social theories about the normative possibilities of economy on the one hand and, on the other, entitlements to self-realization. Moreover, such externally imposed evaluative

---

[2] On entitlements approaches to poverty and well-being, see for example Sen (1999); Saith (2001); and Nussbaum (2003).

criteria do not necessarily correspond to local social categorizations of difference and deprivation, which generally make different kinds of distinctions and which impose boundaries in different places corresponding to the systems of social organization in which such boundaries come to have salience and are put to work. Chronic poverty as a concept has only limited resonance with the kinds of deprivation classifications invoked by members of poor communities, who are more likely to comment on the extreme poor where they have suffered other deprivations or where their status borders on the marginal (Hulme and McKay, 2006). Chronicity in itself or persistent poverty may indeed be too commonplace to be remarked upon in many communities at the periphery of world economies.

The lack of fit between chronic poverty as a category and the kinds of differentiations amongst the poor which people in poor communities consider meaningful stems from current policy orientations which aim to keep people out of poverty, and hence to focus representational energies on policing the analytical line between poor and non-poor. The result is a reliance on social analytical models which either make the boundary visible or facilitate its maintenance: hence for example vulnerability is defined in development social thought not as a state in which negative outcomes are likely, as in the common meaning of the term in English, but as the risk of becoming poor. In this actuarial categorization based on shared vulnerability to risk (Ewald, 1991, p. 199), rather than shared attributes, the attributes of those so categorized are rarely differentiated (Hastrup, 1993, p. 720). This lumping together has the paradoxical effect of equating the social and biological effects of extreme deprivation with the effects of assetlessness for the poor, who are nevertheless assumed to be situated on the margins of potential economic self-reliance. Such conceptual elisions are exemplified in the theoretical arguments of the economist Dasgupta, linking poverty to destitution, and destitution not merely to hunger but to human capacity for labour and hence to income and wealth (Dasgupta, 1993, 1997; Devereux, 2003; Fogel, 2004). This approach not only takes economies too literally, in assuming that the natural extension of human capacity to labour equates to the production of exchange value, after Ricardo and Marx (Gudeman, 2001, p. 101). It reduces humanity to biology, and biology to the reproduction of labour power (cf. Fanon, 1967). Human beings become simply machines within production systems.

In actuality, the causes and effects of extreme deprivation, poverty, and assetlessness must be differentiated. Extreme deprivation associated with destitution is qualitatively and experientially distinct from poverty, even of the chronic or apparently long-lasting kind (cf. Nandy, 2002, p. 115; Devereux, 2003). The important question is not whether assetlessness leads to deprivation, but under what conditions assets become the mediating factor in accessing support entitlements. Access to support may be mediated though exchange frameworks and markets, hence Sen's insight that the Great Bengal

Famine resulted not from an absence of food which was widely available in markets, but from what he termed a 'failure' in 'exchange entitlements' (1981, p. 47). It may also be mediated through a range of social statuses commonly associated with, and often prior to, asset portfolios. The most common of these is gender, in which gender status determines not only one's entitlement to hold various assets, but often the extent to which one can enter into other statuses which have implications for autonomy over one's own capabilities. Other examples where status is prior to asset holding include feudalism or caste-based land holding in village India.

14.3. Unnatural Assets

Assetlessness in the formal sense of absence of personal property and formal land holding were characteristic of foraging societies of southern Africa during the twentieth century, exemplified in the case of the San of Botswana and Namibia. Absence of assets, or rather a social system which did not construe relations between people as mediated by access to things (Strathern, 1985, p. 197), did not entail conditions of poverty (Good, 1999; see also Woodburn, 1982). As long as the San could access their main economic resource, their hunting and gathering territories, and as long as they could obtain additional cash through wage labour for neighbouring cattle herders, they seem to have enjoyed relatively good standards of living. They had considerable autonomy, the freedom to work as they chose, excellent nutrition (Lee, 1979, p. 296)[3] and plenty of leisure time. Indeed, in the 1970s the anthropologist Marshall Sahlins went so far as to claim that contemporary foraging groups were the 'original affluent society' (2004, p. 9). This has long ceased to be the situation. Forcibly resettled San in Namibia and Botswana find themselves excluded from their hunting grounds, unable to gather wild foods, and dependent on cash to mediate access to basic foods and necessities. Leisure ceases to be the desired purpose of productive labour and instead becomes forced through a combination of lack of access to previous productive activities and high unemployment. Poverty, welfare dependency, and destitution result (Good, 1999). Examples such as this demonstrate that relations between poverty and assets are complicated, depending on the social systems in which relationships between assets and entitlements are determined.

Assets are not things 'out there' in the world which have natural exchange values. What count as assets are artefacts of the social systems which determine what are constituted as such and their changing values. Recognition as an asset holder is first and foremost social recognition within a system that

---

[3] Compared to agriculturalists in the same region of Africa. Lee's study also shows that the San groups he worked with in the 1970s were less vulnerable to seasonal food shortages than neighbouring agriculturalists.

permits assets to become convertible. Within real economies, that is social systems as opposed to abstract models of economy, assets are what are accepted as assets, that is as having transactability and conversion value in relation to who is entitled to transact them (Gudeman, 2001). Social and natural capitals for example, the abstract values claimed by development theorists as forms of capital (e.g. Narayan and Pritchett, 1997), are not necessarily utilizable as assets unless they are convertible within actual economies. Natural capital can become convertible through formalization into property. This process of assetification, that is the social process of formalizing the asset status of things (and, in some social systems, persons), depends on political and institutional movements in the organization of the relations between people.[4] The 'mystery of capital', as De Soto acknowledges, does not inhere in capital itself, but within the institutional arrangements though which social relations can be made to bring 'capital' into being. Therefore, the strategy for creating capital is premised neither on production nor technology, although it entails the production of specialized technologies for the creation of capital, which centre on legal reforms and systems, that is on ways in which social relations are organized (2000, p. 9).

14.4. Destitution and Disentitlement

The importance of relationships, the institutional ordering between people and people and people and things, is clearly evident in the example of destitution. Destitution is not an automatic consequence of poverty, an endpoint in an economic process of impoverishment brought about by income failure. It is rather the product of a crisis in social relations. Destitution, associated with social exclusion and marginality and with the loss of the social entitlements within society that a person may have once had, represents sanctioned harm through a recategorization of a person away from previous entitlements (Harriss White, 2002, pp. 4–9). In the absence of wider systems of social support, the consequences of destitution are devastating. Yet despite the prevalence and severity of destitution globally, particularly in the poorest countries in the world, its significance has been consistently underplayed in development thinking.

The oversight of destitution in preference for poverty is explained by the challenges a concept of destitution as a failure of social relations presents for the theoretical underpinnings of the poverty paradigm, with its assumptions of individual economic agency oriented towards growth and the market as the institution capable of springing the poverty trap (see also Nandy,

---

[4] See Marcia Wright's book on the lives of East African slaves and other owned dependants for a sense of how this was organized in the nineteenth century (1993).

2002). In addition, as some theorists see destitution as the extreme end-point of progressive impoverishment, destitution is thought to be encompassed within the poverty paradigm. Such perspectives are profoundly distorting. Destitution, as the state in which people have lost social entitlements, is patently a different kind of social position from poverty, and has different consequences. Destitution might be connected to poverty of one sort or another, but the point is that once the person becomes destitute they have entered a new social categorization which situates them very differently in relation to others. In some instances, as for example in India, this resituation is so extreme as to amount to active social expulsion (Harriss White, 2002, p. 4).

The person locally categorized as destitute has experienced a loss of social placement, of entitlement, within a scheme of social ordering. Their social recategorization situates them outside social relations of entitlement, bringing into sharp relief the importance of moral content and values in determining who gets what, and to what extent the effects of extreme deprivation are socially tolerated. Destitution as a consequence of recategorization of entitlements or a shift in the moral content of social relations highlights the centrality of social relations in determining how people live, that is their deprivations and entitlements (see also Kabeer, 2005). These relations extend far beyond the market frameworks represented in economic models of poverty. Such models of economic relations fail to recognize the social constitution of value and allocations, and hence the social and institutional foundations of poverty and destitution. It is these socially constituted values and allocations which establish the parameters of distribution and compensation, and which ensure that some individuals are more likely than others to become destitute, and will not have the luxury of poverty.

Destitution is not so much a failure of social relations as a categorical shift into a different realm of social relations, into the domain beyond which social obligations cease. Destitution as a categorical transition into the space where social obligation has ended is a process of reordering, too, a social process through which certain individuals are socially resituated through active recategorization. This is not simply a consequence of poverty, but of a special kind of social reorganization. Understanding the social constitution of destitution as process sheds light not only on the differences between poverty and destitution, but on the ways in which the social ordering of allocative entitlements determines social well-being and social harm. Destitution in India has been characterized by Barbara Harriss White as a stage near the end-point of a process of social exclusion and marginalisation. The extent of the desocialization of the destitute is so extreme that destitution is generally experienced as a condition of individuals, the fragments of atomized households. Destitution in India is not an outcome of extreme poverty, although the destitute are extremely poor. It may be a consequence of mental illness, divorce, loss of rights to dependency, and stigmatization. The destitute lack social assets, although they do create their own forms of social organization (2002). Destitution in this example is more than the failure of livelihoods and dependence on transfers, as Devereux proposes for Ethiopia (2003, pp. 8, 11). Neither is it simply a matter of exclusion from access to the labour market which could provide income and hence the route away from poverty. Destitution is a *social status*. Destitution represents the condition in which people become disengaged from the moral obligations of mutuality which constitute the matrix of the social. The destitute have lost their rights to dependent status (Harriss White, 2002, p. 7). This disengagement encompasses kinship, households, and arenas of consumption and exchange. Destitution is thus not merely a highly individual condition (ibid. 3). It is positively antisocial.

Given that destitution is a kind of social status it is not surprising that it is most elaborated in highly unequal and formally differentiated societies such as India. As a shift in social categorizations into a realm beyond support it is of course more visible in countries which do not have widespread systems of emergency assistance and social welfare. Even in social welfare regimes, however, destitution exists and marks a transition point where assetless individuals become so socially disembedded as to be external not only to kinship and social networks but to the established state systems of social support (Pasarro, 1996). Destitution as a social status is also evident in the highly unequal but less formally hierarchical societies in Africa where, as in India, destitution as a status is associated with social and household fragmentation, marginalization, exclusion, and extreme deprivation. Perceiving destitution as a social status rather than an economic condition provides an interesting vantage point for understanding the processes of destitution which again must be apprehended in social terms. Destitution as the termination of entitlements through loss of dependent status is an outcome of the ways in which dependency is constituted in certain contexts for certain social categories. It is not the loss of support in itself which fosters destitution, although this becomes a precipitating cause, so much as the social order which deems certain social categories dependent on others and incapable of subsisting without new relations of dependency being established. What is stripped away from the destitute is the latent right to ongoing relations of dependency. They thus have to rely on the unpredictability and humiliation of charity and alms, and on the very transient relationship between giver and recipient which such transactions convey.

Vulnerability to destitution is not evenly distributed but is an attribute inherent in the unequal ways in which all societies are organized. Certain social categories are at greater risk than others of losing social and economic assets. This is clearly evident in the Indian example, where members of tribal groups and scheduled castes are at increased risk of destitution, along with other pariah categories: widows, sex workers, epileptics, the disabled.[5] Exclusion and marginalization are not in fact indicators of social breakdown, but of the opposite. They are indices of social order (Douglas, 1986) which sanctions social harm for some individuals while it ensures the protection of others. Responses to famine provide a clear example of this. The harm created by famine in terms of social chaos and increased morbidity is not in fact the effect of the famine agent, drought or harvest failure or whatever, but of the ways in which access to alternative sources of food or cash is organized (Sen, 1981; De Waal, 1989). The effects of famine are experienced differently by different social categories: the very same social categories who are vulnerable in everyday life bear the burden of famine-intensified vulnerability. This is evident in village India where 'substantial harms and risks of harm' are unevenly allocated as part of the formal structure of social organization. Torry makes this point explicitly when he states that 'famine adjustments are not radical abnormal breaks with customary behaviour: rather, they *extend ordinary conventions*' (1986, p. 126). That this is the case is not surprising. Society as a way of organizing is built, like all forms of organization, on the elaboration of difference. In the words of Charles Tilly, 'another way of thinking about organizations is to see them as an extreme form of categorical inequality: a frontier extended into a complete perimeter separating ins from outs' (1998, p. 61). Social benefits like social costs accrue along existing lines of social division. The rich get richer, the marginal get excluded. They are also likely to suffer disproportionately from the effects of deprivation, manifested in vastly increased rates of mortality, morbidity, and vulnerability not only to disease, but displacement, dislocation, and dispossession (Farmer, 1996, 1999). These allocations central to social ordering are likely to be justified ideologically in moral and religious terms, hence for example the cultural elaboration of pollution in Hinduism, the inauspiciousness of widows in India and Bangladesh; the marginalization of Roma people in Eastern Europe, and the ongoing stigmatization of people living with HIV and AIDS in many countries (Torry, 1986; Douglas, 1991; Davis, 2006).

14.5. Reordering Entitlements

The micro processes of social differentiation as a practice of social ordering can be clearly observed at household level, within the local social relations of family, not only with reorderings based on the possibilities presented within existing categorizations, for example the gendered category of wife to widow, but from insider to outsider, innocent victim to 'witch other' (Ciekawy, 1998,

---

[5] Nandy comments on the high incidence of death by starvation of tribal children in Maharashtra in 2001, the lack of public condemnation of this state of affairs, and the fact that this occurred within 'a relatively prosperous state' (2002, p. 14).

p. 120). Recent accounts of the social effects of witchcraft in contemporary Africa demonstrate how this process happens and what drives it when families seek to reorder kinship relations, and hence relations of obligation, through witchcraft allegations. This is not to suggest that families accusing others of witchcraft are doing so only in order to alter the relations between them. They are doing so because they perceive these others to have altered, to have come to embody the attributes of witches, and hence the relations between people are already changed. Allegations of witchcraft have different social consequence for accused witches depending on what is done to them. These range from expulsion, execution, the imposition of sanctions, and, in parts of southern and eastern Africa, cleansing rituals which reintegrate alleged witches into social networks (Green, 1997; Green and Mesaki, 2005; Niehaus, 2005, p. 506). Irrespective of what happens to alleged witches, all face recategorization as essentially 'other'. Witches harbour immoral attributes and desires. Their opposition to the social good is such that witches physically embody the inverse of normal human attributes, walking upside down, adopting nocturnal habits, and eating human flesh (Green, 1997, 2005). The social and institutional processes which create the possibilities for categorization are oriented towards the production of 'witch-others' (Ciekawy, 1998, p. 120). It is the othering possibilities of witchcraft which situate it as a strategy within family conflicts and which make witchcraft useful in situations where social order is at stake. In converting kin to stranger, neighbour to demon, allocations and entitlements are profoundly redrafted.

The witch as pre-existing outsider, exemplified by the in-marrying wife within the wider family, is giving way to the witch insider as notions of significant family contract. In Zambia, the anthropologist Elizabeth Colson found that fathers were now liable to be accused of witchcraft by their adult sons and daughters, something previously unimaginable when she had first undertaken research during the 1960s (2000). In Malawi and southern Africa witchcraft disputes are now used as a means of converting the moral content of relationships, transforming kin into strangers and those closest and between whom mutual obligations existed into mortal enemies (Peters, 2002; Niehaus, 2005). What seems to be happening in witchcraft in many countries is an increasing emphasis on the potential for witchcraft within closer groups of kin (Douglas, 1999; Ashforth, 2005). The dynamics of witchcraft provide coherent commentaries on core social values, not only about what sociality is and hence its antithesis, the witch, but by extension concerning the moral content of social relations. It is not then surprising that where witchcraft is utilized against non-kin co-residents within small-scale communities it retains an explicit concern with moral sociality. Isaak Niehaus describes the social context of a spate of accusations of witchcraft against neighbours in a rural community in South Africa during the 1990s. Apart from the escalating violence with which alleged witches were confronted, and the very real threat of severe penalties, including homicide, they faced, the targeting of accusations was notable. Victims of accusation were not only elderly and income poor, they had few dependants. Most lived alone (2005, pp. 200–1).

Niehaus, in an inverted reference to Jane Guyer's classic account of 'wealth in people', that is the importance of dependants in relations of social status and power in West Africa (1996), calls this 'poverty in people' (2005, p. 201). Yet these elderly people were not yet destitute. On the contrary, they seemingly made ends meet and managed to maintain themselves and their social existence without recourse to support from kin and neighbours. It was the apparent self-reliance of these poor individuals which aroused suspicions of witchcraft. How could they maintain themselves alone, without someone to help them? With no grandchildren to fetch and carry? With no helping hands in the fields or in the house? Surely such people must be in control of zombies, the mindless bodies of other people, to undertake this work in secret. Witchcraft here provides a tool for the creation of a moral boundary between witch and victim, moral villager and amoral demon, but it is also being used to make clear statements about how people should live. Aloneness is negatively valued in general. Combined with self-reliance it becomes an affront. The refusal of these older people to become enmeshed in relations of reciprocity and dependency by for example taking in children to help them challenged the normativity of mutual asking for assistance which was highly threatening to other poor people in the community. Witchcraft discourse in these examples and in the strategies of older persons to do without dependants was negatively viewed not merely as antisocial, but as creating atomized households, without social ties—the very kinds of households which are the basis of economic theories of the modern social imaginary. The parallel between witchcraft, individualism, and the market values of consumption is acknowledged in popular representations of witches throughout Africa (e.g. Englund, 1996; Sanders, 2001).

14.6. Poverty and Social Ordering

Witchcraft discourses, in Africa and elsewhere, are commentaries on sociality and hence on the ways in which society as a network of relationships is organized. Like development theories of society, with which they contrast, they represent normative orderings which are morally weighted. This ordering emphasizes the relations of interdependency between people, indeed dependency and responsibility for others as core values. Wealth in people, patronage and clientelism, and the values of kinship are part of this discourse, which is articulated symbolically through the cultural emphasis on food and feeding, inclusive kinship, and extended visiting. In this visioning of social order, households are not perceived as isolated units engaging with other households through market institutions. Neither is there a categorical separation between spheres of production, reproduction, and exchange. These separations are in fact in the process of being created through global incorporation and the international development policies which require modern social ordering, that is the division between conceptual spheres of economy, public sphere, and the private, to be operationalized (Mitchell, 2002; Taylor, 2004). It is these orderings, with their categorical delineation of households and restricted vision of the social, which both require poverty and create it as a problem to be solved through economic transformation.

A consequence of extant economic transitions and the development polices which promote them is to make the market the institutional cornerstone of social organization and, in the process, to render extensive non-market systems of social allocation unsustainable. A result is the increasing tension between social values of inclusion and mutual obligation, and the burden of support for individuals and families who depend on cash for their livelihoods. In situations where there is no alternative but to shrink the family, and hence the pool of obligations, individuated households are being created, through such strategies as witchcraft differentiation, contributing to the creation of the kinds of households as economic agents which conform to the social imaginary of modern capitalism (Wallerstein and Smith, 1992, p. 13). Similar processes of household creation and shrinkage were set in train by the aggressive social policies of industrializing France and England in the nineteenth century, which sought to establish the productive individual enmeshed within the capitalist economy and to ensure the institutional separation between the organizational spheres of production, reproduction, and exchange (Donzelot, 1979; Williams, 1981; Polanyi, 2001; Block and Somers, 2003). These processes of social reorganization required by the separation of economy were for the first time managed by the state. Social policy was born out of the need to create a national economy as an object of policy and management, an economy which depended on the isolation of households as units of engagement and through which populations could be reproduced as labour power. Gender as an organizing principle came into play here, with the ideal of the male household head as provider for a family and household reinforced through regulation which restricted women's access to labour markets and their entitlements to independent social support.

Such organization makes capitalist integration into global markets possible, creating economic opportunities for poor people in poor countries to become part of global value chains in which their product or labour can provide them with some kind of income. It does not necessarily address the problem of chronic poverty because the social determination of value means that agents at the bottom of the global economy cannot determine their worth within it. The implicit theory of social relations in which poverty discourse is embedded rests on the categorical divisions of modernity, economy, public, and private.

Dependency becomes imagined as hierarchical relationship between unproductive persons, who are thus not economic agents, and household heads, breadwinners, market agents. Because dependency is imagined as one way and as the drain of the unproductive on the productive and hence as a cost, it is represented as illegitimate. Indeed, the only valorized activity within this social model is productive, in the sense of producing goods which have market values for exchange. In this construction, the problem of poverty is a problem first and foremost of households as economic units in which relations of interdependency and mutual responsibility are privatized.

As individuation proceeds within this model relations within households become contested as dependency is further delimited in the drive to productivity. In Western societies it is not family division due to witchcraft allegations so much as divorce which creates new atomized households. In the words of Ulrich Beck, 'It is not social position but divorce which is the trap door through which women fall into the "new poverty"...*the spiral of individualisation is thus taking place inside the family*' (1992, p. 89; my emphasis). Legitimate dependency becomes morally loaded and confined to the categories of acceptable dependants: children, the elderly, and people whose disabilities prevent them from achieving the economic ideal of self-reliance (Fraser and Gordon, 1994; Adair, 2002). Livelihoods discourses in development documentation and research are based on these kinds of representations (e.g. Scoones, 1998). As individuals strive to earn a living in a liberalized economic order, those deemed unproductive risk destitution. Policies which foster individuation and investment in individual human capital, such as the promotion of secondary education, may promote the betterment of some individuals but in diverting investment away from supporting other social categories of dependants actually drive the socially differentiating processes of impoverishment and destitution.[6]

14.7. Conclusion: Durable Poverty and Destitution

I have argued that chronic poverty as a concept is useful in highlighting the intractability of poverty, and hence confronting assumptions inherent in theories about growth. Chronic poverty as a framing device has limited explanatory power. It cannot explain why some people stay poor, nor isolate the institutional relations which allocate social costs and benefits inequitably across social categories, indeed which create and reproduce the very social categories to which positive and negative entitlements accrue. Further, in prioritizing duration rather than depth it does not adequately differentiate

---

[6] Beck makes a similar argument for the kinds of social policies and processes which foster individuation, and which therefore render old social models, about gender relations for example, impractical in the sense that they no longer work in practice (1992).

between different dimensions of extreme poverty and their diverse contextually determined causes. The concept of destitution provides a useful comparison. Unlike chronic poverty, which may or may not correspond to local categorizations, some variant of destitution is acknowledged as a state of extreme poverty and social marginalization in many communities, often associated with stigma and with certain social categories. Destitution is different from extreme poverty. It is not a simple consequence of shortfalls in income, but of the moral constitution of entitlements. Entitlements do not exist in the abstract or within ideal institutional forms, despite capability theorizing, but in the constitution of social orders as networks of moral relationships. The content of relationships determines what different categories of person can expect and the kind of values which are allocated to them. A shift in this categorization, as demonstrated in the examples of witchcraft, shifts allocations and entitlements. The process of entitlement shifting is not confined to the use of witchcraft in contemporary Africa, but is central both to poverty theory and to the kinds of policies which are intended to eliminate it. Because allocative entitlements cannot be inclusively achieved through market institutions entitlement shifting and the reorganization of dependency inevitably contribute to extreme poverty and destitution. Exploring destitution as a social status and as the outcome of a social process highlights the centrality of institutions in making differentiation endure. Intractable poverty is also the result of social relations and ordering, not only in which certain people are stigmatized and excluded from opportunity because they are poor, but in the ways in which values are allocated in the global economy. Theorizing *durable*, rather than chronic, poverty might convey the materiality of the institutional factors which keep people poor, and highlight the importance of social relations.

References

Adair, V. (2002), 'Branded with Infamy: Inscriptions of Poverty and Class in the United States', *Signs: Journal of Women in Culture and Society*, 27(2), 451–71.

Ashforth, A. (2005), *Witchcraft, Violence and Democracy in South Africa*, Chicago: University of Chicago Press.

Beck, U. (1992), *Risk Society. Towards a New Modernity*, London: Sage.

Bevan, P. (2003), 'Extending Understanding of Chronic Poverty Dynamics: Towards a Post-Disciplinary Approach', paper presented at 'Staying Poor: Chronic Poverty and Development Policy', Manchester, April.

Block, F., and Somers, F. (2003), 'In the Shadow of Speenhamland; Social Policy and the Old Poor Law', *Politics and Society*, 31(2): 283–323.

Ciekawy, D. (1998), 'Witchcraft in Statecraft: Five Technologies of Power in Colonial and Postcolonial Kenya', *African Studies Review*, 41(3): 119–41.

Colson, E. (2000), 'The Father as Witch', *Africa: Journal of the International African Institute*, 70(3): 333–58.

Dasgupta, P. (1993), *An Enquiry into Wellbeing and Destitution*, Oxford: Clarendon Press.

—— (1997), 'Nutritional Status, the Capacity for Work and Destitution', *Journal of Econometrics*, 77: 5–37.

Davis, P. (2006), 'Poverty in Time: Exploring Poverty Dynamics from Life Histories in Bangladesh', paper presented at CPRC workshop on poverty concepts, Manchester, October.

De Soto, H. (2000), *The Mystery of Capital: Why Capitalism Triumphs in the West and Fails Everywhere Else*, London: Transworld.

Devereux, S. (2003), *Conceptualising Destitution*, IDS Working Paper No. 216, Brighton.

De Waal, A. (1989), *Famine That Kills: Darfur, Sudan 1984–5*, Oxford: Clarendon Press.

Donzelot, J. (1979), *The Policing of Families*, Baltimore: Johns Hopkins University Press.

Douglas, M. (1991), 'Witchcraft and Leprosy: Two Strategies of Exclusion', *Man*, NS 26(4): 723–36.

—— (1999), 'Sorcery Accusations Unleashed: The Lele Revisited 1987', *Africa: Journal of the International African Institute*, 69(2): 177–93.

—— (1986), *How Institutions Think*, Syracuse, NY: Syracuse University Press.

Englund, H. (1996), 'Witchcraft, Modernity and the Person: The Morality of Accumulation in Central Malawi', *Critique of Anthropology*, 16(3): 257–9.

Escobar, A. (1995), *Encountering Development: The Making and Unmaking of the Third World*, Princeton: Princeton University Press.

Ewald, F. (1991), 'Insurance and Risk', in G. Burchell, C. Gordon, and P. Miller (eds.), *The Foucault Effect: Studies in Governmentality*, London: Harvester, 197–210.

Fanon, F. (1967), *The Wretched of the Earth*, London: Penguin.

Farmer, P. (1996), 'On Suffering and Structural Violence: A View from Below', *Daedalus*, 125(1): 261–83.

—— (1999), *Infections and Inequalities: The Modern Plagues*, Berkeley and Los Angeles: University of California Press.

Fogel, W. (2004), *The Escape from Hunger and Premature Death 1700–2100: Europe, America and the Third World*, Cambridge: Cambridge University Press.

Fraser, N. (1993), 'Clintonism, Welfare and the Antisocial Wage: The Emergence of a Neoliberal Political Imaginary', *Rethinking Marxism*, 6(1): 9–23.

—— and Gordon, L. (1994), 'A Genealogy of Dependency: Tracing a Keyword in the US Welfare State', *Signs*, 19(2): 309–36.

Good, A. (1999), 'The State and Extreme Poverty in Botswana: The San and the Destitutes', *Journal of Modern African Studies*, 37(2): 185–205.

Gore, C. (1993), 'Entitlement Relations and "Unruly" Social Practices: A Comment on the Work of Amartya Sen', *Journal of Development Studies*, 29(3): 429–60.

Green, M. (1997), 'Witchcraft Suppression Practices and Movements: Public Politics and the Logic of Purification', *Comparative Studies in Society and History*, 39(2): 319–45.

—— (2005), 'A Discourse on Inequality: Poverty, Public Bads and Entrenching Witchcraft in Post Adjustment Tanzania', *Anthropological Theory*, 5(3): 247–66.

—— (2006), 'Presenting Poverty, Attacking Representations: Anthropological Perspectives on Poverty in Development', *Journal of Development Studies*, 42(7): 1108–29.

Green, M. (2007), 'Delivering Discourse: Some Ethnographic Reflections on the Practice of Policy Making in International Development', *Critical Policy Analysis*, 1(2): 220–34.

—— and Hulme, D. (2005), 'From Correlates and Characteristics to Causes: Thinking about Poverty from a Chronic Poverty Perspective', *World Development*, 33(6): 867–79.

—— and Mesaki, S. (2005), 'The Birth of the "Salon": Poverty, Modernization and Dealing with Witchcraft in Southern Tanzania', *American Ethnologist*, 32(3): 371–88.

Gudeman, S. (2001), *The Anthropology of Economy*, Oxford: Blackwell.

Guyer, J. (1996), 'Wealth in People and Self Realization in Equatorial Guinea', *Man*, NS 28(2): 243–65.

Habermas, J. (1989), *The Structural Transformation of the Public Sphere: An Enquiry into a Category of Bourgeois Society*, London: Polity.

Hardt, A., and Negri, A. (2000), *Empire*, Cambridge, Mass.: Harvard University Press.

Harper, C., Marcus, R., and Moore, K. (2003), 'Enduring Poverty and the Conditions of Childhood: Lifecourse and Intergenerational Poverty Transmissions', *World Development*, 31(3): 535–54.

Harriss, J. (2006), 'Why Understanding of Social Relations Matters More for Policy on Chronic Poverty than Measurement', paper presented to workshop on Chronic Poverty Concepts, University of Manchester, October.

Harriss White, B. (2002), *A Note on Destitution*, Queen Elizabeth House Working Paper No. 86, Oxford.

Hastrup, K. (1993), 'Hunger and the Hardness of Facts', *Man*, NS 28(4): 727–39.

Hulme, D., and McKay, A. (2006), 'Identifying and Measuring Chronic Poverty. Beyond Monetary Measures', paper presented to workshop on Chronic Poverty Concepts, University of Manchester, October.

Hulme, D., and Shepherd, A. (2003), 'Conceptualizing Chronic Poverty', *World Development*, 31(3): 403–24.

Kabeer, N. (2005), 'Snakes, Ladders and Traps: Changing Lives and Livelihoods in Rural Bangladesh (1994–2001)', Chronic Poverty Research Centre Working Paper No. 50, University of Manchester.

Law, J. (1993), *Organising Modernity: Social Order and Social Theory*, Oxford: Blackwell.

Lee, R. (1979), *The !Kung San: Men, Women and Work in a Foraging Society*, Cambridge: Cambridge University Press.

Mitchell, T. (2002), *Rule of Experts: Egypt, Techno-politics, Modernity*, Berkeley and Los Angeles: University of California Press.

Moore, K. (2001), 'Frameworks for Understanding the Intergenerational Transmission of Poverty and Well-Being in Developing Countries', Chronic Poverty Research Centre Working Paper 8, University of Manchester.

Nandy, A. (2002), 'The Beautiful, Expanding Future of Poverty: Popular Economics as a Psychological Defence', *International Studies Review*, 4(2): 107–21.

Narayan, D., and Pritchett, L. (1997), 'Cents and Sociability: Household Income and Social Capital in Rural Tanzania', Policy Research Working Paper No. 1796, Washington: World Bank, Social Development Department and Development Research Group.

Niehaus, I. (2005), 'Witches and Zombies of the South African Lowveld: Discourse, Accusations and Subjective Reality', *Journal of the Royal Anthropological Institute*, 11: 191–210.

Nussbaum, M. C. (2003), 'Capabilities as Fundamental Entitlement: Sen and Social Justice', *Feminist Economics*, 9(2–3): 33–59.

O'Connor, A. (2001), *Poverty Knowledge: Social Science, Social Policy and the Poor in Twentieth Century US History*, Princeton: Princeton University Press.

Pasarro, J. (1996), *The Unequal Homeless*, New York: Routledge.

Peters, P. (2002), 'Bewitching Land: The Role of Land Disputes in Converting Kin to Strangers and Class Formation in Malawi', *Journal of Southern African Studies*, 28(1): 155–78.

Polanyi, K. (2001), *The Great Transformation: The Political and Economic Origins of our Time*, Boston: Beacon Press.

Rabinow, P. (1995), *French Modern: Norms and Forms of the Social Environment*, Chicago: University of Chicago Press.

Sahlins, M. (2004), *Stone Age Economics*, London: Routledge (1st edn. 1974).

Saith, R. (2001), 'Capabilities: The Concept and its Operationalisation', QEH Working Paper Series 66, Queen Elizabeth House, University of Oxford.

Sanders, T. (2001), 'Save our Skins: Adjustment, Morality and the Occult in Tanzania', in H. Moore and T. Sanders (eds.), *Magical Interpretations, Material Realities: Modernity, Witchcraft and the Occult in Postcolonial Africa*, London: Routledge.

Scoones, I. (1998), 'Sustainable Rural Livelihoods: A Framework for Analysis', IDS Working Paper No. 72, Brighton: Institute for Development Studies.

Sen, A. (1981), *Poverty and Famines: An Essay on Entitlement and Deprivation*, London: Oxford University Press.

—— (1999), *Development as Freedom*, Oxford: Oxford University Press.

Shepherd, A. (2006), *A Conceptual Framework for Understanding and Explaining Chronic Poverty*, CPRC Working Paper, Manchester.

Smith, J., and Wallerstein, I. (eds) (1992), 'Households as an institution of the world economy', in Smith, J., and Wallerstein, I. *Creating and Transforming Households: Constraints of the World Economy*, Cambridge: Cambridge University Press, pp. 3–23.

Strathern, M. (1985), 'Kinship and Economy: Constitutive Orders of a Provisional Kind', *American Ethnologist*, 12(20): 191–209.

Taylor, C. (2004), *Modern Social Imaginaries*, Durham, NC: Duke University Press.

Tilly, C. (1998), *Durable Inequality*, Berkeley and Los Angeles: University of California Press.

Torry, W. (1986), 'Morality and Harm: Hindu Peasant Adjustments to Famines', *Social Science Information*, 25(1): 125–60.

Williams, K. (1981), *From Pauperism to Poverty*, London: Routledge and Kegan Paul.

Woodburn, J. (1982), 'Egalitarian Societies', *Man*, NS 17(3): 431–51.

Wright, M. (1993), *Strategies of Slaves and Women: Life Stories from East/ Central Africa*, London: James Currey.

15

Toward an Economic Sociology of Chronic Poverty

*Enhancing the Rigour and Relevance of Social Theory**

Michael Woolcock

The day is not far off when the economic problem will take the back seat where it belongs, and the arena of the heart and the head will be occupied or reoccupied, by our real problems—the problems of life and of human relations, of creation and behaviour and religion.

John Maynard Keynes, *First Annual Report of the Arts Council (1945–46)*

15.1. Introduction

There is now broad agreement among scholars and practitioners alike that the causes, manifestations, and consequences of poverty are multidimensional, i.e. that poverty cannot be adequately defined by very low income alone, but can include various forms of exclusion and marginality from basic services, labour and credit markets, citizenship claims, and agreed-upon human rights provisions (Sen, 1999). As recent scholarship by historians (O'Connor, 2001; Sherman, 2002; Jones, 2004) has shown, conceptions of poverty—i.e. of who is, and who is not, poor[1]—and their corresponding policy response strategies have changed considerably over the centuries, even as many important

* The views expressed in this chapter are those of the author alone, and should not be attributed to the respective organizations (or their executive directors) with which he is affiliated. An early version of this chapter was presented at the CPRC's 'Concepts and Methods for Analysing Poverty Dynamics and Chronic Poverty' conference, held at the University of Manchester in October 2006. I am grateful for the help received from participants at that conference, and to David Hulme for encouraging me to explore the issues raised here.

[1] See also Pritchett (2006) for an interesting discussion on who is *not* poor within the terms of contemporary policy and empirical debates.

methodological debates continue about how best to measure poverty and compare it across different contexts (Deaton, 2001; Iceland, 2005; Brady, 2006; Dercon, 2006), and assess the importance of economic growth to reducing it (Hausmann, Rodrik, and Pritchett, 2005; Kraay, 2005; Ravallion, 2006). Many serious minds are dedicated to exploring and refining these issues, and I am not going to enter that fray, at least not here. For our present purposes, I begin from the simple (and, I hope, relatively non-controversial) premiss that poverty has many dimensions, that among these dimensions income is centrally important, and that inclusive ('pro-poor'[2]) economic growth policies are necessary but insufficient for reducing it.

This chapter, rather, focuses on both expanding and refining the analytical scope of the 'social' (or non-economic) aspects of chronic poverty, and thereby, I hope, enhancing efforts to respond more effectively to it. The argument in this chapter proceeds as follows. In recognizing that poverty is 'multidimensional', today's dominant policy discourses have actually made important, if often underappreciated, steps to incorporate insights from social and political theory, but these (hard-won) gains now need to be consolidated, advanced, and sharpened. Three broad themes in non-economic social science—what I shall call, for simplicity's sake, 'networks', 'exclusion', and 'culture'—have been at the forefront of these important efforts to make initial inroads into shaping contemporary policy discourses, not least at the international level. While further useful insights can certainly be gained from continued research in these areas, building significantly on them requires the incorporation of three additional (and interrelated) realms into the theories of and policy responses to chronic poverty. To constitute a coherent and useful theory, these realms must cumulatively be able to (a) provide a basic but distinctive model of human behaviour, (b) explain how and why poverty persists as part of broader processes of economic prosperity and social change, (c) account for the mechanisms by which power is created, maintained, and challenged, and (d) readily lend themselves to informing (and iteratively learning from) a new generation of supportable poverty reduction policies and practices. These three new realms—which are not actually new, since they are deeply grounded in a long tradition of social theory, and are not posed here in contradistinction to the prevailing themes—are social relations, rules systems, and meaning systems.

These are admittedly ambitious goals, and within the constraints of a single chapter can necessarily only be partially achieved, if at all. I surely have no desire to engage in what could only be a futile quest for a 'grand theory' of chronic poverty, but I am firmly of the conviction that historical events,

---

[2] The precise definition of 'pro-poor' economic growth is itself contentious (see UNDP's International Poverty Centre 'one-pagers', which have explored the core contentious issues), though no one seriously claims that economic growth (however defined) is unnecessary for sustained poverty reduction.

recent intellectual innovations, and fervent political activism have conspired to provide us with a narrow window of opportunity to seriously incorporate social themes into a coherent and supportable strategy for reducing poverty and marginalization, an opportunity not experienced for perhaps forty years (the civil rights movement) or nearly a century (the progressive era). 'Theory' is, of course, but one element shaping the viability of any such strategy, but to the extent that scholars have any comparative advantage in these matters, it is largely in the realm of theory and ideas. So, herewith my contribution, as someone who resides at the awkward nexus of multidisciplinary research and development policy; the chapter will have served its purpose if it provides (even provokes) a basis for further sustained deliberation.

The chapter is structured in six sections. Section 15.2 briefly looks at how poverty generally, and chronic poverty in particular, is explained in the current policy literature, with a focus on 'poverty traps' and (more recently) 'inequality traps'. I will contend here that three strands of scholarship in the non-economic social sciences have exerted quite considerable influence at the level of contemporary policy discourse (and to a lesser extent, practice), and that critics, especially those within these disciplines, have been slow to recognize this fact. Section 15.3 argues that these successes, important as they are, cannot do the heavy intellectual lifting required for a more comprehensive social theory of chronic poverty, and that, as such, a new edifice must be constructed and negotiated for. The key elements of this edifice are nascent within a long history of scholarship across all the social sciences, but, as a package, need to be reframed in order to enhance their most salient and compelling elements, and their prospects of gaining policy traction. These elements, or realms as I shall call them, must not amount to merely yet another 'conceptual framework' for informing 'development policy', but do the work of any serious social theory of economic life. I provide four tests for assessing the efficacy of any such theory. Section 15.4 provides three brief case studies of selected aspects of chronic poverty, to demonstrate both the influence and the limits of prevailing approaches. Section 15.5 provides a spirited (if not detailed) defence of three constituent realms of a broader social theory of chronic poverty, namely systems of social relations, rules, and meaning. Section 15.6 concludes.

15.2. Poverty as a Policy 'Story': Poverty Traps, Inequality Traps

'Poverty' clearly has a long intellectual history (see Geremek, 1994; Beaudoin, 2007), and I cannot possibly hope to do justice to this complex account here. For our purposes, I shall simply summarize the dominant explanation of poverty in developing countries within contemporary policy circles, and then show how aspects of three different bodies of scholarship within non-economic social science have modified (even challenged) that account, and given rise to (and/or themselves been influenced by) particular policy responses. The dominant account of chronic poverty presented by economists, and made manifest in the discourse of international and bilateral development agencies, centres on the notion of 'poverty traps' (Azariadis and Stachurski, 2006). Poverty traps have long been invoked by all manner of social scientists working at all units of analysis—from countries (Sachs, 2005) to individuals (Bowles, Durlauf, and Hoff, 2006)—to explain chronic poverty, or the empirical reality that poverty tends to persist across generations (Hulme and Shepherd, 2003). While many economists (e.g. Easterly, 2006) dispute the presence of poverty traps at the macro level (i.e. a self-perpetuating low-level equilibrium in which a poor country struggles to attract investment, thus cannot provide basic public goods and services, endures sluggish/erratic/negative economic growth, suffers recurrent politics crises, and thus cannot attract investment), there is much stronger support for it at the micro level (Banerjee, Benabou, and Mookherjee, 2006), where poor individuals cannot afford adequate food, education, and healthcare, are thus more often sick and unable to work, and thus less able to earn sufficient income to support themselves and their families.

The dynamics of poverty traps are compounded by pervasive market failures, especially in labour, finance, insurance, and property rights, which generate hugely inefficient outcomes: workers have few incentives to invest in their (or their children's) education (because no one else does); households are unable to find secure places for their savings (leading to investments in, say, livestock, which can die, get sick, or be stolen) or obtain credit at reasonable interest rates (thereby sending them to usurious moneylenders); disasters of all kinds, whether to property or persons, can lead to utter destitution, leading to investments in low-risk but low-return crops and entrepreneurial ventures (Scott, 1976); and informal (at best) property rights mean the few material possessions of the poor cannot be leveraged as security (and are thus rendered 'dead capital', as De Soto, 2000, famously put it). In the absence of formal protections embodied in a legally binding statement of ownership, such possessions can also be expropriated at will (and with no recourse other than vigilantism) by local elites, criminal elements, business interests, or the state.

Presented as such, the microeconomics of poverty traps should be relatively straightforward and non-controversial: this account enjoys strong theoretical backing and empirical support, and its various aspects are readily apparent to anyone who has done fieldwork in developing countries. It can provide a reasonably solid explanation of why individuals with the 'same' demographic attributes at birth in different countries can nonetheless enjoy vastly different life chances (World Bank, 2005) and, more tellingly, why individuals who are 'rich' (i.e. in the upper 10 per cent of the income distribution) in poor countries have life chances vastly inferior to the 'poor' (bottom 10 per cent) in rich countries (Pritchett, 2006). The core problem with the orthodox poverty traps account lies more in the areas of what it cannot adequately explain, and what it does not say (or is unable to say). It struggles, for example, to explain why particular *groups* (e.g. Dalhits in India, Aborigines in Australia) tend to remain chronically poor, why the broad enhancement of material welfare tends to be accompanied by (often severe) conflict (Bates, 2000), why certain groups (e.g., the Roma in Eastern Europe, the residents of 'Zomia'[3] in southeast Asia) who could in fact have access to formal education, financial services, and police protection may nonetheless actively chose to remain outside the purview of the state, and how systemic (as opposed to individual) 'poverty traps' sometimes are actually broken.

In its defence, the broad acceptance currently accorded to the 'multidimensionality' of poverty (alluded to at the start of this chapter) is in some important sense a recognition by policy elites that microeconomics alone cannot fully account for the wide array of factors shaping the causes, manifestations, and consequences of poverty (and especially chronic poverty). Because of its own internal shortcomings, then, and—equally importantly—the compelling nature of key empirical and theoretical insights presented by other disciplines, the recent reports of the major international development agencies (i.e. the World Bank's World Development Reports and the UNDP's Human Development Reports), and the Chronic Poverty Report (funded by the UK government's Department for International Development), have given significant space to the 'non-economic' dimensions of poverty and inequality. While hard-line critics will always find fault with them, the World Development Report 2000/1 (World Bank, 2000), for example, assigned a whole section to covering the political and social dimensions of poverty, while WDR2006 granted an entire chapter (and several sections elsewhere) to historical and political economy considerations of equity and the institutional mechanisms by which it is created and perpetuated (see further discussion below). For their part, recent HDRs have also focused exclusively on considerations of culture and inequality. Their inherent limitations notwithstanding, these documents represent important discursive milestones and opportunities for further advancement, and should be recognized as such by the wider scholarly community.

If 'poverty traps' is the policy shorthand for the microeconomics of poverty, what the WDR2006 (World Bank, 2005; see also

---

[3] 'Zomia' is a title coined by (among others) van Schendel (2002) to refer to the broad expanse of mountainous territory covering northern Burma, Thailand, Malaysia, Laos, northern Vietnam, and southern China, which has, for centuries, been populated by nomadic peoples who have overtly (and, for the most part, successfully) resisted incorporation into the prevailing state, practising 'escape agriculture' and exhibiting an 'escape social structure' (see Scott, forthcoming).

Rao, 2005b[4]) calls 'inequality traps' can be said to be the equivalent for non-economics perspectives. In its simplest form, inequality trap refers to 'durable' (cf. Tilly, 2000) structures of economic, political, and social difference that serve to keep poor people (and, by extension, poor countries) poor. Large economic gaps between rich and poor groups, for example, can give rise to vastly unequal political influence which, over time, can consolidate itself into institutionalized disadvantage and discrimination; it can erode the tax base for public services, with the wealthy purchasing their own private education, healthcare, transport, and security, effectively putting them in a separate 'moral universe' (Skocpol, 1990) to that of the poor, with whom they rarely interact or even come in contact, thereby eroding their elective affinity and sense of shared political interests. Similarly, widening and (seemingly or actually) entrenched inequality can serve to undermine any hope by those at the bottom of the income ladder that 'hard work' and 'playing by the rules', rather than criminal or subversive activity, can yield them (and/or their children) a life of basic dignity (let alone economic advancement).

If one unpacks the intellectual genesis of 'inequality traps', and the pathways by which the idea has become influential in international development circles, it can be said to draw on three strands of research within social science. The first of these can be called 'network isolation', which has its origins in the Chicago School of urban sociology in the early twentieth century but has had its greatest contemporary influence through the work of sociologist William Julius Wilson (1987, 1996) on 'the truly disadvantaged'—i.e. those who, through mutually reinforcing processes of urban deindustrialization and out-migration by the middle classes, find themselves increasingly isolated from the diverse social networks and high-quality public services that provide the vital information, resources, and 'cultural capital' (following Bourdieu) needed to find and keep good jobs and affordable housing. This work is broadly compatible with work by economists on poverty mapping and 'geographical poverty traps' (Jalan and Ravallion, 2002), and with that strand of social capital research in development studies influenced by Robert Putnam[5] (e.g. Isham, 2002; Fafchamps, 2006): for these scholars, it is the social networks that provide the basis of information flows and resource sharing in poor communities, which constitute key elements of their survival and mobility strategies; they also serve to confine the poor to particular (usually spatially isolated) places, wherein their absence of diverse social networks is only consolidated.

---

[4] Sage and Woolcock (2006) also outline what they call 'legal inequality traps', a situation whereby the prevailing rules system—both in its normative and judicial incarnations—serves to keep poor people poor.

[5] See Woolcock and Narayan (2000), who outline four strands of social capital research—communitarian, networks, institutions, and synergy—that have flowed from the work of Robert Putnam.

To the literature on networks, scholars of social policy, especially those in Europe, have succeeded in introducing a discourse on 'social exclusion' into academic and policy debates on poverty (Silver, this volume), arguing that rigid class structures and overt discrimination continue to exert a powerful influence on who has knowledge of, access to, and sustained participation in key mobility mechanisms such as employment, citizenship, and education. Primarily concerned with understanding the social and political processes whereby particular groups and structures are reproduced over time, the social exclusion literature has managed to convey a greater sense of internal coherence and unity than its counterparts on networks (above) and culture (below), though at the expense, perhaps, of sparking energetic (even controversial) debate or driving a concrete operational agenda. Entire academic centres have been established on social exclusion (e.g. at LSE), and it's clear that the language of social exclusion simultaneously stems from, resonates with, and informs pan-European sensibilities on the causes of and responses to poverty in its midst, yet it's hard to identify precise instances of where actual projects or policies in developing countries have been launched on the basis of a 'social exclusion theory'. If one were to extrapolate a little, it could plausibly be argued that the language of 'empowerment' is one discursive manifestation of social exclusion theory, in which case the connections to policy are much more readily apparent (e.g., Stern, Dethier, and Rogers, 2005; Alsop, Holland, and Bertelsen, 2006). Even so, as these citations themselves indicate, the concept of 'empowerment' can and does draw on multiple (sometimes very different) intellectual strands.

For better or worse, various 'cultural explanations' have also had policy salience in discussions of poverty. At one extreme, hard-line 'culture of poverty' advocates (e.g. Murray, 1994) have asserted that the behaviour of the poor themselves is the reason for their misfortune (and thus urge governments to dismantle the welfare state because it only encourages dependency and perpetuates social problems such as teen pregnancy); similarly, influential writers such as Lawrence Harrison and Samuel Huntington (e.g. Harrison and Huntington, 2001) have long argued that 'culture' is the primary determinant of a country's level of prosperity. More sophisticated thinkers (e.g. Portes, 1995; Patterson, 2006) have contended that certain powerful intra-group norms, especially among immigrants and young people, can contribute to poverty by conspiring to undermine achievement ethics, wealth accumulation, and safe sexual practices. Discussions of 'culture' in some policy circles have also been driven by an otherwise laudable concern to protect or promote a certain community's cultural products and artefacts (e.g. its music, food, languages, art, monuments, heritage sites, etc.), but where this has been the case it has tended to overwhelm more detailed and deliberative reflections on the ontological status of culture, in the process perpetuating a false view that 'culture' is something 'out there' in poor communities (preferably in exotic countries) rather than an inherent and ubiquitous feature of life 'in here', i.e. inside even (or especially) the most seemingly bland development agencies and academic departments. These (serious) concerns notwithstanding, the most recent and vibrant literature on culture, poverty, and development policy (e.g. Rao and Walton, 2004) argues for making a concerted effort to incorporate the insights of mainstream anthropology into development theory and practice, a process which has made important first steps but which now needs to be consolidated and expanded (see below).

There are clearly detailed and expansive literatures in each of these three domains, but for our present purposes it is sufficient to note that each has been a key vehicle through which ideas and evidence from mainstream social science have gained some measure of policy traction in poverty debates. Given that such debates are ordinarily dominated by economists, and that non-economist social scientists have long argued that they should be given a voice in such deliberations, it is a noteworthy accomplishment that some measure of influence is beginning to be obtained. These advances ought to be more widely recognized, not least by those who claim, implicitly or explicitly, that major development agencies are immutable to change. Nevertheless, much remains to be done if a fuller and more faithful rendering of social science is to shape the content and direction of poverty policy and the knowledge base on which it rests (assuming this is a desirable objective, which I obviously believe it is). In the sections that follow, I outline the tasks that a social theory of poverty (especially chronic poverty) must be able to accomplish, provide some simple case studies of the types of problems it must be able to address, and identify three substantive issues to which sustained attention should be given if social science scholarship is to have a greater impact on poverty (and other) policy debates in the coming years.

15.3. Tasks of a Social Theory of (Chronic) Poverty

If non-economic social science is to have an expanded role and a more confident voice in policy debates on poverty, it is essential that its theoretical moorings be distinctive and well grounded. In this section, I outline four tasks that I think a comprehensive social theory of poverty—and by extension, chronic poverty—must be able to accomplish. I take this approach because, in my experience, social scientists have to date too frequently chosen (or been forced by necessity) to carve out highly selected aspects of their conceptual and methodological toolkits in their engagements with economists and policy makers, opportunistically finding spaces and moments for inserting them rather than strategically enacting a broader vision. As someone who has spent more than a decade in daily interaction with some of the world's leading poverty economists I am acutely aware that seeking and exploiting opportunistic moments are sometimes all that can be done; still, if (as I have argued above) important groundwork has now been laid and if the prospects appear somewhat brighter regarding the receptivity of the policy community (and economists themselves) to 'non-economic' themes (such as governance, institutions, and participation), then it is important that next steps be taken proactively, rather than reactively.

To this end, I submit the following four tasks that, going forward, a comprehensive theory of (chronic) poverty must be able to accomplish if it is to be distinctive, useful, and supportable to those who design and implement responses to it. First, the theory must provide a basic but distinctive model of human behaviour. If a serious alternative is to be mounted to economic models, then it must be recognized that much of the power (and putative 'rigour') of economics rests on its simple and simplifying assumptions of human behaviour. If social scientists (including economists) wish to resist assertions that humans are utility maximizing and self-interested, and that little, behaviourally, separates the decision-making calculus of Wall Street executives and Kalahari bushmen, then they need to do more than merely assert their disagreement; they must pose a viable alternative.

Second, the theory must be able to explain how and why poverty persists as part of broader processes of economic prosperity and social change. Even if economic growth is, on average, 'good for the poor', a solid theory must also be able to account for the nature and extent of the standard deviation (cf. Ravallion, 2001). Most pragmatically, the policies and social consensus that underpin growth itself will only be politically sustainable if the benefits of growth are widely shared, and if the distributional conflicts accompanying that growth—e.g. through changes in relations between classes and occupational groups—are meaningfully accommodated (Easterly, Ritzen, and Woolcock, 2006).

Third, the theory is obliged to explain the mechanisms by which power is created, maintained, and challenged. Most social scientists will assert vigorously that 'political economy' considerations are an essential component of their theoretical apparatus, but too often the precise mechanisms are left more asserted than demonstrated, with the author being much clearer about what they are 'against' than what they are actually 'for'.

Fourth, the theory must readily lend itself to informing (and iteratively learning from) a new generation of supportable poverty reduction policies, projects, and practices. As more concrete manifestations of social theory are implemented in response to poverty concerns, they should be treated as 'laboratories' for testing (and thereby informing) many of the ideas and hypotheses espoused by scholars.[6]

---

[6] I thank Scott Guggenheim for stressing this point, and indeed for encouraging his own development projects to be subject to this kind of scrutiny.

The veracity of these four criteria for assessing the merits of a given social theory of (chronic) poverty, and my proposal for what the elements of such a theory might comprise, are outlined below, but it is helpful to first present three illustrative cases of the types of concrete poverty problems that the world is currently wrestling with. If nothing else, a serious theory, social or otherwise, must be able to speak sensibly to these types of concerns. The cases themselves are relatively self-explanatory; they are not meant to be 'representative' in any statistical sense, but embodiments of the larger processes and policy dilemmas with which I believe contemporary scholars and practitioners of poverty must engage.

15.4. Three Very Brief Illustrative Cases

Consider these three brief cases—from China, Australia, and Cameroon—of problems confronting today's poverty scholars and practitioners.

15.4.1. *Conflict in rural China*

China's spectacular rates of annual per capita economic growth over the past three decades are widely (and rightly) recognized for the vital role they have played in bringing millions of people out of poverty. Achieving the global poverty reduction targets of the Millennium Development Goals will turn in no small part on large countries like China continuing to sustain such growth rates. Less well appreciated, however, is the enormous amount of everyday conflict that has accompanied China's rapid economic expansion in recent years. In 2004, reports Muldavin (2006), there were 74,000 'uprisings' across the country, a product of environmental destruction, widening inequality, and the forced expropriation of land from villagers by the state to accommodate the seemingly insatiable demands of developers and wealthy city dwellers seeking to escape urban pollution and small apartments. 'Rural unrest is the biggest political problem China faces today', writes Joshua Muldavin, a geographer who is a long-standing student of changes in rural land tenure in China. 'Peasant land loss is a time bomb for the state.'

15.4.2. *Maternal health in Aboriginal communities in Maningrida, Australia[7]*

Many Aboriginal communities in Australia live in 'fourth world' conditions. In isolated towns such as Maningrida (in the Northern Territory), most specialist medical needs are serviced from Darwin, a two-hour flight from

---

[7] A more detailed discussion and analysis of this case is provided in Sage and Woolcock (2008).

Maningrida. In particular, antenatal care, birthing, and postnatal care are all provided for in the city: expectant mothers are flown there for up to four months. Given the prevalence of disease and serious health problems, low life expectancies, and high levels of neonatal deaths among Arnhem Land communities (and the criticism faced by the Australian government in relation to these problems), the free provision of world standard medical care may seem like an extremely generous, progressive, rights-based programme (fulfilling and protecting people's right to health).

Under indigenous law in Arnhem Land communities, however, the 'place of birth' is a key cultural determinant of clan lines, rights, and authority. Women who are expecting a child are obliged, under traditional law, to return to 'their country' to ensure the ongoing connection of their children to the land and to the laws, rights, and responsibilities that are seen to emanate from it. For Australian healthcare authorities, however, these birthing practices are too difficult to regulate or to service. If a woman does not want to go to Darwin, local healthcare authorities persuade and/or cajole her and, ultimately, provide no alternative. Traditional midwives, where they still exist, are not recognized by law, and are considered 'dangerous' by local healthcare authorities. If, in the last instance, a woman refuses to go, the local healthcare authorities present her with a suite of legal disclaimer documents, denying any legal responsibility or liability to the government.

In practice, however, many women continue to travel back to their traditional lands to birth their children. Their actions are 'outlawed' (or at least are outside the law) and so they are given no assistance by local healthcare providers, who are in fact obliged (by law) *not* to help them. Thanks to the breakdown of local communities, and the movement of most communities into constructed towns such as Maningrida, even when traditional healthcare practitioners and midwives do exist, they tend not to be found in outlying areas. There, women continue to experience high levels of birth-related health problems, and high levels of maternal and infant mortality. Conversely, while those women who agree to travel to Darwin do experience better health outcomes, the birth of many children 'off country' serves to undermine traditional norms and increases the conflict between local communities and government services, or between local communities.

15.4.3. *Stopping the spread of AIDS in Cameroon*

The scale of the tragedy of the AIDS pandemic sweeping Africa is relatively well acknowledged, but most of the international energy marshalled in response to it so far has focused on technical matters such as creating incentives for major pharmaceutical companies to produce lower-cost anti-retroviral drugs. Crucially important as these initiatives are, they focus on treating the symptoms of those already infected rather than preventing the spread of AIDS in the first place. Given that AIDS is acquired in the most inti-mate (sexual), primal (parent-to-child), and behavioural (sharing of needles) of ways, effective responses at this level face a barrage of vexing challenges.

Understandings of personal healthcare issues are, in all communities every-where, grounded in broader understandings of how the world works, of basic mechanisms of cause and effect, and of identity and status. For many rural Africans, where there is only one doctor for every 40,000 people but one tradi-tional healer for every 500 people (Rosenthal, 2006), and where cosmologies and community identities are still strongly grounded in an agrarian way of life, engaging in rituals and practices that would cause grave concern to 'mod-ern' public health officials is just a normal part of everyday life. Having infants fed by multiple mothers, for example, is a common practice and part of the naming ceremony whereby a newborn becomes recognized as a member of the group; witchdoctors may counsel anxious patients to ward off evil spirits by making multiple cuts with a shared razor blade. Tribal identity markings and circumcisions may be conducted in similar ways, and in countries such as Cameroon, polygamy is common (with some chiefs having as many as thirty wives).

Responding effectively to the AIDS pandemic in Africa (and elsewhere) thus requires far more than just technical and scientific advances, important as these are. 'If we are only biology, biology, biology, then we are only doing half of our mission,' says Marcel Manny Lobe, director of the new International Reference and Research Centre for HIV-AIDS in Yaoundé. 'We need also to do the sociology and anthropology and then make biological interventions.'[8]

These seemingly different cases from different continents nonetheless share important similarities. First, they show that social relations are central to understanding responses to economic and political change. In China, conflict is a product of resources and livelihoods being expropriated, but even if the expropriation itself is only part of the economic growth strategy, rapid change—and the concomitant processes of conflict it engenders—is only likely to continue. We are accustomed to thinking of conflict as a product of 'failed' development, but here it is both a cause and effect of rising prosperity. Similarly, the enduring power of social relations is vital for understanding the efficacy (or lack thereof) of healthcare interventions, whether in a rich country (Australia) or a poor one (Cameroon), no matter how well intentioned or well resourced the providers. Second, these social relations are embedded within and upheld by rules systems, ranging from everyday social norms and customary legal systems to the formal laws of the state and international agreements. Chinese peasants, Aboriginal mothers-to-be, and Cameroonian AIDS patients carry out their lives within rules systems that are often unclear (by design) to outsiders and which may or may not cohere with the rules

---

[8] Cited in Rosenthal (2006).

systems of other groups or those of the state. When they do not—as in each case here—serious problems ensue. Third, social relations and rules systems are themselves embedded in broader meaning systems encompassing beliefs about how one makes sense of the world, whether and how one effects change, and where one is situated in that world relative to others.

In the cases above, poor Chinese peasants, poor Aboriginal women, and poor Africans are being challenged (forced) to engage with qualitatively different 'modern' sensibilities pertaining to livelihoods, childbirth practices, and public health; as such, the fault line (or policy 'bottleneck') is not so much the absence of material resources (cf. Sachs, 2005) but rather different ways— ontologically and epistemologically—of understanding how the world works. For these types of development problems, which I contend are ubiquitous and omnipresent, the appropriate solution is not technical but political; optimal and legitimate solutions, characteristically unknowable ex ante, can only be arrived at through equitable negotiation and deliberation. In the next section, I elaborate briefly on these three elements—social relations, rules systems, and meaning systems—and argue that they should be the basis of the next stage of efforts to incorporate social and political theory into development policy and practice.

15.5. Elements of an Economic Sociology of Chronic Poverty: Social Relations, Rules Systems, Meaning Systems

To date, I have argued, the dominant scholarly and policy debates on development in general, and poverty in particular, have been most influenced (outside of economics) by studies of networks, social exclusion, and culture. This has occurred not only because of the inherent appeal of the core ideas in these fields, and the passing of historical events which have created greater space for their (actual or potential) receptivity, but because certain key actors and organizations have actively and strategically promoted them (see Bebbington et al., 2004). To the extent human agency can be similarly deployed going forward, the consolidation and extension of these gains, and the incorporation of a still richer body of social science research into understanding poverty dynamics, requires, I suggest, a focus on three additional realms.[9] The three illustrative case studies (above) provide a sense of their practical manifestation; in this section, I provide an overview of their distinctive analytical underpinnings.

[9] My focus on three fields of study, as opposed to some other number, is more a matter of discursive convenience than demonstrated empirical fact. I am conscious that, in quests to render 'big picture' issues in manageable terms, the choice of three factors has a long and sometimes awkward history; Gellner (1988, p. 19), for example, amusingly calls such proclivities 'trinitarianism'.

15.5.1. *Social relations*

Arguing for a focus on 'social relations' as a basis for understanding economic outcomes has its origins at least as far back as Marx (see Farr, 2004), but for our present purposes it should direct our attention to three key sub-issues. First, following (among others) Emirbayer (1997), Tilly (2000), and Rao and Walton (2004), it should help us understand how groups are defined, how 'us–them' boundaries are created, sustained, and transgressed, and how these shift during periods of economic and political transformation. It is in and through groups that identities are formed, and it is a defining feature of modernity that it simultaneously fractures individual identity into multiple (sometimes competing) strands—home/work, citizen/subject, sacred/profane—even as it then requires individuals (and, by extension, communities) to 'manage' these different claims on their time, resources, and loyalty (Gellner, 1988). As Polanyi (1944) famously argued, 'the great transformation' unleashed by the industrial revolution—and whose workings continue to unfold today—rendered separate what had previously been unified.

Second, humans are relentlessly status-oriented beings, constantly assessing their preferences, aspirations, and strategies on the basis of their place in various identity groups and broader communities within which their lives are 'embedded'. Recent work in experimental economics[10] has confirmed what has long been a staple of sociology and social psychology, namely that individual choices and values are heavily influenced by the particular reference groups one believes most salient, and the perceived legitimacy and permeability of the boundaries separating these groups (Haslam, 2004). The direst circumstances of poverty, for example, in which all sense of hope or expectation for escaping it appears to be lost, can itself undermine 'capacities to aspire' (Appadurai, 2004) and thereby contribute to the persistence of inequality traps. Similarly, membership in a stigmatized group (such as a low caste in India) can itself—that is, all other things equal—contribute to low performance on standardized tests.[11]

Third, many key services—such as health, education, and social work—are *necessarily* delivered in and through social relationships (doctor–patient, teacher–student, counsellor–client). There is no short-changing the fact that schooling, for example, whether it is conducted privately, by the state, or by parents at home, essentially takes human interaction between teacher and student over the course of six hours a day, 200 days a year, for twelve years, in order to 'produce' a sufficiently socialized and educated young adult able to take their place in our modern economy and society. Making services work is key to enhancing the welfare of the poor (World Bank, 2003), but—as

[10] Radin and Woolcock (2008) provide an overview of this work and an assessment of its significance for social theory and development.
[11] This literature is surveyed in World Bank (2005).

the case of AIDS in Cameroon above demonstrates—responding effectively, especially where intensely private matters such as sexuality are involved, will entail paying serious attention to the relational aspects of service delivery (Pritchett and Woolcock, 2004), not just technical issues such as the pricing of those services, or administrative issues such as the design of line ministries (important as these are).

15.5.2. Rules systems

While there is a broad consensus that the design and implementation of effective development policy entails 'understanding the rules of the game' in a given context, that equitable outcomes depend on 'levelling the playing field', and that transparent and accountable governance requires 'building the rule of law', there is far less agreement on how anyone can (or might) actually do these things. The international community has a long and unhappy history in such matters (Sage and Woolcock, 2006), in no small part because its programmatic activities have been the logical end product of (i) the prevailing theories for much of the last sixty years (whether emanating from modernization theory, Marxist perspectives, or neoclassical assumptions), and (ii) the imperatives of large development organizations, both of which have combined to encourage (and/or justify) technical assistance strategies centred on 'jumping straight to Weber' (Pritchett and Woolcock, 2004)—that is, implementing, preferably in a single bound, end-state institutional forms deemed to be 'international best practice'.

It is important to note that certain development problems (such as low-cost methods for desalinating water, or engineering techniques for building rural roads in high-rainfall environments) do indeed have technical solutions, and when they are identified it is clearly to everyone's advantage for these to be widely and rapidly disseminated. In such matters, the wheel does not have to be reinvented each time. In a vast range of other cases, however, such as resolving tensions between different ethnic groups or building judicial systems, an entirely different decision-making apparatus is required. The development community is only slowly coming to an appreciation of this, though both its political history and prevailing institutional architecture conspire against it. Nevertheless, social and political theory (and research methods) has a vital role to play here. If 'good governance' and 'making institutions work' for the poor is everyone's seemingly highest priority, then a whole new intellectual software is required. Enhancing the accessibility and quality of justice for the poor; bridging state and non-state justice systems; creating new deliberative spaces for decision making and political reform: these are all vital tasks in the twenty-first century, and ones to which social science is well equipped to speak (see Gibson and Woolcock, 2008, drawing on Habermas).

Rules systems constitute everything from constitutions and contracts to languages and social norms—they are all human inventions to regulate behaviour, facilitate exchange, and (at best) constrain elite power. As such, efforts to introduce some version of them into settings where they have not previously existed requires a theoretical framework considerably different from those used to set exchange rates, build bridges, or design pension systems. Similarly, rules systems themselves—most graphically apartheid, but also laws that deny widows any inheritance or gender norms that encourage girls to leave school early—can lie at the heart of 'legal inequality traps' (Sage and Woolcock, 2006, 2008) that keep poor people poor. 'Breaking' such traps is a vital, if vexing, development challenge.

15.5.3. *Meaning systems*

This final realm of enquiry is an extension of the best work on culture and development (e.g. Rao and Walton, 2004). Here the concern is with understanding how people make sense of what happens in the world and to them; how they understand the role of their own agency (vis-à-vis 'social structures' and 'the fates') in shaping their life chances and opportunities; and how they engage with (and are affected by) difference and change. In order to realize these ambitious goals, it will be necessary to engage more systematically with the most recent work on cultural 'frames' and 'repertoires' (e.g. Lamont and Small, 2006), which seeks to understand how people navigate/negotiate institutional boundaries and power differentials, and how they learn (or not) the 'language'/mannerisms required to negotiate them.

Such knowledge is also important for coming to terms with apparent anomalies in the behaviour of marginalized groups. Some such groups, as our Cameroon example above shows, actively resist or subvert practices that are 'clearly' in their best interests, not out of ignorance or defiance but because their particular frame of understanding places a higher value on upholding community norms, or because, more radically, the 'superior' practice directly contravenes their cosmology (e.g. when villagers refuse to immunize their children because they believe puncturing the skin with a needle allows evil spirits to enter). In important work done by Scott (1985) and Gledhill (2000), marginalized groups do in fact actively defy those above them, but in ways that are less visible to those people and/or that subtly give the marginalized a slightly stronger negotiating position (e.g. by refusing to allow customary law to be codified; if it was, they would, as illiterates, probably lose to formally trained lawyers). Mediating between very different ways of understanding the world is a task fraught with ethical and political difficulties: one cannot unilaterally accept that 'traditional ways' are inherently virtuous (e.g. child marriage, female circumcision, bride burning, capital punishment), yet neither can one assume that forcibly (by decree or conditionality requirements) implementing 'modern' approaches in a single bound is desirable (or even possible). Reconciling these tensions is not merely an uncomfortable (or 'soft') component of development; it *is* development. Moreover, because the development business is inherently one of encounters between people with such vastly different power, expectations, and philosophies, effective strategies to reduce poverty must therefore give a much more prominent place to perspectives that can help 'manage' these encounters in the most equitable and accountable manner. A greater focus on 'meaning systems' is a step in this direction.

Finally, I argue that a focus on social relations, rules systems, and meaning systems satisfies the four criteria (outlined above) that a rigorous and relevant social theory must be able to meet. Cumulatively, they (a) provide a clear but distinctive model of human behaviour, (b) explain how and why poverty persists as part of broader processes of economic prosperity and social change, (c) account for the mechanisms by which power is created, maintained, and challenged, and (d) readily lend themselves to informing (and iteratively learning from) a new generation of supportable poverty reduction policies and practices.

15.6. Conclusion: Development as 'Good Struggles'

Amongst policy-oriented non-economists (such as myself), it is common to read arguments to the effect that policies enacted in response to poverty would be more effective if only they adopted a more 'social' and/or 'political' approach, yet much of the intellectual energy that accompanies this call tends to be long on critiques of (what is assumed to be) economic orthodoxy and short on coherent and supportable alternatives. On the rare occasions that viable alternatives are in fact submitted by non-economists, they seek to distance themselves as far as possible from economics and its putative associations with 'neo-liberalism'. These strident polarities make for easy contrasts and witticisms, but in doing so they simultaneously manage to (a) sell short the positive contributions their own disciplines could (and should) be making to poverty knowledge and practice, and (b) underappreciate the progress that has been made over the last ten years, both within economics itself and with respect to the policy traction that particular social concepts have been able to secure. Scholars are trained to be sceptics, but in this instance at least there is a reasonable basis for optimism that hard-won gains can be consolidated and built upon.

For this to happen, I have argued that social scientists need to have greater confidence in the content and usefulness of their theories and methods. While the history and organizational imperatives of the large contemporary development agencies will continue (for the foreseeable future) to construe problems and solutions in largely technocratic terms (Scott, 1998)—and thereby privilege those disciplines (such as economics and engineering) most conducive to this—the appropriate response from social scientists should be to speak concretely to actual policy problems, not (as seems to be so often the case) engage in endless 'critiques' and/or presentations of yet more 'conceptual frameworks' (cf. Pieterse, 2001). The three illustrative cases presented above demand real responses; all are at the centre of contemporary policy debates, speaking directly to some of the most pressing and vexing development concerns of the twenty-first century: economic and political transformation, the plight of indigenous groups, responding to the AIDS pandemic. Social theory can and should speak directly and constructively to these concerns.

Economics alone cannot solve these problems, but it will probably be *part of* an answer; the challenge for social scientists is to articulate coherent and supportable theories that speak confidently to those aspects on which it has a clear comparative advantage. One such aspect is that class of problems—and they are legion—for which there is no technical solution; indeed, where the belief that there is a technical solution (i.e. if only more smart people could be recruited and resources given to them) is itself a major part of the problem (Pritchett and Woolcock, 2004). Worrying more about social relations, rules systems, and meaning systems will be central to addressing such concerns. Where a given development issue (e.g. race relations)—or some aspect of a given development issue (e.g. student–teacher relations as part of a broader debate on 'education')—entails crafting spaces for dialogue and negotiation, the opportunity is ripe for entry by detailed contributions by social scientists. In this sense, and because effective responses in these instances will primarily come about through equitable political contestation rather than technical analysis, much of development can be said to be about facilitating 'good struggles' (Adler, Sage, and Woolcock, 2007). Creating the space for such a contribution, however, is as important as being able to speak sensibly to it.

References

Adler, Daniel, Sage, Caroline, and Woolcock, Michael (2007), 'Interim Institutions and the Development Process: Opening Spaces for Reform in Indonesia and Cambodia', mimeo.

Alsop, Ruth, Holland, Jeremy, and Bertelsen, Mette (eds.) (2006), *Empowerment in Practice: From Analysis to Implementation*, Washington: World Bank.

Appadurai, Ajun (2004), 'The Capacity to Aspire: Culture and the Terms of Recognition', in Vijayendra Rao and Michael Walton (eds.), *Culture and Public Action*, Stanford, Calif.: Stanford University Press, 59–84.

Azariadis, Costas, and Stachurski, John (2006), 'Poverty Traps', in Philippe Aghion and Steven Durlauf (eds.), *Handbook of Economic Growth*, vol. i/a, Amsterdam: Elsevier Science, 295–384.

Banerjee, Abhijit, Benabou, Roland, and Mookherjee, Dilip (eds.) (2006), *Understanding Poverty*, New York: Oxford University Press.

Bates, Robert (2000), *Violence and Prosperity: The Political Economy of Development*, New York: Norton.

Beaudoin, Steven (2007), *Poverty in World History*, London: Routledge.

Bebbington, Anthony, Guggenheim, Scott, Olson, Elizabeth, and Woolcock, Michael (2004), 'Understanding Social Capital Debates at the World Bank', *Journal of Development Studies*, 40(5): 33–64.

Bowles, Samuel, Durlauf, Steven, and Hoff, Karla (eds.) (2006), *Poverty Traps*, Princeton: Princeton University Press.

Brady, Michael (forthcoming), *Politicizing Poverty, Socializing Equality*.

Deaton, Angus (2001), 'Counting the World's Poor: Problems and Possible Solutions', *World Bank Research Observer*, 16(2): 125–47.

Dercon, Stefon (2006), 'Measuring Poverty', in David Clark (ed.), *Elgar Companion to Development Studies*, London: Edward Elgar.

De Soto, Hernando (2000), *The Mystery of Capital: Why Capitalism Succeeds in the West and Fails Everywhere Else*, New York: Basic Books.

Easterly, William (2006), 'Reliving the 50s: The Big Push, Poverty Traps, and Takeoffs in Economic Development', *Journal of Economic Growth*, 11(4): 289–318.

——Ritzen, Jozef, and Woolcock, Michael (2006), 'Social Cohesion, Institutions and Growth', *Economics & Politics*, 18(2): 103–20.

Emirbayer, Mustafa (1997), 'Manifesto for a Relational Sociology', *American Journal of Sociology*, 103(2): 281–317.

Fafchamps, Marcel (2006), 'Development and Social Capital', *Journal of Development Studies*, 42(7): 1180–98.

Farr, James (2004), 'Social Capital: A Conceptual History', *Political Theory*, 32(1): 6–33.

Gellner, Ernest (1988), *Plough, Sword and Book: The Structure of Human History*, Chicago: University of Chicago Press.

Geremek, Bronislaw (1994), *Poverty: A History*, Oxford: Blackwell.

Gibson, Christopher, and Woolcock, Michael (2008), 'Empowerment, Deliberative Development, and Local Level Politics in Indonesia: Participatory Projects as a Source of Countervailing Power', *Studies in Comparative International Developement*, 43(2): 151–80.

Gledhill, John (2000), *Power and its Disguises*, London: Pluto Press.

Harrison, Lawrence, and Huntington, Samuel (eds.) (2001), *Culture Matters: How Values Shape Human Progress*, New York: Basic Books.

Haslam, S. Alexander (2004), *Psychology in Organizations: The Social Identity Approach*, 2nd edn., New York: Sage Publications.

Hausmann, Ricardo, Rodrik, Dani, and Pritchett, Lant (2004), 'Growth Accelerations', NBER Working Paper No. 10050, Cambridge.

Hulme, David, and Shepherd, Andrew (2003), 'Conceptualizing Chronic Poverty', *World Development*, 31(3): 403–24.

Iceland, John (2005), *Poverty in America*, Berkeley and Los Angeles: University of California Press.

Isham, Jonathan (2002), 'The Effects of Social Capital on Fertilizer Adoption: Evidence from Rural Tanzania', *Journal of African Economies*, 11(1): 39–60.

Jalan, Jyotsna, and Ravallion, Martin (2002), 'Geographical Poverty Traps? A Micro Model of Consumption Growth in Rural China', *Journal of Applied Econometrics*, 17: 329–46.

Jones, Gareth Steadman (2004), *An End to Poverty? A Historical Debate*, London: Profile Books.

Kraay, Aart (2005), 'Economic Growth and Poverty Reduction', Policy Research Working Paper, Washington: World Bank.

Lamont, Michele, and Small, Mario Luis (2006), 'How Culture Matters for Poverty: Thickening our Understanding', in David Harris and Ann Lin (eds.), *The Colors of Poverty*, New York: Russell Sage Foundation.

Muldavin, Joshua (2006), 'In Rural China, a Time Bomb is Ticking', *International Herald Tribune*, 1 January, available at <http://www.iht.com/articles/2006/01/01/opinion/edmuldavin.php>.

Murray, Charles (1994), *Losing Ground: American Social Policy, 1950–1980*, 2nd edn., New York: Perseus Publishing.

Newman, Mark, Barabasi, Albert-Laszlo, and Watts, Duncan (eds.) (2006), *The Structure and Dynamics of Networks*, Princeton: Princeton University Press.

O'Connor, Alice (2001), *Poverty Knowledge: Social Science and Social Policy and the Poor in Twentieth Century U.S. History*, Princeton: Princeton University Press.

Patterson, Orlando (2006), 'A Poverty of the Mind', *New York Times*, 26 March, available at <http://select.nytimes.com/search/restricted/article?res=F30C1EF63C540C758ED-DAA0894DE404482>.

Pieterse, Jan Nederveen (2001), *Development Theory: Deconstructions/Reconstructions*, London: Sage Publications.

Polanyi, Karl (1944), *The Great Transformation*, Boston: Beacon Press.

Portes, Alejandro (ed.) (1995), *The Economic Sociology of Immigration: Essays on Networks, Ethnicity and Entrepreneurship*, New York: Russell Sage Foundation.

—— (2006), 'Institutions and Development: A Conceptual Reanalysis', *Population and Development Review*, 32(2): 233–62.

Pritchett, Lant (2006), 'Who is *not* Poor? Dreaming of a World Truly Free of Poverty', *World Bank Research Observer*, 21(1): 1–23.

—— and Woolcock, Michael (2004), 'Solutions when the Solution is the Problem: Arraying the Disarray in Development', *World Development*, 32(2): 191–212.

Radin, Elizabeth, and Woolcock, Michael (2008), 'Social Capital and Economic Development Revisited: Integrating Science, Social Science, and Practice', in Dario Castiglione, Jan van Deth, and Guglielmo Wolleb (eds.), *Handbook of Social Capital*, New York: Oxford University Press.

Rao, Vijayendra (2005a), 'Symbolic Public Goods and the Coordination of Collective Action: A Comparison of Local Development in India and Indonesia', Policy Research Working Paper No. 3685, Washington: World Bank.

—— (2005b), 'On Inequality Traps and Development Policy', *Development Outreach*, 8(1): 10–13.

—— and Walton, Michael (eds.) (2004), *Culture and Public Action*, Palo Alto, Calif.: Stanford University Press.

Ravallion, Martin (2001), 'Growth, Inequality and Poverty: Looking beyond Averages', *World Development*, 29(11): 1803–15.

Ravallion, Martin (2006), 'Poverty and Growth', in David Clark (ed.), *Elgar Companion to Development Studies*, London: Edward Elgar.

Rosenthal, Elisabeth (2006), 'Traditional Ways Spread AIDS in Africa, Experts Say', *New York Times*, 21 November, available at <http://www.nytimes.com/2006/11/21/world/africa/21cameroon.html?ex=1171602000&en=6947e1e902f2b1b7&ei=5070>.

Sachs, Jeffrey (2005), *The End of Poverty: Economic Possibilities for our Time*, New York: Penguin.

Sage, Caroline, and Woolcock, Michael (2006), 'Rules Systems and the Development Process', in Caroline Sage and Michael Woolcock (eds.), *World Bank Legal Review: Law, Equity and Development*, Amsterdam: Martinus Nijhoff.

———— (forthcoming), 'Breaking Legal Inequality Traps: New Approaches to Building Justice Systems for the Poor in Developing Countries', in Anis Dani and Arjan de Haan (eds.), *Inclusive States: Social Policy and Structural Inequalities*, Washington: World Bank.

Scott, James (1976), *The Moral Economy of the Peasant: Rebellion and Resistance in Southeast Asia*, New Haven: Yale University Press.

—— (1985), *Weapons of the Weak: Everyday Forms of Peasant Resistance*, New Haven: Yale University Press.

—— (1998), *Seeing Like a State: Why Certain Schemes to Improve the Human Condition Have Failed*, New Haven: Yale University Press.

—— (forthcoming), *Why Civilizations Can't Climb Hills*, New Haven: Yale University Press.

Sen, Amartya (1999), *Development as Freedom*, New York: Knopf.

Sherman, Sandra (2002), *Imagining Poverty: Quantification and the Decline of Paternalism*, Columbus, Oh.: Ohio State University Press.

Skocpol, Theda (1990), 'Sustainable Social Policy: Fighting Poverty without Poverty Programs', *American Prospect*, 1(2): 58–70.

Stern, Nicholas, Dethier, Jean-Jacques, and Rogers, F. Halsey (2005), *Growth and Empowerment: Making Development Happen*, Cambridge, Mass.: MIT Press.

Tilly, Charles (2000), *Durable Inequalities*, Berkeley and Los Angeles: University of California Press.

van Schendel, Willem (2002), 'Geographies of Knowing, Geographies of Ignorance: Jumping Scale in Southeast Asia', *Environment and Planning D: Society and Space*, 20: 647–68.

Wilson, William Julius (1987), *The Truly Disadvantaged: The Inner City, the Underclass, and Public Policy*, Chicago: University of Chicago Press.

—— (1996), *When Work Disappears: The World of the New Urban Poor*, New York: Knopf.

Woolcock, Michael, and Narayan, Deepa (2000), 'Social Capital: Implications for Development Theory, Research, and Policy', *World Bank Research Observer*, 15(2): 225–49.

World Bank (2000), *World Development Report 2000/01: Attacking Poverty*, New York: Oxford University Press.

—— (2003), *World Development Report 2004: Making Services Work for Poor People*, New York: Oxford University Press.

—— (2005), *World Development Report 2006: Equity and Development*, New York: Oxford University Press.

Index

Index

Index

Index